Classics of Western Thought

Classics of Western Thought

UNDER THE GENERAL EDITORSHIP OF
Thomas H. Greer
MICHIGAN STATE UNIVERSITY

I. *The Ancient World*

EDITED BY *Stebelton H. Nulle*
MICHIGAN STATE UNIVERSITY

II. *Middle Ages, Renaissance, and Reformation*

EDITED BY *Karl F. Thompson*
MICHIGAN STATE UNIVERSITY

III. *The Modern World,* ENLARGED EDITION

EDITED BY *Charles Hirschfeld*
RICHMOND COLLEGE,
CITY UNIVERSITY OF NEW YORK

EDITED BY

Stebelton H. Nulle

MICHIGAN STATE UNIVERSITY

CLASSICS OF WESTERN THOUGHT

*The
Ancient
World*

Harcourt, Brace & World, Inc.

New York / Chicago / San Francisco / Atlanta

PA 3621 .N8

General Introduction

The editors of this three-volume series strongly believe that the best means of introducing students to their humanistic heritage is through a selection of original writings by the great minds of the Western tradition. It is for this purpose that we have brought together what we regard as classics of the Western tradition—of Western *thought*, in the broad sense. This collection of primary documents is intended for use in college-level courses in humanities or in the history of civilization, normally in company with a brief narrative text. One such text, designed especially for use with these volumes, is Thomas H. Greer's *A Brief History of Western Man* (Harcourt, Brace & World, 1968).

The volume and range of documents in Western civilization are, of course, enormous, and good reasons can always be advanced for making one selection over another. We have decided to restrict our own choice to what is truly *classic*, that is to say, valuable both for its intrinsic merit and for having exerted a paramount influence on its own and later times. We have, therefore, selected writings that reveal judgment applied to observation and that display creative thought and literary skill. In deciding upon the length and quantity of selections, we have aimed to keep in balance two purposes: to make each document *long enough* to give a substantial view of the author's ideas and to offer, at the same time, a substantial *number* of the foremost writers. (In a few instances we have omitted a familiar classic because the full text is readily available in satisfactory and inexpensive paperback editions, as for example, Homer's *Iliad*.)

The documents appear for the most part in chronological order and are arranged in three manageable volumes: *The Ancient World* (Volume One); *Middle Ages, Renaissance, and Reformation* (Volume Two); and *The Modern World* (Volume Three). Each document is introduced by a brief account of the author's life, of his role in the shaping of the Western tradition, and of the significance of the particular work. As in the selection of the writings themselves, we have kept student and teacher continually in mind.

We believe that the chief merit of these volumes is that they are guided by our aggregate experience of many years in the classroom—teaching college and university courses in humanities and in the history of civilization.

THOMAS H. GREER

Preface

In this first volume of *Classics of Western Thought* are gathered some
of the best thought and expression of the ancient Mediterranean
world, spanning a period of more than a thousand years (from Amos
to Augustine). Given the restricted number of selections, we can do
no more than sample the cultural treasures of these earlier societies,
for we are heirs to a legacy of unparalleled richness, whose sources
are spread over the whole of classical antiquity.

First, we shall follow the Greeks in their search for rational answers
to the problems of truth and beauty, of freedom and justice. Then
we shall mark the Roman vision of a wider human concord, a community of mankind resting upon government and law. Justly they
could boast with the elder Pliny that the mission of Rome was "to
give to humanity human culture, and in a word become for all
peoples in the whole world their one and only country." Lastly, we
shall witness the Judeo-Christian perception of God's oneness and
the aspiration for a moral order in which his will is realized in the
affairs of mankind.

To be sure, Hellenic culture was not without its irrational elements, but it was the moderation, harmony, and balance of the Greek
classical ideal that spread throughout the Mediterranean world,
finding expression in literature and the arts (what we now call the
humanities), and (among a cultivated few at least) as a way of life.
The Romans, adapting, interpreting, and extending Hellenic culture, also succeeded where Athens had failed, thus giving mankind
their own ideal of a universal human order which has never been
forgotten.

But soon a feeling of profound malaise spread throughout the
ancient world. A sense of failure and defeat and a realization of the
imperfect nature of secular life led to an urgent search for supernatural meaning and guidance, and ultimately to the rise of Christianity. Gone was the Hellenic sense of the uniqueness of man—a
being neither god nor beast; gone was the confidence in the

potential excellence of full humanity; and gone was the bold reliance upon reason. Now there was a new religion, proclaiming faith in man's spiritual nature and eternal destiny: a religion based on revelations and expressed in rituals. The ideal of saintliness replaced the classical image of the high-minded man, doing his utmost to fulfill his latent human powers. The Middle Ages had arrived.

Despite the fluctuations of passing centuries, the ideals we identify with ancient Greece, Rome, and Judaea were to live on in radically altered times, and today they still offer answers to the perennial questions of value and meaning that beset us in the thermonuclear age.

STEBELTON H. NULLE

Contents

Classics of Western Thought

Sophocles

1

Oedipus Rex

The chief literary achievement of Athens in the Golden Age and one of the noblest products of the human imagination is Attic tragedy. The way was prepared for it by a unique circumstance: an extraordinary, self-conscious maturity of outlook on the part of the Athenian populace provided a climate in which poets of genius, through the medium of tragedy, found an audience of taste and feeling. These poets interpreted the Hellenic traditions and ideals and offered their own insights into the nature of man's life and destiny.

The three dramatists regarded by the Greeks themselves as supreme were Aeschylus, Euripides, and Sophocles (ca. 496–406 B.C.). Throughout his long life Sophocles had every advantage: aristocratic birth, wealth, good looks, success, and, above all, the boon of having lived in Athens during the Golden Age. Of the more than one hundred plays he wrote, however, only seven survive. *Oedipus Rex* dates from about 429 B.C. (the year of Pericles' death); it is regarded as his masterpiece and is certainly one of the half-dozen great tragedies of all time.

The story of this drama is drawn from a well-known Greek legend. As interpreted by Sophocles, the play concerns man's relation to the divine order. Since divine order and justice are considered identical, Oedipus, who unintentionally broke the moral code guaranteed by the Olympian gods, is made to suffer horribly. Whether or not his punishment is just, by mere human standards, is irrelevant to the judgment of the gods. It is their will that man should know himself and thus realize his limitations. At the end of the play, the blind Oedipus, having learned of the moral code through suffering, emerges a wiser man, more aware of life's meaning than the confident, proud ruler he was at the beginning.

This was not the private viewpoint of Sophocles alone. The sentiments

Sophocles, *Oedipus Rex*, trans. Albert Cook, in *Ten Greek Plays*, ed. L. R. Lind (New York: Houghton Mifflin, 1957), 117–53. Copyright by Albert Cook. Reprinted by permission.

of the Chorus, whose role was to comment upon and to express general opinion, showed that the belief that man should know himself was part of the consciousness of the folk. The corollary of this attitude helped to make possible the miracle of Periclean Athens: that man has within himself a potential enabling him to face harsh realities, even the prospect of ultimate doom, with courage and dignity. Both the suffering of Oedipus—evoking the emotions of pity and terror—and his grandeur in adversity are of the essence of tragedy. This Greek attitude—standing in awe and wonder at the uniqueness of man and his inherent moral stature—is also of the essence of humanism.

CHARACTERS

OEDIPUS, *king of Thebes*
A PRIEST
CREON, *brother-in-law of Oedipus*
CHORUS *of Theban elders*
TEIRESIAS, *a prophet*
JOCASTA, *sister of Creon, wife of Oedipus*
MESSENGER
SERVANT *of Laius, father of Oedipus*
SECOND MESSENGER
(*silent*) ANTIGONE *and* ISMENE, *daughters of Oedipus*

SCENE   *Before the palace of Oedipus at Thebes. In front of the large central doors, an altar; and an altar near each of the two side doors. On the altar steps are seated suppliants—old men, youths, and young boys—dressed in white tunics and cloaks, their hair bound with white fillets. They have laid on the altars olive branches wreathed with wool-fillets.*

The old PRIEST OF ZEUS *stands alone facing the central doors of the palace. The doors open, and* OEDIPUS, *followed by two attendants who stand at either door, enters and looks about.*

OEDIPUS   O children, last born stock of ancient Cadmus,
What petitions are these you bring to me
With garlands on your suppliant olive branches?
The whole city teems with incense fumes,

Teems with prayers for healing and with groans.
Thinking it best, children, to hear all this
Not from some messenger, I came myself,
The world renowned and glorious Oedipus.
But tell me, aged priest, since you are fit
To speak before these men, how stand you here,
In fear or want? Tell me, as I desire
To do my all; hard hearted I would be
To feel no sympathy for such a prayer.

   PRIEST   O Oedipus, ruler of my land, you see
How old we are who stand in supplication
Before your altars here, some not yet strong
For lengthy flight, some heavy with age,
Priests, as I of Zeus, and choice young men.
The rest of the tribe sits with wreathed branches,
In market places, at Pallas' two temples,
And at prophetic embers by the river.
The city, as you see, now shakes too greatly
And cannot raise her head out of the depths
Above the gory swell. She wastes in blight,
Blight on earth's fruitful blooms and grazing flocks,
And on the barren birth pangs of the women.
The fever god has fallen on the city,
And drives it, a most hated pestilence
Through whom the home of Cadmus is made empty.
Black Hades is enriched with wails and groans.
Not that we think you equal to the gods
These boys and I sit suppliant at your hearth,
But judging you first of men in the trials of life,
And in the human intercourse with spirits:—
You are the one who came to Cadmus' city
And freed us from the tribute which we paid
To the harsh-singing Sphinx. And that you did
Knowing nothing else, unschooled by us.
But people say and think it was some god
That helped you to set our life upright.
Now Oedipus, most powerful of all,
We all are turned here toward you, we beseech you,
Find us some strength, whether from one of the gods
You hear an omen, or know one from a man.

For the experienced I see will best
Make good plans grow from evil circumstance.
Come, best of mortal men, raise up the state.
Come, prove your fame, since now this land of ours
Calls you savior for your previous zeal.
O never let our memory of your reign
Be that we first stood straight and later fell,
But to security raise up this state.
With favoring omen once you gave us luck;
Be now as good again; for if henceforth
You rule as now, you will be this country's king,
Better it is to rule men than a desert,
Since nothing is either ship or fortress tower
Bare of men who together dwell within.

   OEDIPUS   O piteous children, I am not ignorant
Of what you come desiring. Well I know
You are all sick, and in your sickness none
There is among you as sick as I,
For your pain comes to one man alone,
To him and to none other, but my soul
Groans for the state, for myself, and for you.
You do not wake a man who is sunk in sleep;
Know that already I have shed many tears,
And travelled many wandering roads of thought.
Well have I sought, and found one remedy;
And this I did: the son of Menoeceus,
Creon, my brother-in-law, I sent away
Unto Apollo's Pythian halls to find
What I might do or say to save the state.
The days are measured out that he is gone;
It troubles me how he fares. Longer than usual
He has been away, more than the fitting time.
But when he comes, then evil I shall be,
If all the god reveals I fail to do.

   PRIEST   You speak at the right time. These men just now
Signal to me that Creon is approaching.

   OEDIPUS   O Lord Apollo, grant that he may come
In saving fortune shining as in eye.

   PRIEST   Glad news he brings, it seems, or else his head
Would not be crowned with leafy, berried bay.

OEDIPUS We will soon know. He is close enough to hear.—
Prince, my kinsman, son of Menoeceus,
What oracle do you bring us from the god?
     CREON A good one. For I say that even burdens
If they chance to turn out right, will all be well.
     OEDIPUS Yet what is the oracle? Your present word
Makes me neither bold nor apprehensive
     CREON If you wish to hear in front of this crowd
I am ready to speak, or we can go within.
     OEDIPUS Speak forth to all. The sorrow that I bear
Is greater for these men than for my life.
     CREON May I tell you what I heard from the god?
Lord Phoebus clearly bids us to drive out,
And not to leave uncured within this country,
A pollution we have nourished in our land.
     OEDIPUS With what purgation? What kind of misfortune?
     CREON Banish the man, or quit slaughter with slaughter
In cleansing, since this blood rains on the state.
     OEDIPUS Who is this man whose fate the god reveals?
     CREON Laius, my lord, was formerly the guide
Of this our land before you steered this city.
     OEDIPUS I know him by hearsay, but I never saw him.
     CREON Since he was slain, the god now plainly bids us
To punish his murderers, whoever they may be.
     OEDIPUS Where are they on the earth? How shall we find
This indiscernible track of ancient guilt?
     CREON In this land, said Apollo. What is sought
Can be apprehended; the unobserved escapes.
     OEDIPUS Did Laius fall at home on this bloody end?
Or in the fields, or in some foreign land?
     CREON As a pilgrim, the god said, he left his tribe
And once away from home, returned no more.
     OEDIPUS Was there no messenger, no fellow wayfarer
Who saw, from whom an inquirer might get aid?
     CREON They are all dead, save one, who fled in fear
And he knows only one thing sure to tell.
     OEDIPUS What is that? We may learn many facts from one
If we might take for hope a short beginning.
     CREON Robbers, Apollo said, met there and killed him
Not by the strength of one, but many hands.

OEDIPUS   How did the robber unless something from here
Was at work with silver, reach this point of daring?
CREON   These facts are all conjecture. Laius dead,
There rose in evils no avenger for him.
OEDIPUS   But when the king had fallen slain, what trouble
Prevented you from finding all this out?
CREON   The subtle-singing Sphinx made us let go
What was unclear to search at our own feet.
OEDIPUS   Well then, I will make this clear afresh
From the start. Phoebus was right, you were right
To take this present interest in the dead.
Justly it is you see me as your ally
Avenging alike this country and the god.
Not for the sake of some distant friends,
But for myself I will disperse this filth.
Whoever it was who killed that man
With the same hand may wish to do vengeance on me.
And so assisting Laius I aid myself.
But hurry quickly, children, stand up now
From the altar steps, raising these suppliant boughs.
Let someone gather Cadmus' people here
To learn that I will do all, whether at last
With Phoebus' help we are shown saved or fallen.
PRIEST   Come, children, let us stand. We came here
First for the sake of what this man proclaims.
Phoebus it was who sent these prophecies
And he will come to save us from the plague.

CHORUS

O sweet-tongued voice of Zeus, in what spirit do you come
From Pytho rich in gold
To glorious Thebes? I am torn on the rack, dread shakes my fearful
    mind,
Apollo of Delos, hail!
As I stand in awe of you, what need, either new
Do you bring to the full for me, or old in the turning times of the
    year?
Tell me, O child of golden Hope, undying Voice!

First on you do I call, daughter of Zeus, undying Athene
And your sister who guards our land,
Artemis, seated upon the throne renowned of our circled Place,
And Phoebus who darts afar;
Shine forth to me, thrice warder-off of death;
If ever in time before when ruin rushed upon the state,
The flame of sorrow you drove beyond our bounds, come also now.

O woe! Unnumbered that I bear
The sorrows are! My whole host is sick, nor is there a sword of
   thought
To ward off pain. The growing fruits
Of glorious earth wax not, nor women
Withstand in childbirth shrieking pangs.
Life on life you may see, which, like the well-winged bird,
Faster than stubborn fire, speed
To the strand of the evening god.

Unnumbered of the city die.
Unpitied babies bearing death lie unmoaned on the ground.
Grey-haired mothers and young wives
From all sides at the altar's edge
Lift up a wail beseeching, for their mournful woes.
The prayer for healing shines blent with a grieving cry;
Wherefore, O golden daughter of Zeus,
Send us your succour with its beaming face.

Grant that fiery Ares, who now with no brazen shield
Flames round me in shouting attack
May turn his back in running flight from our land,
May be borne with fair wind
To Amphitrite's great chamber
Or to the hostile port
Of the Thracian surge.
For even if night leaves any ill undone
It is brought to pass and comes to be in the day.
O Zeus who bear the fire
And rule the lightning's might,
Strike him beneath your thunderbolt with death!

O lord Apollo, would that you might come and scatter forth
Untamed darts from your twirling golden bow;
Bring succour from the plague; may the flashing
Beams come of Artemis,
With which she glances through the Lycian hills.
Also on him I call whose hair is held in gold,
Who gives a name to this land,
Bacchus of winy face, whom maidens hail!
Draw near with your flaming Maenad band
And the aid of your gladsome torch
Against the plague, dishonoured among the gods.

OEDIPUS   You pray; if for what you pray you would be willing
To hear and take my words, to nurse the plague,
You may get succour and relief from evils.
A stranger to this tale I now speak forth,
A stranger to the deed, for not alone
Could I have tracked it far without some clue,
But now that I am enrolled a citizen
Latest among the citizens of Thebes
To all you sons of Cadmus I proclaim
Whoever of you knows at what man's hand
Laius, the son of Labdacus, met his death,
I order him to tell me all, and even
If he fears, to clear the charge and he will suffer
No injury, but leave the land unharmed.
If someone knows the murderer to be an alien
From foreign soil, let him not be silent;
I will give him a reward, my thanks besides.
But if you stay in silence and from fear
For self or friend thrust aside my command,
Here now from me what I shall do for this;
I charge that none who dwell within this land
Whereof I hold the power and the throne
Give this man shelter whoever he may be,
Or speak to him, or share with him in prayer
Or sacrifice, or serve him lustral rites,
But drive him, all, out of your homes, for he
Is this pollution on us, as Apollo
Revealed to me just now in oracle.

I am therefore the ally of the god
And of the murdered man. And now I pray
That the murderer, whether he hides alone
Or with his partners, may, evil coward,
Wear out in luckless ills his wretched life.
I further pray, that, if at my own hearth
He dwells known to me in my own home,
I may suffer myself the curse I just now uttered.
And you I charge to bring all this to pass
For me, and for the god, and for our land
Which now lies fruitless, godless, and corrupt.
Even if Phoebus had not urged this affair,
Not rightly did you let it go unpurged
When one both noble and a king was murdered!
You should have sought it out. Since now I reign
Holding the power which he had held before me,
Having the selfsame wife and marriage bed—
And if his seed had not met barren fortune
We should be linked by offspring from one mother;
But as it was, fate leapt upon his head.
Therefore in this, as if for my own father
I fight for him, and shall attempt all
Searching to seize the hand which shed that blood,
For Labdacus' son, before him Polydorus,
And ancient Cadmus, and Agenor of old.
And those who fail to do this, I pray the gods
May give them neither harvest from their earth
Nor children from their wives, but may they be
Destroyed by a fate like this one, or a worse.
You other Thebans, who cherish these commands,
May Justice, the ally of a righteous cause,
And all the gods be always on your side.
  CHORUS   By the oath you laid on me, my king, I speak.
I killed not Laius, nor can show who killed him.
Phoebus it was who sent this question to us,
And he should answer who has done the deed.
  OEDIPUS   Your words are just, but to compel the gods
In what they do not wish, no man can do.
  CHORUS   I would tell what seems to me our second course.
  OEDIPUS   If there is a third, fail not to tell it too.

CHORUS   Lord Teiresias I know, who sees this best
Like lord Apollo; in surveying this,
One might, my lord, find out from him most clearly.
   OEDIPUS   Even this I did not neglect; I have done it already.
At Creon's word I twice sent messengers.
It is a wonder he has been gone so long.
   CHORUS   And also there are rumors, faint and old.
   OEDIPUS   What are they? I must search out every tale.
   CHORUS   They say there were some travellers who killed him.
   OEDIPUS   So I have heard, but no one sees a witness.
   CHORUS   If his mind knows a particle of fear
He will not long withstand such curse as yours.
   OEDIPUS   He fears no speech who fears not such a deed.
   CHORUS   But here is the man who will convict the guilty.
Here are these men leading the divine prophet
In whom alone of men the truth is born.
   OEDIPUS   O you who ponder all, Teiresias,
Both what is taught and what cannot be spoken,
What is of heaven and what trod on the earth,
Even if you are blind, you know what plague
Clings to the state, and, master, you alone
We find as her protector and her saviour.
Apollo, if the messengers have not told you,
Answered our question, that release would come
From this disease only if we make sure
Of Laius' slayers and slay them in return
Or drive them out as exiles from the land.
But you now, grudge us neither voice of birds
Nor any way you have of prophecy.
Save yourself and the state; save me as well.
Save everything polluted by the dead.
We are in your hands; it is the noblest task
To help a man with all your means and powers.
   TEIRESIAS   Alas! Alas! How terrible to be wise,
Where it does the seer no good. Too well I know
And have forgot this, or would not have come here.
   OEDIPUS   What is this? How fainthearted you have come!
   TEIRESIAS   Let me go home; it is best for you to bear
Your burden, and I mine, if you will heed me.

OEDIPUS   You speak what is lawless, and hateful to the state
Which raised you, when you deprive her of your answer.

TEIRESIAS   And I see that your speech does not proceed
In season; I shall not undergo the same.

OEDIPUS   Don't by the gods turn back when you are wise,
When all we suppliants lie prostrate before you.

TEIRESIAS   And all unwise; I never shall reveal
My evils, so that I may not tell yours.

OEDIPUS   What do you say? You know, but will not speak?
Would you betray us and destroy the state?

TEIRESIAS   I will not hurt you or me. Why in vain
Do you probe this? You will not find out from me.

OEDIPUS   Worst of evil men, you would enrage
A stone itself. Will you never speak,
But stay so untouched and so inconclusive?

TEIRESIAS   You blame my anger and do not see that
With which you live in common, but upbraid me.

OEDIPUS   Who would not be enraged to hear these words
By which you now dishonor this our city?

TEIRESIAS   Of itself this will come, though I hide it in silence.

OEDIPUS   Then you should tell me what it is will come.

TEIRESIAS   I shall speak no more. If further you desire,
Rage on in wildest anger of your soul.

OEDIPUS   I shall omit nothing I understand
I am so angry. Know that you seem to me
Creator of the deed and worker too
In all short of the slaughter; if you were not blind,
I would say this crime was your work alone.

TEIRESIAS   Really? Abide yourself by the decree
You just proclaimed, I tell you! From this day
Henceforth address neither these men nor me.
You are the godless defiler of this land.

OEDIPUS   You push so bold and taunting in your speech;
And how do you think to get away with this?

TEIRESIAS   I have got away. I nurse my strength in truth.

OEDIPUS   Who taught you this? Not from your art you got it.

TEIRESIAS   From you. You had me speak against my will.

OEDIPUS   What word? Say again, so I may better learn.

TEIRESIAS   Didn't you get it before? Or do you bait me?

OEDIPUS   I don't remember it. Speak forth again.

TEIRESIAS   You are the slayer whom you seek, I say.

OEDIPUS   Not twice you speak such bitter words unpunished.

TEIRESIAS   Shall I speak more to make you angrier still?

OEDIPUS   Do what you will, your words will be in vain.

TEIRESIAS   I say you have forgot that you are joined
With those most dear to you in deepest shame
And do not see where you are in sin.

OEDIPUS   Do you think you will always say such things in joy?

TEIRESIAS   Surely, if strength abides in what is true.

OEDIPUS   It does, for all but you, this not for you
Because your ears and mind and eyes are blind.

TEIRESIAS   Wretched you are to make such taunts, for soon
All men will cast the selfsame taunts on you.

OEDIPUS   You live in entire night, could do no harm
To me or any man who sees the day.

TEIRESIAS   Not at my hands will it be your fate to fall.
Apollo suffices, whose concern it is to do this.

OEDIPUS   Are these devices yours, or are they Creon's?

TEIRESIAS   Creon is not your trouble; you are yourself.

OEDIPUS   O riches, empire, skill surpassing skill
In all the numerous rivalries of life,
How great a grudge there is stored up against you
If for this kingship, which the city gave,
Their gift, not my request, into my hands—
For this, the trusted Creon, my friend from the start
Desires to creep by stealth and cast me out
Taking a seer like this, a weaver of wiles,
A crooked swindler who has got his eyes
On gain alone, but in his art is blind.
Come, tell us, in what clearly are you a prophet?
How is it, when the weave-songed bitch was here
You uttered no salvation for these people?
Surely the riddle then could not be solved
By some chance comer; it needed prophecy.
You did not clarify that with birds
Or knowledge from a god; but when I came,
The ignorant Oedipus, I silenced her,
Not taught by birds, but winning by my wits,
Whom you are now attempting to depose,

Thinking to minister near Creon's throne.
I think that to your woe you and that plotter
Will purge the land, and if you were not old
Punishment would teach you what you plot.
    CHORUS It seems to us, O Oedipus our king,
Both this man's words and yours were said in anger.
Such is not our need, but to find out
How best we shall discharge Apollo's orders.
    TEIRESIAS Even if you are king, the right to answer
Should be free to all; of that I too am king.
I live not as your slave, but as Apollo's.
And not with Creon's wards shall I be counted.
I say, since you have taunted even my blindness,
You have eyes, but see not where in evil you are
Nor where you dwell, nor whom you are living with.
Do you know from whom you spring? And you forget
You are an enemy to your own kin
Both those beneath and those above the earth.
Your mother's and father's curse, with double goad
And dreaded foot shall drive you from this land.
You who now see straight shall then be blind,
And there shall be no harbour for your cry
With which all Mount Cithaeron soon shall ring,
When you have learned the wedding where you sailed
At home, into no port, by voyage fair.
A throng of other ills you do not know
Shall equal you to yourself and to your children.
Throw mud on this, on Creon, on my voice—
Yet there shall never be a mortal man
Eradicated more wretchedly than you.
    OEDIPUS Shall these unbearable words be heard from him?
Go to perdition! Hurry! Off, away,
Turn back again and from this house depart.
    TEIRESIAS If you had not called me, I should not have come.
    OEDIPUS I did not know that you would speak such folly
Or I would not soon have brought you to my house.
    TEIRESIAS And such a fool I am, as it seems to you.
But to the parents who bore you I seem wise.
    OEDIPUS What parents? Wait! What mortals gave me birth?
    TEIRESIAS This day shall be your birth and your destruction.

OEDIPUS   All things you say in riddles and unclear.

TEIRESIAS   Are you not he who best can search this out?

OEDIPUS   Mock, if you wish, the skill that made me great.

TEIRESIAS   This is the very fortune that destroyed you.

OEDIPUS   Well, if I saved the city, I do not care.

TEIRESIAS   I am going now. You, boy, be my guide.

OEDIPUS   Yes, let him guide you. Here you are in the way.
When you are gone you will give no more trouble.

TEIRESIAS   I go when I have said what I came to say
Without fear of your frown; you cannot destroy me.
I say, the very man whom you long seek
With threats and announcements about Laius' murder—
This man is here. He seems an alien stranger,
But soon he shall be revealed of Theban birth,
Nor at this circumstance shall he be pleased.
He shall be blind who sees, shall be a beggar
Who now is rich, shall make his way abroad
Feeling the ground before him with a staff.
He shall be revealed at once as brother
And father to his own children, husband and son
To his mother, his father's kin and murderer.
Go in and ponder that. If I am wrong,
Say then that I know nothing of prophecy.

CHORUS

Who is the man the Delphic rock said with oracular voice
Unspeakable crimes performed with his gory hands?
It is time for him now to speed
His foot in flight, more strong
Than horses swift as the storm.
For girt in arms upon him springs
With fire and lightning, Zeus' son
And behind him, terrible,
Come the unerring Fates.

From snowy Parnassus just now the word flashed clear
To track the obscure man by every way,
For he wanders under the wild
Forest, and into caves
And cliff rocks, like a bull,

Reft on his way, with care on care
Trying to shun the prophecy
Come from the earth's mid-navel,
But about him flutters the ever living doom.

Terrible, terrible things the wise bird-augur stirs.
I neither approve nor deny, at a loss for what to say,
I flutter in hopes and fears, see neither here nor ahead;
For what strife has lain
On Labdacus' sons or Polybus' that I have found ever before
Or now, whereby I may run for the sons of Labdacus
In sure proof against Oedipus' public fame
As avenger for dark death?

Zeus and Apollo surely understand and know
The affairs of mortal men, but that a mortal seer
Knows more than I, there is no proof. Though a man
May surpass a man in knowledge,
Never shall I agree, till I see the word true, when men blame
     Oedipus,
For there came upon him once clear the winged maiden
And wise he was seen, by sure test sweet for the state.
So never shall my mind judge him evil guilt.

     CREON   Men of our city, I have heard dread words
That Oedipus our king accuses me.
I am here indignant. If in the present troubles
He thinks that he has suffered at my hands
One word or deed tending to injury
I do not crave the long-spanned age of life
To bear this rumor, for it is no simple wrong
The damage of this accusation brings me;
It brings the greatest, if I am called a traitor
To you and my friends, a traitor to the state.
     CHORUS   Come now, for this reproach perhaps was forced
By anger, rather than considered thought.
     CREON   And was the idea voiced that my advice
Persuaded the prophet to give false accounts?
     CHORUS   Such was said. I know not to what intent.
     CREON   Was this accusation laid against me
From straightforward eyes and straightforward mind?

CHORUS   I do not know. I see not what my masters do;
But here he is now, coming from the house.

OEDIPUS   How dare you come here? Do you own a face
So bold that you can come before my house
When you are clearly the murderer of this man
And manifestly pirate of my throne?
Come, say before the gods, did you see in me
A coward or a fool, that you plotted this?
Or did you think I would not see your wiles
Creeping upon me, or knowing, would not ward off?
Surely your machination is absurd
Without a crowd of friends to hunt a throne
Which is captured only by wealth and many men.

CREON   Do you know what you do? Hear answer to your charges
On the other side. Judge only what you know.

OEDIPUS   Your speech is clever, but I learn it ill
Since I have found you harsh and grievous toward me.

CREON   This very matter hear me first explain.

OEDIPUS   Tell me not this one thing: you are not false.

CREON   If you think stubbornness a good possession
Apart from judgment, you do not think right.

OEDIPUS   If you think you can do a kinsman evil
Without the penalty, you have no sense.

CREON   I agree with you. What you have said is just.
Tell me what you say you have suffered from me.

OEDIPUS   Did you, or did you not, advise my need
Was summoning that prophet person here?

CREON   And still is. I hold still the same opinion.

OEDIPUS   How long a time now has it been since Laius—

CREON   Performed what deed? I do not understand.

OEDIPUS   —Disappeared to his ruin at deadly hands.

CREON   Far in the past the count of years would run.

OEDIPUS   Was this same seer at that time practising?

CREON   As wise as now, and equally respected.

OEDIPUS   At that time did he ever mention me?

CREON   Never when I stood near enough to hear.

OEDIPUS   But did you not make inquiry of the murder?

CREON   We did, of course, and got no information.

OEDIPUS   How is it that this seer did not utter this then?

CREON   When I don't know, as now, I would keep still.

OEDIPUS This much you know full well, and so should speak:—
CREON What is that? If I know, I will not refuse.
OEDIPUS This: If he had not first conferred with you
He never would have said that I killed Laius.
CREON If he says this, you know yourself, I think;
I learn as much from you as you from me.
OEDIPUS Learn then: I never shall be found a slayer.
CREON What then, are you the husband of my sister?
OEDIPUS What you have asked is plain beyond denial.
CREON Do you rule this land with her in equal sway?
OEDIPUS All she desires she obtains from me.
CREON Am I with you two not an equal third?
OEDIPUS In just that do you prove a treacherous friend.
CREON No, if, like me, you reason with yourself.
Consider this fact first: would any man
Choose, do you think, to have his rule in fear
Rather than doze unharmed with the same power?
For my part I have never been desirous
Of being king instead of acting king.
Nor any other man has, wise and prudent.
For now I obtain all from you without fear.
If I were king, I would do much unwilling.
How then could kingship sweeter be for me
Than rule and power devoid of any pain?
I am not yet so much deceived to want
Goods besides those I profitably enjoy.
Now I am hailed and gladdened by all men.
Now those who want from you speak out to me,
Since all their chances' outcome dwells therein.
How then would I relinquish what I have
To get those gains? My mind runs not so bad.
I am prudent yet, no lover of such plots,
Nor would I ever endure others' treason.
And first as proof of this go on to Pytho;
See if I told you truly the oracle.
Next proof: see if I plotted with the seer;
If you find so at all, put me to death
With my vote for my guilt as well as yours.
Do not convict me just on unclear conjecture.
It is not right to think capriciously

The good are bad, nor that the bad are good.
It is the same to cast out a noble friend,
I say, as one's own life, which best he loves.
The facts, though, you will safely know in time,
Since time alone can show the just man just,
But you can know a criminal in one day.

CHORUS   A cautious man would say he has spoken well.
O king, the quick to think are never sure.

OEDIPUS   When the plotter, swift, approaches me in stealth
I too in counterplot must be as swift.
If I wait in repose, the plotter's ends
Are brought to pass and mine will then have erred.

CREON   What do you want then? To cast me from the land?

OEDIPUS   Least of all that. My wish is you should die,
Not flee to exemplify what envy is.

CREON   Do you say this? Will you neither trust nor yield?

OEDIPUS   [No, for I think that you deserve no trust.]

CREON   You seem not wise to me.

OEDIPUS   I am for me.

CREON   You should be for me too.

OEDIPUS   No, you are evil.

CREON   Yes, if you understand nothing.

OEDIPUS   Yet I must rule.

CREON   Not when you rule badly.

OEDIPUS   O city, city!

CREON   It is my city too, not yours alone.

CHORUS   Stop, princes. I see Jocasta coming
Out of the house at the right time for you.
With her you must settle the dispute at hand.

JOCASTA   O wretched men, what unconsidered feud
Of tongues have you aroused? Are you not ashamed,
The state so sick, to stir up private ills?
Are you not going home? And you as well?
Will you turn a small pain into a great?

CREON   My blood sister, Oedipus your husband
Claims he will judge against me two dread ills:
Thrust me from the fatherland or take and kill me.

OEDIPUS   I will, my wife; I caught him in the act
Doing evil to my person with evil skill.

CREON   Now may I not rejoice but die accursed
If ever I did any of what you accuse me.

JOCASTA   O, by the gods, believe him, Oedipus.
First, in reverence for his oath to the gods,
Next, for my sake and theirs who stand before you.

CHORUS   Hear my entreaty, lord. Consider and consent.

OEDIPUS   What wish should I then grant?

CHORUS   Respect the man, no fool before, who now in oath is strong.

OEPIDUS   You know what you desire?

CHORUS   I know.

OEDIPUS   Say what you mean.

CHORUS   Your friend who has sworn do not dishonour
By casting guilt for dark report.

OEDIPUS   Know well that when you ask this grant from me,
You ask my death or exile from the land.

CHORUS   No, by the god foremost among the gods,
The Sun, may I perish by the utmost doom
Godless and friendless, if I have this in mind.
But ah, the withering earth wears down
My wretched soul, if to these ills
Of old are added ills from both of you.

OEDIPUS   Then let him go, though surely I must die
Or be thrust dishonoured from this land by force.
Your grievous voice I pity, not that man's;
Wherever he may be, he will be hated.

CREON   Sullen you are to yield, as you are heavy
When you exceed in wrath. Natures like these
Are justly sorest for themselves to bear.

OEDIPUS   Will you not go and leave me?

CREON   I am on my way.
You know me not, but these men see me just.

CHORUS   O queen, why do you delay to bring this man indoors?

JOCASTA   I want to learn what happened here.

CHORUS   Unknown suspicion rose from talk, and the unjust devours.

JOCASTA   In both of them?

CHORUS   Just so.

JOCASTA   What was the talk?

CHORUS   Enough, enough! When the land is pained
It seems to me at this point we should stop.

OEDIPUS   Do you see where you have come? Though your intent
Is good, you slacken off and blunt my heart.

CHORUS   O lord, I have said not once alone,
Know that I clearly would be mad
And wandering in mind, to turn away
You who steered along the right,
When she was torn with trouble, our beloved state.
O may you now become in health her guide.

JOCASTA   By the gods, lord, tell me on what account
You have set yourself in so great an anger.

OEDIPUS   I shall tell you, wife; I respect you more than these men.
Because of Creon, since he has plotted against me.

JOCASTA   Say clearly, if you can; how started the quarrel?

OEDIPUS   He says that I stand as the murderer of Laius.

JOCASTA   He knows himself, or learned from someone else?

OEDIPUS   No, but he sent a rascal prophet here.
He keeps his own mouth clean in what concerns him.

JOCASTA   Now free yourself of what you said, and listen.
Learn from me, no mortal man exists
Who knows prophetic art for your affairs,
And I shall briefly show you proof of this:
An oracle came once to Laius. I do not say
From Phoebus himself, but from his ministers
That his fate would be at his son's hand to die—
A child, who would be born from him and me.
And yet, as the rumour says, they were strangers,
Robbers who killed him where three highways meet.
But three days had not passed from the child's birth
When Laius pierced and tied together his ankles,
And cast him by others' hands on a pathless mountain.
Therein Apollo did not bring to pass
That the child murder his father, nor for Laius
The dread he feared, to die at his son's hand.
Such did prophetic oracles determine.
Pay no attention to them. For the god
Will easily make clear the need he seeks.

OEDIPUS   What wandering of soul, what stirring of mind
Holds me, my wife, in what I have just heard!

JOCASTA   What care has turned you back that you say this?

OEDIPUS   I thought I heard you mention this, that Laius
Was slaughtered at the place where three highways meet.

JOCASTA   That was the talk. The rumour has not ceased.

OEDIPUS   Where is this place where such a sorrow was?

JOCASTA   The country's name is Phocis. A split road
Leads to one place from Delphi and Daulia.

OEDIPUS   And how much time has passed since these events?

JOCASTA   The news was heralded in the city scarcely
A little while before you came to rule.

OEDIPUS   O Zeus, what have you planned to do to me?

JOCASTA   What passion is this in you, Oedipus?

OEDIPUS   Don't ask me that yet. Tell me about Laius.
What did he look like? How old was he when murdered?

JOCASTA   A tall man, with his hair just brushed with white.
His shape and form differed not far from yours.

OEDIPUS   Alas! Alas! I think unwittingly
I have just laid dread curses on my head.

JOCASTA   What are you saying? I shrink to behold you, lord.

OEDIPUS   I am terribly afraid the seer can see.
That will be clearer if you say one thing more.

JOCASTA   Though I shrink, if I know what you ask, I will answer.

OEDIPUS   Did he set forth with few attendants then,
Or many soldiers, since he was a king?

JOCASTA   They were five altogether among them.
One was a herald. One chariot bore Laius.

OEDIPUS   Alas! All this is clear now. Tell me, my wife,
Who was the man who told these stories to you?

JOCASTA   One servant, who alone escaped, returned.

OEDIPUS   Is he by chance now present in our house?

JOCASTA   Not now. Right from the time when he returned
To see you ruling and Laius dead,
Touching my hand in suppliance, he implored me
To send him to fields and to pastures of sheep
That he might be farthest from the sight of this city.
So I sent him away, since he was worthy
For a slave, to bear a greater grant than this.

OEDIPUS   How then could he return to us with speed?

JOCASTA   It can be done. But why would you order this?

OEDIPUS   O lady, I fear I have said too much.
On this account I now desire to see him.
   JOCASTA   Then he shall come. But I myself deserve
To learn what it is that troubles you, my lord.
   OEDIPUS   And you shall not be prevented, since my fears
Have come to such a point. For who is closer
That I may speak to in this fate than you?
Polybus of Corinth was my father,
My mother, Dorian Merope. I was held there
Chief citizen of all, till such a fate
Befell me—as it is, worthy of wonder,
But surely not deserving my excitement.
A man at a banquet overdrunk with wine
Said in drink I was a false son to my father.
The weight I held that day I scarcely bore,
But on the next day I went home and asked
My father and mother of it. In bitter anger
They took the reproach from him who had let it fly.
I was pleased at their actions; nevertheless
The rumour always rankled; and spread abroad.
In secret from mother and father I set out
Toward Delphi. Phoebus sent me away ungraced
In what I came for, but other wretched things
Terrible and grievous, he revealed in answer;
That I must wed my mother and produce
An unendurable race to for men to see,
That I should kill the father who begot me.
When I heard this response, Corinth I fled
Henceforth to measure her land by stars alone.
I went where I should never see the disgrace
Of my evil oracles be brought to pass,
And on my journey to that place I came
At which you say this king had met his death.
My wife, I shall speak the truth to you. My way
Led to a place close by the triple road.
There a herald met me, and a man
Seated on colt-drawn chariot, as you said.
There both the guide and the old man himself
Thrust me with driving force out of the path.
And I in anger struck the one who pushed me,

The driver. Then the old man, when he saw me,
Watched when I passed, and from his chariot
Struck me full on the head with double goad.
I paid him back and more. From this very hand
A swift blow of my staff rolled him right out
Of the middle of his seat onto his back.
I killed them all. But if relationship
Existed between this stranger and Laius,
What man now is wretcheder than I?
What man is cursed by a more evil fate?
No stranger or citizen could now receive me
Within his home, or even speak to me,
But thrust me out; and no one but myself
Brought down these curses on my head.
The bed of the slain man I now defile
With hands that killed him. Am I evil by birth?
Am I not utterly vile if I must flee
And cannot see my family in my flight
Nor tread my homeland soil, or else be joined
In marriage to my mother, kill my father,
Polybus, who sired me and brought me up?
Would not a man judge right to say of me
That this was sent on me by some cruel spirit?
O never, holy reverence of the gods,
May I behold that day, but may I go
Away from mortal men, before I see
Such a stain of circumstance come to me.
    CHORUS   My lord, for us these facts are full of dread.
Until you hear the witness, stay in hope.
    OEDIPUS   And just so much is all I have of hope,
Only to wait until the shepherd comes.
    JOCASTA   What, then, do you desire to hear him speak?
    OEDIPUS   I will tell you, if his story is found to be
The same as yours, I would escape the sorrow.
    JOCASTA   What unusual word did you hear from me?
    OEDIPUS   You said he said that they were highway robbers
Who murdered him. Now, if he still says
The selfsame number, I could not have killed him,
Since one man does not equal many men.
But if he speaks of a single lonely traveller,

The scale of guilt now clearly falls to me.

JOCASTA However, know the word was set forth thus
And it is not in him now to take it back;
This tale the city heard, not I alone.
But if he diverges from his previous story,
Even then, my lord, he could not show Laius' murder
To have been fulfilled properly. Apollo
Said he would die at the hands of my own son.
Surely that wretched child could not have killed him,
But he himself met death some time before.
Therefore, in any prophecy henceforth
I would not look to this side or to that.

OEDIPUS Your thoughts ring true, but still let someone go
To summon the peasant. Do not neglect this.

JOCASTA I shall send without delay. But let us enter.
I would do nothing that did not please you.

CHORUS

May fate come on me as I bear
Holy pureness in all word and deed,
For which the lofty striding laws were set down,
Born through the heavenly air
Whereof the Olympian sky alone the father was;
No mortal spawn of mankind gave them birth,
Nor may oblivion ever lull them down;
Mighty in them the god is, and he does not age.

Pride breeds the tyrant.
Pride, once overfilled with many things in vain,
Neither in season nor fit for man,
Scaling the sheerest height
Hurls to a dire fate
Where no foothold is found.
I pray the god may never stop the rivalry
That works well for the state.
The god as my protector I shall never cease to hold.

But if a man goes forth haughty in word or deed
With no fear of the Right
Nor pious to the spirits' shrines,

May evil doom seize him
For his ill-fated pride,
If he does not fairly win his gain
Or works unholy deeds,
Or, in bold folly lays on the sacred profane hands.
For when such acts occur, what man may boast
Ever to ward off from his life darts of the gods?
If practices like these are in respect,
Why then must I dance the sacred dance?

Never again in worship shall I go
To Delphi, holy navel of the earth,
Nor to the temple at Abae,
Nor to Olympia,
If these prophecies do not become
Examples for all men.
O Zeus, our king, if so you are rightly called,
Ruler of all things, may they not escape
You and your forever deathless power.
Men now hold light the fading oracles
Told about Laius long ago
And nowhere is Apollo clearly honored;
Things divine are going down to ruin.

JOCASTA Lords of this land, the thought has come to me
To visit the spirits' shrines, bearing in hand
These suppliant boughs and offerings of incense.
For Oedipus raises his soul too high
With all distresses; nor, as a sane man should,
Does he confirm the new by things of old,
But stands at the speaker's will if he speaks terrors.
And so, because my advice can do no more,
To you, Lycian Apollo—for you are nearest—
A suppliant, I have come here with these prayers,
That you may find some pure deliverance for us:
We all now shrink to see him struck in fear,
That man who is the pilot of our ship.
MESSENGER Strangers, could I learn from one of you
Where is the house of Oedipus the king?
Or best, if you know, say where he is himself.

CHORUS   This is his house, stranger; he dwells inside;
This woman is the mother of his children.

MESSENGER   May she be always blessed among the blest,
Since she is the fruitful wife of Oedipus.

JOCASTA   So may you, stranger, also be. You deserve
As much for your graceful greeting. But tell me
What you have come to search for or to show.

MESSENGER   Good news for your house and your husband, lady.

JOCASTA   What is it then? And from whom have you come?

MESSENGER   From Corinth. And the message I will tell
Will surely gladden you—and vex you, perhaps.

JOCASTA   What is it? What is this double force it holds?

MESSENGER   The men who dwell in the Isthmian country
Have spoken to establish him their king.

JOCASTA   What is that? Is not old Polybus still ruling?

MESSENGER   Not he. For death now holds him in the tomb.

JOCASTA   What do you say, old man? Is Polybus dead?

MESSENGER   If I speak not the truth, I am ready to die.

JOCASTA   O handmaid, go right away and tell your master
The news. Where are you, prophecies of the gods?
For this man Oedipus has trembled long,
And shunned him lest he kill him. Now the man
Is killed by fate and not by Oedipus.

OEDIPUS   O Jocasta, my most beloved wife,
Why have you sent for me within the house?

JOCASTA   Listen to this man, and while you hear him, think
To what have come Apollo's holy prophecies.

OEDIPUS   Who is this man? Why would he speak to me?

JOCASTA   From Corinth he has come, to announce that your father
Polybus no longer lives, but is dead.

OEDIPUS   What do you say, stranger? Tell me this yourself.

MESSENGER   If I must first announce my message clearly,
Know surely that the man is dead and gone.

OEDIPUS   Did he die by treachery or chance disease?

MESSENGER   A slight scale tilt can lull the old to rest.

OEDIPUS   The poor man, it seems, died by disease.

MESSENGER   And by the full measure of lengthy time.

OEDIPUS   Alas, alas! Why then do any seek
Pytho's prophetic art, my wife, or hear
The shrieking birds on high, by whose report

I was to slay my father? Now he lies
Dead beneath the earth, and here am I
Who have not touched the blade. Unless in longing
For me he died, and in this sense was killed by me.
Polybus has packed away these oracles
In his rest in Hades. They are now worth nothing.

JOCASTA Did I not tell you that some time ago?

OEDIPUS You did, but I was led astray by fear.

JOCASTA Henceforth put nothing of this on your heart.

OEDIPUS Why must I not still shrink from my mother's bed?

JOCASTA What should man fear, whose life is ruled by fate,
For whom there is clear foreknowledge of nothing?
It is best to live by chance, however you can.
Be not afraid of marriage with your mother;
Already many mortals in their dreams
Have shared their mother's bed. But he who counts
This dream as nothing, easiest bears his life.

OEDIPUS All that you say would be indeed propitious,
If my mother were not alive. But since she is,
I still must shrink, however well you speak.

JOCASTA And yet your father's tomb is a great eye.

OEDIPUS A great eye indeed. But I fear her who lives.

MESSENGER Who is this woman that you are afraid of?

OEDIPUS Merope, old man, with whom Polybus lived.

MESSENGER What is it in her that moves you to fear?

OEDIPUS A dread oracle, stranger, sent by the god.

MESSENGER Can it be told, or must no other know?

OEDIPUS It surely can. Apollo told me once
That I must join in intercourse with my mother
And shed with my own hands my father's blood.
Because of this, long since I have kept far
Away from Corinth—and happily—but yet
It would be most sweet to see my parents' faces.

MESSENGER Was this your fear in shunning your own city?

OEDIPUS I wished, too, old man, not to slay my father.

MESSENGER Why then have I not freed you from this fear,
Since I have come with friendly mind, my lord?

OEDIPUS Yes, and take thanks from me, which you deserve.

MESSENGER And this is just the thing for which I came,
That when you got back home I might fare well.

OEDIPUS   Never shall I go where my parents are.

MESSENGER   My son, you clearly know not what you do.

OEDIPUS   How is that, old man? By the gods, let me know.

MESSENGER   If for these tales you shrink from going home.

OEDIPUS   I tremble lest what Phoebus said comes true.

MESSENGER   Lest you incur pollution from your parents?

OEDIPUS   That is the thing, old man, that always haunts me.

MESSENGER   Well, do you know that surely you fear nothing?

OEDIPUS   How so? If I am the son of those who bore me.

MESSENGER   Since Polybus was no relation to you.

OEDIPUS   What do you say? Was Polybus not my father?

MESSENGER   No more than this man here but just so much.

OEDIPUS   How does he who begot me equal nothing?

MESSENGER   That man was not your father, any more than I am.

OEDIPUS   Well then, why was it he called me his son?

MESSENGER   Long ago he got you as a gift from me.

OEDIPUS   Though from another's hand, yet so much he loved me!

MESSENGER   His previous childlessness led him to that.

OEDIPUS   Had you bought or found me when you gave me to him?

MESSENGER   I found you in Cithaeron's folds and glens.

OEDIPUS   Why were you travelling in those regions?

MESSENGER   I guarded there a flock of mountain sheep.

OEDIPUS   Were you a shepherd, wandering for pay?

MESSENGER   Yes, and your saviour too, child, at that time.

OEDIPUS   What pain gripped me, that you took me in your arms?

MESSENGER   The ankles of your feet will tell you that.

OEDIPUS   Alas, why do you mention that old trouble?

MESSENGER   I freed you when your ankles were pierced together.

OEDIPUS   A terrible shame from my swaddling clothes I got.

MESSENGER   Your very name you got from this misfortune.

OEDIPUS   By the gods, did my mother or father do it? Speak.

MESSENGER   I know not. He who gave you knows better than I.

OEDIPUS   You didn't find me, but took me from another?

MESSENGER   That's right. Another shepherd gave you to me.

OEDIPUS   Who was he? Can you tell me who he was?

MESSENGER   Surely. He belonged to the household of Laius.

OEDIPUS   The man who ruled this land once long ago?

MESSENGER   Just so. He was a herd in that man's service.

OEDIPUS   Is this man still alive, so I could see him?

MESSENGER   You dwellers in this country should know best.

OEDIPUS   Is there any one of you who stand before me
Who knows the shepherd of whom this man speaks?
If you have seen him in the fields or here,
Speak forth; the time has come to find this out.

CHORUS   I think the man you seek is no one else
Than the shepherd you were so eager to see before.
Jocasta here might best inform us that.

OEDIPUS   My wife, do you know the man we just ordered
To come here? Is it of him that this man speaks?

JOCASTA   Why ask of whom he spoke? Think nothing of it.
Brood not in vain on what has just been said.

OEDIPUS   It could not be that when I have got such clues,
I should not shed clear light upon my birth.

JOCASTA   Don't, by the gods, investigate this more
If you care for your own life. I am sick enough.

OEDIPUS   Take courage. Even if I am found a slave
For three generations, your birth will not be base.

JOCASTA   Still, I beseech you, hear me. Don't do this.

OEDIPUS   I will hear of nothing but finding out the truth.

JOCASTA   I know full well and tell you what is best.

OEDIPUS   Well, then, this best, for some time now, has given me
pain.

JOCASTA   O ill-fated man, may you never know who you are.

OEDIPUS   Will someone bring the shepherd to me here?
And let this lady rejoice in her opulent birth.

JOCASTA   Alas, alas, hapless man. I have this alone
To tell you, and nothing else forevermore.

CHORUS   O Oedipus, where has the woman gone
In the rush of her wild grief? I am afraid
Evil will break forth out of this silence.

OEDIPUS   Let whatever will break forth. I plan to see
The seed of my descent, however small.
My wife, perhaps, because a noblewoman
Looks down with shame upon my lowly birth.
I would not be dishonoured to call myself
The son of Fortune, giver of the good.
She is my mother. The years, her other children,
Have marked me sometimes small and sometimes great.
Such was I born! I shall prove no other man,
Nor shall I cease to search out my descent.

CHORUS

If I am a prophet and can know in mind,
Cithaeron, by tomorrow's full moon
You shall not fail, by mount Olympus,
To find that Oedipus, as a native of your land,
Shall honour you for nurse and mother.
And to you we dance in choral song because you bring
Fair gifts to him our king.
Hail, Phoebus, may all this please you.

Who, child, who bore you in the lengthy span of years?
One close to Pan who roams the mountain woods,
One of Apollo's bedfellows?
For all wild pastures in mountain glens to him are dear.
Was Hermes your father, who Cyllene sways,
Or did Bacchus, dwelling on the mountain peaks,
Take you a foundling from some nymph
Of those by springs of Helicon, with whom he sports the most?

OEDIPUS   If I may guess, although I never met him,
I think, elders, I see that shepherd coming
Whom we have long sought, as in the measure
Of lengthy age he accords with him we wait for.
Besides, the men who lead him I recognize
As servants of my house. You may perhaps
Know better than I if you have seen him before.
CHORUS   Be assured, I know him as a shepherd
As trusted as any other in Laius' service.
OEDIPUS   Stranger from Corinth, I will ask you first,
Is this the man you said?
MESSENGER   You are looking at him.
OEDIPUS   You there, old man, look here and answer me
What I shall ask you. Were you ever with Laius?
SERVANT   I was a slave, not bought but reared at home.
OEDIPUS   What work concerned you? What was your way of life?
SERVANT   Most of my life I spent among the flocks.
OEDIPUS   In what place most of all was your usual pasture?
SERVANT   Sometimes Cithaeron, or the ground nearby.
OEDIPUS   Do you know this man before you here at all?
SERVANT   Doing what? And of what man do you speak?

OEDIPUS The one before you. Have you ever had congress with him?

SERVANT Not to say so at once from memory.

MESSENGER That is no wonder, master, but I shall remind him,
Clearly, who knows me not; yet well I know
That he knew once the region of Cithaeron.
He with a double flock and I with one
Dwelt there in company for three whole years
During the six months' time from spring to fall.
When winter came, I drove into my fold
My flock, and he drove his to Laius' pens.
Do I speak right, or did it not happen so?

SERVANT You speak the truth, though it was long ago.

MESSENGER Come now, do you recall you gave me then
A child for me to rear as my own son?

SERVANT What is that? Why do you ask me this?

MESSENGER This is the man, my friend, who then was young.

SERVANT Go to destruction! Will you not be quiet?

OEDIPUS Come, scold him not, old man. These words of yours
Deserve a scolding more than this man's do.

SERVANT In what, most noble master, do I wrong?

OEDIPUS Not to tell of the child he asks about.

SERVANT He speaks in ignorance, he toils in vain.

OEDIPUS If you will not speak freely, you will under torture.

SERVANT Don't, by the gods, outrage an old man like me.

OEDIPUS Will someone quickly twist back this fellow's arms?

SERVANT Alas, what for? What do you want to know?

OEDIPUS Did you give this man the child of whom he asks?

SERVANT I did. Would I had perished on that day!

OEDIPUS You will come to that unless you tell the truth.

SERVANT I come to far greater ruin if I speak.

OEDIPUS This man, it seems, is trying to delay.

SERVANT Not I. I said before I gave it to him.

OEDIPUS Where did you get it? At home or from someone else?

SERVANT It was not mine. I got him from a man.

OEDIPUS Which of these citizens? Where did he live?

SERVANT O master, by the gods, ask me no more.

OEDIPUS You are done for if I ask you this again.

SERVANT Well then, he was born of the house of Laius.

OEDIPUS One of his slaves, or born of his own race?

SERVANT   Alas, to speak I am on the brink of horror.
OEDIPUS   And I to hear. But still it must be heard.
SERVANT   Well, then, they say it was his child. Your wife
Who dwells within could best say how this stands.
OEDIPUS   Was it she who gave him to you?
SERVANT   Yes, my lord.
OEDIPUS   For what intent?
SERVANT   So I could put it away.
OEDIPUS   When she bore him, the wretch.
SERVANT   She feared bad oracles.
OEDIPUS   What were they?
SERVANT   They said he should kill his father.
OEDIPUS   Why did you give him up to this old man?
SERVANT   I pitied him, master, and thought he would take him
away
To another land, the one from which he came.
But he saved him for greatest woe. If you are he
Whom this man speaks of, you were born curst by fate.
   OEDIPUS   Alas, alas! All things are now come true.
O light, for the last time now I look upon you;
I am shown to be born from those I ought not to have been.
I married the woman I should not have married,
I killed the man whom I should not have killed.

   CHORUS

Alas, generations of mortal men!
How equal to nothing do I number you in life!
Who, O who, is the man
Who bears more of bliss
Than just the seeming so,
And then, like a waning sun, to fall away?
When I know your example,
Your guiding spirit, yours, wretched Oedipus,
I call no mortal blest.

He is the one, O Zeus,
Who peerless shot his bow and won well-fated bliss,
Who destroyed the hook-clawed maiden,
The oracle-singing Sphinx,
And stood a tower for our land from death;

For this you are called our king,
Oedipus, are highest-honoured here,
And over great Thebes hold sway.

And now who is more wretched for men to hear,
Who so lives in wild plagues, who dwells in pains,
In utter change of life?
Alas for glorious Oedipus!
The selfsame port of rest
Was gained by bridegroom father and his son,
How, O how did your father's furrows ever bear you, suffering man?
How have they endured silence for so long?

You are found out, unwilling, by all-seeing Time.
It judges your unmarried marriage where for long
Begetter and begot have been the same.
Alas, child of Laius,
Would I had never seen you.
As one who pours from his mouth a dirge I wail,
To speak the truth, through you I breathed new life,
And now through you I lulled my eye to sleep.

SECOND MESSENGER   O men most honoured always of this land
What deeds you shall hear, what shall you behold!
What grief shall stir you up, if by your kinship
You are still concerned for the house of Labdacus!
I think neither Danube nor any other river
Could wash this palace clean, so many ills
Lie hidden there which now will come to light.
They were done by will, not fate; and sorrows hurt
The most when we ourselves appear to choose them.
   CHORUS   What we heard before causes no little sorrow.
What can you say which adds to that a burden?
   SECOND MESSENGER   This is the fastest way to tell the tale;
Hear it: Jocasta, your divine queen, is dead.
   CHORUS   O sorrowful woman! From what cause did she die?
   SECOND MESSENGER   By her own hand. The most painful of the
   action
Occurred away, not for your eyes to see.
But still, so far as I have memory
You shall learn the sufferings of that wretched woman:

How she passed on through the door enraged
And rushed straight forward to her nuptial bed,
Clutching her hair's ends with both her hands.
Once inside the doors she shut herself in
And called on Laius, who has long been dead,
Having remembrance of their seed of old
By which he died himself and left her a mother
To bear an evil brood to his own son.
She moaned the bed on which by double curse
She bore husband to husband, children to child.
How thereafter she perished I do not know,
For Oedipus burst in on her with a shriek,
And because of him we could not see her woe.
We looked on him alone as he rushed around.
Pacing about, he asked us to give him a sword,
Asked where he might find the wife no wife,
A mother whose plowfield bore him and his children.
Some spirit was guiding him in his frenzy,
For none of the men who are close at hand did so.
With a horrible shout, as if led on by someone,
He leapt on the double doors, from their sockets
Broke hollow bolts aside, and dashed within.
There we beheld his wife hung by her neck
From twisted cords, swinging to and fro.
When he saw her, wretched man, he terribly groaned
And slackened the hanging noose. When the poor woman
Lay on the ground, what happened was dread to see.
He tore the golden brooch pins from her clothes,
And raised them up, and struck his own eyeballs,
Shouting such words as these "No more shall you
Behold the evils I have suffered and done.
Be dark from now on, since you saw before
What you should not, and knew not what you should."
Moaning such cries, not once but many times
He raised and struck his eyes. The bloody pupils
Bedewed his beard. The gore oozed not in drops,
But poured in a black shower, a hail of blood.
From both of them these woes have broken out,
Not for just one, but man and wife together.
The bliss of old that formerly prevailed

Was bliss indeed, but now upon this day
Lamentation, madness, death, and shame—
No evil that can be named is not at hand.
   CHORUS Is the wretched man in any rest now from pain?
   SECOND MESSENGER He shouts for someone to open up the doors
And show to all Cadmeans his father's slayer,
His mother's—I should not speak the unholy word.
He says he will hurl himself from the land, no more
To dwell cursed in the house by his own curse.
Yet he needs strength and someone who will guide him.
His sickness is too great to bear. He will show it to you
For the fastenings of the doors are opening up,
And such a spectacle you will soon behold
As would make even one who abhors it take pity.
   CHORUS O terrible suffering for men to see,
Most terrible of all that I
Have ever come upon. O wretched man,
What madness overcame you, what springing daimon
Greater than the greatest for men
Has caused your evil-daimoned fate?
Alas, alas, grievous one,
But I cannot bear to behold you, though I desire
To ask you much, much to find out,
Much to see,
You make me shudder so!
   OEDIPUS Alas, alas, I am grieved!
Where on earth, so wretched, shall I go?
Where does my voice fly through the air,
O Fate, where have you bounded?
   CHORUS To dreadful end, not to be heard or seen.

   OEDIPUS O cloud of dark
That shrouds me off, has come to pass, unspeakable,
Invincible, that blows no favoring blast.
Woe,
O woe again, the goad that pierces me,
Of the sting of evil now, and memory of before.
   CHORUS No wonder it is that among so many pains
You should both mourn and bear a double evil.
   OEDIPUS Ah, friend,
You are my steadfast servant still,

You still remain to care for me, blind.
Alas! Alas!
You are not hid from me; I know you clearly,
And though in darkness, still I hear your voice.
    CHORUS O dreadful doer, how did you so endure
To quench your eyes? What daimon drove you on?

    OEDIPUS Apollo it was, Apollo, friends
Who brought to pass these evil, evil woes of mine.
The hand of no one struck my eyes but wretched me.
For why should I see,
When nothing sweet there is to see with sight?
    CHORUS This is just as you say.
    OEDIPUS What more is there for me to see,
My friends, what to love,
What joy to hear a greeting?
Lead me at once away from here,
Lead me away, friends, wretched as I am,
Accursed, and hated most
Of mortals to the gods.
    CHORUS Wretched alike in mind and in your fortune,
How I wish that I had never known you.

    OEDIPUS May he perish, whoever freed me
From fierce bonds on my feet,
Snatched me from death and saved me, doing me no joy.
For if then I had died, I should not be
So great a grief to friends and to myself.
    CHORUS This also is my wish.
    OEDIPUS I would not have come to murder my father,
Nor have been called among men
The bridegroom of her from whom I was born.
But as it is I am godless, child of unholiness,
Wretched sire in common with my father.
And if there is any evil older than evil left,
It is the lot of Oedipus.
    CHORUS I know not how I could give you good advice,
For you would be better dead than living blind.

    OEDIPUS That how things are was not done for the best—
Teach me not this, or give me more advice.

If I had sight, I know not with what eyes
I could ever face my father among the dead,
Or my wretched mother. What I have done to them
Is too great for a noose to expiate.
Do you think the sight of my children would be a joy
For me to see, born as they were to me?
No, never for these eyes of mine to see.
Nor the city, nor the tower, nor the sacred
Statues of gods; of these I deprive myself,
Noblest among the Thebans, born and bred,
Now suffering everything. I tell you all
To exile me as impious, shown by the gods
Untouchable and of the race of Laius.
When I uncovered such a stain on me,
Could I look with steady eyes upon the people?
No, no! And if there were a way to block
The spring of hearing, I would not forbear
To lock up wholly this my wretched body.
I should be blind and deaf.—For it is sweet
When thought can dwell outside our evils.
Alas, Cithaeron, why did you shelter me?
Why did you not take and kill me at once, so I
Might never reveal to men whence I was born?
O Polybus, O Corinth, O my father's halls,
Ancient in fable, what an outer fairness,
A festering of evils, you raised in me.
For now I am evil found, and born of evil.
O the three paths! Alas the hidden glen,
The grove of oak, the narrow triple roads
That drank from my own hands my father's blood.
Do you remember any of the deeds
I did before you then on my way here
And what I after did? O wedlock, wedlock!
You gave me birth, and then spawned in return
Issue from the selfsame seed; you revealed
Father, brother, children, in blood relation,
The bride both wife and mother, and whatever
Actions are done most shameful among men.
But it is wrong to speak what is not good to do.
By the gods, hide me at once outside our land,

Or murder me, or hurl me in the sea
Where you shall never look on me again.
Come, venture to lay your hands on this wretched man.
Do it. Be not afraid. No mortal man
There is, except myself, to bear my evils.

    CHORUS Here is Creon, just in time for what you ask
To work and to advise, for he alone
Is left in place of you to guard the land.

    OEDIPUS Alas, what word, then, shall I tell this man?
What righteous ground of trust is clear in me,
As in the past in all I have done him evil?

    CREON Oedipus, I have not come to laugh at you,
Nor to reproach you for your former wrongs.

(To the attendants)

If you defer no longer to mortal offspring,
Respect at least the all-nourishing flame
Of Apollo, lord of the sun. Fear to display
So great a pestilence, which neither earth
Nor holy rain nor light will well receive.
But you, conduct him to the house at once.
It is most pious for the kin alone
To hear and to behold the family sins.

    OEDIPUS By the gods, since you have plucked me from my fear,
Most noble, facing this most vile man,
Hear me one word—I will speak for you, not me.

    CREON What desire do you so persist to get?

    OEDIPUS As soon as you can, hurl me from this land
To where no mortal man will ever greet me.

    CREON I would do all this, be sure. But I want first
To find out from the god what must be done.

    OEDIPUS His oracle, at least, is wholly clear;
Leave me to ruin, an impious parricide.

    CREON Thus spake the oracle. Still, as we stand
It is better to find out sure what we should do.

    OEDIPUS Will you inquire about so wretched a man?

    CREON Yes. You will surely put trust in the god.

    OEDIPUS I order you and beg you, give the woman
Now in the house such burial as you yourself
Would want. Do last rites justly for your kin.

But may this city never be condemned—
My father's realm—because I live within.
Let me live in the mountains where Cithaeron
Yonder has fame of me, which father and mother
When they were alive established as my tomb.
There I may die by those who sought to kill me.
And yet this much I know, neither a sickness
Nor anything else can kill me. I would not
Be saved from death, except for some dread evil.
Well, let my fate go wherever it may.
As for my sons, Creon, assume no trouble;
They are men and will have no difficulty
Of living wherever they may be.
O my poor grievous daughters, who never knew
Their dinner table set apart from me,
But always shared in everything I touched—
Take care of them for me, and first of all
Allow me to touch them and bemoan our ills.
Grant it, lord,
Grant it, noble. If with my hand I touch them
I would think I had them just as when I could see.

(*Creon's attendants bring in* ANTIGONE *and* ISMENE.)

What's that?
By the gods, can it be I hear my dear ones weeping?
And have you taken pity on me, Creon?
Have you had my darling children sent to me?
Do I speak right?
    CREON   You do. For it was I who brought them here,
Knowing this present joy your joy of old.
    OEDIPUS   May you fare well. For their coming may the spirit
That watches over you be better than mine.
My children, where are you? Come to me, come
Into your brother's hands, that brought about
Your father's eyes, once bright, to see like this.
Your father, children, who, seeing and knowing nothing,
Became a father whence he was got himself.
I weep also for you—I cannot see you—
To think of the bitter life in days to come
Which you will have to lead among mankind.

What citizens' gatherings will you approach?
What festivals attend, where you will not cry
When you go home, instead of gay rejoicing?
And when you arrive at marriageable age,
What man, my daughters, will there be to chance you,
Incurring such reproaches on his head,
Disgraceful to my children and to yours?
What evil will be absent, when your father
Killed his own father, sowed seed in her who bore him,
From whom he was born himself, and equally,
Has fathered you whence he himself was born.
Such will be the reproaches. Who then will wed you?
My children, there is no one for you. Clearly
You must decay in barrenness, unwed.
Son of Menoeceus—since you are alone
Left as a father to them, for we who produced them
Are both in ruin—see that you never let
These girls wander as beggars without husbands,
Let them not fall into such woes as mine.
But pity them, seeing how young they are
To be bereft of all except your aid.
Grant this, my noble friend, with a touch of your hand.
My children, if your minds were now mature,
I would give you much advice. But, pray this for me,
To live as the time allows, to find a life
Better than that your siring father had.

CREON You have wept enough here, come, and go inside the house.

OEDIPUS I must obey, though nothing sweet.

CREON   All things are good in their time.

OEDIPUS Do you know in what way I go?

CREON   Tell me, I'll know when I hear.

OEDIPUS Send me outside the land.

CREON   You ask what the god will do.

OEDIPUS But to the gods I am hated.

CREON   Still, it will soon be done.

OEDIPUS Then you agree?

CREON   What I think not I would not say in vain.

OEDIPUS Now lead me away.

CREON   Come then, but let the children go.

OEDIPUS   Do not take them from me.

CREON   Wish not to govern all,
For what you ruled will not follow you through life.

CHORUS   Dwellers in native Thebes, behold this Oedipus
Who solved the famous riddle, was your mightiest man.
What citizen on his lot did not with envy gaze?
See to how great a surge of dread fate he has come!
So I would say a mortal man, while he is watching
To see the final day, can have no happiness
Till he pass the bound of life, nor be relieved of pain.

Herodotus

——————— *2* ———————

History

Attic tragedy was only one form of Hellenic humanism in the Golden Age. The same century saw the emergence of history (i.e., the written record of contemporary events—in prose) as a new way of preserving the deeds of men from oblivion; epic poetry had been the old form. It is interesting that the name of the Muse of history, Clio, means "the celebrator." The appearance of history might be described as part of the Greek spirit of inquiry, seeking to do for man what the nature-philosophers had done for the physical world. But the immediate inspiration for the earliest surviving prose work of Western literature was patriotic: the great national effort of the Persian Wars (490–445 B.C.).

Herodotus (*ca.* 484–425 B.C.), called the "Father of History" (though he was not actually the first historian), was born at Halicarnassus in Caria— a Greek city chafing under Persian control. After an unsuccessful revolt on the part of the inhabitants, Herodotus went into exile, and, although he loved Athens and made it his home, he spent much of his life wandering through the lands of the eastern Mediterranean.

It was at this time that he set out to record the great happenings of the Persian Wars. His main object was to depict the rival worlds of Greece and Persia as seen through a single mind; for this purpose he put together the great mass of material he had gathered on his travels in one grand composition. This bold and original undertaking he called *historiē* ("researches"). Judged by modern historical standards, his *History* is defective in many ways; it is, however, a work of striking impartiality and tolerance. Although Herodotus gives us the patriotic saga of Thermopylae (one of the selections included here), he treats the enemy and its culture with respect.

Herodotus, *The History of Herodotus,* trans. George Rawlinson (London: Murray, 1880), I, 163–68, 205–08, 210, 212–14; II, 441–44, 509–13; IV, 162–71, 174–80.

Herodotus wrote his *History* to be recited before a listening public, not to be read privately, and it is in this manner, as a teller of tales, that he made his living. However skeptical he might have been of some of his particulars, the form of his work was determined by the necessity of keeping the interest of his audience. As a consequence it is full of fascinating stories, often drawn from the folklore of the Near East—as are the two stories in this selection. Both are also examples of the pattern congenial to Greek tradition: the moral sequence of prosperity-presumption-ruin.

ACCOUNT OF THE GREEKS AT THERMOPYLAE

King Xerxes pitched his camp in the region of Malis called Trachinia, while on their side the Greeks occupied the straits. These straits the Greeks in general call Thermopylae (the Hot Gates); but the natives, and those who dwell in the neighbourhood, call them Pylae (the Gates). Here then the two armies took their stand; the one master of all the region lying north of Trachis, the other of the country extending southward of that place to the verge of the continent.

The Greeks who at this spot awaited the coming of Xerxes were the following:—From Sparta, three hundred men-at-arms: from Arcadia, a thousand Tegeans and Mantineans, five hundred of each people; a hundred and twenty Orchomenians, from the Arcadian Orchomenus; and a thousand from other cities: from Corinth, four hundred men: from Phlius, two hundred: and from Mycenae eighty. Such was the number from the Peloponnese. There were also present, from Boeotia, seven hundred Thespians and four hundred Thebans.

Besides these troops, the Locrians of Opus and the Phocians had obeyed the call of their countrymen, and sent, the former all the force they had, the latter a thousand men. For envoys had gone from the Greeks at Thermopylae among the Locrians and Phocians, to call on them for assistance, and to say—"They were themselves but the vanguard of the host, sent to precede the main body, which might every day be expected to follow them. The sea was in good keeping, watched by the Athenians, the Eginetans, and the rest of the fleet. There was no cause why they should fear; for after all the invader was not a god but a man; and there never had been, and never would be, a man who was not liable to misfortunes from the very day of his birth, and those misfortunes greater in proportion to his own greatness. The assailant therefore, being only a mortal, must needs fall from his glory." Thus urged, the Locrians and the Phocians had come with their troops to Trachis.

The various nations had each captains of their own under whom they served; but the one to whom all especially looked up, and who had the command of the entire force, was the Lacedaemonian, Leonidas.

Leonidas had come to be king of Sparta quite unexpectedly.

Having two elder brothers, Cleomenes and Dorieus, he had no thought of ever mounting the throne. However, when Cleomenes died without male offspring, as Dorieus was likewise deceased, having perished in Sicily, the crown fell to Leonidas, who was older than Cleombrotus, the youngest of the sons of Anaxandridas, and, moreover, was married to the daughter of Cleomenes. He had now come to Thermopylae, accompanied by the three hundred men which the law assigned him, whom he had himself chosen from among the citizens, and who were all of them fathers with sons living. On his way he had taken the troops from Thebes, whose number I have already mentioned, and who were under the command of Leontiades the son of Eurymachus. The reason why he made a point of taking troops from Thebes, and Thebes only, was that the Thebans were strongly suspected of being well inclined to the Medes. Leonidas therefore called on them to come with him to the war, wishing to see whether they would comply with his demand, or openly refuse, and disclaim the Greek alliance. They, however, though their wishes leant the other way, nevertheless sent the men.

The force with Leonidas was sent forward by the Spartans in advance of their main body, that the sight of them might encourage the allies to fight, and hinder them from going over to the Medes, as it was likely they might have done had they seen that Sparta was backward. They intended presently, when they had celebrated the Carneian festival, which was what now kept them at home, to leave a garrison in Sparta, and hasten in full force to join the army. The rest of the allies also intended to act similarly; for it happened that the Olympic festival fell exactly at this same period. None of them looked to see the contest at Thermopylae decided so speedily; wherefore they were content to send forward a mere advanced guard. Such accordingly were the intentions of the allies.

The Greek forces at Thermopylae, when the Persian army drew near to the entrance of the pass, were seized with fear; and a council was held to consider about a retreat. It was the wish of the Peloponnesians generally that the army should fall back upon the Peloponnese, and there guard the Isthmus. But Leonidas, who saw with what indignation the Phocians and Locrians heard of this plan, gave his voice for remaining where they were, while they sent envoys to the several cities to ask for help, since they were too few to make a stand against an army like that of the Medes.

While this debate was going on, Xerxes sent a mounted spy to observe the Greeks, and note how many they were, and see what they were doing. He had heard, before he came out of Thessaly, that a few men were assembled at this place, and that at their head were certain Lacedaemonians, under Leonidas, a descendant of Hercules. The horseman rode up to the camp, and looked about him, but did not see the whole army; for such as were on the further side of the wall (which had been rebuilt and was now carefully guarded) it was not possible for him to behold; but he observed those on the outside, who were encamped in front of the rampart. It chanced that at this time the Lacedaemonians held the outer guard, and were seen by the spy, some of them engaged in gymnastic exercises, others combing their long hair. At this the spy greatly marvelled, but he counted their number, and when he had taken accurate note of everything, he rode back quietly; for no one pursued after him, nor paid any heed to his visit. So he returned, and told Xerxes all that he had seen.

Upon this, Xerxes, who had no means of surmising the truth—namely, that the Spartans were preparing to do or die manfully—but thought it laughable that they should be engaged in such employments, sent and called to his presence Demaratus the son of Ariston, who still remained with the army. When he appeared, Xerxes told him all that he had heard, and questioned him concerning the news, since he was anxious to understand the meaning of such behaviour on the part of the Spartans. Then Demaratus said—

"I spake to thee, O King! concerning these men long since, when we had but just begun our march upon Greece; thou, however, didst only laugh at my words, when I told thee of all this, which I saw would come to pass. Earnestly do I struggle at all times to speak truth to thee, sire; and now listen to it once more. These men have come to dispute the pass with us; and it is for this that they are now making ready. 'Tis their custom, when they are about to hazard their lives, to adorn their heads with care. Be assured, however, that if thou canst subdue the men who are here and the Lacedaemonians who remain in Sparta, there is no other nation in all the world which will venture to lift a hand in their defence. Thou hast now to deal with the first kingdom and town in Greece, and with the bravest men."

Then Xerxes, to whom what Demaratus said seemed altogether to surpass belief, asked further, "How it was possible for so small an army to contend with his?"

"O King!" Demaratus answered, "let me be treated as a liar, if matters fall not out as I say."

But Xerxes was not persuaded any the more. Four whole days he suffered to go by, expecting that the Greeks would run away. When, however, he found on the fifth that they were not gone, thinking that their firm stand was mere impudence and recklessness, he grew wroth, and sent against them the Medes and Cissians, with orders to take them alive and bring them into his presence. Then the Medes rushed forward and charged the Greeks, but fell in vast numbers: others however took the places of the slain, and would not be beaten off, though they suffered terrible losses. In this way it became clear to all, and especially to the King, that though he had plenty of combatants, he had but very few warriors. The struggle, however, continued during the whole day.

Then the Medes, having met so rough a reception, withdrew from the fight; and their place was taken by the band of Persians under Hydarnes, whom the King called his "Immortals": they, it was thought, would soon finish the business. But when they joined battle with the Greeks, 'twas with no better success than the Median detachment—things went much as before—the two armies fighting in a narrow space, and the barbarians using shorter spears than the Greeks, and having no advantage from their numbers. The Lacedaemonians fought in a way worthy of note, and showed themselves far more skilful in fight than their adversaries, often turning their backs, and making as though they were all flying away, on which the barbarians would rush after them with much noise and shouting, when the Spartans at their approach would wheel round and face their pursuers, in this way destroying vast numbers of the enemy. Some Spartans likewise fell in these encounters, but only a very few. At last the Persians, finding that all their efforts to gain the pass availed nothing, and that, whether they attacked by divisions or in any other way, it was to no purpose, withdrew to their own quarters.

During these assaults, it is said that Xerxes, who was watching the battle, thrice leaped from the throne on which he [sat], in terror for his army.

Next day the combat was renewed, but with no better success on the part of the barbarians. The Greeks were so few that the barbarians hoped to find them disabled, by reason of their wounds, from offering any further resistance; and so they once more attacked them. But the Greeks were drawn up in detachments according to their cities, and bore the brunt of the battle in turns,—all except the Phocians, who had been stationed on the mountain to guard the pathway. So, when the Persians found no difference between that day and the preceding, they again retired to their quarters.

Now, as the King was in a great strait, and knew not how he should deal with the emergency, Ephialtes, the son of Eurydêmus, a man of Malis, came to him and was admitted to a conference. Stirred by the hope of receiving a rich reward at the King's hands, he had come to tell him of the pathway which led across the mountain to Thermopylae; by which disclosure he brought destruction on the band of Greeks who had there withstood the barbarians.

.   .   .

The Greeks at Thermopylae received the first warning of the destruction which the dawn would bring on them from the seer Megistias, who read their fate in the victims as he was sacrificing. After this, deserters came in and brought the news that the Persians were marching round by the hills; it was still night when the men arrived. Last of all, the scouts came running down from the heights and brought in the same accounts when the day was just beginning to break. Then the Greeks held a council to consider what they should do, and here opinions were divided: some were strong against quitting their post, while others contended to the contrary.

So, when the council had broken up, part of the troops departed and went their ways homeward to their several states; part however resolved to remain and to stand by Leonidas to the last.

It is said that Leonidas himself sent away the troops who departed because he tendered their safety, but thought it unseemly that either he or his Spartans should quit the post which they had been especially sent to guard. For my own part, I incline to think that Leonidas gave the order, because he perceived the allies to be out of heart and unwilling to encounter the danger to which his own mind was made up. He therefore commanded them to retreat, but said that he himself could not draw back with honour; knowing that if he stayed glory awaited him and that Sparta in that case would not lose her prosperity. For when the Spartans, at the very beginning of the war, sent to consult the oracle concerning it, the answer which they received from the Pythoness was, "that either Sparta must be overthrown by the barbarians or one of her kings must perish." . . .

The remembrance of this answer, I think, and the wish to secure the whole glory for the Spartans, caused Leonidas to send the allies away. . . .

So the allies, when Leonidas ordered them to retire, obeyed him and forthwith departed. Only the Thespians and the Thebans remained with the Spartans; and of these the Thebans were kept back by Leonidas as hostages, very much against their will. The Thespians, on the contrary, stayed entirely of their own accord, refusing to retreat, and declaring that they would not forsake Leonidas and his followers. So they abode with the Spartans and died with them. Their leader was Demophilus, the son of Diadromes.

At sunrise Xerxes made libations, after which he waited until the time when the forum is wont to fill and then began his advance. Ephialtes had instructed him thus, as the descent of the mountain is much quicker and the distance much shorter than the way round the hills, and the ascent. So the barbarians under Xerxes began to draw nigh; and the Greeks under Leonidas, as they now went forth determined to die, advanced much further than on previous days, until they reached the more open portion of the pass. Hitherto they had held their station within the wall and from this had gone forth to fight at the point where the pass was the narrowest. Now they joined battle beyond the defile and carried slaughter among the barbarians, who fell in heaps. Behind them the captains of the squadrons, armed with whips, urged their men forward with continual blows. Many were thrust into the sea, and there perished; a still greater number were trampled to death by their own soldiers. No one heeded the dying. For the Greeks, reckless of their own safety and desperate, since they knew that as the mountain had been crossed their destruction was nigh at hand, exerted themselves with the most furious valour against the barbarians.

By this time the spears of the greater number were all shivered, and with their swords they hewed down the ranks of the Persians; and here, as they strove, Leonidas fell fighting bravely, together with many other famous Spartans whose names I have taken care to learn on account of their great worthiness, as indeed I have those of all the three hundred. There fell too at the same time very many famous Persians: among them two sons of Darius. . . . Thus two brothers of Xerxes here fought and fell.

And now there arose a fierce struggle between the Persians and the Lacedaemonians over the body of Leonidas, in which the Greeks four times drove back the enemy, and at last by their great bravery succeeded in bearing off the body. This combat was scarcely ended when the Persians with Ephialtes approached; and the Greeks, informed that they drew nigh, made a change in the manner of their fighting. Drawing back into the narrowest part of the pass, and retreating even behind the cross wall, they posted themselves upon a hillock, where they stood all drawn up together in one close body, except only the Thebans. The hillock whereof I speak is at the entrance of the straits, where the stone lion stands which was set up in honour of Leonidas. Here they defended themselves to the last, such as still had swords using them, and the others resisting with their hands and teeth; till the barbarians, who in part had pulled down the wall and attacked them in front, in part had gone round and now encircled them upon every side, overwhelmed and buried the remnant which was left beneath showers of missile weapons.

Thus nobly did the whole body of Lacedaemonians and Thespians behave; but nevertheless one man is said to have distinguished himself above all the rest: to wit, Dieneces the Spartan. A speech which he made before the Greeks engaged the Medes remains on record. One of the Trachinians told him, "Such was the number of the barbarians that when they shot forth their arrows the sun would be darkened by their multitude," Dieneces, not at all frightened at these words, but making light of the Median numbers, answered, "Our Trachinian friend brings us excellent tidings. If the Medes darken the sun, we shall have our fight in the shade." . . .

The slain were buried where they fell; and in their honour, nor less in honour of those who died before Leonidas sent the allies away, an inscription was set up which said,

> "Here did four thousand men from Pelops' land
> Against three-hundred myriads bravely stand."

This was in honour of all. Another was for the Spartans alone:

> "Go, stranger, and to Lacedaemon tell
> That here, obeying her behests, we fell."

CROESUS-SOLON STORIES

[Croesus, king of Lydia (560–546 B.C.)] made war in turn upon every Ionian and Aeolian state, bringing forward, where he could, a substantial ground of complaint; where such failed him, advancing some poor excuse.

In this way he made himself master of all the Greek cities in Asia, and forced them to become his tributaries.

• • •

Croesus, afterwards, in the course of many years, brought under his sway almost all the nations to the west of the Halys. The Lycians and Cilicians alone continued free; all the other tribes he reduced and held in subjection. . . .

When all these conquests had been added to the Lydian empire, and the prosperity of Sardis was now at its height, there came thither, one after another, all the sages of Greece living at the time, and among them Solon, the Athenian. He was on his travels, having left Athens to be absent ten years, under the pretence of wishing to see the world, but really to avoid being forced to repeal any of the laws which, at the request of the Athenians, he had made for them. Without his sanction the Athenians could not repeal them, as they had bound themselves under a heavy curse to be governed for ten years by the laws which should be imposed on them by Solon.

On this account, as well as to see the world, Solon set out upon his travels, in the course of which he went to Egypt to the court of Amasis, and also came on a visit to Croesus at Sardis. Croesus received him as his guest, and lodged him in the royal palace. On the third or fourth day after, he bade his servants conduct Solon over his treasuries, and show him all their greatness and magnificence. When he had seen them all, and, so far as time allowed, inspected them, Croesus addressed this question to him. "Stranger of Athens, we have heard much of thy wisdom and of thy travels through many lands, from love of knowledge and a wish to see the world. I am curious therefore to inquire of thee, whom, of all the men that thou hast seen, thou deemest the most happy?" This he asked because he thought himself the happiest of mortals: but Solon answered him without flattery, according to his true sentiments, "Tellus of Athens, sire." Full of astonishment at what he heard, Croesus demanded sharply, "And wherefore dost thou deem Tellus happiest?" To which the other replied, "First, because his country was flourishing in his days, and he himself had sons both beautiful and good, and he lived to see children born to each of them, and these children all grew up; and further because, after a life spent in what our people look upon as comfort, his end was surpassingly glorious. In a battle between the Athenians and their neighbours near Eleusis, he came to the assistance of his countrymen, routed the foe, and died upon the field most gallantly. The Athenians gave him a public funeral on the spot where he fell, and paid him the highest honours."

Thus did Solon admonish Croesus by the example of Tellus, enumerating the manifold particulars of his happiness. When he had ended, Croesus inquired a second time, who after Tellus seemed to him the happiest, expecting that at any rate, he would be given the second place. "Cleobis and Bito," Solon answered; "they were of Argive race; their fortune was enough for their wants, and they were besides endowed with so much bodily strength that they had both gained prizes at the Games. Also this tale is told of them:— There was a great festival in honour of the goddess Juno at Argos, to which their mother must needs be taken in a car. Now the oxen did not come home from the field in time: so the youths, fearful of being too late, put the yoke on their own necks, and themselves drew the car in which their mother rode. Five and forty furlongs did they draw her, and stopped before the temple. This deed of theirs was witnessed by the whole assembly of worshippers, and then their life closed in the best possible way. Herein, too, God showed forth most evidently, how much better a thing for man death is than life. For the Argive men, who stood around the car, extolled the vast strength of the youths; and the Argive women extolled the mother who was blessed with such a pair of sons; and the mother herself, overjoyed at the deed and at the praises it had won, standing straight before the image, besought the goddess to bestow on Cleobis and Bito, the sons who had so mightily honoured her, the highest blessing to which mortals can attain. Her prayer ended, they offered sacrifice and partook of the holy banquet, after which the two youths fell asleep in the temple. They never woke more, but so passed from the earth. The Argives, looking on them as among the best of men, caused statues of them to be made, which they gave to the shrine at Delphi."

When Solon had thus assigned these youths the second place, Croesus broke in angrily, "What, stranger of Athens, is my happiness, then, so utterly set at naught by thee, that thou dost not even put me on a level with private men?"

"Oh! Croesus," replied the other, "thou askedst a question concerning the condition of man, of one who knows that the power above us is full of jealousy, and fond of troubling our lot. A long life gives one to witness much, and experience much oneself, that one would not choose. Seventy years I regard as the limit of the life of man. In these seventy years are contained, without reckoning intercalary months, twenty-five thousand and two hundred days. Add an intercalary month to every other year, that the seasons may come round at the right time, and there will be, besides the seventy years, thirty-five such months, making an addition of one thousand and fifty days. The whole number of the days contained in the seventy years will thus be twenty-six thousand two hundred and fifty, whereof not one but will produce events unlike the rest. Hence man is wholly accident. For thyself, oh! Croesus, I see that thou art wonderfully rich, and art the lord of many nations; but with respect to that whereon thou questionest me, I have no answer to give, until I hear that thou hast closed thy life happily. For assuredly he who possesses great store of riches is no nearer happiness than he who has what suffices for his daily needs, unless it so hap that luck attend upon him, and so he continue in the enjoyment of all his good things to the end of life. For many of the wealthiest men have been unfavoured of fortune, and many whose means were moderate have had excellent luck. Men of the former class excel those of the latter but in two respects; these last excel the former in many. The wealthy man is better able to content his desires, and to bear up against a sudden buffet of calamity. The other has less ability to withstand these evils (from which, however, his good luck keeps him clear), but he enjoys all these following blessings: he is whole of limb, a stranger to disease, free from misfortune, happy in his children, and comely to look upon. If, in addition to all this, he end his life well, he is of a truth the man of whom thou art in search, the man who may rightly be termed happy. Call him, however, until he die, not happy but fortunate. Scarcely, indeed, can any man unite all these advantages: as there is no country which contains within it all that it needs, but each, while it possesses some things, lacks others, and the best country is that which contains the most; so no single human being is complete in every respect—something is always lacking. He who unites the greatest number of advantages, and retaining them to the day of his death, then dies peaceably, that man alone, sire, is, in my judgment, entitled to bear the name of 'happy.' But in every matter it behoves us to mark well the end: for oftentimes God gives men a gleam of happiness, and then plunges them into ruin."

Such was the speech which Solon addressed to Croesus, a speech which brought him neither largess nor honour. The king saw him depart with much indifference, since he thought that a man must be an arrant fool who made no account of present good, but bade men always wait and mark the end.

After Solon had gone away a dreadful vengeance, sent of God, came upon Croesus, to punish him, it is likely, for deeming himself the happiest of men. First he had a dream in the night, which foreshowed him truly the evils that were about to befall him in the person of his son. For Croesus had two sons, one blasted by a natural defect, being deaf and dumb; the other, distinguished far above all his co-mates in every pursuit. The name of the last was Atys. It was this son concerning whom he dreamt a dream, that he would die by the blow of an iron weapon. When he woke, he considered earnestly with himself, and, greatly alarmed at the dream, instantly made his son take a wife; and whereas in former years the youth had been wont to command the Lydian forces in the field, he now would not suffer him to accompany them. All the spears and javelins, and weapons used in the wars, he removed out of the male apartments, and laid them in heaps in the chambers of the women, fearing lest perhaps one of the weapons that hung against the wall might fall and strike him.

Now it chanced that while he was making arrangements for the wedding, there came to Sardis a man under a misfortune, who had upon him the stain of blood. He was by race a Phrygian, and belonged to the family of the king. Presenting himself at the palace of Croesus, he prayed to be admitted to purification according to the customs of the country.

. . .

Then the king sent for Adrastus, the Phrygian, and said to him, "Adrastus, when thou wert smitten with the rod of affliction—no reproach, my friend—I purified thee, and have taken thee to live with me in my palace, and have been at every charge. Now, therefore, it behoves thee to requite the good offices which thou hast received at my hands by consenting to go with my son on this hunting party, and to watch over him, if perchance you should be attacked upon the road by some band of daring robbers. Even apart from this, it were right for thee to go where thou mayest make thyself famous by noble deeds. They are the heritage of thy family, and thou too art so stalwart and strong."

Adrastus answered, "Except for thy request, oh! king, I would rather have kept away from this hunt; for methinks it ill beseems a man under a misfortune such as mine to consort with his happier compeers; and besides, I have no heart to it. On many grounds I had stayed behind; but, as thou urgest it, and I am bound to pleasure thee (for truly it does behove me to requite thy good offices), I am content to do as thou wishest. For thy son, whom thou givest into my charge, be sure thou shalt receive him back safe and sound, so far as depends upon a guardian's carefulness."

Thus assured, Croesus let them depart, accompanied by a band of picked youths, and well provided with dogs of chace. When they reached Olympus, they scattered in quest of the animal; he was soon found, and the hunters, drawing round him in a circle, hurled their weapons at him. Then the stranger, the man who had been purified of blood, whose name was Adrastus, he also hurled his spear at the boar, but missed his aim, and struck Atys. Thus was the son of Croesus slain by the point of an iron weapon, and the warning of the vision was fulfilled. Then one ran to Sardis to

bear the tidings to the king, and he came and informed him of
the combat and of the fate that had befallen his son.

If it was a heavy blow to the father to learn that his child was
dead, it yet more strongly affected him to think that the very man
whom he himself once purified had done the deed. In the violence
of his grief he called aloud on Jupiter Catharsius, to be a witness
of what he had suffered at the stranger's hands. Afterwards he
invoked the same god as Jupiter Ephistius and Hetaereus—using
the one term because he had unwittingly harboured in his house
the man who had now slain his son; and the other, because the
stranger, who had been sent as his child's guardian, had turned out
his most cruel enemy.

Presently the Lydians arrived, bearing the body of the youth,
and behind them followed the homicide. He took his stand in
front of the [corpse], and, stretching forth his hand to Croesus, delivered himself into his power with earnest entreaties that he would
sacrifice him upon the body of his son—"his former misfortune was
burthen enough; now that he had added to it a second, and had
brought ruin on the man who purified him, he could not bear to
live." Then Croesus, when he heard these words, was moved with
pity towards Adrastus, notwithstanding the bitterness of his own
calamity; and so he answered, "Enough, my friend; I have all the
revenge that I require, since thou givest sentence of death against
thyself. But in sooth it is not thou who hast injured me, except
so far as thou hast unwittingly dealt the blow. Some god is the
author of my misfortune, and I was forewarned of it a long time
ago."

* * *

At the end of this time the grief of Croesus was interrupted
by intelligence from abroad. He learnt that Cyrus, the son of
Cambyses, had destroyed the empire of Astyages, the son of
Cyaxares; and that the Persians were becoming daily more powerful. This led him to consider with himself whether it were possible
to check the growing power of that people before it came to a
head. With this design he resolved to make instant trial of the
several oracles in Greece, and of the one in Libya. So he sent his
messengers in different directions, some to Delphi, some to Abae
in Phocis, and some to Dodôna; others to the oracle of Amphiaraüs;

others to that of Trophonius; others, again, to Branchidae in Milesia. These were the Greek oracles which he consulted. To Libya he sent another embassy, to consult the oracle of Ammon. These messengers were sent to test the knowledge of the oracles, that, if they were found really to return true answers, he might send a second time, and inquire if he ought to attack the Persians.

The messengers who were despatched to make trial of the oracles were given the following instructions: they were to keep count of the days from the time of their leaving Sardis, and, reckoning from that date, on the hundredth day they were to consult the oracles, and to inquire of them what Croesus the son of Alyattes, king of Lydia, was doing at that moment. The answers given them were to be taken down in writing, and brought back to him. None of the replies remain on record except that of the oracle at Delphi. There, the moment that the Lydians entered the sanctuary, and before they put their questions, the Pythoness thus answered them in hexameter verse:—

"I can count the sands, and I can measure the ocean;
I have ears for the silent, and know what the dumb man meaneth;
Lo! on my sense there striketh the smell of a shell-covered tortoise,
Boiling now on the fire, with the flesh of a lamb, in a cauldron,—
Brass is the vessel below, and brass the cover above it."

These words the Lydians wrote down at the mouth of the Pythoness as she prophesied, and then set off on their return to Sardis. When all the messengers had come back with the answers which they had received, Croesus undid the rolls, and read what was written in each. Only one approved itself to him, that of the Delphic oracle. This he had no sooner heard than he instantly made an act of adoration, and accepted it as true, declaring that the Delphic was the only really oracular shrine, the only one that had discovered in what way he was in fact employed. For on the departure of his messengers he had set himself to think what was most impossible for any one to conceive of his doing, and then, waiting till the day agreed on came, he acted as he had determined. He took a tortoise and a lamb, and cutting them in pieces with his own hands, boiled them both together in a brazen cauldron, covered over with a lid which was also of brass.

Such then was the answer returned to Croesus from Delphi. What the answer was which the Lydians who went to the shrine of Amphiaraüs and performed the customary rites, obtained of the oracle there, I have it not in my power to mention, for there is no record of it. All that is known is, that Croesus believed himself to have found there also an oracle which spoke the truth.

After this Croesus, having resolved to propitiate the Delphic god with a magnificent sacrifice, offered up three thousand of every kind of sacrificial beast, and besides made a huge pile, and placed upon it couches coated with silver and with gold, and golden goblets, and robes and vests of purple; all which he burnt in the hope of thereby making himself more secure of the favour of the god. Further he issued his orders to all the people of the land to offer a sacrifice according to their means. When the sacrifice was ended, the king melted down a vast quantity of gold, and ran it into ingots, making them six palms long, three palms broad, and one palm in thickness. The number of ingots was a hundred and seventeen, four being of refined gold, in weight two talents and a half, the others of pale gold, and in weight two talents. He also caused a statue of a lion to be made in refined gold, the weight of which was ten talents. At the time when the temple of Delphi was burnt to the ground, this lion fell from the ingots on which it was placed; it now stands in the Corinthian treasury, and weighs only six talents and a half, having lost three talents and a half by the fire.

On the completion of these works, Croesus sent them away to Delphi, and with them two bowls of an enormous size, one of gold, the other of silver, which used to stand, the latter upon the right, the former upon the left, as one entered the temple.

. . .

These were the offerings sent by Croesus to Delphi. To the shrine of Amphiaraüs, with whose valour and misfortune he was acquainted, he sent a shield entirely of gold, and a spear, also of solid gold, both head and shaft. They were still existing in my day at Thebes, laid up in the temple of Ismenian Apollo.

The messengers who had the charge of conveying these treasures to the shrines, received instructions to ask the oracles whether Croesus should go to war with the Persians, and if so, whether he should strengthen himself by the forces of an ally. Accordingly, when they had reached their destinations and presented the gifts, they proceeded to consult the oracles in the following terms:—

"Croesus, king of Lydia and other countries, believing that these are the only real oracles in all the world, has sent you such presents as your discoveries deserved, and now inquires of you whether he shall go to war with the Persians, and if so, whether he shall strengthen himself by the forces of a confederate." Both the oracles agreed in the tenor of their reply, which was in each case a prophecy that if Croesus attacked the Persians, he would destroy a mighty empire, and a recommendation to him to look and see who were the most powerful of the Greeks, and to make alliance with them.

At the receipt of these oracular replies Croesus was overjoyed, and feeling sure now that he would destroy the empire of the Persians, he sent once more to Pytho, and presented to the Delphians, the number of whom he had ascertained, two gold staters apiece. In return for this the Delphians granted to Croesus and the Lydians the privilege of precedency in consulting the oracle, exemption from all charges, the most honourable seat at the festivals, and the perpetual right of becoming at pleasure citizens of their town.

After sending these presents to the Delphians, Croesus a third time consulted the oracle, for having once proved its truthfulness, he wished to make constant use of it. The question whereto he now desired an answer was—"Whether his kingdom would be of long duration?" The following was the reply of the Pythoness:—

> "Wait till the time shall come when a mule is monarch of Media;
> Then, thou delicate Lydian, away to the pebbles of Hermus;
> Haste, oh! haste thee away, nor blush to behave like a coward."

Of all the answers that had reached him, this pleased him far the best, for it seemed incredible that a mule should ever come to be king of the Medes, and so he concluded that the sovereignty would never depart from himself or his seed after him. Afterwards he turned his thoughts to the alliance which he had been recommended to contract, and sought to ascertain by inquiry which was the most powerful of the Grecian states. His inquiries pointed out to him two states as pre-eminent above the rest. These were the Lacedaemonians and the Athenians, the former of Doric the latter of Ionic blood.

. . .

He then disbanded the army—consisting of mercenary troops— which had been engaged with the Persians and had since accompanied him to his capital, and let them depart to their homes, never imagining that Cyrus, after a battle in which victory had been so evenly balanced, would venture to march upon Sardis.

While Croesus was still in this mind, all the suburbs of Sardis were found to swarm with snakes, on the appearance of which the horses left feeding in the pasture-grounds, and flocked to the suburbs to eat them. The king, who witnessed the unusual sight, regarded it very rightly as a prodigy. He therefore instantly sent messengers to the soothsayers of Telmessus, to consult them upon the matter. His messengers reached the city, and obtained from the Telmessians an explanation of what the prodigy portended, but fate did not allow them to inform their lord; for ere they entered Sardis on their return, Croesus was a prisoner. What the Telmessians had declared was, that Croesus must look for the entry of an army of foreign invaders into his country, and that when they came they would subdue the native inhabitants; since the snake, said they, is a child of earth, and the horse a warrior and a foreigner. Croesus was already a prisoner when the Telmessians thus answered his inquiry, but they had no knowledge of what was taking place at Sardis, or of the fate of the monarch.

Cyrus, however, when Croesus broke up so suddenly from his quarters after the battle at Pteria, conceiving that he had marched away with the intention of disbanding his army, considered a little, and soon saw that it was advisable for him to advance upon Sardis with all haste, before the Lydians could get their forces together a second time. Having thus determined, he lost no time in carrying out his plan. He marched forward with such speed that he was himself the first to announce his coming to the Lydian king. That monarch, placed in the utmost difficulty by the turn of events which had gone so entirely against all his calculations, nevertheless led out the Lydians to battle. In all Asia there was not at that time a braver or more warlike people. Their manner of fighting was on horseback; they carried long lances, and were clever in the management of their steeds.

The two armies met in the plain before Sardis.

. . .

The combat was long; but at last, after a great slaughter on both sides, the Lydians turned and fled. They were driven within their walls, and the Persians laid siege to Sardis.

Thus the siege began. Meanwhile Croesus, thinking that the place would hold out no inconsiderable time, sent off fresh heralds to his allies from the beleaguered town. His former messengers had been charged to bid them assemble at Sardis in the course of the fifth month; they whom he now sent were to say that he was already besieged, and to beseech them to come to his aid with all possible speed. Among his other allies Croesus did not omit to send to Lacedaemon.

It chanced, however, that the Spartans were themselves just at this time engaged in a quarrel with the Argives about a place called Thyrea. . . .

Although the Spartans were engaged with these matters when the herald arrived from Sardis to entreat them to come to the assistance of the besieged king, yet, notwithstanding, they instantly set to work to afford him help. They had completed their preparations, and the ships were just ready to start, when a second message informed them that the place had already fallen, and that Croesus was a prisoner. Deeply grieved at his misfortune, the Spartans ceased their efforts.

. . .

Thus was Sardis taken by the Persians, and Croesus himself fell into their hands, after having reigned fourteen years, and been besieged in his capital fourteen days; thus too did Croesus fulfil the oracle, which said that he should destroy a mighty empire,— by destroying his own. Then the Persians who had made Croesus prisoner brought him before Cyrus. Now a vast pile had been raised by his orders, and Croesus, laden with fetters, was placed upon it, and with him twice seven of the sons of the Lydians. I know not whether Cyrus was minded to make an offering of the first-fruits to some god or other, or whether he had vowed a vow and was performing it, or whether, as may well be, he had heard that Croesus was a holy man, and so wished to see if any of the heavenly powers would appear to save him from being burnt alive. However it might be, Cyrus was thus engaged, and Croesus was already on the pile, when it entered his mind in the depth of his woe that there was a divine warning in the words which had come to him from the lips of Solon, "No one while he lives is happy." When this thought smote him he fetched a long breath, and breaking his deep silence, groaned out aloud, thrice uttering the name of Solon. Cyrus caught the sounds, and bade the interpreters inquire of Croesus who it was he called on. They drew near and asked him, but he held his peace, and for a long time made no answer to their questionings, until at length, forced to say something, he exclaimed, "One I would give much to see converse with every monarch." Not knowing what he meant by this reply, the interpreters begged him to explain himself; and as they pressed for an answer, and grew to be troublesome, he told them how, a long time before, Solon, an Athenian, had come and seen all his splendour, and made light of it; and how whatever he had said to him had fallen out exactly as he foreshowed, although it was nothing that especially concerned him, but applied to all mankind alike, and most to those who seemed to themselves happy. Meanwhile, as he thus spoke, the pile was lighted, and the outer portion began to blaze. Then Cyrus, hearing from the interpreters what Croesus had said, relented, bethinking himself that he too was a man, and that it was a fellow-man, and one who had once been as blessed by fortune as himself, that he was burning alive; afraid, moreover, of retribution, and full of the thought that whatever is human is insecure. So he bade them quench the blazing fire as quickly as they could, and take down Croesus and the other Lydians, which they tried to do, but the flames were not to be mastered.

Then, the Lydians say that Croesus, perceiving by the efforts made to quench the fire that Cyrus had relented, and seeing also that all was in vain, and that the men could not get the fire under, called with a loud voice upon the god Apollo, and prayed him, if he had ever received at his hands any acceptable gift, to come to his aid, and deliver him from his present danger. As thus with tears he besought the god, suddenly, though up to that time the sky had been clear and the day without a breath of wind, dark clouds gathered, and the storm burst over their heads with rain of such violence, that the flames were speedily extinguished. Cyrus, convinced by this that Croesus was a good man and a favourite of heaven, asked him after he was taken off the pile, "Who it was that had persuaded him to lead an army into his country, and so become his foe rather than continue his friend?" to which Croesus made answer as follows: "What I did, oh! king, was to thy advantage and to my own loss. If there be blame, it rests with the god of the

Greeks, who encouraged me to begin the war. No one is so foolish
as to prefer . . . war, in which, instead of sons burying their
fathers, fathers bury their sons. But the gods willed it so."

Thus did Croesus speak. Cyrus then ordered his fetters to be
taken off, and made him sit down near himself, and paid him
much respect, looking upon him, as did also the courtiers, with a
sort of wonder.

. . . . .

THE RING OF POLYCRATES

While Cambyses was carrying on this war in Egypt, the Lacedaemonians likewise sent a force to Samos against Polycrates, the
son of Aeaces, who had by insurrection made himself master of
that island. At the outset he divided the state into three parts, and
shared the kingdom with his brothers, Pantagnôtus and Syloson;
but later, having killed the former and banished the latter, who
was the younger of the two, he held the whole island. Hereupon
he made a contract of friendship with Amasis, the Egyptian king,
sending him gifts, and receiving from him others in return. In a
little while his power so greatly increased, that the fame of it went
abroad throughout Ionia and the rest of Greece. Wherever he
turned his arms, success waited on him. He had a fleet of a hundred
penteconters, and bowmen to the number of a thousand. Herewith
he plundered all, without distinction of friend or foe; for he
argued that a friend was better pleased if you gave him back what
you had taken from him, than if you spared him at the first. He
captured many of the islands, and several towns upon the mainland. Among his other doings he overcame the Lesbians in a sea-
fight, when they came with all their forces to the help of Miletus,
and made a number of them prisoners. These persons, laden with
fetters, dug the moat which surrounds the castle at Samos.

The exceeding good fortune of Polycrates did not escape the
notice of Amasis, who was much disturbed thereat. When therefore
his successes continued increasing, Amasis wrote him the following
letter, and sent it to Samos. "Amasis to Polycrates thus sayeth: It
is a pleasure to hear of a friend and ally prospering; but thy
exceeding prosperity does not cause me joy, forasmuch as I know
that the gods are envious. My wish for myself, and for those whom
I love, is, to be now successful, and now to meet with a check;

thus passing through life amid alternate good and ill, rather than with perpetual good fortune. For never yet did I hear tell of any one succeeding in all his undertakings, who did not meet with calamity at last, and come to utter ruin. Now, therefore, give ear to my words, and meet thy good luck in this way: bethink thee which of all thy treasures thou valuest most and canst least bear to part with; take it, whatsoever it be, and throw it away, so that it may be sure never to come any more into the sight of man. Then, if thy good fortune be not thenceforth chequered with ill, save thyself from harm by again doing as I have counselled."

When Polycrates read this letter, and perceived that the advice of Amasis was good, he considered carefully with himself which of the treasures that he had in store it would grieve him most to lose. After much thought he made up his mind that it was a signet-ring which he was wont to wear, an emerald set in gold, the workmanship of Theodore, son of Têlecles, a Samian. So he determined to throw this away; and, manning a penteconter, he went on board, and bade the sailors put out into the open sea. When he was now a long way from the island, he took the ring from his finger, and, in the sight of all those who were on board, flung it into the deep. This done, he returned home, and gave vent to his sorrow.

Now it happened five or six days afterwards that a fisherman caught a fish so large and beautiful, that he thought it well deserved to be made a present of to the king. So he took it with him to the gate of the palace, and said that he wanted to see Polycrates. Then Polycrates allowed him to come in; and the fisherman gave him the fish with these words following—"Sir king, when I took this prize, I thought I would not carry it to market, though I am a poor man who live by my trade. I said to myself, it is worthy of Polycrates and his greatness; and so I brought it here to give it to you." This speech pleased the king, who thus spoke in reply:— "Thou didst right well, friend; and I am doubly indebted, both for the gift, and for the speech. Come now, and sup with me." So the fisherman went home, esteeming it a high honour that he had been asked to sup with the king. Meanwhile the servants, on cutting open the fish, found the signet of their master in its belly. No sooner did they see it than they seized upon it, and hastening to Polycrates with great joy, restored it to him, and told him in what way it had been found. The king, who saw something providential in the matter, forthwith wrote a letter to Amasis, telling him all that had happened, what he had himself done, and what had been the upshot—and despatched the letter to Egypt.

When Amasis had read the letter of Polycrates, he perceived that it does not belong to man to save his fellow-man from the fate which is in store for him: likewise he felt certain that Polycrates would end ill, as he prospered in everything, even finding what he had thrown away. So he sent a herald to Samos, and dissolved the contract of friendship. This he did, that when the great and heavy misfortune came, he might escape the grief which he would have felt if the sufferer had been his bond-friend.

About the time of Cambyses' last sickness, the following events happened. There was a certain Oroetes, a Persian, whom Cyrus had made governor of Sardis. This man conceived a most unholy wish. He had never suffered wrong or had an ill word from Polycrates the Samian—nay, he had not so much as seen him in all his life; yet, notwithstanding, he conceived the wish to seize him and put him to death. This wish, according to the account which the most part give, arose from what happened one day as he was sitting with another Perisian in the gate of the king's palace. The man's name was Mitrobates, and he was ruler of the satrapy of Dascyleium. He and Oroetes had been talking together, and from talking they fell to quarrelling and comparing their merits; whereupon Mitrobates said to Oroetes reproachfully, "Art thou worthy to be called a man, when, near as Samos lies to thy government, and easy as it is to conquer, thou hast omitted to bring it under the dominion of the king? Easy to conquer, said I? Why, a mere common citizen, with the help of fifteen men-at-arms, mastered the island, and is still king of it." Oroetes, they say, took this reproach greatly to heart; but, instead of seeking to revenge himself on the man by whom it was uttered, he conceived the desire of destroying Polycrates, since it was on Polycrates' account that the reproach had fallen on him.

Another less common version of the story is that Oroetes sent a herald to Samos to make a request, the nature of which is not stated; Polycrates was at the time reclining in the apartment of the males, and Anacreon the Teian was with him; when therefore the herald came forward to converse, Polycrates, either out of studied contempt for the power of Oroetes, or it may be merely by chance, was lying with his face turned away towards the wall; and so he lay all the time that the herald spake, and when he ended, did not even vouchsafe him a word.

Such are the two reasons alleged for the death of Polycrates; it is open to all to believe which they please. What is certain is, that Oroetes, while residing at Magnesia on the Maeander, sent a Lydian, by name Myrsus, the son of Gyges, with a message to Polycrates at Samos, well knowing what that monarch designed. For Polycrates entertained a design which no other Greek, so far as we know, ever formed before him, unless it were Minos the Cnossian, and those (if there were any such) who had the mastery of the Egaean at an earlier time—Polycrates, I say, was the first of mere human birth who conceived the design of gaining the empire of the sea, and aspired to rule over Ionia and the islands. Knowing then that Polycrates was thus minded, Oroetes sent his message, which ran as follows:—

"Oroetes to Polycrates thus sayeth: I hear thou raisest thy thoughts high, but thy means are not equal to thy ambition. Listen then to my words, and learn how thou mayest at once serve thyself and preserve me. King Cambyses is bent on my destruction—of this I have warning from a sure hand. Come thou, therefore, and fetch me away, me and all my wealth—share my wealth with me, and then, so far as money can aid, thou mayest make thyself master of the whole of Greece. But if thou doubtest of my wealth, send the trustiest of thy followers, and I will show my treasures to him."

Polycrates, when he heard this message, was full of joy, and straightway approved the terms; but, as money was what he chiefly desired, before stirring in the business he sent his secretary, Maeandrius, son of Maeandrius, a Samian, to look into the matter. This was the man who, not very long afterwards, made an offering at the temple of Juno of all the furniture which had adorned the male apartments in the palace of Polycrates, an offering well worth seeing. Oroetes learning that one was coming to view his treasures, contrived as follows:—he filled eight great chests almost brimful of stones, and then covering over the stones with gold, corded the chests, and so held them in readiness. When Maeandrius arrived, he was shown this as Oroetes' treasure, and having seen it returned to Samos.

On hearing his account, Polycrates, notwithstanding many warnings given him by the soothsayers, and much dissuasion of his friends, made ready to go in person. Even the dream which visited his daughter failed to check him. She had dreamed that she saw her father hanging high in air, washed by Jove, and anointed by the sun. Having therefore thus dreamed, she used every effort to prevent her father from going; even as he went on board his penteconter crying after him with words of evil omen. Then Polycrates threatened her that, if he returned in safety, he would keep her unmarried many years. She answered, "Oh! that he might perform his threat; far better for her to remain long unmarried than to be bereft of her father!"

Polycrates, however, making light of all the counsel offered him, set sail and went to Oroetes. Many friends accompanied him; among the rest, Democêdes, the son of Calliphon, a native of Crotona, who was a physician, and the best skilled in his art of all men then living. Polycrates, on his arrival at Magnesia, perished miserably, in a way unworthy of his rank and of his lofty schemes. For, if we except the Syracusans, there has never been one of the Greek tyrants who was to be compared with Polycrates for magnificence. Oroetes, however, slew him in a mode which is not fit to be described, and then hung his dead body upon a cross. His Samian followers Oroetes let go free, bidding them thank him that they were allowed their liberty; the rest, who were in part slaves, in part free foreigners, he alike treated as his slaves by conquest. Then was the dream of the daughter of Polycrates fulfilled; for Polycrates, as he hung upon the cross, and rain fell on him, was washed by Jupiter; and he was anointed by the sun, when his own moisture overspread his body. And so the vast good fortune of Polycrates came at last to the end which Amasis the Egyptian king had prophesied in days gone by.

Thucydides

3

History of the Peloponnesian War

As the Persian Wars, narrated by Herodotus, were the prelude to Greek glory, the Peloponnesian War (431–404 B.C.) between Athens and Sparta brought suffering and disaster to Greece. To record and analyze that bitter struggle of Greek against Greek fell to a younger historian, Thucydides (ca. 471–ca. 400 B.C.). Born in Athens to rank and wealth, Thucydides was elected a general in 423 B.C. and given command against the Spartans in the north Aegean. For allowing himself to be outmaneuvered by the enemy's best general, he was exiled and did not return to Athens until 404. He spent his years of exile recording the tragedy of his own times: the Peloponnesian War. Behind his narrative lay a special purpose. Why had Athens, with the fairest prospects of victory, been beaten? In essence, Thucydides' *History* is an analysis of the causes of the Athenian defeat; hence it has been well described as a study in the pathology of imperialism and war.

Thucydides' own reflections on issues and motives are found in the forty or more set speeches for which the *History* is famous. These speeches, which appear as direct quotations but were written by Thucydides, are a familiar expository device in ancient literature; like the oration and the dialogue, they must be accounted for by the importance of the spoken word in Greek culture. Thucydides claimed that he "put into the mouth of the speaker the sentiments proper to the occasion, expressed as I thought he would be likely to express them." The most famous speech is Pericles' Funeral Oration, reprinted here, which is a eulogy of Athens as the noblest product of man's reason. Another famous passage, also included here, is the Melian Dialogue, where the monstrous realities of the conflict are stripped bare. To the question, "Why did Athens fall?" Thucydides

Thucydides, *History of the Peloponnesian War*, trans. Benjamin Jowett (Boston: Lothrop, 1883), 115–24, 398–407.

answers that Periclean moderation had been abandoned for barbarous extremism.

Thucydides says he composed his *History* as "a thing to possess and keep forever." It is accurate, impartial, and meditative, conveying a stark picture of man's moral degeneration and disillusionment when he sacrifices the life of reason for wealth and power. There is none of the sentiment or supernaturalism which makes Herodotus entertaining, but lovers of Thucydides' Olympian detachment and historical outlook have hailed him as the supreme historian of all time.

During the same winter, in accordance with an old national custom, the funeral of those who first fell in this war was celebrated by the Athenians at the public charge. The ceremony is as follows: Three days before the celebration they erect a tent in which the bones of the dead are laid out, and every one brings to his own dead any offering which he pleases. At the time of the funeral the bones are placed in chests of cypress wood, which are conveyed on hearses; there is one chest for each tribe. They also carry a single empty litter decked with a pall for all whose bodies are missing, and cannot be recovered after the battle. The procession is accompanied by any one who chooses, whether citizen or stranger, and the female relatives of the deceased are present at the place of interment and make lamentation. The public sepulchre is situated in the most beautiful spot outside the walls; there they always bury those who fall in war; only after the battle of Marathon the dead, in recognition of their pre-eminent valor, were interred on the field. When the remains have been laid in the earth, some man of known ability and high reputation, chosen by the city, delivers a suitable oration over them; after which the people depart. Such is the manner of interment; and the ceremony was repeated from time to time throughout the war. Over those who were the first buried Pericles was chosen to speak. At the fitting moment he advanced from the sepulchre to a lofty stage, which had been erected in order that he might be heard as far as possible by the multitude, and spoke as follows:—

Pericles

FUNERAL SPEECH

"Most of those who have spoken here before me have commended the lawgiver who added this oration to our other funeral customs; it seemed to them a worthy thing that such an honor should be given at their burial to the dead who have fallen on the field of battle. But I should have preferred that, when men's deeds have been brave, they should be honored in deed only, and with such an honor as this public funeral, which you are now witnessing. Then the reputation of many would not have been imperilled on the eloquence or want of eloquence of one, and their virtues believed or not as he spoke well or ill. For it is difficult to say neither too little nor too much; and even moderation is apt not to give the impression of truthfulness. The friend of the dead who knows the facts is likely to think that the words of the speaker fall short of his knowledge and of his wishes; another who is not so well informed, when he hears of anything which surpasses his own powers, will be envious and will suspect exaggeration. Mankind are tolerant of the praises of others so long as each hearer thinks that he can do as well or nearly as well himself, but, when the speaker rises above him, jealousy is aroused and he begins to be incredulous. However, since our ancestors have set the seal of their approval upon the practice, I must obey, and to the utmost of my power shall endeavor to satisfy the wishes and beliefs of all who hear me.

"I will speak first of our ancestors, for it is right and becoming that now, when we are lamenting the dead, a tribute should be paid to their memory. There has never been a time when they did not inhabit this land, which by their valor they have handed down from generation to generation, and we have received from them a free state. But if they were worthy of praise, still more were our fathers, who added to their inheritance, and after many a struggle transmitted to us their sons this great empire. And we ourselves assembled here to-day, who are still most of us in the vigor of life, have chiefly done the work of improvement, and have richly endowed our city with all things, so that she is sufficient for herself both in peace and war. Of the military exploits by which our various possessions were acquired, or of the energy with which we or our fathers drove back the tide of war, Hellenic or Barbarian, I will not speak; for the tale would be long and is familiar to you. But before I praise the dead, I should like to point out by what principles of action we rose to power, and under what institutions and through what manner of life our empire became great. For I conceive that such thoughts are not unsuited to the occasion, and that this numerous assembly of citizens and strangers may profitably listen to them.

"Our form of government does not enter into rivalry with the institutions of others. We do not copy our neighbors, but are an example to them. It is true that we are called a democracy, for the administration is in the hands of the many and not of the few. But while the law secures equal justice to all alike in their private disputes, the claim of excellence is also recognized; and when a citizen is in any way distinguished, he is preferred to the public service, not as a matter of privilege, but as the reward of merit. Neither is poverty a bar, but a man may benefit his country whatever be the obscurity of his condition. There is no exclusiveness in our public life, and in our private intercourse we are not suspicious of one another, nor angry with our neighbor if he does what he likes; we do not put on sour looks at him which, though harmless, are not pleasant. While we are thus unconstrained in our private intercourse, a spirit of reverence pervades our public acts; we are prevented from doing wrong by respect for authority and for the laws, having an especial regard to those which are ordained for the protection of the injured as well as to those unwritten laws which bring upon the transgressor of them the reprobation of the general sentiment.

"And we have not forgotten to provide for our weary spirits many relaxations from toil; we have regular games and sacrifices throughout the year; at home the style of our life is refined; and the delight which we daily feel in all these things helps to banish melancholy. Because of the greatness of our city the fruits of the whole earth flow in upon us; so that we enjoy the goods of other countries as freely as of our own.

"Then, again, our military training is in many respects superior to that of our adversaries. Our city is thrown open to the world, and we never expel a foreigner or prevent him from seeing or learning anything of which the secret if revealed to an enemy might profit him. We rely not upon management or trickery, but upon our own hearts and hands. And in the matter of education, whereas they from early youth are always undergoing laborious exercises which are to make them brave, we live at ease, and yet are equally ready to face the perils which they face. And here is the proof. The Lacedaemonians come into Attica not by themselves, but with their whole confederacy following; we go alone into a neighbor's country; and although our opponents are fighting for their homes and we on a foreign soil, we have seldom any difficulty in overcoming them. Our enemies have never yet felt our united strength; the care of a navy divides our attention, and on land we are obliged to send our own citizens everywhere. But they, if they meet and defeat a part of our army, are as proud as if they had routed us all, and when defeated they pretend to have been vanquished by us all.

"If then we prefer to meet danger with a light heart but without laborious training, and with a courage which is gained by habit and not enforced by law, are we not greatly the gainers? Since we do not anticipate the pain, although, when the hour comes, we can be as brave as those who never allow themselves to rest; and thus too our city is equally admirable in peace and in war. For we are lovers of the beautiful, yet simple in our tastes, and we cultivate the mind without loss of manliness. Wealth we employ, not for talk and ostentation, but when there is a real use for it. To avow poverty with us is no disgrace: the true disgrace is in doing nothing to avoid it. An Athenian citizen does not neglect the state because he takes care of his own household; and even those of us who are engaged in business have a very fair idea of politics. We alone regard a man who takes no interest in public affairs, not as a harmless, but as a useless character; and if few of us are originators, we are all sound judges of a policy. The great impediment to action is, in our opinion, not discussion, but the want of that knowledge which is gained by discussion preparatory to action. For we have a peculiar power of thinking before we act and of acting too, whereas other men are courageous from ignorance but hesitate upon reflection. And they are surely to be esteemed the bravest spirits who, having the clearest sense both of the pains and pleasures of life, do not on that account shrink from danger. In doing good, again, we are unlike others; we make our friends by conferring, not by receiving favors. Now he who confers a favor is the firmer friend, because he would fain by kindness keep alive the memory of an obligation; but the recipient is colder in his feelings, because he knows that in requiting another's generosity he will not be winning gratitude, but only paying a debt. We alone do good to our neighbors not upon a calculation of interest, but in the confidence of freedom and in a frank and fearless spirit. To sum up: I say that Athens is the school of Hellas, and that the individual Athenian in his own person seems to have the power of adapting himself to the most varied forms of action with the utmost versatility and grace. This is no passing and idle word, but truth and fact; and the assertion is verified by the position to which these qualities have raised the state. For in the hour of trial Athens alone among her contemporaries is superior to the report of her. No enemy who comes against her is indignant at the reverses which he sustains at the hands of such a city; no subject complains that his masters are unworthy of him. And we shall assuredly not be without witnesses; there are mighty monuments of our power which will make us the wonder of this and of succeeding ages; we shall not need the praises of Homer or of any other panegyrist whose poetry may please for the moment, although his representation of the facts will not bear the light of day. For we have compelled every land and every sea to open a path for our valor, and have everywhere planted eternal memorials of our friendship and of our enmity. Such is the city for whose sake these men nobly fought and died; they could not bear the thought that she might be taken from them; and every one of us who survive should gladly toil on her behalf.

"I have dwelt upon the greatness of Athens because I want to show you that we are contending for a higher prize than those who enjoy none of these privileges, and to establish by manifest proof the merit of these men whom I am now commemorating. Their loftiest praise has been already spoken. For in magnifying the city I have magnified them, and men like them whose virtues made her glorious. And of how few Hellenes can it be said as of them, that their deeds when weighed in the balance have been found equal to their fame! Methinks that a death such as theirs has been gives the true measure of a man's worth; it may be the first revelation of his virtues, but is at any rate their final seal. For even those who come short in other ways may justly plead the valor with which they have fought for their country; they have blotted out the evil with the good, and have benefited the state more by their public services than they have injured her by their private actions. None of these men were enervated by wealth or hesitated to resign the pleasures of life; none of them put off the evil day in the hope, natural to poverty, that a man, though poor, may one day become rich. But, deeming that the punishment of their enemies was sweeter than any of these things, and that they could fall in no nobler cause, they determined at the hazard of their lives to be honorably avenged, and to leave the rest. They resigned to hope their unknown chance of happiness; but in the face of death they resolved to rely upon themselves alone. And when the moment came they were minded to resist and suffer, rather than to fly and save their lives; they ran away from the word of dishonor, but on the battle-field their feet stood fast, and in an instant, at the height of their fortune, they passed away from the scene, not of their fear, but of their glory.

"Such was the end of these men; they were worthy of Athens, and the living need not desire to have a more heroic spirit although they may pray for a less fatal issue. The value of such a spirit is not to be expressed in words. Any one can discourse to you for ever about the advantages of a brave defence which you know already. But instead of listening to him I would have you day by day fix your eyes upon the greatness of Athens, until you become filled with the love of her; and when you are impressed by the spectacle of her glory, reflect that this empire has been acquired by men who knew their duty and had the courage to do it, who in the hour of conflict had the fear of dishonor always present to them, and who, if ever they failed in an enterprise, would not allow their virtues to be lost to their country, but freely gave their lives to her as the fairest offering which they could present at her feast. The sacrifice which they collectively made was individually repaid to them; for they received again each one for himself a praise which grows not old, and the noblest of all sepulchres—I speak not of that in which their remains are laid, but of that in which their glory survives, and is proclaimed always and on every fitting occasion both in word and deed. For the whole earth is the sepulchre of famous men; not only are they commemorated by columns and inscriptions in their own country, but in foreign lands there dwells also an unwritten memorial of them, graven not on stone but in the hearts of men. Make them your examples, and, esteeming courage to be freedom and freedom to be happiness, do not weigh too nicely the perils of war. The unfortunate who has no hope of a change for the better has less reason to throw away his life than the prosperous who, if he survive, is always liable to a change for the worse, and to whom any accidental fall makes the most serious difference. To a man of spirit, cowardice and disaster coming together are far more bitter than death, striking him unperceived at a time when he is full of courage and animated by the general hope.

"Wherefore I do not now commiserate the parents of the dead who stand here; I would rather comfort them. You know that your life has been passed amid manifold vicissitudes; and that they may be deemed fortunate who have gained most honor, whether an honorable death like theirs, or an honorable sorrow like yours, and whose days have been so ordered that the term of their happiness is likewise the term of their life. I know how hard it is to make you feel this, when the good fortune of others will too often remind you of the gladness which once lightened your hearts. And sorrow is felt at the want of those blessings, not which a man never knew, but which were a part of his life before they were taken from him. Some of you are of an age at which they may hope to have other children, and they ought to bear their sorrow better; not only will the children who may hereafter be born make them forget their own lost ones, but the city will be doubly a gainer. She will not be left desolate, and she will be safer. For a man's counsel cannot have equal weight or worth, when he alone has no children to risk in the general danger. To those of you who have passed their prime, I say; 'Congratulate yourselves that you have been happy during the greater part of your days; remember that your life of sorrow will not last long, and be comforted by the glory of those who are gone. For the love of honor alone is ever young, and not riches, as some say, but honor is the delight of men when they are old and useless.'

"To you who are the sons and brothers of the departed, I see that the struggle to emulate them will be an arduous one. For all men praise the dead, and, however pre-eminent your virtue may be, hardly will you be thought, I do not say to equal, but even to approach them. The living have their rivals and detractors, but when a man is out of the way, the honor and good-will which he receives is unalloyed. And, If I am to speak of womanly virtues to those of you who will henceforth be widows, let me sum them up in one short admonition: To a woman not to show more weakness than is natural to her sex is a great glory, and not to be talked about for good or for evil among men.

"I have paid the required tribute, in obedience to the law, making use of such fitting words as I had. The tribute of deeds has been paid in part; for the dead have been honorably interred, and it remains only that their children should be maintained at the public charge until they are grown up; this is the solid prize with which, as with a garland, Athens crowns her sons living and dead, after a struggle like theirs. For where the rewards of virtue are greatest, there the noblest citizens are enlisted in the service of the state. And now, when you have duly lamented, every one his own dead, you may depart."

Such was the order of the funeral celebrated in this winter, with the end of which ended the first year of the Peloponnesian War.

MELIAN DIALOGUE

The Melians are colonists of the Lacedaemonians who would not submit to Athens like the other islanders. At first they were neutral and took no part. But when the Athenians tried to coerce them by ravaging their lands they were driven into open hostilities. The generals, Cleomedes the son of Lycomedes and Tisias the son of Tisimachus, encamped with the Athenian forces on the island. But before they did the country any harm they sent envoys to negotiate with the Melians. Instead of bringing these envoys before the people, the Melians desired them to explain their errand to the magistrates and to the chief men. They spoke as follows:—

"Since we are not allowed to speak to the people, lest, forsooth, they should be deceived by seductive and unanswerable arguments which they would hear set forth in a single uninterrupted oration (for we are perfectly aware that this is what you mean in bringing us before a select few), you who are sitting here may as well make assurance yet surer. Let us have no set speeches at all, but do you reply to each several statement of which you disapprove, and criticise it at once. Say first of all how you like this mode of proceeding."

The Melian representatives answered:—"The quiet interchange of explanations is a reasonable thing, and we do not object to that. But your warlike movements, which are present not only to our fears but to our eyes, seem to belie your words. We see that, although you may reason with us, you mean to be our judges; and that at the end of the discussion, if the justice of our cause prevail and we therefore refuse to yield, we may expect war; if we are convinced by you, slavery."

"ATH. 'Nay, but if you are only going to argue from fancies about the future, or if you meet us with any other purpose than that of looking your circumstances in the face and saving your city, we have done; but if this is your intention we will proceed.'

MEL. 'It is an excusable and natural thing that men in our position should have much to say and should indulge in many fancies. But we admit that this conference has met to consider the question of our preservation; and therefore let the argument proceed in the manner which you propose.'

ATH. 'Well, then, we Athenians will use no fine words; we will not go out of our way to prove at length that we have a right to rule, because we overthrew the Persians; or that we attack you now because we are suffering any injury at your hands. We should not convince you if we did; nor must you expect to convince us by arguing that, although a colony of the Lacedaemonians, you have taken no part in their expeditions, or that you have never done us any wrong. But you and we should say what we really think, and aim only at what is possible, for we both alike know that into the discussion of human affairs the question of justice only enters where the pressure of necessity is equal, and that the powerful exact what they can, and the weak grant what they must.'

MEL. 'Well, then, since you set aside justice and invite us to speak of expediency, in our judgment it is certainly expedient that you should respect a principle which is for the common good; and that to every man when in peril a reasonable claim should be accounted a claim of right, and any plea which he is disposed to urge, even if failing of the point a little, should help his cause. Your interest in this principle is quite as great as ours, inasmuch as you, if you fall, will incur the heaviest vengeance, and will be the most terrible example to mankind.

ATH. 'The fall of our empire, if it should fall, is not an event to which we look forward with dismay; for ruling states such as Lacedaemon are not cruel to their vanquished enemies. And we are fighting not so much against the Lacedaemonians as against our own subjects who may some day rise up and overcome their former masters. But this is a danger which you may leave to us. And we will now endeavor to show that we have come in the interests of our empire, and that in what we are about to say we are only seeking the preservation of your city. For we want to make you ours with the least trouble to ourselves, and it is for the interests of us both that you should not be destroyed.'

MEL. 'It may be your interest to be our masters, but how can it be ours to be your slaves?'

ATH. 'To you the gain will be that by submission you will avert the worst; and we shall be all the richer for your preservation.'

MEL. 'But must we be your enemies? Will you not receive us as friends if we are neutral and remain at peace with you?'

ATH. 'No, your enmity is not half so michievous to us as your friendship; for the one is in the eyes of our subjects an argument of our power, the other of our weakness.'

MEL. 'But are your subjects really unable to distinguish between states in which you have no concern, and those which are chiefly your own colonies, and in some cases have revolted and been subdued by you?'

ATH. 'Why, they do not doubt that both of them have a good deal to say for themselves on the score of justice, but they think that states like yours are left free because they are able to defend themselves, and that we do not attack them because we dare not. So that your subjection will give us an increase of security, as well as an extension of empire. For we are masters of the sea, and you who are islanders, and insignificant islanders too, must not be allowed to escape us.'

MEL. 'But do you not recognize another danger? For once more, since you drive us from the plea of justice and press upon us your doctrine of expediency, we must show you what is for our interest, and, if it be for yours also, may hope to convince you:—Will you not be making enemies of all who are now neutrals? When they see how you are treating us they will expect you some day to turn against them; and if so, are you not strengthening the enemies whom you already have, and bringing upon you others who, if they could help, would never dream of being your enemies at all?'

ATH. 'We do not consider our really dangerous enemies to be any of the peoples inhabiting the mainland who, secure in their freedom, may defer indefinitely any measures of precaution which they take against us, but islanders who, like you, happen to be under no control, and all who may be already irritated by the necessity of submission of our empire—these are our real enemies, for they are the most reckless and most likely to bring themselves as well as us into a danger which they cannot but foresee.'

MEL. 'Surely then, if you and your subjects will brave all this risk, you to preserve your empire and they to be quit of it, how base and cowardly it would be in us, who retain our freedom, not to do and suffer anything rather than be your slaves.'

ATH. 'Not so, if you calmly reflect: for you are not fighting against equals to whom you cannot yield without disgrace, but you are taking counsel whether or no you shall resist an overwhelming force. The question is not one of honor but of prudence.'

MEL. 'But we know that the fortune of war is sometimes impartial, and not always on the side of numbers. If we yield now all is over; but if we fight there is yet a hope that we may stand upright.'

ATH. 'Hope is a good comforter in the hour of danger, and when men have something else to depend upon, although hurtful, she is not ruinous. But when her spendthrift nature has induced them to stake their all, they see her as she is in the moment of their fall, and not till then. While the knowledge of her might enable them to beware of her, she never fails. You are weak and a single turn of the scale might be your ruin. Do not you be thus deluded; avoid the error of which so many are guilty, who, although they might still be saved if they would take the natural means, when visible grounds of confidence forsake them, have recourse to the invisible, to prophecies and oracles and the like, which ruin men by the hopes which they inspire in them.'

MEL. 'We know only too well how hard the struggle must be against your power, and against fortune, if she does not mean to be impartial. Nevertheless we do not despair of fortune; for we hope to stand as high as you in the favor of heaven, because we are righteous, and you against whom we contend are unrighteous; and we are satisfied that our deficiency in power will be compensated by the aid of our allies the Lacedaemonians; they cannot refuse to help us, if only because we are their kinsmen, and for the sake of their own honor. And therefore our confidence is not so utterly blind as you suppose.'

ATH. 'As for the Gods, we expect to have quite as much of their favor as you: for are we not doing or claiming anything which goes beyond common opinion about divine or men's desires about human things. For of the Gods we believe, and of men we know, that by a law of their nature wherever they can rule they will. This law was not made by us, and we are not the first who have acted upon it; we did but inherit it, and shall bequeath it to all time, and we know that you and all mankind, if you were as strong as we are, would do as we do. So much for the Gods; we have told you why we expect to stand as high in their good opinion as you. And then as to the Lacedaemonians—when you imagine that out of very shame they will assist you, we admire the simplicity of your idea, but we do not envy you the folly of it. The Lacedaemonians are exceedingly virtuous among themselves, and according to their national standard of morality. But in respect of their dealings with others, although many things might be said, a word is enough to describe them—of all men whom we know they are the most notorious for identifying what is pleasant with what is honorable, and what is expedient with what is just. But how inconsistent is such a character with your present blind hope of deliverance!'

MEL. 'That is the very reason why we trust them; they will look to their interest, and therefore will not be willing to betray the Melians, who are their own colonists, lest they should be distrusted by their friends in Hellas and play into the hands of their enemies.'

ATH. 'But do you not see that the path of expediency is safe, whereas justice and honor involve danger in practice, and such dangers the Lacedaemonians seldom care to face?'

MEL. 'On the other hand, we think that whatever perils there may be, they will be ready to face them for our sakes, and will consider danger less dangerous where we are concerned. For if they need our aid we are close at hand, and they can better trust our loyal feeling because we are their kinsmen.' . . .

ATH. 'If you are wise you will not run this risk; you ought to see that there can be no disgrace in yielding to a great city which invites you to become her ally on reasonable terms, keeping your own land, and merely paying tribute; and that you will certainly gain no honour if, having to choose between two alternatives, safety and war, you obstinately prefer the worse. To maintain our rights against equals, to be politic with superiors, and to be moderate towards inferiors is the path of safety. Reflect once more when we have withdrawn, and say to yourselves over and over again that you are deliberating about your one and only country, which may be saved or may be destroyed by a single decision.'

The Athenian envoys returned to the army; and the generals, when they found that the Melians would not yield, immediately commenced hostilities. They surrounded the town of Melos with a wall, dividing the work among the several contingents. They then left troops of their own and of the allies to keep guard both by land and by sea, and retired with the greater part of their army; the remainder carried on the blockade.

About the same time the Argives made an inroad into Phliasia, and lost nearly eighty men, who were caught in an ambuscade by the Phliasians and the Argive exiles. The Athenian garrison in Pylos took much spoil from the Lacedaemonians; nevertheless, the latter did not renounce the peace and go to war, but only notified by a proclamation that if any one of their own people had a mind to make reprisals on the Athenians he might. The Corinthians next declared war upon the Athenians on some private grounds, but the rest of the Peloponnesians did not join them. The Melians took that part of the Athenian wall which looked towards the agora by a night assault, killed a few men, and brought in as much corn and other necessaries as they could; they then retreated and remained inactive. After this the Athenians set a better watch. So the summer ended.

In the following winter the Lacedaemonians had intended to make an expedition into the Argive territory, but finding that the sacrifices which they offered at the frontier were unfavorable they returned home. The Argives, suspecting that the threatened invasion was instigated by citizens of their own, apprehended some of them; others however escaped.

About the same time the Melians took another part of the Athenian wall; for the fortifications were insufficiently guarded. Whereupon the Athenians sent fresh troops, under the command of Philocrates the son of Demeas. The place was now closely invested, and there was treachery among the citizens themselves. So the Melians were induced to surrender at discretion. The Athenians thereupon put to death all who were of military age, and made slaves of the women and children. They then colonized the island, sending thither five hundred settlers of their own.

Xenophon

4

The Constitution of the Lacedaemonians

Athens was not the only polis extolled beyond its own borders. Lacedaemon (better known as Sparta), also had its admirers, particularly among aristocrats and the well-to-do. In the late fifth century B.C. pro-Spartan sentiment was conspicuous in the coterie about Socrates and among supporters of the reactionary regime set up in Athens by the victorious Spartans in 404 B.C.

One of the members of this circle was Xenophon (*ca.* 434–*ca.* 355 B.C.), a middle-class property-holding Athenian. After the downfall of the reactionary party he enlisted with other Greeks as a mercenary in the pay of a prince who claimed the throne of Persia. The collapse of the expedition led to a long, grim retreat northward to the Black Sea and safety. Later he campaigned under the King of Sparta against the Persians, but when the latter became the allies of Athens, he was exiled and his property confiscated. For the next twenty years Xenophon lived in retirement in Spartan-held territory as a country gentleman, hunting and writing vigorously.

His best-known work is the *Anabasis,* a spirited account of the great retreat, of which he had been the leader; but he also wrote three rather banal books about Socrates, a long history continuing from where Thucydides left off, and other works. His *Constitution of the Lacedaemonians,* drawn upon for the following selection, is the best general account of the Spartan way of life, with which he was familiar.

Not long after Xenophon's death, this regimented society—whose creation is attributed to Lycurgus, an ancient and legendary lawgiver—broke down forever. Of all the distinction won by Sparta at Thermopylae and in the Peloponnesian War, nothing remained but a high tradition—a tradition destined for a long life. Through Xenophon and Plato, and later Plutarch,

Xenophon, *The Constitution of the Lacedaemonians,* in *The Minor Works of Xenophon,* trans. J. S. Watson (London: Bell [Bohn Classical Library], 1878), 204–09, 212–23.

the aristocratic Spartan ideal of breeding and discipline was transmitted to the modern ruling classes of England and continental Europe, whose education, ever since the fifteenth century, has been based on the Greek and Roman classics.

THE REGULATIONS OF LYCURGUS RESPECTING MARRIAGE AND THE TREATMENT OF CHILDREN

But reflecting once how Sparta, one of the least populous of states, had proved the most powerful and celebrated city in Greece, I wondered by what means this result had been produced. When I proceeded, however, to contemplate the institutions of the Spartans, I wondered no longer.

Lycurgus, who made laws for them, by obedience to which they have flourished, I not only admire, but consider to have been in the fullest sense a wise man; for he rendered his country preëminent in prosperity, not by imitating other states, but by making ordinances contrary to those of most governments.

With regard, for example, to the procreation of children, that I may begin from the beginning, other people feed their young women, who are about to produce offspring, and who are of the class regarded as well brought up, on the most moderate quantity of vegetable food possible, and on the least possible quantity of meat, while they either keep them from wine altogether, or allow them to use it only when mixed with water; and as the greater number of the men engaged in trades are sedentary, so the rest of the Greeks think it proper that their young women should sit quiet and spin wool. But how can we expect that women thus treated should produce a vigorous progeny? Lycurgus, on the contrary, thought that female slaves were competent to furnish clothes; and, considering that the production of children was the noblest duty of the free, he enacted, in the first place, that the female should practise bodily exercises no less than the male sex; and he then appointed for the women contests with one another, just as for the men, expecting that when both parents were rendered strong, a stronger offspring would be born from them.

Observing, too, that the men of other nations, when women

were united to husbands, associated with their wives during the early part of their intercourse without restraint, he made enactments quite at variance with this practice; for he ordained that a man should think it shame to be seen going in to his wife, or coming out from her. When married people meet in this way, they must feel stronger desire for the company of one another, and whatever offspring is produced must thus be rendered far more robust than if the parents were satiated with each other's society.

In addition to these regulations, he also took from the men the liberty of marrying when each of them pleased, and appointed that they should contract marriages only when they were in full bodily vigour, deeming this injunction also conducive to the production of an excellent offspring. Seeing also that if old men chanced to have young wives, they watched their wives with the utmost strictness, he made a law quite opposed to this feeling; for he appointed that an old man should introduce to his wife whatever man in the prime of life he admired for his corporeal and mental qualities, in order that she might have children by him. If, again, a man was unwilling to associate with his wife, and yet was desirous of having proper children, he made a provision also with respect to him, that whatever woman he saw likely to have offspring, and of good disposition, he might, on obtaining the consent of her husband, have children by her. Many similar permissions he gave; for the women are willing to have two families, and the men to receive brothers to their children, who are equal to them in birth and standing, but have no claim to share in their property.

Let him who wishes, then, consider whether Lycurgus, in thus making enactments different from those of other legislators, in regard to the procreation of children, secured for Sparta a race of men eminent for size and strength.

ON THE TRAINING AND EDUCATION OF CHILDREN

Having given this account of the procreation of children, I wish also to detail the education of those of both sexes. Of the other Greeks, those who say that they bring up their sons best set slaves over them to take charge of them, as soon as the children can understand what is said to them, and send them, at the same time, to schoolmasters, to learn letters, and music, and the exercises of the palaestra. They also render their children's feet delicate by the use of sandals, and weaken their bodies by changes of clothes; and as to food, they regard their appetite as the measure of what they are to take. But Lycurgus, instead of allowing each citizen to set slaves as guardians over his children, appointed a man to have the care of them all, one of those from whom the chief magistrates are chosen; and he is called the paedonomus. He invested this man with full authority to assemble the boys, and, if he found that any one was negligent of his duties, to punish him severely. He assigned him also some of the grown-up boys as scourge-bearers, that they might inflict whatever chastisement was necessary; so that great dread of disgrace, and great willingness to obey, prevailed among them.

Instead, also, of making their feet soft with sandals, he enacted that they should harden them by going without sandals; thinking that, if they exercised themselves in this state, they would go up steep places with far greater ease, and descend declivities with greater safety; and that they would also leap, and skip, and run faster unshod, if they had their feet inured to doing so, than shod. Instead of being rendered effeminate, too, by a variety of dresses, he made it a practice that they should accustom themselves to one dress throughout the year; thinking that they would thus be better prepared to endure cold and heat.

As to food, he ordained that they should exhort the boys to take only such a quantity as never to be oppressed with repletion, and not to be strangers to living somewhat frugally; supposing that, being thus brought up, they would be the better able, if they should be required, to support toil under a scarcity of supplies, would be the more likely to persevere in exertion, should it be imposed on them, on the same quantity of provisions, and would be less desirous of sauces, more easily satisfied with any kind of food, and pass their lives in greater health. He also considered that the fare which rendered the body slender would be more conducive to increasing its stature than that which expanded it with nutriment. Yet that the boys might not suffer too much from hunger, Lycurgus, though he did not allow them to take what they wanted without trouble, gave them liberty to steal certain things to relieve the cravings of nature; and he made it honourable to steal as many cheeses as possible. That he did not give them leave to form schemes for getting food because he was at a loss what to allot them, I suppose no one is ignorant; as it is evident that he who designs to steal must be wakeful during the night, and use deceit, and lay plots; and, if he would gain anything of consequence, must employ spies. All these things, therefore, it is plain that he taught the children from a desire to render them more dexterous in securing provisions, and better qualified for warfare.

Some one may say, "Why, then, if he thought it honourable to steal, did he inflict a great number of stripes on him who was caught in the [act]?" I answer, that in other things which men teach, they punish him who does not follow his instructions properly; and that the Lacedaemonians accordingly punished those who were detected as having attempted to steal in an improper manner. These boys he gave in charge to others to scourge them at the altar of Diana Orthia; designing to show by this enactment that it is possible for a person, after enduring pain for a short time, to enjoy pleasure with credit for a long time. It is also shown by this punishment that, where there is need of activity, the inert person benefits himself the least, and occasions himself most trouble.

In order, too, that the boys, in case of the paedonomus being absent, may never be in want of a president, he appointed that whoever of the citizens may happen at any time to be present is to assume the direction of them, and to enjoin whatever he may think advantageous for them, and punish them if they do anything wrong. By doing this, Lycurgus has also succeeded in rendering the boys much more modest; for neither boys nor men respect any one so much as their rulers. And that if, on any occasion, no full-grown man happen to be present, the boys may not even in that case be without a leader, he ordained that the most active of the grown-up youths take the command of each band; so that the boys there are never without a superintendent.

It appears to me that I must say something also of the boys as objects of affection; for this has likewise some reference to education. Among the other Greeks, a man and boy either form a union, as among the Boeotians, and associate together, or, as among the Eleians, the men gain the favour of the youths by means of attentions bestowed upon them; but there are some of the Greeks who prohibit the suitors for the boys' favours from having the least conversation with them. But Lycurgus, acting contrary to all these people also, thought proper, if any man, being himself such as he ought to be, admired the disposition of a youth, and made it his object to render him a faultless friend, and to enjoy his society, to bestow praise upon him, and regarded this as the most excellent kind of education; but if any man showed that his affections were fixed only on the bodily attractions of a youth, Lycurgus, considering this as most unbecoming, appointed that at Lacedaemon suitors for the favours of boys should abstain from intimate connexion with them, not less strictly than parents abstain from such intercourse with their children, or children of the same family from that with one another. That such a state of things is disbelieved by some, I am not surprised; for in most states the laws are not at all adverse to the love of youths; but Lycurgus, for his part, took such precautions with reference to it.

.   .   .

MEALS TAKEN IN PUBLIC. ON TEMPERANCE

The employments which Lycurgus appointed for each period of life have now been almost all specified. What mode of living he instituted for all the citizens, I will next endeavour to explain.

Lycurgus, then, having found the Spartans, like the other Greeks, taking their meals at home, and knowing that most were guilty of excess at them, caused their meals to be taken in public, thinking that his regulations would thus be less likely to be transgressed. He appointed them such a quantity of food, that they should neither be overfed nor feel stinted. Many extraordinary supplies are also furnished from what is caught in hunting, and for these the rich sometimes contribute bread; so that the table is never without provisions, as long as they design the meal to last, and yet is never expensive.

Having put a stop likewise to all unnecessary drinking, which weakens alike the body and the mind, he gave permission that every one should drink when he was thirsty, thinking that the drink would thus be most innoxious and most pleasant. When they take their meals together in this manner, how can any one ruin either himself or his family by gluttony or drunkenness? In other states, equals in age generally associate together, and with them modesty has but very little influence; but Lycurgus, at Sparta, mixed citizens of different ages, so that the younger are for the most part instructed by the experience of the older. It is a custom at these public meals, that whatever any one has done to his honour in the community is related; so that insolence, or disorder from intoxication, or any indecency in conduct or language, has there no opportunity of showing itself. The practice of taking meals away from home is also attended with these advantages, that the people are obliged to walk in taking their departure homewards, and to be careful that they may not stagger from the effects of wine, knowing that they will not remain where they dined, and that they must conduct themselves in the night just as in the day; for it is not allowable for any one who is still liable to military duty to walk with a torch.

As Lycurgus observed, too, that those who, after taking food, exercise themselves, become well-complexioned, plump, and robust, while those who are inactive are puffy, unhealthy-looking, and feeble, he did not neglect to give attention to that point; and as he perceived that when any one engages in labour from his own inclination, he proves himself to have his body in efficient condition, he ordered that the oldest in each place of exercise should take care that those belonging to it should never be overcome by taking too much food. With regard to this matter, he appears to me to have been by no means mistaken; for no one would easily find men more healthy, or more able-bodied, than the Spartans; for they exercise themselves alike in their legs, in their hands, and in their shoulders.

ORDINANCES REGARDING CHILDREN, SLAVES, AND PROPERTY

In the following particulars, also, he made enactments contrary to the usage of most states; for in other communities each individual has the control over his own children, and servants, and property; but Lycurgus, wishing to order things so that the citizens might enjoy some advantage from one another, unattended with any reciprocal injury, ordained that each should have authority not only over his own children, but over those of others. But when a person is conscious that his fellow-citizens are fathers of the children over whom he exercises authority, he must exercise it in such a way as he would wish it to be exercised over his own. If a boy, on any occasion, receive blows from another boy, and complain of that boy to his father, it is considered dishonourable in the father not to inflict additional blows on his son. Thus they trust to one another to impose nothing disgraceful on the children.

He enacted also that a person might use his neighbour's servants, if he had need of them. He introduced, too, a community of property in hunting-dogs; so that those who require them call on their

owner to hunt, who, if he is not at leisure to hunt himself, cheerfully sends them out. They use horses also in like manner; for
whoever is sick, or wants a vehicle, or desires to go to some place
speedily, takes possession of a horse, if he sees one anywhere, and,
after making proper use of it, restores it.

Nor, in regard to the following point, did he allow that which
is customary among other people should be practised among his
countrymen. For when men, from being overtaken by night in
hunting, are in want of provisions, unless they have previously
furnished themselves with them, he directed that, in such a case,
those who have partaken of what they need, leave the rest ready for
use, and that those who require a supply, having opened the seals,
and taken as much as they want, seal the remainder up again and
leave it. As they share thus, then, with one another, those who
possess but little participate, whenever they are in need, in all the
produce of the country.

RESTRICTIONS ON THE EMPLOYMENTS OF THE LACEDAEMONIANS

The following practices, too, Lycurgus established in Sparta, at
variance with those of the rest of Greece. In other communities
all gain as much by traffic as they can; one cultivates land, another
trades by sea, another engages in general commerce, another maintains himself by art. But at Sparta, Lycurgus prohibited free men
from having any connexion with traffic, and enjoined them to consider as their only occupation whatever secures freedom to states.
How, indeed, could wealth be eagerly sought in a community where
he had appointed that the citizens should contribute equally to
their necessary maintenance, and should take their meals in common, and had thus provided that they should not desire wealth with
a view to sensual gratifications? Nor had they, moreover, to get
money for the sake of clothing; for they think themselves adorned,
not by expensive raiment, but by a healthy personal appearance.
Nor have they to gather money for the purpose of spending it on
those who eat with them, since he has made it more honourable
for a person to serve his neighbours by bodily exertion, than by
putting himself to pecuniary expense; making it apparent that the
one proceeds from the mind, and the other from fortune.

From acquiring money by unjust means, he prohibited them
by such methods as the following. He instituted, in the first place,

such a kind of money, that, even if but ten minae came into a house, it could never escape the notice either of masters or of servants; for it would require much room, and a carriage to convey it. In the next place, gold and silver are searched after, and, if they are discovered anywhere, the possessor of them is punished. How, then, could gain by traffic be an object of pursuit, in a state where the possession of money occasions more pain than the use of it affords pleasure?

OBEDIENCE TO THE MAGISTRATES AND LAWS

That at Sparta the citizens pay the strictest obedience to the magistrates and laws, we all know. I suppose, however, that Lycurgus did not attempt to establish such an excellent order of things, until he had brought the most powerful men in the state to be of the same mind with regard to it. I form my opinion on this consideration, that, in other states, the more influential men are not willing even to appear to fear the magistrates, but think that such fear is unbecoming free men; but in Sparta, the most powerful men not only put themselves under the magistrates, but even count it an honour to humble themselves before them, and to obey, when they are called upon, not walking, but running; supposing that if they themselves are the first to pay exact obedience, others will follow their example; and such has been the case. It is probable, also, that the chief men established the magistracy of the Ephori, in conjunction with Lycurgus, as they must have been certain that obedience is of the greatest benefit, alike in a state, and in an army, and in a family; and they doubtless considered that the greater power magistrates have, the greater effect will they produce on the citizens in enforcing obedience. The Ephori, accordingly, have full power to impose a fine on whomsoever they please, and to exact the fine without delay; they have power also to degrade magistrates even while they are in office, and to put them in prison, and to bring them to trial for their life. Being possessed of such authority, they do not, like the magistrates in other states, always permit those who are elected to offices to rule during the whole year as they choose, but, like despots and presidents in gymnastic contests, punish on the instant whomsoever they find acting at all contrary to the laws.

Though there were many other excellent contrivances adopted

by Lycurgus, to induce the citizens to obey the laws, the most excellent of all appears to me to be, that he did not deliver his laws to the people until he had gone, in company with the most eminent of his fellow-citizens, to Delphi, and consulted the god whether it would be more beneficial and advantageous for Sparta to obey the laws which he had made. As the god replied that it would be more beneficial in every way, he at once delivered them, deciding that it would be not only illegal, but impious, to disobey laws sanctioned by the oracle.

INFAMY AND PENALTIES OF COWARDICE

It is deserving of admiration, too, in Lycurgus, that he made it a settled principle in the community, that an honourable death is preferable to a dishonourable life; for whoever pays attention to the subject will find that fewer of those who hold this opinion die than of those who attempt to escape danger by flight. Hence we may say with truth, that safety attends for a much longer period on valour than on cowardice; for valour is not only attended with less anxiety and greater pleasure, but is also more capable of assisting and supporting us. It is evident, too, that good report accompanies valour; for almost everybody is willing to be in alliance with the brave.

How he contrived that such sentiments should be entertained, it is proper not to omit to mention. He evidently, then, intended a happy life for the brave, and a miserable one for the cowardly. In other communities, when a man acts as a coward, he merely brings on himself the name of coward, but the coward goes to the same market, and sits or takes exercise, if he pleases, in the same place with the brave men; at Lacedaemon, however, every one would be ashamed to admit a coward into the same tent with him, or to allow him to be his opponent in a match at wrestling. Frequently, too, a person of such a character, when they choose opposite parties to play at ball, is left without any place; and in forming a chorus he is thrust into the least honourable position. On the road he must yield the way to others, and at public meetings he must rise up, even before his juniors. His female relatives he must maintain at home, and they must pay the penalty of his want of spirit; he is also not allowed to have his hearth without a wife, and must at the same time pay a fine for being in that condition. He must not walk abroad anointed, or imitate the manners of persons of blameless character; else he will have to receive stripes from his betters. Since, then, such disgrace is inflicted on cowards, I do not at all wonder that death is preferred at Sparta to a life so dishonourable and infamous.

HONOURS PAID TO OLD AGE. ENCOURAGEMENT OF VIRTUE

Lycurgus seems to me to have provided also, with great judgment, how virtue might be practised even to old age; for by adding to his other enactments the choice of senators at an advanced stage of life, he caused honour and virtue not to be disregarded even in old age.

It is worthy of admiration in him, too, that he attached consideration to the old age of the well-deserving; for by making the old men arbiters in the contest for superiority in mental qualifications, he rendered their old age more honourable than the vigour of those in the meridian of life. This contest is deservedly held in the greatest esteem among the people, for gymnastic contests are attended with honour, but they concern only bodily accomplishments; the contest for distinction in old age involves a decision respecting merits of the mind. In proportion, therefore, as the mind is superior to the body, so much are contests for mental eminence more worthy of regard than those concerning bodily superiority.

Is it not highly worthy of admiration, also, in Lycurgus, that when he saw that those who are disinclined to practice virtue are not qualified to increase the power of their country, he obliged all the citizens of Sparta to cultivate every kind of virtue publicly. As private individuals, accordingly, who practise virtue, are superior in it to those who neglect it, so Sparta is naturally superior in virtue to all other states, as it is the only one that engages in a public cultivation of honour and virtue. Is it not also deserving of commendation, that, when other states punish any person that injures another, Lycurgus inflicted no less punishment on any one that openly showed himself regardless of becoming as good a man as possible? He thought, as it appears, that by those who make others slaves, or rob them, or steal anything, the individual sufferers only are injured, but that by the unprincipled and cowardly whole communities are betrayed; so that he appears to me to have justly imposed the heaviest penalties on such characters.

He also imposed on his countrymen an obligation, from which there is no exception, of practising every kind of political virtue;

for he made the privileges of citizenship equally available to all those who observed what was enjoined by the laws, without taking any account either of weakness of body or scantiness of means; but if any one was too indolent to perform what the laws prescribed, Lycurgus appointed that he should be no longer counted in the number of equally privileged citizens.

That these laws are extremely ancient is certain; for Lycurgus is said to have lived in the time of the Heracleidae; but, ancient as they are, they are still very new to other communities; for, what is the most wonderful of all things, all men extol such institutions, but no state thinks proper to imitate them.

OF THE LACEDAEMONIAN ARMY

The regulations which I have mentioned are beneficial alike in peace and in war; but if any one wishes to learn what he contrived better than other legislators with reference to military proceedings, he may attend to the following particulars.

In the first place, then, the Ephori give the cavalry and infantry public notice of the years during which they must join the army, as well as the artisans; for the Lacedaemonians provide themselves in the field with an abundance of all those things which people use in a city; and of whatever instruments an army may require in common, orders are given to bring some on waggons, and others on beasts of burden, as by this arrangement anything left behind is least likely to escape notice.

For engagements in the field he made the following arrangements. He ordered that each soldier should have a purple robe and a brazen shield; for he thought that such a dress had least resemblance to that of women, and was excellently adapted for the field of bottle, as it is soonest made splendid, and is longest in growing soiled. He permitted also those above the age of puberty to let their hair grow, as he thought that they thus appeared taller, more manly, and more terrible in the eyes of the enemy.

When they were thus equipped, he divided them into six morae of cavalry and heavy-armed infantry. Each of these morae of the citizens has one polemarch, four centurions, eight captains of fifty, and sixteen enomotarchs. The men of these morae are sometimes, according to the command issued, formed in enomotiae, sometimes by threes, sometimes by sixes. As to what most people imagine, that the arrangement of the Lacedaemonians under arms is extremely complex, they conceive the exact contrary to what is the fact; for in the Lacedaemonian order the officers are placed in the front ranks, and each rank is in a condition to perform everything which it is necessary for it to perform. So easy is it to understand this arrangement, that no one, who can distinguish one man from another, would fail of learning it; for it is assigned to some to lead, and enjoined on others to follow. Shiftings of place, by which the companies are extended or deepened, are ordered by the word of the enomotarch, as by a herald; and in these there is nothing in the least difficult to learn. But how it is possible for men in this arrangement, even if they are thrown into confusion, to fight with an enemy presenting themselves on any quarter alike, it is not so easy to understand, except for those who have been brought up under the institution of Lycurgus. The Lacedaemonians do with the greatest ease what appears extremely difficult to other men that are even accustomed to arms. For when they march in column, one enomotia follows in the rear of another; and if, when they are in this order, a body of the enemy shows itself in front, orders are given to each enomotarch to bring up his enomotia to the front on the left; and this movement is made throughout the whole army, until it presents itself in full array against the enemy. But if again, while they are in this order, the enemy should show themselves in the rear, each rank performs an evolution, that the strongest may always be presented to the enemy.

But when the commander is on the left, they do not in that case consider themselves in a worse condition, but sometimes even in a better; for if an enemy should attempt to encompass them, he would come round, not on the defenceless, but on the armed side. If on any occasion, again, it should appear advantageous, for any particular object, that the commander should occupy the right wing, they wheel the troop towards the wing, and manoeuvre the main body, until the commander is on the right, and the rear becomes the left. But if, again, a body of the enemy appear on the right, marching in column, they do nothing else but turn each century round, like a ship, so as to front the enemy; and thus the century which was in the rear comes to the right. But if the enemy approach on the left, they do not allow them to come near, but repulse them, or turn their centuries round to face the enemy; and thus again the century that was in the rear takes its place on the left.

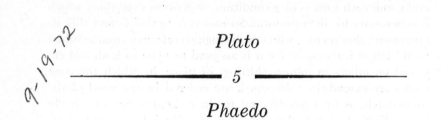

Plato

5

Phaedo

Neither Socrates nor Jesus, the most famous and most beloved teachers of the ancient world, left any written works. For our knowledge of both we must depend mainly upon the evidence of disciples, who saw them as beings without human parallel. In the case of Socrates, our primary source is Plato, in whose dialogues the Athenian sage is the foremost figure.

Socrates (*ca.* 470–399 B.C.) lived at Athens, in an age that was, like our own, one of intellectual and moral unrest. The most venerable orthodoxies were exposed to radical criticism and revaluation, especially by a group of teachers known as the Sophists. Socrates himself contributed to the shaking of popular beliefs by constantly questioning everyone he met; his challenging of tradition was largely responsible for the fact that he was brought to trial and put to death.

But his place in history does not rest upon this negative basis. Socrates had no doubt at all that truth exists, as the following selection amply proves. Truth is in the possession of every man, hidden under smug self-satisfaction and narrow dogmatism, and needs only to be liberated by the judicious examination and testing of opinion. This "Socratic method" aimed at revealing eternal principles of human conduct, upon which personal happiness and social stability depend. Socrates' mode of truth-seeking (dialectic) is illustrated in *Phaedo,* a dialogue that ranks among the masterworks of Western literature.

As Plato tells us, Socrates spends the last hours before his execution in comforting his friends. Persisting in his outlook and method, he tells them that behind the immediate world of appearances lies the unseen eternal order. It is for this, the eternal world, that men should live; the souls of men who have lived wisely will at last rejoin the eternal world when freed by death.

Plato, *Phaedo,* in *The Dialogues of Plato,* trans. Benjamin Jowett (Oxford: Clarendon Press, 1953), Steph. 1–5, 8–13, 25–28, 30–34, 65–66.

Centuries later this philosophy was to contribute mightily to the intellectual capital of Christianity; but, since Socrates subjected everything to the test of reason and based morality upon human values, he is also regarded as a leading spirit in the rationalist and humanist tradition.

PERSONS OF THE DIALOGUE

PHAEDO, *who is the narrator of the Dialogue to*
ECHECRATES *of Phlius*
SOCRATES
ATTENDANT OF THE PRISON
APOLLODORUS
SIMMIAS
CEBES
CRITO

SCENE *The Prison of Socrates*
PLACE OF THE NARRATION *Phlius*

ECHECRATES Were you yourself, Phaedo, in the prison with Socrates on the day when he drank the poison?

PHAEDO Yes, Echecrates, I was.

ECH. I should so like to hear about his death. What did he say in his last hours? We were informed that he died by taking poison, but no one knew anything more; for no Phliasian ever goes to Athens now, and it is a long time since any stranger from Athens has found his way hither; so that we had no clear account.

PHAED. Did you not hear of the proceedings at the trial?

ECH. Yes; some one told us about the trial, and we could not understand why, having been condemned, he should have been put to death, not at the time, but long afterwards. What was the reason of this?

PHAED. An accident, Echecrates: the stern of the ship which the Athenians send to Delos happened to have been crowned on the day before he was tried.

ECH. What is this ship?

PHAED.   It is the ship in which, according to Athenian tradition, Theseus went to Crete when he took with him the fourteen youths, and was the saviour of them and of himself. And they are said to have vowed to Apollo at the time, that if they were saved they would send a yearly mission to Delos. Now this custom still continues, and the whole period of the voyage to and from Delos, beginning when the priest of Apollo crowns the stern of the ship, is a holy season, during which the city is not allowed to be polluted by public executions; and when the vessel is detained by contrary winds, the time spent in going and returning is very considerable. As I was saying, the ship was crowned on the day before the trial, and this was the reason why Socrates lay in prison and was not put to death until long after he was condemned.

ECH.   What was the manner of his death, Phaedo? What was said or done? And which of his friends were with him? Or did the authorities forbid them to be present—so that he had no friends near him when he died?

PHAED.   No; there were several of them with him.

ECH.   If you have nothing to do, I wish that you would tell me what passed, as exactly as you can.

PHAED.   I have nothing at all to do, and will try to gratify your wish. To be reminded of Socrates is always the greatest delight to me, whether I speak myself or hear another speak of him.

ECH.   You will have listeners who are of the same mind with you, and I hope that you will be as exact as you can.

PHAED.   I had a singular feeling at being in his company. For I could hardly believe that I was present at the death of a friend, and therefore I did not pity him, Echecrates; he died so fearlessly, and his words and bearing were so noble and gracious, that to me he appeared blessed. I thought that in going to the other world he could not be without a divine call, and that he would be happy, if any man ever was, when he arrived there; and therefore I did not pity him as might have seemed natural at such an hour. But I had not the pleasure which I usually feel in philosophical discourse (for philosophy was the theme of which we spoke). I was pleased, but in the pleasure there was also a strange admixture of pain; for I reflected that he was soon to die, and this double feeling was shared by us all; we were laughing and weeping by turns, especially the excitable Apollodorus—you know the sort of man?

ECH.   Yes.

PHAED. He was quite beside himself, and I and all of us were greatly moved.

ECH. Who were present?

PHAED. Of native Athenians there were, besides Apollodorus, Critobulus and his father Crito, Hermogenes, Epigenes, Aeschines, Antisthenes; likewise Ctesippus of the deme of Paeania, Menexenus, and some others; Plato, if I am not mistaken, was ill.

ECH. Were there any strangers?

PHAED. Yes, there were; Simmias the Theban, and Cebes, and Phaedondes; Euclid and Terpsion, who came from Megara.

ECH. And was Aristippus there, and Cleombrotus?

PHAED. No, they were said to be in Aegina.

ECH. Any one else?

PHAED. I think that these were nearly all.

ECH. Well, and what did you talk about?

PHAED. I will begin at the beginning, and endeavour to repeat the entire conversation. On the previous days we had been in the habit of assembling early in the morning at the court in which the trial took place, and which is not far from the prison. There we used to wait talking with one another until the opening of the doors (for they were not opened very early); then we went in and generally passed the day with Socrates. On the last morning we assembled sooner than usual, having heard on the day before when we quitted the prison in the evening that the sacred ship had come from Delos; and so we arranged to meet very early at the accustomed place. On our arrival the jailer who answered the door, instead of admitting us, came out and told us to stay until he called us. 'For the Eleven,' he said, 'are now with Socrates; they are taking off his chains, and giving orders that he is to die to-day.' He soon returned and said that we might come in. On entering we found Socrates just released from chains, and Xanthippè, whom you know, sitting by him, and holding his child in her arms. When she saw us she uttered a cry and said, as women will: 'O Socrates, this is the last time that either you will converse with your friends, or they with you.' Socrates turned to Crito and said: 'Crito, let some one take her home.' Some of Crito's people accordingly led her away, crying out and beating herself. And when she was gone, Socrates, sitting up on the couch, bent and rubbed his leg, saying, as he was rubbing: How singular is the thing called pleasure, and how curiously related to pain, which might be thought to be the opposite of it; for they are never present to a man at the same instant, and yet he who pursues either is generally compelled to take the other; their bodies are two, but they are joined by a single head. And I cannot help thinking that if Aesop had remembered them, he would have made a fable about God trying to reconcile their strife, and how, when he could not, he fastened their heads together; and this is the reason why when one comes the other follows: as I know by my own experience now, when after the pain in my leg which was caused by the chain pleasure appears to succeed.

Upon this Cebes said: I am glad, Socrates, that you have mentioned the name of Aesop. For it reminds me of a question which has been asked by many, and was asked of me only the day before yesterday by Evenus the poet—he will be sure to ask it again, and therefore if you would like me to have an answer ready for him, you may as well tell me what I should say to him:—he wanted to know why you, who never before wrote a line of poetry, now that you are in prison are turning Aesop's fables into verse, and also composing that hymn in honour of Apollo.

Tell him, Cebes, he replied, what is the truth—that I had no idea of rivalling him or his poems; to do so as I knew, would be no easy task. But I wanted to see whether I could purge away a scruple which I felt about the meaning of certain dreams. In the course of my life I have often had intimations in dreams 'that I should compose music.' The same dream came to me sometimes in one form, and sometimes in another, but always saying the same or nearly the same words: 'Cultivate and make music,' said the dream. And hitherto I had imagined that this was only intended to exhort and encourage me in the study of philosophy, which has been the pursuit of my life, and is the noblest and best of music. The dream was bidding me do what I was already doing, in the same way that the competitor in a race is bidden by the spectators to run when he is already running. But I was not certain of this; for the dream might have meant music in the popular sense of the word, and being under sentence of death, and the festival giving me a respite, I thought that it would be safer for me to satisfy the scruple, and, in obedience to the dream, to compose a few verses before I departed. And first I made a hymn in honour of the god of the festival, and then considering that a poet, if he is really to be a poet, should not only put together words, but should invent stories, and that I have no invention, I took some fables of Aesop, which I had ready at hand and which I knew—they were the first I came upon—and turned them into verse. Tell this to Evenus, Cebes, and bid him be of good cheer; say that I would have him come after me if he be a wise man, and not tarry; and that to-day I am likely to be going, for the Athenians say that I must.

Simmias said: What a message for such a man! having been a frequent companion of his I should say that, as far as I know him, he will never take your advice unless he is obliged.

Why, said Socrates,—is not Evenus a philosopher?

I think that he is, said Simmias.

Then he, or any man who has the spirit of philosophy, will be willing to die; but he will not take his own life, for that is held to be unlawful.

Here he changed his position, and put his legs off the couch on to the ground, and during the rest of the conversation he remained sitting.

Why do you say, enquired Cebes, that a man ought not to take his own life, but that the philosopher will be ready to follow the dying?

Socrates replied: And have you, Cebes and Simmias, who are the disciples of Philolaus, never heard him speak of this?

Yes, but his language was obscure, Socrates.

My words, too, are only an echo; but there is no reason why I should not repeat what I have heard: and indeed, as I am going to another place, it is very meet for me to be thinking and talking of the nature of the pilgrimage which I am about to make. What can I do better in the interval between this and the setting of the sun?

. . .

And now, O my judges, I desire to prove to you that the real philosopher has reason to be of good cheer when he is about to die, and that after death he may hope to obtain the greatest good in the other world. And how this may be, Simmias and Cebes, I will endeavour to explain. For I deem that the true votary of philosophy is likely to be misunderstood by other men; they do not perceive that he is always pursuing death and dying; and if this be so, and he has had the desire of death all his life long, why when his time comes should be repine at that which he has been always pursuing and desiring?

Simmias said laughingly: Though not in a laughing humour,

you have made me laugh, Socrates; for I cannot help thinking that the many when they hear your words will say how truly you have described philosophers, and our people at home will likewise say that the life which philosophers desire is in reality death, and that they have found them out to be deserving of the death which they desire. *Gives a sense of the dialectic method*

And they are right, Simmias, in thinking so, with the exception of the words 'they have found them out'; for they have not found out either what is the nature of that death which the true philosopher deserves, or how he deserves or desires death. But enough of them:—let us discuss the matter among ourselves. Do we believe that there is such a thing as death?

To be sure, replied Simmias.

Plato's idea Begin

Is it not the separation of soul and body? And to be dead is the completion of this; when the soul exists in herself, and is released from the body and the body is released from the soul, what is this but death?

Just so, he replied.

There is another question, which will probably throw light on our present enquiry if you and I can agree about it:—Ought the philosopher to care about the pleasures—if they are to be called pleasures—of eating and drinking?

Certainly not, answered Simmias.

And what about the pleasures of love—should he care for them? By no means.

And will he think much of the other ways of indulging the body, for example, the acquisition of costly raiment, or sandals, or other adornments of the body? Instead of caring about them, does he not rather despise anything more than nature needs? What do you say?

I should say that the true philosopher would despise them.

Would you not say that he is entirely concerned with the soul and not with the body? He would like, as far as he can, to get away from the body and to turn to the soul.

Quite true.

In matters of this sort philosophers, above all other men, may be observed in every sort of way to dissever the soul from the communion of the body.

Very true.

Whereas, Simmias, the rest of the world are of opinion that to him who has no sense of pleasure and no part in bodily pleasure, life is not worth having; and that he who is indifferent about them is as good as dead. 3) *Men Knew thru Reasoning*

That is also true. 4) *Reincarnation*

What again shall we say of the actual acquirement of knowledge? —is the body, if invited to share in the enquiry, a hinderer or a helper? I mean to say, have sight and hearing any truth in them? Are they not, as the poets are always telling us, inaccurate witnesses? and yet, if even they are inaccurate and indistinct, what is to be said of the other senses?—for you will allow that they are the best of them?

Certainly, he replied.

Then when does the soul attain truth?—for in attempting to consider anything in company with the body she is obviously deceived.

True.

Then must not true existence be revealed to her in thought, if at all?

Yes.

And thought is best when the mind is gathered into herself and none of these things trouble her—neither sounds nor sights nor pain nor any pleasure,—when she takes leave of the body, and has as little as possible to do with it, when she has no bodily sense or desire, but is aspiring after true being?

Certainly.

And in this the philosopher dishonours the body; his soul runs away from his body and desires to be alone and by herself?

That is true.

Well, but there is another thing, Simmias: Is there or is there not an absolute justice?

Assuredly there is.

And an absolute beauty and absolute good?

Of course.

But did you ever behold any of them with your eyes?

Certainly not.

Or did you ever reach them with any other bodily sense?—and I speak not of these alone, but of absolute greatness, and health, and strength, and of the essence or true nature of everything. Has the reality of them ever been perceived by you through the bodily organs? or rather, is not the nearest approach to the knowledge of their several natures made by him who so orders his intellectual vision as to have the most exact conception of the essence of each thing which he considers?

Certainly.

And he attains to the purest knowledge of them who goes to each with the mind alone, not introducing or intruding in the act of thought, sight, or any other sense together with reason, but with the very light of the mind in her own clearness searches into the very truth of each; he who has got rid, as far as he can, of eyes and ears and, so to speak, of the whole body, these being in his opinion distracting elements which when they infect the soul hinder her from acquiring truth and knowledge—who, if not he, is likely to attain to the knowledge of true being?

What you say has a wonderful truth in it, Socrates, replied Simmias.

And when real philosophers consider all these things, will they not be led to make a reflection which they will express in words something like the following? 'Have we not found,' they will say, 'a path of thought which seems to bring us and our argument to the conclusion, that while we are in the body, and while the soul is infected with the evils of the body, our desire will not be satisfied? and our desire is of the truth. For the body is a source of endless trouble to us by reason of the mere requirement of food; and is liable also to diseases which overtake and impede us in the search after true being: it fills us full of loves, and lusts, and fears, and fancies of all kinds, and endless foolery, and in fact, as men say, takes away from us the power of thinking at all. Whence come wars, and fightings, and factions? whence but from the body and the lusts of the body? Wars are occasioned by the love of money, and money has to be acquired for the sake and in the service of the body; and by reason of all these impediments we have no time to give to philosophy; and, last and worst of all, even if we are at leisure and betake ourselves to some speculation, the body is always breaking in upon us, causing turmoil and confusion in our enquiries, and so amazing us that we are prevented from seeing the truth. It has been proved to us by experience that if we would have pure knowledge of anything we must be quit of the body—the soul in herself must behold things in themselves; and then we shall attain the wisdom which we desire, and of which we say that we are lovers; not while we live, but after death; for if while in company with the body, the soul cannot have pure knowledge, one of two things follows—either knowledge is not to be attained at all, or, if at all, after death. For then, and not till then, the soul will be parted from the body and exist in herself alone. In this present life, I reckon that we make the nearest approach to knowledge when we have the least possible intercourse or communion with the body, and are not surfeited with the bodily nature, but keep ourselves pure until the hour when God himself is pleased to release us. And thus having got rid of the foolishness of the body we shall be pure and hold converse with the pure, and know of ourselves the clear light everywhere, which is no other than the light of truth.' For the impure are not permitted to approach the pure. These are the sort of words, Simmias, which the true lovers of knowledge cannot help saying to one another and thinking. You would agree; would you not?

Undoubtedly, Socrates.

But, O my friend, if this be true, there is great reason to hope that, going whither I go, when I have come to the end of my journey, I shall attain that which has been the pursuit of my life. And therefore I go on my way rejoicing, and not I only, but every other man who believes that his mind has been made ready and that he is in a manner purified.

Certainly, replied Simmias.

And what is purification but the separation of the soul from the body, as I was saying before; the habit of the soul gathering and collecting herself into herself from all sides out of the body; the dwelling in her own place alone, as in another life, so also in this, as far as she can;—the release of the soul from the chains of the body?

Very true, he said.

And this separation and release of the soul from the body is termed death?

To be sure, he said.

And the true philosophers, and they only, are ever seeking to release the soul. Is not the separation and release of the soul from the body their especial study?

That is true.

And, as I was saying at first, there would be a ridiculous contradiction in men studying to live as nearly as they can in a state of death, and yet repining when it comes upon them.

Clearly.

He argues then that
the body is mortal & soul immortal

$P'106$

And the true philosophers, Simmias, are always occupied in the practice of dying, wherefore also to them least of all men is death terrible. Look at the matter thus:—if they have been in every way the enemies of the body, and are wanting to be alone with the soul, when this desire of theirs is granted, how inconsistent would they be if they trembled and repined, instead of rejoicing at their departure to that place where, when they arrive, they hope to gain that which in life they desired—and this was wisdom—and at the same time to be rid of the company of their enemy. Many a man has been willing to go to the world below animated by the hope of seeing there an earthly love, or wife, or son, and conversing with them. And will he who is a true lover of wisdom, and is strongly persuaded in like manner that only in the world below he can worthily enjoy her, still repine at death? Will he not depart with joy? Surely he will, O my friend, if he be a true philosopher. For he will have a firm conviction that there, and there only, he can find wisdom in her purity. And if this be true, he would be very absurd, as I was saying, if he were afraid of death.

He would indeed, replied Simmias.

And when you see a man who is repining at the approach of death, is not his reluctance a sufficient proof that he is not a lover of wisdom, but a lover of the body, and probably at the same time a lover of either money or power, or both?

Quite so, he replied.

And is not courage, Simmias, a quality which is specially characteristic of the philosopher?

Certainly.

There is temperance again, which even by the vulgar is supposed to consist in the control and regulation of the passions, and in the sense of superiority to them—is not temperance a virtue belonging to those only who despise the body, and who pass their lives in philosophy?

Most assuredly.

For the courage and temperance of other men, if you will consider them, are really a contradiction.

How so?

Well, he said, you are aware that death is regarded by men in general as a great evil.

Very true, he said.

And do not courageous men face death because they are afraid of yet greater evils?

That is quite true.

Then all but the philosophers are courageous only from fear, and because they are afraid; and yet that a man should be courageous from fear, and because he is a coward, is surely a strange thing.

Very true.

And are not the temperate exactly in the same case? They are temperate because they are intemperate—which might seem to be a contradiction, but is nevertheless the sort of thing which happens with this foolish temperance. For there are pleasures which they are afraid of losing; and in their desire to keep them, they abstain from some pleasures, because they are overcome by others; and although to be conquered by pleasure is called by men intemperance, to them the conquest of pleasure consists in being conquered by pleasure. And that is what I mean by saying that, in a sense, they are made temperate through intemperance.

Such appears to be the case.

Yet the exchange of one fear or pleasure or pain for another fear or pleasure or pain, and of the greater for the less, as if they were coins, is not the exchange of virtue. O my blessed Simmias, is there not one true coin for which all things ought to be exchanged?—and that is wisdom; and only in exchange for this, and in company with this, is anything truly bought or sold, whether courage or temperance or justice. And is not all true virtue the companion of wisdom, no matter what fears or pleasures or other similar goods or evils may or may not attend her? But the virtue which is made up of these goods, when they are severed from wisdom and exchanged with one another, is a shadow of virtue only, nor is there any freedom or health or truth in her; but in the true exchange there is a purging away of all these things, and temperance, and justice, and courage, and wisdom herself are the purgation of them. The founders of the mysteries would appear to have had a real meaning, and were not talking nonsense when they intimated in a figure long ago that he who passes unsanctified and uninitiated into the world below will lie in a slough, but that he who arrives there after initiation and purification will dwell with the gods. For 'many,' as they say in the mysteries, 'are the thyrsus-bearers, but few are the mystics,'—meaning, as I interpret the words, 'the true philosophers.'

In the number of whom, during my whole life, I have been seeking, according to my ability, to find a place;—whether I have sought in a right way or not, and whether I have succeeded or not, I shall truly know in a little while, if God will, when I myself arrive in the other world—such is my belief. And therefore I maintain that I am right, Simmias and Cebes, in not grieving or repining at parting from you and my masters in this world, for I believe that I shall equally find good masters and friends in another world. But most men do not believe this saying; if then I succeed in convincing you by my defence better than I did the Athenian judges, it will be well.

.   .   .

And were we not saying long ago that the soul when using the body as an instrument of perception, that is to say, when using the sense of sight or hearing or some other sense (for the meaning of perceiving through the body is perceiving through the senses)—were we not saying that the soul too is then dragged by the body into the region of the changeable, and wanders and is confused; the world spins round her, and she is like a drunkard, when she touches change?

Very true.

But when returning into herself she reflects, then she passes into the other world, the region of purity, and eternity, and immortality, and unchangeableness, which are her kindred, and with them she ever lives, when she is by herself and is not let or hindered; then she ceases from her erring ways, and being in communion with the unchanging is unchanging. And this state of the soul is called wisdom?

That is well and truly said, Socrates, he replied.

And to which class is the soul more nearly alike and akin, as far as may be inferred from this argument, as well as from the preceding one?

I think, Socrates, that, in the opinion of every one who follows the argument, the soul will be infinitely more like the unchangeable —even the most stupid person will not deny that.

And the body is more like the changing?

Yes.

Yet once more consider the matter in another light: When the soul and the body are united, then nature orders the soul to rule and govern, and the body to obey and serve. Now which of these two functions is akin to the divine? and which to the mortal? Does not the divine appear to you to be that which naturally orders and rules, and the mortal to be that which is subject and servant?

True.

And which does the soul resemble?

The soul resembles the divine, and the body the mortal—there can be no doubt of that, Socrates.

Then reflect, Cebes: of all which has been said is not this the conclusion?—that the soul is in the very likeness of the divine, and immortal, and intellectual, and uniform, and indissoluble, and unchangeable; and that the body is in the very likeness of the human, and mortal, and unintellectual, and multiform, and dissoluble, and changeable. Can this, my dear Cebes, be denied? *p. 108*

It cannot.

But if it be true, then is not the body liable to speedy dissolution? and is not the soul almost or altogether indissoluble?

Certainly.

And do you further observe, that after a man is dead, the body, or visible part of him, which is lying in the visible world, and is called a corpse, and would naturally be dissolved and decomposed and dissipated, is not dissolved or decomposed at once, but may remain for some time, nay even for a long time, if the constitution be sound at the time of death, and the season of the year favourable? For the body when shrunk and embalmed, as the manner is in Egypt, may remain almost entire through infinite ages; and even in decay, there are still some portions, such as the bones and ligaments, which are practically indestructible:—Do you agree?

Yes.

And is it likely that the soul, which is invisible, in passing to the place of the true Hades, which like her is invisible, and pure, and noble, and on her way to the good and wise God, whither, if God will, my soul is also soon to go,—that the soul, I repeat, if this be her nature and origin, will be blown away and destroyed immediately on quitting the body, as the many say? That can never be, my dear Simmias and Cebes. The truth rather is, that the soul which is pure at departing and draws after her no bodily taint, having never voluntarily during life had connection with the body, which she is ever avoiding, herself gathered into herself;—and making such abstraction her perpetual study—which means that she

has been a true disciple of philosophy; and therefore has in fact
been always engaged in the practice of dying? For is not philosophy
the study of death?—

Certainly—

That soul, I say, herself invisible, departs to the invisible world
—to the divine and immortal and rational: thither arriving, she is
secure of bliss and is released from the error and folly of men,
their fears and wild passions and all other human ills, and for ever
dwells, as they say of the initiated, in company with the gods. Is
not this true, Cebes?

Yes, said Cebes, beyond a doubt.

But the soul which has been polluted, and is impure at the time
of her departure, and is the companion and servant of the body
always, and is in love with and fascinated by the body and by the
desires and pleasures of the body, until she is led to believe that the
truth only exists in a bodily form, which a man may touch and see
and taste, and use for the purposes of his lusts,—the soul, I mean,
accustomed to hate and fear and avoid the intellectual principle,
which to the bodily eye is dark and invisible, and can be attained
only by philosophy;—do you suppose that such a soul will depart
pure and unalloyed?

Impossible, he replied.

She is held fast by the corporeal, which the continual association
and constant care of the body have wrought into her nature.

Very true.

And this corporeal element, my friend, is heavy and weighty
and earthy, and is that element of sight by which a soul is depressed
and dragged down again into the visible world, because she is afraid
of the invisible and of the world below—prowling about tombs and
sepulchres, near which, as they tell us, are seen certain ghostly
apparitions of souls which have not departed pure, but are cloyed
with sight and therefore visible.

That is very likely, Socrates.

Yes, that is very likely, Cebes; and these must be the souls, not of
the good, but of the evil, which are compelled to wander about
such places in payment of the penalty of their former evil way of
life; and they continue to wander until through the craving after
the corporeal which never leaves them, they are imprisoned finally
in another body. And they may be supposed to find their prisons
in the same natures which they have had in their former lives.

What natures do you mean, Socrates?

What I mean is that men who have followed after gluttony, and wantonness, and drunkenness, and have had no thought of avoiding them, would pass into asses and animals of that sort. What do you think?

I think such an opinion to be exceedingly probable.

And those who have chosen the portion of injustice, and tyranny, and violence, will pass into wolves, or into hawks and kites;—whither else can we suppose them to go?

Yes, said Cebes; with such natures, beyond question.

And there is no difficulty, he said, in assigning to all of them places answering to their several natures and propensities?

There is not, he said.

Some are happier than others; and the happiest both in themselves and in the place to which they go are those who have practised the civil and social virtues which are called temperance and justice, and are acquired by habit and attention without philosophy and mind.

Why are they the happiest?

Because they may be expected to pass into some gentle and social kind which is like their own, such as bees or wasps or ants, or back again into the form of man, and just and moderate men may be supposed to spring from them.

Very likely.

No one who has not studied philosophy and who is not entirely pure at the time of his departure is allowed to enter the company of the Gods, but the lover of knowledge only. And this is the reason, Simmias and Cebes, why the true votaries of philosophy abstain from all fleshly lusts, and hold out against them and refuse to give themselves up to them,—not because they fear poverty or the ruin of their families, like the lovers of money, and the world in general; nor like the lovers of power and honour, because they dread the dishonour or disgrace of evil deeds.

No, Socrates, that would not become them, said Cebes.

No indeed, he replied; and therefore they who have any care of their own souls, and do not merely live moulding and fashioning the body, say farewell to all this; they will not walk in the ways of the blind: and when philosophy offers them purification and release from evil, they feel that they ought not to resist her influence, and whither she leads they turn and follow.

What do you mean, Socrates?

I will tell you, he said. The lovers of knowledge are conscious that the soul was simply fastened and glued to the body—until philosophy received her, she could only view real existence through the bars of a prison, not in and through herself; she was wallowing in the mire of every sort of ignorance, and by reason of lust had become the principal accomplice in her own captivity. This was her original state; and then, as I was saying, and as the lovers of knowledge are well aware, philosophy, seeing how terrible was her confinement, of which she was to herself the cause, received and gently comforted her and sought to release her, pointing out that the eye and the ear and the other senses are full of deception, and persuading her to retire from them, and abstain from all but the necessary use of them, and be gathered up and collected into herself, bidding her trust in herself and her own pure apprehension of pure existence, and to mistrust whatever comes to her through other channels and is subject to variation; for such things are visible and tangible, but what she sees in her own nature is intelligible and invisible. And the soul of the true philosopher thinks that she ought not to resist this deliverance, and therefore abstains from pleasures and desires and pains and fears, as far as she is able; reflecting that when a man has great joys or sorrows or fears or desires, he suffers from them, not merely the sort of evil which might be anticipated—as for example, the loss of his health or property which he has sacrificed to his lusts—but an evil greater far, which is the greatest and worst of all evils, and one of which he never thinks.

What is it, Socrates? said Cebes.

The evil is that when the feeling of pleasure or pain is most intense, every soul of man imagines the objects of this intense feeling to be then plainest and truest: but this is not so, they are really the things of sight.

Very true.

And is not this the state in which the soul is most enthralled by the body?

How so?

Why, because each pleasure and pain is a sort of nail which nails and rivets the soul to the body, until she becomes like the body, and believes that to be true which the body affirms to be true; and from agreeing with the body and having the same delights she is obliged to have the same habits and haunts, and is not likely ever to be pure at her departure to the world below, but is always infected by the body; and so she sinks into another body and there germinates and grows, and has therefore no part in the communion of the divine and pure and simple.

Most true, Socrates, answered Cebes.

And this, Cebes, is the reason why the true lovers of knowledge are temperate and brave; and not for the reason which the world gives.

Certainly not.

Certainly not! The soul of a philosopher will reason in quite another way; she will not ask philosophy to release her in order that when released she may deliver herself up again to the thraldom of pleasures and pains, doing a work only to be undone again, weaving instead of unweaving her Penelope's web. But she will calm passion, and follow reason, and dwell in the contemplation of her, beholding the true and divine (which is not matter of opinion), and thence deriving nourishment. Thus she seeks to live while she lives, and after death she hopes to go to her own kindred and to that which is like her, and to be freed from human ills. Never fear, Simmias and Cebes, that a soul which has been thus nurtured and has had these pursuits, will at her departure from the body be scattered and blown away by the winds and be nowhere and nothing.

. . .

When he had spoken these words, he arose and went into a chamber to bathe; Crito followed him, and told us to wait. So we remained behind, talking and thinking of the subject of discourse, and also of the greatness of our sorrow; he was like a father of whom we were being bereaved, and we were about to pass the rest of our lives as orphans. When he had taken the bath his children were brought to him—(he had two young sons and an elder one); and the women of the family also came, and he talked to them and gave them a few directions in the presence of Crito; then he dismissed them and returned to us.

Now the bow of sunset was near, for a good deal of time had passed while he was within. When he came out, he sat down with us again after his bath, but not much was said. Soon the jailer, who was the servant of the Eleven, entered and stood by him, saying:—To you, Socrates, whom I know to be the noblest and gentlest and best of all who ever came to this place, I will not impute the angry feelings of other men, who rage and swear at me, when, in obedience to the authorities, I bid them drink the poison—indeed, I am sure that you will not be angry with me; for others, as you are aware, and not I, are to blame. And so fare you well, and try to bear lightly what must needs be—you know my errand. Then bursting into tears he turned away and went out.

Socrates looked at him, and said: I return your good wishes, and will do as you bid. Then turning to us, he said, How charming the man is: since I have been in prison he has always been coming to see me, and at times he would talk to me, and was as good to me as could be, and now see how generously he sorrows on my account. We must do as he says, Crito; and therefore let the cup be brought, if the poison is prepared: if not, let the attendant prepare some.

Yet, said Crito, the sun is still upon the hill-tops, and I know that many a one has taken the draught late, and after the announcement has been made to him, he has eaten and drunk, and enjoyed the society of his beloved; do not hurry—there is time enough.

Socrates said: Yes, Crito, and they of whom you speak are right in so acting, for they think that they will be gainers by the delay; but I am right in not following their example, for I do not think that I should gain anything by drinking the poison a little later; I should only be ridiculous in my own eyes for sparing and saving a life which is already forfeit. Please then to do as I say, and not to refuse me.

Crito made a sign to the servant, who was standing by; and he went out, and having been absent for some time, returned with the jailer carrying the cup of poison. Socrates said: You, my good friend, who are experienced in these matters, shall give me directions how I am to proceed. The man answered: You have only to walk about until your legs are heavy, and then to lie down, and the poison will act. At the same time he handed the cup to Socrates, who in the easiest and gentlest manner, without the least fear or change of colour or feature, looking at the man with all his eyes, Echecrates, as his manner was, took the cup and said: What do you say about making a libation out of this cup to any god? May I, or not? The man answered: We only prepare, Socrates, just so much as we deem enough. I understand, he said: but I may and must ask the gods to prosper my journey from this to the other world—even so—and so be it according to my prayer. Then raising the cup to his lips, quite readily and cheerfully he drank off the poison. And hitherto most of us had been able to control our sorrow; but now when we saw him drinking, and saw too that he had finished the draught, we could no longer forbear, and in spite of myself my own tears were flowing fast; so that I covered my face and wept, not for him, but at the thought of my own calamity in having to part from such a friend. Nor was I the first; for Crito, when he found himself unable to restrain his tears, had got up, and I followed; and at that moment, Apollodorus, who had been weeping all the time, broke out in a loud and passionate cry which made cowards of us all. Socrates alone retained his calmness: What is this strange outcry? he said. I sent away the women mainly in order that they might not misbehave in this way, for I have been told that a man should die in peace. Be quiet then, and have patience. When we heard his words we were ashamed, and refrained our tears; and he walked about until, as he said, his legs began to fail, and then he lay on his back, according to the directions, and the man who gave him the poison now and then looked at his feet and legs; and after a while he pressed his foot hard, and asked him if he could feel; and he said, No; and then his leg, and so upwards and upwards, and showed us that he was cold and stiff. And he felt them himself, and said: When the poison reaches the heart, that will be the end. He was beginning to grow cold about the groin, when he uncovered his face, for he had covered himself up, and said—they were his last words—he said: Crito, I owe a cock to Asclepius; will you remember to pay the debt? The debt shall be paid, said Crito; is there anything else? There was no answer to this question; but in a minute or two a movement was heard, and the attendants uncovered him; his eyes were set, and Crito closed his eyes and mouth.

Such was the end, Echecrates, of our friend; concerning whom I may truly say, that of all the men of his time whom I have known, he was the wisest and justest and best.

Plato

6

The Republic

The trial and death of Socrates came as a profound shock to his most brilliant disciple, Plato (*ca.* 427–*ca.* 347 B.C.). Born a member of the Athenian ruling class, he grew up in an atmosphere of war and revolution. He had seen the discredited Athenian democracy go down in ruin and had looked hopefully to a government by gentlemen (some of them his relatives) to restore order and justice—only to be disillusioned by the incompetence of the Thirty Tyrants installed by Sparta. The death of Plato's revered master turned him from a life of prospective public service, normal for an aristocrat, to the propagation and application of the Socratic ideals. After a prolonged absence from the city following the events described in the *Phaedo,* he returned to Athens in 387; he gathered about himself a community of young disciples, teaching them the principles of his revered master.

The basic human problem, it seemed to Plato, was this: How can society be reconstituted so that men may know happiness and justice? To facilitate a formal inquiry into this problem, Plato instituted a school in a private garden on the outskirts of Athens, called the Academy. The Academy was to be used to train philosopher-statesmen who, he hoped, would one day govern Athens. Soon, however, it became not only a pan-Hellenic center for study and research, but a magnet for the world at large; as such it was to exist for almost a thousand years.

Here, until his death, Plato taught and developed the thought of Socrates and continued to write the dialogues; among them were the *Phaedo* (preceding selection) and *The Republic,* from which the following passages are taken. Although the Spartan polity is taken as an imperfect working model, the central thesis of *The Republic* is that government is a task only for those qualified; that the disinterested lover of truth,

Plato, *The Republic,* trans. F. M. Cornford (New York and London: Oxford University Press, Inc., 1945), 103–11, 148–50, 152–58, 163–64, 176–79, 227–31, 234. Reprinted by permission of the publishers.

the philosopher, alone is qualified to govern; and that until philosophy
and political power meet in one authority there will be no end of human
misery.

The Republic is a discussion of great intellectual richness and breadth,
and, as Plato's most widely read work, it has exercised a profound influence upon Western thought. To many it is known only as a utopian
program, the first of its kind in the literature of the West; but to others,
perhaps reflecting upon the social horrors and stupidities of the twentieth
century, it is regarded as the greatest work of political philosophy ever
written.

The dialogue as a whole is concerned with the nature of justice and
how a just social order may be realized. Socrates (the "I" of the dialogue)
develops the true meaning of justice and draws an unforgettable picture
of an ideal society in which it has been made real. The selection given
here deals with the proposed ruling élite (called Guardians); with the
roles and relations of men, women, and children; with the central place
of philosophy in human affairs; and, in the famous allegory of the cave,
with the crucial function of philosophers as educators and governors. The
persons who participate in the imaginary dialogue are, besides Socrates
himself, Glaucon and Adeimantus, the brothers of Plato. The scene is
the house of a mutual friend in the Piraeus.

———————————

[Earlier in the dialogue, the discussion has turned about the pre-
liminary education of the Guardians, ending at the age of twenty,
intended to develop a harmony of mental, physical, and "philosophic" elements in their character. As we begin the selected
passage, Socrates moves on to a higher level of training: to the
"kingly science" that fits the best for rule.]

Good, said Socrates; and what is the next point to be settled? Is
it not the question, which of these Guardians are to be rulers and
which are to obey?

No doubt, said Glaucon.

Well, it is obvious that the elder must have authority over the
young, and that the rulers must be the best.

Yes.

And as among farmers the best are those with a natural turn for farming, so, if we want the best among our Guardians, we must take those naturally fitted to watch over a commonwealth. They must have the right sort of intelligence and ability; and also they must look upon the commonwealth as their special concern—the sort of concern that is felt for something so closely bound up with oneself that its interests and fortunes, for good or ill, are held to be identical with one's own.

Exactly.

So the kind of men we must choose from among the Guardians will be those who, when we look at the whole course of their lives, are found to be full of zeal to do whatever they believe is for the good of the commonwealth and never willing to act against its interest.

Yes, they will be the men we want.

We must watch them, I think, at every age and see whether they are capable of preserving this conviction that they must do what is best for the community, never forgetting it or allowing themselves to be either forced or bewitched into throwing it over.

How does this throwing over come about?

I will explain. When a belief passes out of the mind, a man may be willing to part with it, if it is false and he has learnt better, or unwilling, if it is true.

I see how he might be willing to let it go; but you must explain how he can be unwilling.

Where is your difficulty? Don't you agree that men are unwilling to be deprived of good, though ready enough to part with evil? Or that to be deceived about the truth is evil, to possess it good? Or don't you think that possessing truth means thinking of things as they really are?

You are right. I do agree that men are unwilling to be robbed of a true belief.

When that happens to them, then, it must be by theft, or violence, or bewitchment.

Again I do not understand.

Perhaps my metaphors are too high-flown. I call it theft when one is persuaded out of one's belief or forgets it. Argument in the one case, and time in the other, steal it away without one's knowing what is happening. You understand now?

Yes.

And by violence I mean being driven to change one's mind by pain or suffering.

That too I understand, and you are right.

And bewitchment, as I think you would agree, occurs when a man is beguiled out of his opinion by the allurements of pleasure or scared out of it under the spell of panic.

Yes, all delusions are like a sort of bewitchment.

As I said just now, then, we must find out who are the best guardians of this inward conviction that they must always do what they believe to be best for the commonwealth. We shall have to watch them from earliest childhood and set them tasks in which they would be most likely to forget or to be beguiled out of this duty. We shall then choose only those whose memory holds firm and who are proof against delusion.

Yes.

We must also subject them to ordeals of toil and pain and watch for the same qualities there. And we must observe them when exposed to the test of yet a third kind of bewitchment. As people lead colts up to alarming noises to see whether they are timid, so these young men must be brought into terrifying situations and then into scenes of pleasure, which will put them to severer proof than gold tried in the furnace. If we find one bearing himself well in all these trials and resisting every enchantment, a true guardian of himself, preserving always that perfect rhythm and harmony of being which he has acquired from his training in music and poetry, such a one will be of the greatest service to the commonwealth as well as to himself. Whenever we find one who has come unscathed through every test in childhood, youth, and manhood, we shall set him as a Ruler to watch over the commonwealth; he will be honoured in life, and after death receive the highest tribute of funeral rites and other memorials. All who do not reach this standard we must reject. And that, I think, my dear Glaucon, may be taken as an outline of the way in which we shall select Guardians to be set in authority as Rulers.

I am very much of your mind.

These, then, may properly be called Guardians in the fullest sense, who will ensure that neither foes without shall have the power, nor friends within the wish, to do harm. Those young men whom up to now we have been speaking of as Guardians, will be

better described as Auxiliaries, who will enforce the decisions of
the Rulers.

I agree.

Now, said I, can we devise something in the way of those convenient fictions we spoke of earlier, a single bold flight of invention, which we may induce the community in general, and if
possible the Rulers themselves, to accept?

What kind of fiction?

Nothing new; something like an Eastern tale of what, according
to the poets, has happened before now in more than one part of
the world. The poets have been believed; but the thing has not
happened in our day, and it would be hard to persuade anyone
that it could ever happen again.

You seem rather shy of telling this story of yours.

With good reason, as you will see when I have told it.

Out with it; don't be afraid.

Well, here it is; though I hardly know how to find the courage
or the words to express it. I shall try to convince, first the Rulers
and the soldiers, and then the whole community, that all that
nurture and education which we gave them was only something
they seemed to experience as it were in a dream. In reality they
were the whole time down inside the earth, being moulded and
fostered while their arms and all their equipment were being fashioned also; and at last, when they were complete, the earth sent
them up from her womb into the light of day. So now they must
think of the land they dwell in as a mother and nurse, whom they
must take thought for and defend against any attack, and of their
fellow citizens as brothers born of the same soil.

You might well be bashful about coming out with your fiction.

No doubt; but still you must hear the rest of the story. It is true,
we shall tell our people in this fable, that all of you in this land
are brothers; but the god who fashioned you mixed gold in the
composition of those among you who are fit to rule, so that they
are of the most precious quality; and he put silver in the Auxiliaries, and iron and brass in the farmers and craftsmen. Now, since
you are all of one stock, although your children will generally be
like their parents, sometimes a golden parent may have a silver
child or a silver parent a golden one, and so on with all the other
combinations. So the first and chief injunction laid by heaven upon
the Rulers is that, among all the things of which they must show

themselves good guardians, there is none that needs to be so carefully watched as the mixture of metals in the souls of the children.
If a child of their own is born with an alloy of iron or brass, they
must, without the smallest pity, assign him the station proper to
his nature and thrust him out among the craftsmen or the farmers.
If, on the contrary, these classes produce a child with gold or silver
in his composition, they will promote him, according to his value,
to be a Guardian or an Auxiliary. They will appeal to a prophecy
that ruin will come upon the state when it passes into the keeping
of a man of iron or brass. Such is the story; can you think of any
device to make them believe it?

Not in the first generation; but their sons and descendants might
believe it, and finally the rest of mankind.

Well, said I, even so it might have a good effect in making them
care more for the commonwealth and for one another; for I think
I see what you mean.

So, I continued, we will leave the success of our story to the care
of popular tradition; and now let us arm these sons of Earth and
lead them, under the command of their Rulers, to the site of our
city. There let them look round for the best place to fix their
camp, from which they will be able to control any rebellion against
the laws from within and to beat off enemies who may come from
without like wolves to attack the fold. When they have pitched
their camp and offered sacrifice to the proper divinities, they must
arrange their sleeping quarters; and these must be sufficient to
shelter them from winter cold and summer heat.

Naturally. You mean they are going to live there?

Yes, said I; but live like soldiers, not like men of business.

What is the difference?

I will try to explain. It would be very strange if a shepherd were
to disgrace himself by keeping, for the protection of his flock, dogs
who were so ill-bred and badly trained that hunger or unruliness
or some bad habit or other would set them worrying the sheep
and behaving no better than wolves. We must take every precaution against our Auxiliaries treating the citizens in any such way
and, because they are stronger, turning into savage tyrants instead
of friendly allies; and they will have been furnished with the best
of safeguards, if they have really been educated in the right way.

But surely there is nothing wrong with their education.

We must not be too positive about that, my dear Glaucon; but we can be sure of what we said not long ago, that if they are to have the best chance of being gentle and humane to one another and to their charges, they must have the right education, whatever that may be.

We were certainly right there.

Then besides that education, it is only common sense to say that the dwellings and other belongings provided for them must be such as will neither make them less perfect Guardians nor encourage them to maltreat their fellow citizens.

True.

With that end in view, let us consider how they should live and be housed. First, none of them must possess any private property beyond the barest necessaries. Next, no one is to have any dwelling or store-house that is not open for all to enter at will. Their food, in the quantities required by men of temperance and courage who are in training for war, they will receive from the other citizens as the wages of their guardianship, fixed so that there shall be just enough for the year with nothing over; and they will have meals in common and all live together like soldiers in a camp. Gold and silver, we shall tell them, they will not need, having the divine counterparts of those metals always in their souls as a god-given possession, whose purity it is not lawful to sully by the acquisition of that mortal dross, current among mankind, which has been the occasion of so many unholy deeds. They alone of all the citizens are forbidden to touch and handle silver or gold, or to come under the same roof with them, or wear them as ornaments, or drink from vessels made of them. This manner of life will be their salvation and make them the saviours of the commonwealth. If ever they should come to possess land of their own and houses and money, they will give up their guardianship for the management of their farms and households and become tyrants at enmity with their fellow citizens instead of allies. And so they will pass all their lives in hating and being hated, plotting and being plotted against, in much greater fear of their enemies at home than of any foreign foe, and fast heading for the destruction that will soon overwhelm their country with themselves. For all these reasons let us say that this is how our Guardians are to be housed and otherwise provided for, and let us make laws accordingly.

By all means, said Glaucon.

Here Adeimantus interposed. Socrates, he said, how would you meet the objection that you are not making these people particularly happy? It is their own fault too, if they are not; for they are really masters of the state, and yet they get no good out of it as other rulers do, who own lands, build themselves fine houses with handsome furniture, offer private sacrifices to the gods, and entertain visitors from abroad; who possess, in fact, that gold and silver you spoke of, with everything else that is usually thought necessary for happiness. These people seem like nothing so much as a garrison of mercenaries posted in the city and perpetually mounting guard.

Yes, I said, and what is more they will serve for their food only without getting a mercenary's pay, so that they will not be able to travel on their own account or to make presents to a mistress or to spend as they please in other ways, like the people who are commonly thought happy. You have forgotten to include these counts in your indictment, and many more to the same effect.

Well, take them as included now.

And you want to hear the answer?

Yes.

We shall find one, I think, by keeping to the line we have followed so far. We shall say that, though it would not be surprising if even these people were perfectly happy under such conditions, our aim in founding the commonwealth was not to make any one class specially happy, but to secure the greatest possible happiness for the community as a whole. We thought we should have the best chance of finding justice in a state so constituted, just as we should find injustice where the constitution was of the worst possible type; we could then decide the question which has been before us all this time. For the moment, we are constructing, as we believe, the state which will be happy as a whole, not trying to secure the well-being of a select few; we shall study a state of the opposite kind presently. It is as if we were colouring a statue and someone came up and blamed us for not putting the most beautiful colours on the noblest parts of the figure; the eyes, for instance, should be painted crimson, but we had made them black. We should think it a fair answer to say: Really, you must not expect us to paint eyes so handsome as not to look like eyes at all. This applies to all the parts: the question is whether, by giving each its proper colour, we make the whole beautiful. So too, in the present case, you must not press us to endow our Guardians with a happiness that will make them anything rather than guardians. We could quite easily clothe our farmers in gorgeous robes, crown them with gold, and invite them to till the soil at their pleasure; or we might set our potters to lie on couches by their fire, passing round the wine and making merry, with their wheel at hand to work at whenever they felt so inclined. We could make all the rest happy in the same sort of way, and so spread this well-being through the whole community. But you must not put that idea into our heads; if we take your advice, the farmer will be no farmer, the potter no longer a potter; none of the elements that make up the community will keep its character. In many cases this does not matter so much: if a cobbler goes to the bad and pretends to be what he is not, he is not a danger to the state; but, as you must surely see, men who make only a vain show of being guardians of the laws and of the commonwealth bring the whole state to utter ruin, just as, on the other hand, its good government and well-being depend entirely on them. We, in fact, are making genuine Guardians who will be the last to bring harm upon the commonwealth; if our critic aims rather at producing a happiness like that of a party of peasants feasting at a fair, what he has in mind is something other than a civic community. So we must consider whether our aim in establishing Guardians is to secure the greatest possible happiness for them, or happiness is something of which we should watch the development in the whole commonwealth. If so, we must compel these Guardians and Auxiliaries of ours to second our efforts; and they, and all the rest with them, must be induced to make themselves perfect masters each of his own craft. In that way, as the community grows into a well-ordered whole, the several classes may be allowed such measure of happiness as their nature will compass.

I think that is an admirable reply.

. . .

We must go back, then, said Socrates, to a subject which ought, perhaps, to have been treated earlier in its proper place; though, after all, it may be suitable that the women should have their turn on the stage when the men have quite finished their performance, especially since you are so insistent. In my judgement, then, the question under what conditions people born and educated as we have described should possess wives and children, and how they should treat them, can be rightly settled only by keeping to the course on which we started them at the outset. We undertook to put these men in the position of watch-dogs guarding a flock. Suppose we follow up the analogy and imagine them bred and reared in the same sort of way. We can then see if that plan will suit our purpose.

How will that be?

In this way. Which do we think right for watch-dogs: should the females guard the flock and hunt with the males and take a share in all they do, or should they be kept within doors as fit for no more than bearing and feeding their puppies, while all the hard work of looking after the flock is left to the males?

They are expected to take their full share, except that we treat them as not quite so strong.

Can you employ any creature for the same work as another, if you do not give them both the same upbringing and education?

No.

Then, if we are to set women to the same tasks as men, we must teach them the same things. They must have the same two branches of training for mind and body and also be taught the art of war, and they must receive the same treatment.

That seems to follow.

Possibly, if these proposals were carried out, they might be ridiculed as involving a good many breaches of custom.

They might indeed.

The most ridiculous—don't you think?—being the notion of women exercising naked along with the men in the wrestling-schools; some of them elderly women too, like the old men who still have a passion for exercise when they are wrinkled and not very agreeable to look at.

Yes, that would be thought laughable, according to our present notions.

Now we have started on this subject, we must not be frightened of the many witticisms that might be aimed at such a revolution, not only in the matter of bodily exercise but in the training of women's minds, and not least when it comes to their bearing arms and riding on horseback. Having begun upon these rules, we must not draw back from the harsher provisions. The wits may be asked to stop being witty and try to be serious; and we may remind them

that it is not so long since the Greeks, like most foreign nations
of the present day, thought it ridiculous and shameful for men
to be seen naked. When gymnastic exercises were first introduced
in Crete and later at Sparta, the humorists had their chance to
make fun of them; but when experience had shown that nakedness is better uncovered than muffled up, the laughter died down
and a practice which the reason approved ceased to look ridiculous
to the eye. This shows how idle it is to think anything ludicrous
but what is base. One who tries to raise a laugh at any spectacle
save that of baseness and folly will also, in his serious moments,
set before himself some other standard than goodness of what deserves to be held in honour.

Most assuredly.

The first thing to be settled, then, is whether these proposals are
feasible; and it must be open to anyone, whether a humorist or
serious-minded, to raise the question whether, in the case of mankind, the feminine nature is capable of taking part with the other
sex in all occupations, or in none at all, or in some only; and in
particular under which of these heads this business of military
service falls. Well begun is half done, and would not this be the
best way to begin?

Yes.

Shall we take the other side in this debate and argue against
ourselves? We do not want the adversary's position to be taken
by storm for lack of defenders.

I have no objection.

Let us state his case for him. "Socrates and Glaucon," he will
say, "there is no need for others to dispute your position; you yourselves, at the very outset of founding your commonwealth, agreed
that everyone should do the one work for which nature fits him."
Yes, of course; I suppose we did. "And isn't there a very great
difference in nature between man and woman?" Yes, surely. "Does
not that natural difference imply a corresponding difference in the
work to be given to each?" Yes. . . .

If, then, we find that either the male sex or the female is specially
qualified for any particular form of occupation, then that occupation, we shall say, ought to be assigned to one sex or the other.
But if the only difference appears to be that the male begets and
the female brings forth, we shall conclude that no difference between man and woman has yet been produced that is relevant to

our purpose. We shall continue to think it proper for our Guardians and their wives to share in the same pursuits.

And quite rightly.

The next thing will be to ask our opponent to name any profession or occupation in civic life for the purposes of which woman's nature is different from man's.

That is a fair question.

He might reply, as you did just now, that it is not easy to find a satisfactory answer on the spur of the moment, but that there would be no difficulty after a little reflection.

Perhaps.

Suppose, then, we invite him to follow us and see if we can convince him that there is no occupation concerned with the management of social affairs that is peculiar to women. We will confront him with a question: When you speak of a man having a natural talent for something, do you mean that he finds it easy to learn, and after a little instruction can find out much more for himself; whereas a man who is not so gifted learns with difficulty and no amount of instruction and practice will make him even remember what he has been taught? Is the talented man one whose bodily powers are readily at the service of his mind, instead of being a hindrance? Are not these the marks by which you distinguish the presence of a natural gift for any pursuit?

Yes, precisely.

Now do you know of any human occupation in which the male sex is not superior to the female in all these respects? Need I waste time over exceptions like weaving and watching over saucepans and batches of cakes, though women are supposed to be good at such things and get laughed at when a man does them better?

It is true, he replied, in almost everything one sex is easily beaten by the other. No doubt many women are better at many things than many men; but taking the sexes as a whole, it is as you say.

To conclude, then, there is no occupation concerned with the management of social affairs which belongs either to woman or to man, as such. Natural gifts are to be found here and there in both creatures alike; and every occupation is open to both, so far as their natures are concerned, though woman is for all purposes the weaker.

Certainly.

. . .

It follows that one woman will be fitted by nature to be a Guardian, another will not; because these were the qualities for which
we selected our men Guardians. So for the purpose of keeping watch
over the commonwealth, woman has the same nature as man, save
in so far as she is weaker.

So it appears.

It follows that women of this type must be selected to share the
life and duties of Guardians with men of the same type, since they
are competent and of a like nature, and the same natures must be
allowed the same pursuits.

Yes.

We come round, then, to our former position, that there is nothing contrary to nature in giving our Guardians' wives the same
training for mind and body. The practice we proposed to establish
was not impossible or visionary, since it was in accordance with
nature. Rather, the contrary practice which now prevails turns out
to be unnatural.

So it appears.

Well, we set out to inquire whether the plan we proposed was
feasible and also the best. That it is feasible is now agreed; we
must next settle whether it is the best.

Obviously.

Now, for the purpose of producing a woman fit to be a Guardian,
we shall not have one education for men and another for women,
precisely because the nature to be taken in hand is the same.

True.

What is your opinion on the question of one man being better
than another? Do you think there is no such difference?

Certainly I do not.

And in this commonwealth of ours which will prove the better
men—the Guardians who have received the education we described,
or the shoemakers who have been trained to make shoes?

It is absurd to ask such a question.

Very well. So these Guardians will be the best of all the citizens?

By far.

And these women the best of all the women?

Yes.

Can anything be better for a commonwealth than to produce in
it men and women of the best possible type?

No.

And that result will be brought about by such a system of mental and bodily training as we have described?

Surely.

We may conclude that the institution we proposed was not only practicable, but also the best for the commonwealth.

Yes.

The wives of our Guardians, then, must strip for exercise, since they will be clothed with virtue, and they must take their share in war and in the other social duties of guardianship. They are to have no other occupation; and in these duties the lighter part must fall to the women, because of the weakness of their sex. The man who laughs at naked women, exercising their bodies for the best of reasons, is like one that "gathers fruit unripe," for he does not know what it is that he is laughing at or what he is doing. There will never be a finer saying than the one which declares that whatever does good should be held in honour, and the only shame is in doing harm.

That is perfectly true. . . . So far, then, in regulating the position of women, we may claim to have come safely through with one hazardous proposal, that male and female Guardians shall have all occupations in common. The consistency of the argument is an assurance that the plan is a good one and also feasible. We are like swimmers who have breasted the first wave without being swallowed up.

Not such a small wave either.

You will not call it large when you see the next.

Let me have a look at the next one, then.

Here it is: a law which follows from that principle and all that has gone before, namely that, of these Guardians, no one man and one woman are to set up house together privately: wives are to be held in common by all; so too are the children, and no parent is to know his own child, nor any child his parent.

It will be much harder to convince people that that is either a feasible plan or a good one.

As to its being a good plan, I imagine no one would deny the immense advantage of wives and children being held in common, provided it can be done. I should expect dispute to arise chiefly over the question whether it is possible.

There may well be a good deal of dispute over both points.

You mean, I must meet attacks on two fronts. I was hoping to escape one by running away: if you agreed it was a good plan, then I should only have had to inquire whether it was feasible.

No, we have seen through that manœuvre. You will have to defend both positions.

Well, I must pay the penalty for my cowardice. But grant me one favour. Let me indulge my fancy, like one who entertains himself with idle day-dreams on a solitary walk. Before he has any notion how his desires can be realized, he will set aside that question, to save himself the trouble of reckoning what may or may not be possible. He will assume that his wish has come true, and amuse himself with settling all the details of what he means to do then. So a lazy mind encourages itself to be lazier than ever; and I am giving way to the same weakness myself. I want to put off till later that question, how the thing can be done. For the moment, with your leave, I shall assume it to be possible, and ask how the Rulers will work out the details in practice; and I shall argue that the plan, once carried into effect, would be the best thing in the world for our commonwealth and for its Guardians. That is what I shall now try to make out with your help, if you will allow me to postpone the other question.

Very good; I have no objection.

Well, if our Rulers are worthy of the name, and their Auxiliaries likewise, these latter will be ready to do what they are told, and the Rulers, in giving their commands, will themselves obey our laws and will be faithful to their spirit in any details we leave to their discretion.

No doubt.

It is for you, then, as their lawgiver, who have already selected the men, to select for association with them women who are so far as possible of the same natural capacity. Now since none of them will have any private home of his own, but they will share the same dwelling and eat at common tables, the two sexes will be together; and meeting without restriction for exercise and all through their upbringing, they will surely be drawn towards union with one another by a necessity of their nature—necessity is not too strong a word, I think?

Not too strong for the constraint of love, which for the mass of mankind is more persuasive and compelling than even the necessity of mathematical proof.

Exactly. But in the next place, Glaucon, anything like unregulated unions would be a profanation in a state whose citizens lead the good life. The Rulers will not allow such a thing.

No, it would not be right.

Clearly, then, we must have marriages, as sacred as we can make them; and this sanctity will attach to those which yield the best results.

Certainly. . . .

This, then, Glaucon, is the manner in which the Guardians of your commonwealth are to hold their wives and children in common. Must we not next find arguments to establish that it is consistent with our other institutions and also by far the best plan?

Yes, surely.

We had better begin by asking what is the greatest good at which the lawgiver should aim in laying down the constitution of a state, and what is the worst evil. We can then consider whether our proposals are in keeping with that good and irreconcilable with the evil.

By all means.

Does not the worst evil for a state arise from anything that tends to rend it asunder and destroy its unity, while nothing does it more good than whatever tends to bind it together and make it one?

That is true.

And are not citizens bound together by sharing in the same pleasures and pains, all feeling glad or grieved on the same occasions of gain or loss; whereas the bond is broken when such feelings are no longer universal, but any event of public or personal concern fills some with joy and others with distress?

Certainly.

And this disunion comes about when the words "mine" and "not mine," "another's" and "not another's" are not applied to the same things throughout the community. The best ordered state will be the one in which the largest number of persons use these terms in the same sense, and which accordingly most nearly resembles a single person. When one of us hurts his finger, the whole extent of those bodily connexions which are gathered up in the soul and unified by its ruling element is made aware and it all shares as a whole in the pain of the suffering part; hence we say that the man has a pain in his finger. The same thing is true of the pain or pleasure felt when any other part of the person suffers or is relieved.

Yes; I agree that the best organized community comes nearest to that condition.

And so it will recognize as a part of itself the individual citizen to whom good or evil happens, and will share as a whole in his joy or sorrow.

.   .   .

But really, Socrates, Glaucon continued, if you are allowed to go on like this, I am afraid you will forget all about the question you thrust aside some time ago: whether a society so constituted can ever come into existence, and if so, how. No doubt, if it did exist, all manner of good things would come about. I can even add some that you have passed over. Men who acknowledged one another as fathers, sons, or brothers and always used those names among themselves would never desert one another; so they would fight with unequalled bravery. And if their womenfolk went out with them to war, either in the ranks or drawn up in the rear to intimidate the enemy and act as a reserve in case of need, I am sure all this would make them invincible. At home, too, I can see many advantages you have not mentioned. But, since I admit that our commonwealth would have all these merits and any number more, if once it came into existence, you need not describe it in further detail. All we have now to do is to convince ourselves that it can be brought into being and how.

This is a very sudden onslaught, said I; you have no mercy on my shilly-shallying. Perhaps you do not realize that, after I have barely escaped the first two waves, the third, which you are now bringing down upon me, is the most formidable of all. When you have seen what it is like and heard my reply, you will be ready to excuse the very natural fears which made me shrink from putting forward such a paradox for discussion.

The more you talk like that, he said, the less we shall be willing to let you off from telling us how this constitution can come into existence; so you had better waste no more time.

Well, said I, let me begin by reminding you that what brought us to this point was our inquiry into the nature of justice and injustice.

True; but what of that?

Merely this: suppose we do find out what justice is, are we going to demand that a man who is just shall have a character which exactly corresponds in every respect to the ideal of justice? Or shall we be satisfied if he comes as near to the ideal as possible and has in him a larger measure of that quality than the rest of the world?

That will satisfy me.

If so, when we set out to discover the essential nature of justice and injustice and what a perfectly just and a perfectly unjust man would be like, supposing them to exist, our purpose was to use them as ideal patterns: we were to observe the degree of happiness or unhappiness that each exhibited, and to draw the necessary inference that our own destiny would be like that of the one we most resembled. We did not set out to show that these ideals could exist in fact.

That is true.

Then suppose a painter had drawn an ideally beautiful figure complete to the last touch, would you think any the worse of him, if he could not show that a person as beautiful as that could exist?

No, I should not.

Well, we have been constructing in discourse the pattern of an ideal state. Is our theory any the worse, if we cannot prove it possible that a state so organized should be actually founded?

Surely not.

That, then, is the truth of the matter. But if, for your satisfaction, I am to do my best to show under what conditions our ideal would have the best chance of being realized, I must ask you once more to admit that the same principle applies here. Can theory ever be fully realized in practice? Is it not in the nature of things that action should come less close to truth than thought? People may not think so; but do you agree or not?

I do.

Then you must not insist upon my showing that this construction we have traced in thought could be reproduced in fact down to the last detail. You must admit that we shall have found a way to meet your demand for realization, if we can discover how a state might be constituted in the closest accordance with our description. Will not that content you? It would be enough for me.

And for me too.

Then our next attempt, it seems, must be to point out what defect in the working of existing states prevents them from being so organized, and what is the least change that would effect a transformation into this type of government—a single change if possible, or perhaps two; at any rate let us make the changes as few and insignificant as may be.

By all means.

Well, there is one change which, as I believe we can show, would bring about this revolution—not a small change, certainly, nor an easy one, but possible.

What is it?

I have now to confront what we called the third and greatest wave. But I must state my paradox, even though the wave should break in laughter over my head and drown me in ignominy. Now mark what I am going to say.

Go on.

Unless either philosophers become kings in their countries or those who are now called kings and rulers come to be sufficiently inspired with a genuine desire for wisdom; unless, that is to say, political power and philosophy meet together, while the many natures who now go their several ways in the one or the other direction are forcibly debarred from doing so, there can be no rest from troubles, my dear Glaucon, for states, nor yet, as I believe, for all mankind; nor can this commonwealth which we have imagined ever till then see the light of day and grow to its full stature. This it was that I have so long hung back from saying; I knew what a paradox it would be, because it is hard to see that there is no other way of happiness either for the state or for the individual.

Paradox

. . .

Next, said I, here is a parable to illustrate the degrees in which our nature may be enlightened or unenlightened. Imagine the condition of men living in a sort of cavernous chamber underground, with an entrance open to the light and a long passage all down the cave. Here they have been from childhood, chained by the leg and also by the neck, so that they cannot move and can see only what is in front of them, because the chains will not let them turn their heads. At some distance higher up is the light of a fire burning behind them; and between the prisoners and the fire is a track with a parapet built along it, like the screen at a puppet-show, which hides the performers while they show their puppets over the top.

I see, said he.

Now behind this parapet imagine persons carrying along various artificial objects, including figures of men and animals in wood or stone or other materials, which project above the parapet. Naturally, some of these persons will be talking, others silent.

It is a strange picture, he said, and a strange sort of prisoners.

Like ourselves, I replied; for in the first place prisoners so confined would have seen nothing of themselves or of one another, except the shadows thrown by the fire-light on the wall of the Cave facing them, would they?

Not if all their lives they had been prevented from moving their heads.

And they would have seen as little of the objects carried past.

Of course.

Now, if they could talk to one another, would they not suppose that their words referred only to those passing shadows which they saw?

Necessarily.

And suppose their prison had an echo from the wall facing them? When one of the people crossing behind them spoke, they could only suppose that the sound came from the shadow passing before their eyes.

No doubt.

In every way, then, such prisoners would recognize as reality nothing but the shadows of those artificial objects.

Inevitably.

Now consider what would happen if their release from the chains and the healing of their unwisdom should come about in this way. Suppose one of them set free and forced suddenly to stand up, turn his head, and walk with eyes lifted to the light; all these movements would be painful, and he would be too dazzled to make out the objects whose shadows he had been used to see. What do you think he would say, if someone told him that what he had formerly seen was meaningless illusion, but now, being somewhat nearer to reality and turned towards more real objects, he was getting a truer view? Suppose further that he were shown the various objects being carried by and were made to say, in reply to questions, what each of them was. Would he not be perplexed and believe the objects now shown him to be not so real as what he formerly saw?

Yes, not nearly so real.

And if he were forced to look at the fire-light itself, would not his eyes ache, so that he would try to escape and turn back to the things which he could see distinctly, convinced that they really were clearer than these other objects now being shown to him?

Yes.

And suppose someone were to drag him away forcibly up the steep and rugged ascent and not let him go until he had hauled him out into the sunlight, would he not suffer pain and vexation at such treatment, and, when he had come out into the light, find his eyes so full of its radiance that he could not see a single one of the things that he was now told were real?

Certainly he would not see them all at once.

He would need, then, to grow accustomed before he could see things in that upper world. At first it would be easiest to make out shadows, and then the images of men and things reflected in water, and later on the things themselves. After that, it would be easier to watch the heavenly bodies and the sky itself by night, looking at the light of the moon and stars rather than the Sun and the Sun's light in the day-time.

Yes, surely.

Last of all, he would be able to look at the Sun and contemplate its nature, not as it appears when reflected in water or any alien medium, but as it is in itself in its own domain.

No doubt.

And now he would begin to draw the conclusion that it is the Sun that produces the seasons and the course of the year and controls everything in the visible world, and moreover is in a way the cause of all that he and his companions used to see.

Clearly he would come at last to that conclusion.

Then if he called to mind his fellow prisoners and what passed for wisdom in his former dwelling-place, he would surely think himself happy in the change and be sorry for them. They may have had a practice of honouring and commending one another, with prizes for the man who had the keenest eye for the passing shadows and the best memory for the order in which they followed or accompanied one another, so that he could make a good guess as to which was going to come next. Would our released prisoner be likely to covet those prizes or to envy the men exalted to honour and power in the Cave? Would he not feel like Homer's Achilles, that he would far sooner "be on earth as a hired servant in the

house of a landless man" or endure anything rather than go back
to his old beliefs and live in the old way?

Yes, he would prefer any fate to such a life.

Now imagine what would happen if he went down again to take
his former seat in the Cave. Coming suddenly out of the sunlight,
his eyes would be filled with darkness. He might be required once
more to deliver his opinion on those shadows, in competition with
the prisoners who had never been released, while his eyesight was
still dim and unsteady; and it might take some time to become
used to the darkness. They would laugh at him and say that he had
gone up only to come back with his sight ruined; it was worth no
one's while even to attempt the ascent. If they could lay hands on
the man who was trying to set them free and lead them up, they
would kill him.

Yes, they would.

Every feature in this parable, my dear Glaucon, is meant to fit
our earlier analysis. The prison dwelling corresponds to the region
revealed to us through the sense of sight, and the fire-light within
it to the power of the Sun. The ascent to see the things in the
upper world you may take as standing for the upward journey of
the soul into the region of the intelligible; then you will be in
possession of what I surmise, since that is what you wish to be told.
Heaven knows whether it is true; but this, at any rate, is how it
appears to me. In the world of knowledge, the last thing to be
perceived and only with great difficulty is the essential Form of
Goodness. Once it is perceived, the conclusion must follow that,
for all things, this is the cause of whatever is right and good; in
the visible world it gives birth to light and to the lord of light,
while it is itself sovereign in the intelligible world and the parent
of intelligence and truth. Without having had a vision of this Form
no one can act with wisdom, either in his own life or in matters
of state.

So far as I can understand, I share your belief. . . .

You will see, then, Glaucon, that there will be no real injustice
in compelling our philosophers to watch over and care for the other
citizens. We can fairly tell them that their compeers in other states
may quite reasonably refuse to collaborate: there they have sprung
up, like a self-sown plant, in despite of their country's institutions;
no one has fostered their growth, and they cannot be expected to

show gratitude for a care they have never received. "But," we shall
say, "it is not so with you. We have brought you into existence
for your country's sake as well as for your own, to be like leaders
and king-bees in a hive; you have been better and more thoroughly
educated than those others and hence you are more capable of playing your part both as men of thought and as men of action. You
must go down, then, each in his turn, to live with the rest and let
your eyes grow accustomed to the darkness. You will then see a
thousand times better than those who live there always; you will
recognize every image for what it is and know what it represents,
because you have seen justice, beauty, and goodness in their reality;
and so you and we shall find life in our commonwealth no mere
dream, as it is in most existing states, where men live fighting one
another about shadows and quarrelling for power, as if that were a
great prize; whereas in truth government can be at its best and
free from dissension only where the destined rulers are least
desirous of holding office."

Aristotle

7

Nicomachean Ethics

Today many people accept the idea that morals are relative—relative, that is, to the cultural environment; but most influential Greek thinkers rejected this view. They believed it possible to arrive, rationally, at values true for all times and places. That their endeavor was carried on so brilliantly is one of the marvels of Western culture.

In this achievement no one took a greater part than Aristotle (384–322 B.C.). He was born at Stagira in Chalcidice, and his father was physician to the King of Macedon. From the age of seventeen to the death of Plato, twenty years later, he studied under the master at the Academy; he then spent three years as tutor to the young Alexander of Macedon. In 335 he set up his famous Lyceum at Athens, a rival school to the Academy. During the next dozen years he taught and lectured, while producing a wealth of writing. But upon Alexander's death in 323 he was forced by the anti-Macedonian party to flee Athens, and he died in exile a year later.

Throughout his works, covering a wide range of subjects, Aristotle was concerned (as was Plato) with the search for reality, for objective truth; but, more down-to-earth than Plato, he sought to show that sense objects are no less real than the world of Forms or Ideas. In the *Nicomachean Ethics,* where he deals with the problem of the good life, values are therefore tested by his observation of things as they are, rather than by Plato's vision of the ideal.

Although Aristotle constantly strove for permanent and universal values, the *Ethics* reflects the conditions peculiar to Hellenic life. Thus, ancient ideals are always aristocratic—concerned with the good life for the perceptive few, not for the indifferent masses. It is not always easy for the modern reader, after many centuries of Christian and democratic influences, to understand the Aristotelian "high-minded man" or the virtues he represents, discussed in the following selection. Nevertheless, the book

Aristotle, *The Nicomachean Ethics,* trans. F. H. Peters (London: Kegan Paul, Trench, Truebner, 1886), 1–4, 12–17, 23–27, 36–38, 41–55, 113–19.

has made a lasting impression on Western thought and conduct; to this day, wherever the all-round amateur is prized, wherever manners are appreciated, and wherever narrow professionalism is deplored, the spirit of the *Ethics* still lives.

Every art and every kind of inquiry, and likewise every act and purpose, seems to aim at some good: and so it has been well said that the good is that at which everything aims.

But a difference is observable among these aims or ends. What is aimed at is sometimes the exercise of a faculty, sometimes a certain result beyond that exercise. And where there is an end beyond the act, there the result is better than the exercise of the faculty.

Now since there are many kinds of actions and many arts and sciences, it follows that there are many ends also; *e.g.* health is the end of medicine, ships of shipbuilding, victory of the art of war, and wealth of economy.

But when several of these are subordinated to some one art or science,—as the making of bridles and other trappings to the art of horsemanship, and this in turn, along with all else that the soldier does, to the art of war, and so on,—then the end of the master-art is always more desired than the ends of the subordinate arts, since these are pursued for its sake. And this is equally true whether the end in view be the mere exercise of a faculty or something beyond that, as in the above instances.

If then in what we do there be some end which we wish for on its own account, choosing all the others as means to this, but not every end without exception as a means to something else (for so we should go on *ad infinitum,* and desire would be left void and objectless),—this evidently will be the good or the best of all things.

And surely from a practical point of view it much concerns us to know this good; for then, like archers shooting at a definite mark, we shall be more likely to attain what we want.

If this be so, we must try to indicate roughly what it is, and first of all to which of the arts or sciences it belongs.

It would seem to belong to the supreme art or science, that one which most of all deserves the name of master-art or master-science.

Now Politics seems to answer to this description. For it prescribes which of the sciences a state needs, and which each man shall study, and up to what point; and to it we see subordinated even the highest arts, such as economy, rhetoric, and the art of war.

Since then it makes use of the other practical sciences, and since it further ordains what men are to do and from what to refrain, its end must include the ends of the others, and must be the proper good of man.

For though this good is the same for the individual and the state, yet the good of the state seems a grander and more perfect thing both to attain and to secure; and glad as one would be to do this service for a single individual, to do it for a people and for a number of states is nobler and more divine.

This then is the aim of the present inquiry, which is a sort of political inquiry.

We must be content if we can attain to so much precision in our statement as the subject before us admits of; for the same degree of accuracy is no more to be expected in all kinds of reasoning than in all kinds of manufacture.

Now what is noble and just (with which Politics deals) is so various and so uncertain, that some think these are merely conventional and not natural distinctions.

There is a similar uncertainty also about what is good, because good things often do people harm: men have before now been ruined by wealth, and have lost their lives through courage.

Our subject, then, and our data being of this nature, we must be content if we can indicate the truth roughly and in outline, and if, in dealing with matters that are not amenable to immutable laws, and reasoning from premises that are but probable, we can arrive at probable conclusions.

. . .

Leaving these matters, then, let us return once more to the question, what this good can be of which we are in search.

It seems to be different in different kinds of action and in different arts,—one thing in medicine and another in war, and so on. What then is the good in each of these cases? Surely that for the sake of which all else is done. And that in medicine is health, in war is victory, in building is a house,—a different thing in each different case, but always, in whatever we do and in whatever we choose, the end. For it is always for the sake of the end that all else is done.

If then there be one end of all that man does, this end will be the realizable good,—or these ends, if there be more than one.

Our argument has thus come round by a different path to the same point as before. This point we must try to explain more clearly.

We see that there are many ends. But some of these are chosen only as means, as wealth, flutes, and the whole class of instruments. And so it is plain that not all ends are final.

But the best of all things must, we conceive, be something final.

If then there be only one final end, this will be what we are seeking,—or if there be more than one, then the most final of them.

Now that which is pursued as an end in itself is more final than that which is pursued as means to something else, and that which is never chosen as means than that which is chosen both as an end in itself and as means, and that is strictly final which is always chosen as an end in itself and never as means.

Happiness seems more than anything else to answer to this description: for we always choose it for itself, and never for the sake of something else; while honour and pleasure and reason, and all virtue or excellence, we choose partly indeed for themselves (for, apart from any result, we should choose each of them), but partly also for the sake of happiness, supposing that they will help to make us happy. But no one chooses happiness for the sake of these things, or as a means to anything else at all.

We seem to be led to the same conclusion when we start from the notion of self-sufficiency.

The final good is thought to be self-sufficing [or all-sufficing]. In applying this term we do not regard a man as an individual leading a solitary life, but we also take account of parents, children, wife, and, in short, friends and fellow-citizens generally, since man is naturally a social being. Some limit must indeed be set to this; for if you go on to parents and descendants and friends of friends, you will never come to a stop. But this we will consider further on: for the present we will take self-sufficing to mean what by itself makes life desirable and in want of nothing. And happiness is believed to answer to this description.

And further, happiness is believed to be the most desirable thing in the world, and that not merely as one among other good things: if it were merely one among other good things [so that other things could be added to it], it is plain that the addition of the least of other goods must make it more desirable; for the addition becomes a surplus of good, and of two goods the greater is always more desirable.

Thus it seems that happiness is something final and self-sufficing, and is the end of all that man does.

But perhaps the reader thinks that though no one will dispute the statement that happiness is the best thing in the world, yet a still more precise definition of it is needed.

This will best be gained, I think, by asking, What is the function of man? For as the goodness and the excellence of a piper or a sculptor, or the practiser of any art, and generally of those who have any function or business to do, lies in that function, so man's good would seem to lie in his function, if he has one.

But can we suppose that, while a carpenter and a cobbler has a function and a business of his own, man has no business and no function assigned him by nature? Nay, surely as his several members, eye and hand and foot, plainly have each his own function, so we must suppose that man also has some function over and above all these.

What then is it?

Life evidently he has in common even with the plants, but we want that which is peculiar to him. We must exclude, therefore, the life of mere nutrition and growth.

Next to this comes the life of sense; but this too he plainly shares with horses and cattle and all kinds of animals.

There remains then the life whereby he acts—the life of his rational nature, with its two sides or divisions, one rational as obeying reason, the other rational as having and exercising reason.

But as this expression is ambiguous, we must be understood to mean thereby the life that consists in the exercise of the faculties; for this seems to be more properly entitled to the name.

The function of man, then, is exercise of his vital faculties [or soul] on one side in obedience to reason, and on the other side with reason.

But what is called the function of a man of any profession and the function of a man who is good in that profession are generically the same, *e.g.* of a harper and of a good harper; and this holds in all cases without exception, only that in the case of the latter his superior excellence at his work is added; for we say a harper's function is to harp, and a good harper's to harp well.

Man's function then being, as we say, a kind of life—that is to say, exercise of his faculties and action of various kinds with reason —the good man's function is to do this well and beautifully [or nobly].

But the function of anything is done well when it is done in accordance with the proper excellence of that thing.

Putting all this together, then, we find that the good of man is exercise of his faculties in accordance with excellence or virtue, or, if there be more than one, in accordance with the best and most complete virtue.

But there must also be a full term of years for this exercise; for one swallow or one fine day does not make a spring, nor does one day or any small space of time make a blessed or happy man.

This, then, may be taken as a rough outline of the good; for this, I think, is the proper method.

·   ·   ·

Are we, then, to call no man happy as long as he lives, but to wait for the end, as Solon said?

And, supposing we have to allow this, do we mean that he actually is happy after he is dead? Surely that is absurd, especially for us who say that happiness is a kind of activity or life.

But if we do not call the dead man happy, and if Solon meant not this, but that only then could we safely apply the term to a man, as being now beyond the reach of evil and calamity, then here too we find some ground for objection. For it is thought that both good and evil may in some sort befall a dead man (just as they may befall a living man, although he is unconscious of them), e.g. honours rendered to him, or the reverse of these, and again the prosperity or the misfortune of his children and all his descendants.

But this, too, has its difficulties; for after a man has lived happily to a good old age, and ended as he lived, it is possible that many changes may befall him in the persons of his descendants, and that some of them may turn out good and meet with the good fortune they deserve, and others the reverse. It is evident too that the degree in which the descendants are related to their ancestors may vary to any extent. And it would be a strange thing if the dead man were to change with these changes and become happy and miserable by turns. But it would also be strange to suppose that the dead are not affected at all, even for a limited time, by the fortunes of their posterity.

But let us return to our former question; for its solution will, perhaps, clear up this other difficulty.

The saying of Solon may mean that we ought to look for the end and then call a man happy, not because he now is, but because he once was happy.

But surely it is strange that when he is happy we should refuse to say what is true of him, because we do not like to apply the term to living men in view of the changes to which they are liable, and because we hold happiness to be something that endures and is little liable to change, while the fortunes of one and the same man often undergo many revolutions: for, it is argued, it is plain that, if we follow the changes of fortune, we shall call the same man happy and miserable many times over, making the happy man "a sort of chameleon and one who rests on no sound foundation."

We reply that it cannot be right thus to follow fortune. For it is not in this that our weal or woe lies; but, as we said, though the life of man needs these gifts of fortune, yet it is the excellent employment of his powers that constitutes his happiness, as the reverse of this constitutes his misery.

But the discussion of this difficulty leads to a further confirmation of our account. For nothing human is so constant as the excellent exercise of our faculties. The sciences themselves seem to be less abiding. And the highest of these exercises are the most abiding, because the happy are occupied with them most of all and most continuously (for this seems to be the reason why we do not forget how to do them).

The happy man, then, as we define him, will have this required property of permanence, and all through life will preserve his character; for he will be occupied continually, or with the least possible interruption, in excellent deeds and excellent speculations; and, whatever his fortune be, he will take it in the noblest fashion, and bear himself always and in all things suitably, since he is truly good and "foursquare without a flaw."

But the dispensations of fortune are many, some great, some small. The small ones, whether good or evil, plainly are of no weight in the scale; but the great ones, when numerous, will make life happier if they be good; for they help to give a grace to life themselves, and their use is noble and good; but, if they be evil, will enfeeble and spoil happiness; for they bring pain, and often impede the exercise of our faculties.

But nevertheless true worth shines out even here, in the calm endurance of many great misfortunes, not through insensibility, but through nobility and greatness of soul. And if it is what man does that determines the character of his life, as we said, then no happy man will become miserable, for he will never do what is hateful and base. For we hold that the man who is truly good and wise will bear with dignity whatever fortune sends, and will always make the best of his circumstances, as a good general will turn the forces at his command to the best account, and a good shoemaker will make the best shoe that can be made out of a given piece of leather, and so on with all other crafts.

If this be so, the happy man will never become miserable, though he will not be truly happy if he meets with the fate of Priam.

But yet he is not unstable and lightly changed: he will not be moved from his happiness easily, nor by any ordinary misfortunes, but only by many heavy ones; and after such, he will not recover his happiness again in a short time, but if at all, only in a considerable period, which has a certain completeness, and in which he attains to great and noble things.

We shall meet all objections, then, if we say that a happy man is "one who exercises his faculties in accordance with perfect excellence, being duly furnished with external goods, not for any chance time, but for a full term of years": to which perhaps we should add, "and who shall continue to live so, and shall die as he lived," since the future is veiled to us, but happiness we take to be the end and in all ways perfectly final or complete.

If this be so, we may say that those living men are blessed or perfectly happy who both have and shall continue to have these characteristics, but happy as men only.

•   •   •

But our present inquiry has not, like the rest, a merely speculative aim; we are not inquiring merely in order to know what excellence or virtue is, but in order to become good; for otherwise it would profit us nothing. We must ask therefore about these acts, and see of what kind they are to be; for, as we said, it is they that determine our habits or character.

.   .   .

First of all, then, we must observe that, in matters of this sort, to fall short and to exceed are alike fatal. This is plain (to illustrate what we cannot see by what we can see) in the case of strength and health. Too much and too little exercise alike destroy strength, and to take too much meat and drink, or to take too little, is equally ruinous to health, but the fitting amount produces and increases and preserves them. Just so, then, is it with temperance also, and courage, and the other virtues. The man who shuns and fears everything and never makes a stand, becomes a coward; while the man who fears nothing at all, but will face anything, becomes foolhardy. So, too, the man who takes his fill of any kind of pleasure, and abstains from none, is a profligate, but the man who shuns all (like him whom we call a "boor") is devoid of sensibility. For temperance and courage are destroyed both by excess and defect, but preserved by moderation.

.   .   .

But here we may be asked what we mean by saying that men can become just and temperate only by doing what is just and temperate: surely, it may be said, if their acts are just and temperate, they themselves are already just and temperate, as they are grammarians and musicians if they do what is grammatical and musical.

We may answer, I think, firstly, that this is not quite the case even with the arts. A man may do something grammatical [or write something correctly] by chance, or at the prompting of another person: he will not be grammatical till he not only does something grammatical, but also does it grammatically [or like a grammatical person], *i.e.* in virtue of his own knowledge of grammar.

But, secondly, the virtues are not in this point analogous to the arts. The products of art have their excellence in themselves, and so it is enough if when produced they are of a certain quality; but in the case of the virtues, a man is not said to act justly or temperately [or like a just or temperate man] if what he does merely be of a certain sort—he must also be in a certain state of mind when he does it; *i.e.*, first of all, he must know what he is doing; secondly, he must choose it, and choose it for itself; and, thirdly, his act must be the expression of a formed and stable character. Now, of these conditions, only one, the knowledge, is necessary for the possession of any art; but for the possession of the virtues knowledge is of little or no avail, while the other conditions that result from repeatedly doing what is just and temperate are not a little important, but all-important.

The thing that is done, therefore, is called just or temperate when it is such as the just or temperate man would do; but the man who does it is not just or temperate, unless he also does it in the spirit of the just or the temperate man.

It is right, then, to say that by doing what is just a man becomes just, and temperate by doing what is temperate, while without doing thus he has no chance of ever becoming good.

But most men, instead of doing thus, fly to theories, and fancy that they are philosophizing and that this will make them good, like a sick man who listens attentively to what the doctor says and then disobeys all his orders. This sort of philosophizing will no more produce a healthy habit of mind than this sort of treatment will produce a healthy habit of body.

· · ·

We have thus found the genus to which virtue belongs; but we want to know, not only that it is a trained faculty, but also what species of trained faculty it is.

We may safely assert that the virtue or excellence of a thing causes that thing both to be itself in good condition and to perform its function well. The excellence of the eye, for instance, makes both the eye and its work good; for it is by the excellence of the eye that we see well. So the proper excellence of the horse makes a horse what he should be, and makes him good at running, and carrying his rider, and standing a charge.

If, then, this holds good in all cases, the proper excellence or virtue of man will be a habit or trained faculty that makes a man good and makes him perform his function well.

How this is to be done we have already said, but we may exhibit the same conclusion in another way, by inquiring what the nature of this virtue is.

Now, if we have any quantity, whether continuous or discrete, it is possible to take either a larger [or too large], or a smaller [or too small], or an equal [or fair] amount, and that either absolutely or relatively to our own needs.

By an equal or fair amount I understand a mean amount, or one that lies between excess and deficiency.

By the absolute mean, or mean relatively to the thing itself, I understand that which is equidistant from both extremes, and this is one and the same for all.

By the mean relatively to us I understand that which is neither too much nor too little for us; and this is not one and the same for all.

For instance, if ten be larger [or too large] and two be smaller [or too small], if we take six we take the mean relatively to the thing itself [or the arithmetical mean]; for it exceeds one extreme by the same amount by which it is exceeded by the other extreme: and this is the mean in arithmetical proportion.

But the mean relatively to us cannot be found in this way. If ten pounds of food is too much for a given man to eat, and two pounds too little, it does not follow that the trainer will order him six pounds: for that also may perhaps be too much for the man in question, or too little; too little for Milo, too much for the beginner. The same holds true in running and wrestling.

And so we may say generally that a master in any art avoids what is too much and what is too little, and seeks for the mean and chooses it—not the absolute but the relative mean.

Every art or science, then, perfects its work in this way, looking to the mean and bringing its work up to this standard; so that people are wont to say of a good work that nothing could be taken from it or added to it, implying that excellence is destroyed by excess or deficiency, but secured by observing the mean. And good artists, as we say, do in fact keep their eyes fixed on this in all that they do.

Virtue therefore, since like nature it is more exact and better than any art, must also aim at the mean—virtue of course meaning moral virtue or excellence; for it has to do with passions and actions, and it is these that admit of excess and deficiency and the mean. For instance, it is possible to feel fear, confidence, desire, anger, pity, and generally to be affected pleasantly and painfully, either too much or too little, in either case wrongly; but to be thus affected at the right times, and on the right occasions, and towards the right persons, and with the right object, and in the right fashion, is the mean course and the best course, and these are characteristics of virtue. And in the same way our outward acts also admit of excess and deficiency, and the mean or due amount.

Virtue, then, has to deal with feelings or passions and with outward acts, in which excess is wrong and deficiency also is blamed, but the mean amount is praised and is right—both of which are characteristics of virtue.

Virtue, then, is a kind of moderation inasmuch as it aims at the mean or moderate amount.

Again, there are many ways of going wrong (for evil is infinite in nature, to use a Pythagorean figure, while good is finite), but only one way of going right; so that the one is easy and the other hard—easy to miss the mark and hard to hit. On this account also, then, excess and deficiency are characteristic of vice, hitting the mean is characteristic of virtue:

"Goodness is simple, ill takes any shape."

Virtue, then, is a habit or trained faculty of choice, the characteristic of which lies in observing the mean relatively to the persons concerned, and which is guided by reason, *i.e.* by the judgment of the prudent man.

And it is a moderation, firstly, inasmuch as it comes in the middle or mean between two vices, one on the side of excess, the other on the side of defect; and, secondly, inasmuch as, while these vices fall short of or exceed the due measure in feeling and in action, it finds and chooses the mean, middling, or moderate amount.

Regarded in its essence, therefore, or according to the definition of its nature, virtue is a moderation or middle state, but viewed in its relation to what is best and right it is the extreme of perfection.

But it is not all actions nor all passions that admit of moderation; there are some whose very names imply badness, as malevolence, shamelessness, envy, and, among acts, adultery, theft, murder. These and all other like things are blamed as being bad in themselves, and not merely in their excess or deficiency. It is impossible therefore to go right in them; they are always wrong: rightness and wrongness in such things (*e.g.* in adultery) does not depend upon whether it is the right person and occasion and manner, but the mere doing of any one of them is wrong.

It would be equally absurd to look for moderation or excess or deficiency in unjust cowardly or profligate conduct; for then there would be moderation in excess or deficiency, and excess in excess, and deficiency in deficiency.

The fact is that just as there can be no excess or deficiency in temperance or courage because the mean or moderate amount is, in a sense, an extreme, so in these kinds of conduct also there can be no moderation or excess or deficiency, but the acts are wrong however they be done. For, to put it generally, there cannot be moderation in excess or deficiency, nor excess or deficiency in moderation.

But it is not enough to make these general statements [about virtue and vice]: we must go on and apply them to particulars [*i.e.* to the several virtues and vices]. For in reasoning about matters of conduct general statements are too vague, and do not convey so much truth as particular propositions. It is with particulars that conduct is concerned: our statements, therefore, when applied to these particulars, should be found to hold good.

These particulars then [*i.e.* the several virtues and vices and the several acts and affections with which they deal], we will take from the following table.

Moderation in the feelings of fear and confidence is courage: of those that exceed, he that exceeds in fearlessness has no name (as often happens), but he that exceds in confidence is foolhardy, while he that exceeds in fear, but is deficient in confidence, is cowardly.

Moderation in respect of certain pleasures and also (though to a less extent) certain pains is temperance, while excess is profligacy. But defectiveness in the matter of these pleasures is hardly ever found, and so this sort of people also have as yet received no name: let us put them down as "void of sensibility."

In the matter of giving and taking money, moderation is liberality, excess and deficiency are prodigality and illiberality. But these two vices exceed and fall short in contrary ways: the prodigal exceeds in spending, but falls short in taking; while the illiberal man exceeds in taking, but falls short in spending.

(For the present we are but giving an outline or summary, and aim at nothing more; we shall afterwards treat these points in greater detail.)

But, besides these, there are other dispositions in the matter of money: there is a moderation which is called magnificence (for the magnificent is not the same as the liberal man: the former deals with large sums, the latter with small), and an excess which is called bad taste or vulgarity, and a deficiency which is called meanness; and these vices differ from those which are opposed to liberality: how they differ will be explained later.

With respect to honour and disgrace, there is a moderation which is high-mindedness, an excess which may be called vanity, and a deficiency which is little-mindedness.

But just as we said that liberality is related to magnificence, differing only in that it deals with small sums, so here there is a virtue related to high-mindedness, and differing only in that it is concerned with small instead of great honours. A man may have a due desire for honour, and also more or less than a due desire: he that carries this desire to excess is called ambitious, he that has not enough of it is called unambitious, but he that has the due amount has no name. There are also no abstract names for the characters, except "ambition," corresponding to ambitious. And on this account those who occupy the extremes lay claim to the middle place. And in common parlance, too, the moderate man is sometimes called ambitious and sometimes unambitious, and sometimes the ambitious man is praised and sometimes the unambitious. Why this is we will explain afterwards; for the present we will follow out our plan and enumerate the other types of character.

In the matter of anger also we find excess and deficiency and moderation. The characters themselves hardly have recognized names, but as the moderate man is here called gentle, we will call his character gentleness; of those who go into extremes, we may take the term wrathful for him who exceeds, with wrathfulness for the vice, and wrathless for him who is deficient, with wrathfulness for his character.

Besides these, there are three kinds of moderation, bearing some resemblance to one another, and yet different. They all have to do with intercourse in speech and action, but they differ in that one has to do with the truthfulness of this intercourse, while the other two have to do with its pleasantness—one of the two with pleasantness in matters of amusement, the other with pleasantness in all the relations of life. We must therefore speak of these qualities also in order that we may the more plainly see how, in all cases, moderation is praiseworthy, while the extreme courses are neither right nor praiseworthy, but blamable.

In these cases also names are for the most part wanting, but we must try, here as elsewhere, to coin names ourselves, in order to make our argument clear and easy to follow.

In the matter of truth, then, let us call him who observes the mean a true (or truthful) person, and observance of the mean truth (or truthfulness): pretence, when it exaggerates, may be called boasting, and the person a boaster; when it understates, let the names be irony and ironical.

With regard to pleasantness in amusement, he who observes the mean may be called witty, and his character wittiness; excess may be called buffoonery, and the man a buffoon; while boorish may stand for the person who is deficient, and boorishness for his character.

With regard to pleasantness in the other affairs of life, he who makes himself properly pleasant may be called friendly, and his moderation friendliness; he that exceeds may be called obsequious if he have no ulterior motive but a flatterer if he has an eye to his own advantage; he that is deficient in this respect, and always makes himself disagreeable, may be called a quarrelsome or peevish fellow.

Moreover, in mere emotions and in our conduct with regard to them, there are ways of observing the mean; for instance, shame is not a virtue, but yet the modest man is praised. For in these matters also we speak of this man as observing the mean, of that man as going beyond it (as the shame-faced man whom the least thing makes shy), while he who is deficient in the feeling, or lacks it altogether, is called shameless; but the term modest is applied to him who observes the mean.

Righteous indignation, again, hits the mean between envy and malevolence. These have to do with feelings of pleasure and pain at what happens to our neighbours. A man is called righteously indignant when he feels pain at the sight of undeserved prosperity, but your envious man goes beyond him and is pained by the sight of any one in prosperity, while the malevolent man is so far from being pained that he actually exults in the sight of prosperous iniquity.

But we shall have another opportunity of discussing these matters.

As for justice, the term is used in more senses than one; we will, therefore, after disposing of the above questions, distinguish these various senses, and show how each of these kinds of justice is a kind of moderation.

And then we will treat of the intellectual virtues in the same way.

There are, as we said, three classes of disposition, viz. two kinds of vice, one marked by excess, the other by deficiency, and one kind of virtue, the observance of the mean.

Now, the extreme dispositions are opposed both to the mean or moderate disposition and to one another, while the moderate disposition is opposed to both the extremes. Just as a quantity which is equal to a given quantity is also greater when compared with a less, and less when compared with a greater quantity, so the mean or moderate dispositions exceed as compared with the defective dispositions, and fall short as compared with the excessive dispositions, both in feeling and in action; *e.g.* the courageous man seems foolhardy as compared with the coward, and cowardly as compared with the foolhardy; and similarly the temperate man appears profligate in comparison with the insensible, and insensible in comparison with the profligate man; and the liberal man appears prodigal by the side of the illiberal man, and illiberal by the side of the prodigal man.

And so the extreme characters try to displace the mean or moderate character, and each represents him as falling into the opposite extreme, the coward calling the courageous man foolhardy, the foolhardy calling him coward, and so on in other cases.

But while the mean and the extremes are thus opposed to one another, the extremes are still more contrary to each other than to the mean; for they are further removed from one another than from the mean, as that which is greater than a given magnitude is further from that which is less, and that which is less is further from that which is greater, than either the greater or the less is from that which is equal to the given magnitude.

Sometimes, again, an extreme, when compared with the mean, has a sort of resemblance to it, as foolhardiness to courage, or prodigality to liberality; but there is the greatest possible dissimilarity between the extremes.

Again, "things that are as far as possible removed from each other" is the accepted definition of contraries, so that the further things are removed from each other the more contrary they are.

In comparison with the mean, however, it is sometimes the deficiency that is the more opposed, and sometimes the excess; *e.g.* foolhardiness, which is excess, is not so much opposed to courage as cowardice, which is deficiency; but insensibility, which is lack of feeling, is not so much opposed to temperance as profligacy, which is excess.

The reasons for this are two. One is the reason derived from the nature of the matter itself: since one extreme is, in fact, nearer and more similar to the mean, we naturally do not oppose it to the mean so strongly as the other; *e.g.* as foolhardinees seems more similar to courage and nearer to it, and cowardice more dissimilar, we speak of cowardice as the opposite rather than the other: for that which is further removed from the mean seems to be more opposed to it.

This, then, is one reason, derived from the nature of the thing itself. Another reason lies in ourselves: and it is this—those things to which we happen to be more prone by nature appear to be more opposed to the mean: *e.g.* our natural inclination is rather towards indulgence in pleasure, and so we more easily fall into profligate than into regular habits: those courses, then, in which we are more apt to run to great lengths are spoken of as more opposed to the mean; and thus profligacy, which is an excess, is more opposed to temperance than the deficiency is.

We have sufficiently explained, then, that moral virtue is moderation or observance of the mean, and in what sense, viz. (1) as holding a middle position between two vices, one on the side of excess, and the other on the side of deficiency, and (2) as aiming at the mean or moderate amount both in feeling and in action.

And on this account it is a hard thing to be good; for finding the middle or the mean in each case is a hard thing, just as finding the middle or centre of a circle is a thing that is not within the power of everybody, but only of him who has the requisite knowledge.

· · ·

High-mindedness would seem from its very name to have to do with great things; let us first ascertain what these are.

It will make no difference whether we consider the quality itself, or the man who exhibits the quality.

By a high-minded man we seem to mean one who claims much and deserves much: for he who claims much without deserving it is a fool; but the possessor of a virtue is never foolish or silly. The man we have described, then, is high-minded.

He who deserves little and claims little is temperate [or modest], but not high-minded: for high-mindedness [or greatness of soul] implies greatness, just as beauty implies stature; small men may be neat and well proportioned, but cannot be called beautiful.

He who claims much without deserving it is vain (though not every one who claims more than he deserves is vain).

He who claims less than he deserves is little-minded, whether his deserts be great or moderate, or whether they be small and he claims still less: but this little-mindedness is most conspicuous in him whose deserts are great; for what would he do if his deserts were less than they are?

The high-minded man, then, in respect of the greatness of his deserts occupies an extreme position, but in that he behaves as he ought, observes the mean; for he claims that which he deserves, while all the others claim too much or too little.

But now if he deserves much and claims much, and most of all deserves and claims the greatest things, there will be one thing with which he will be especially concerned. For desert has reference to external good things. Now, the greatest of external good things we may assume to be that which we render to the Gods as their due, and that which people in high stations most desire, and which is the prize appointed for the noblest deeds. But the thing that answers to this description is honour, which, we may safely say, is the greatest of all external goods. Honours and dishonours, therefore, are the field in which the high-minded man behaves as he ought.

And indeed we may see, without going about to prove it, that honour is what high-minded men are concerned with; for it is honour that great men claim and deserve.

The little-minded man falls short, whether we compare his claims with his own deserts or with what the high-minded man claims for himself.

The vain or conceited man exceeds what is due to himself, though he does not exceed the high-minded man in his claims.

But the high-minded man, as he deserves the greatest things, must be a perfectly good or excellent man; for the better man always deserves the greater things, and the best possible man the greatest possible things. The really high-minded man, therefore, must be a good or excellent man. And indeed greatness in every virtue or excellence would seem to be necessarily implied in being a high-minded or great-souled man.

It would be equally inconsistent with the high-minded man's character to run along swinging his arms, and to commit an act of injustice; for what thing is there for love of which he would do anything unseemly, seeing that all things are of little account to him?

Survey him point by point and you will find that the notion of a high-minded man that is not a good or excellent man is utterly absurd. Indeed, if we were not good, he could not be worthy of honour; for honour is the prize of virtue, and is rendered to the good as their due.

High-mindedness, then, seems to be the crowning grace, as it were, of the virtues; it makes them greater, and cannot exist without them. And on this account it is a hard thing to be truly high-minded; for it is impossible without the union of all the virtues.

The high-minded man, then, exhibits his character especially in the matter of honours and dishonours and at great honour from good men he will be moderately pleased, as getting nothing more than his due, or even less; for no honour can be adequate to complete virtue; but nevertheless he will accept it, as they have nothing greater to offer him. But honour from ordinary men and on trivial grounds he will utterly despise; for that is not what he deserves. And dishonour likewise he will make light of; for he will never merit it.

But though it is especially in the matter of honours, as we have said, that the high-minded man displays his character, yet he will also observe the mean in his feelings with regard to wealth and power and all kinds of good and evil fortune, whatever may befall him, and will neither be very much exalted by prosperity, nor very much cast down by adversity; seeing that not even honour affects him as if it were a very important thing. For power and wealth are desirable for honour's sake (at least, those who have them wish to gain honour by them). He then who thinks lightly of honour must think lightly of them also.

And so high-minded men seem to look down upon everything.

But the gifts of fortune also are commonly thought to contribute to high-mindedness. For those who are well born are thought worthy of honour, and those who are powerful or wealthy; for they are in a position of superiority, and that which is superior in any good thing is always held in greater honour. And so these things do make people more high-minded in a sense; for such people find honour from some. But in strictness it is only the good man that is worthy of honour, though he that has both goodness and good fortune is commonly thought to be more worthy of honour. Those, however, who have these good things without virtue, neither have any just claim to great things, nor are properly to be called high-minded; for neither is possible without complete virtue.

But those who have these good things readily come to be super-cilious and insolent. For without virtue it is not easy to bear the gifts of fortune becomingly; and so, being unable to bear them, and thinking themselves superior to everybody else, such people look down upon others, and yet themselves do whatever happens to please them. They imitate the high-minded man without being really like him, and they imitate him where they can; that is to say, they do not exhibit virtue in their acts, but they look down upon others. Only the high-minded man never looks down upon others without justice (for he estimates them correctly), while most men do so for quite irrelevant reasons.

The high-minded man is not quick to run into petty dangers, and indeed does not love danger, since there are few things that he much values; but he is ready to incur a great danger, and when-ever he does so is unsparing of his life, as a thing that is not worth keeping at all costs.

It is his nature to confer benefits, but he is ashamed to receive them; for the former is the part of a superior, the latter of an inferior. And when he has received a benefit, he is apt to confer a greater in return; for thus his creditor will become his debtor and be in the position of a recipient of his favour.

It is thought, moreover, that such men remember those on whom they have conferred favours better than those from whom they have received them; for the recipient of a benefit is inferior to the benefactor, but such a man wishes to be in the position of a superior. So he likes to be reminded of the one, but dislikes to be reminded of the other; and this is the reason why we read that Thetis would not mention to Zeus the services she had done him, and why the Lacedaemonians, in treating with the Athenians, reminded them of the benefits received by Sparta rather than of those conferred by her.

It is characteristic of the high-minded man, again, never or re-luctantly to ask favours, but to be ready to confer them, and to be lofty in his behaviour to those who are high in station and favoured by fortune, but affable to those of the middle ranks; for it is a difficult thing and a dignified thing to assert superiority over the former, but easy to assert it over the latter. A haughty demeanour in dealing with the great is quite consistent with good breeding, but in dealing with those of low estate is brutal, like showing off one's strength upon a cripple.

Another of his characteristics is not to rush in wherever honour is to be won, nor to go where others take the lead, but to hold aloof and to shun an enterprise, except when great honour is to be gained, or a great work to be done—not to do many things, but great things and notable.

Again, he must be open in his hate and in his love; for concealment shows fear.

He must care for truth more than for what men will think of him, and speak and act openly; he will not hesitate to say all that he thinks, as he looks down upon mankind. So he will speak the truth, except when he speaks ironically; and irony he will employ in speaking to the generality of men.

Another of his characteristics is that he cannot fashion his life to suit another, except he be a friend; for that is servile: and so all flatterers or hangers on of great men are of a slavish nature, and men of low natures become flatterers.

Nor is he easily moved to admiration; for nothing is great to him.

He readily forgets injuries; for it is not consistent with his character to brood on the past, especially on past injuries, but rather to overlook them.

He is no gossip; he will neither talk about himself nor about others; for he cares not that men should praise him, nor that others should be blamed (though, on the other hand, he is not very ready to bestow praise); and so he is not apt to speak evil of others, not even of his enemies, except with the express purpose of giving offence.

When an event happens that cannot be helped or is of slight importance, he is the last man in the world to cry out or to beg for help; for that is the conduct of a man who thinks these events very important.

He loves to possess beautiful things that bring no profit, rather than useful things that pay; for this is characteristic of the man whose resources are in himself.

Further, the character of the high-minded man seems to require that his gait should be slow, his voice deep, his speech measured; for a man is not likely to be in a hurry when there are few things in which he is deeply interested, nor excited when he holds nothing to be of very great importance: and these are the causes of a high voice and rapid movements.

This, then, is the character of the high-minded man.

But he that is deficient in this quality is called little-minded; he that exceeds, vain or conceited.

Aristotle

8

Politics

The Greek polis and its culture were the affair of a small minority of
privileged citizens who, ideally, placed honor and the esteem of their
peers above power and profit. This fact is abundantly reflected in the
writings of Plato, Thucydides, and Xenophon. All these writers held anti-
democratic views. Aristotle, growing up as he did in Macedonian court
circles, had no democratic sympathies, as evidenced in the *Ethics;* to him
the Athenian politics of the Periclean Age would be contrary to all reason.

Aristotle held that ethics and politics were complementary ways of
going about the same thing: attainment of the good life for man, or
rather for men capable of attaining it. This aspiration is the subject of
his *Politics,* which, for most readers, stands next in interest to the *Ethics.*

Aristotle believes that man is a "political animal" and that his moral
character can be perfected only in the community life of the polis. But
what kind of polis? The selection that follows gives Aristotle's concept of
the ideal state. Its purpose would not be rule by the many, equality for
all, or a high material standard of life, but rather promotion of the good
life for "high-minded" citizens—just as a modern community might aim
to produce industrial wares.

Nowhere are the limitations of Greek political speculation better demon-
strated than in Aristotle's inability to divorce his reasoning from the
actualities of his time. Despite his learning, he did not realize that the
day of the small city-state was past, and he lacked the wide-ranging imagination of his pupil, Alexander, whose career and policy pointed dramatically
to the emergence of the great leader and the great state.

Aristotle, *Politics,* trans. Benjamin Jowett, in *The Works of Aristotle,* ed. W. D.
Ross (Oxford: Clarendon Press, 1921), Book VII, 278–97.

He who would duly inquire about the best form of a state ought first to determine which is the most eligible life; while this remains uncertain the best form of the state must also be uncertain; for, in the natural order of things, those may be expected to lead the best life who are governed in the best manner of which their circumstances admit. We ought therefore to ascertain, first of all, which is the most generally eligible life, and then whether the same life is or is not best for the state and for individuals.

Assuming that enough has been already said in discussions outside the school concerning the best life, we will now only repeat what is contained in them. Certainly no one will dispute the propriety of that partition of goods which separates them into three classes, viz. external goods, goods of the body, and goods of the soul, or deny that the happy man must have all three. For no one would maintain that he is happy who has not in him a particle of courage or temperance or justice or prudence, who is afraid of every insect which flutters past him, and will commit any crime, however great, in order to gratify his lust of meat or drink, who will sacrifice his dearest friend for the sake of half-a-farthing, and is as feeble and false in mind as a child or a madman. These propositions are almost universally acknowledged as soon as they are uttered, but men differ about the degree or relative superiority of this or that good. Some think that a very moderate amount of virtue is enough, but set no limit to their desires of wealth, property, power, reputation, and the like. To whom we reply by an appeal to facts, which easily prove that mankind do not acquire or preserve virtue by the help of external goods, but external goods by the help of virtue, and that happiness, whether consisting in pleasure or virtue, or both, is more often found with those who are most highly cultivated in their mind and in their character, and have only a moderate share of external goods, than among those who possess external goods to a useless extent but are deficient in higher qualities; and this is not only matter of experience, but, if reflected upon, will easily appear to be in accordance with reason. For, whereas external goods have a limit, like any other instrument, and all things useful are of such a nature that where there is too much of them they must either do harm, or at any rate be of no use, to their possessors, every good of the soul, the greater it is, is also of greater use, if the epithet useful as well as noble is appropriate to such subjects. No proof is required to show that the best state of one thing in relation to another corresponds in degree of excellence to the interval between the natures of which we say that these very states are states: so that, if the soul is more noble than our possessions or our bodies, both absolutely and in relation to us, it must be admitted that the best state of either has a similar ratio to the other. Again, it is for the sake of the soul that goods exernal and goods of the body are eligible at all, and all wise men ought to choose them for the sake of the soul, and not the soul for the sake of them.

Let us acknowledge then that each one has just so much of happiness as he has of virtue and wisdom, and of virtuous and wise action. God is a witness to us of this truth, for he is happy and blessed, not by reason of any external good, but in himself and by reason of his own nature. And herein of necessity lies the difference between good fortune and happiness; for external goods come of themselves, and chance is the author of them, but no one is just or temperate by or through chance. In like manner, and by a similar train of argument, the happy state may be shown to be that which is best and which acts rightly; and rightly it cannot act without doing right actions, and neither individual nor state can do right actions without virtue and wisdom. Thus the courage, justice, and wisdom of a state have the same form and nature as the qualities which give the individual who possesses them the name of just, wise, or temperate.

Thus much may suffice by way of preface: for I could not avoid touching upon these questions, neither could I go through all the arguments affecting them; these are the business of another science.

Let us assume then that the best life, both for individuals and states, is the life of virtue, when virtue has external goods enough for the performance of good actions. If there are any who controvert our assertion, we will in this treatise pass them over, and consider their objections hereafter.

There remains to be discussed the question, Whether the happiness of the individual is the same as that of the state, or different? Here again there can be no doubt—no one denies that they are the same. For those who hold that the well-being of the individual consists in his wealth, also think that riches make the happiness of the whole state, and those who value most highly the life of a tyrant deem that city the happiest which rules over the greatest number; while they who approve an individual for his virtue say that the more virtuous a city is, the happier it is. Two points here present themselves for consideration: first (1), which is the more eligible life, that of a citizen who is a member of a state, or that of an alien who has no political ties; and again (2), which is the best form of constitution or the best condition of a state, either on the supposition that political privileges are desirable for all, or for a majority only? Since the good of the state and not of the individual is the proper subject of political thought and speculation, and we are engaged in a political discussion, while the first of these two points has a secondary interest for us, the latter will be the main subject of our inquiry.

Now it is evident that the form of government is best in which every man, whoever he is, can act best and live happily. But even those who agree in thinking that the life of virtue is the most eligible raise a question, whether the life of business and politics is or is not more eligible than one which is wholly independent of external goods, I mean than a contemplative life, which by some is maintained to be the only one worthy of a philosopher. For these two lives—the life of the philosopher and the life of the statesman—appear to have been preferred by those who have been most keen in the pursuit of virtue, both in our own and in other ages. Which is the better is a question of no small moment; for the wise man, like the wise state, will necessarily regulate his life according to the best end. There are some who think that while a despotic rule over others is the greatest injustice, to exercise a constitutional rule over them, even though not unjust, is a great impediment to a man's individual well-being. Others take an opposite view; they maintain that the true life of man is the practical and political, and that every virtue admits of being practised, quite as much by statesmen and rulers as by private individuals. Others, again, are of opinion that arbitrary and tyrannical rule alone consists with happiness; indeed, in some states the entire aim both of the laws and of the constitution is to give men despotic power over their neighbours. And, therefore, although in most cities the laws may be said generally to be in a chaotic state, still, if they aim at anything, they aim at the maintenance of power: thus in Lacedaemon and Crete the system of education and the greater part of the laws are framed with a view to war. And in all nations which are able to gratify their ambition military power is held in esteem, for example among the Scythians and Persians and Thracians and Celts. In some nations there are even laws tending to stimulate the warlike virtues, as at Carthage, where we are told that men obtain the honour of wearing as many armlets as they have served campaigns. There was once a law in Macedonia that he who had not killed an enemy should wear a halter, and among the Scythians no one who had not slain his man was allowed to drink out of the cup which was handed round at a certain feast. Among the Iberians, a warlike nation, the number of enemies whom a man has slain is indicated by the number of obelisks which are fixed in the earth round his tomb; and there are numerous practices among other nations of a like kind, some of them established by law and others by custom. Yet to a reflecting mind it must appear very strange that the statesman should be always considering how he can dominate and tyrannize over others, whether they will or not. How can that which is not even lawful be the business of the statesman or the legislator? Unlawful it certainly is to rule without regard to justice, for there may be might where there is no right. The other arts and sciences offer no parallel; a physician is not expected to persuade or coerce his patients, nor a pilot the passengers in his ship. Yet most men appear to think that the art of despotic government is statesmanship, and what men affirm to be unjust and inexpedient in their own case they are not ashamed of practising towards others; they demand just rule for themselves, but where other men are concerned they care nothing about it. Such behaviour is irrational; unless the one party is, and the other is not, born to serve, in which case men have a right to command, not indeed all their fellows, but only those who are intended to be subjects; just as we ought not to hunt mankind, whether for food or sacrifice, but only the animals which may be hunted for food or sacrifice, this is to say, such wild animals as are eatable. And surely there may be a city happy in isolation, which we will assume to be well-governed (for it is quite possible that a city thus isolated might be well-administered and have good laws); but such a city would not be constituted with any view to war or the conquest of enemies—all that sort of thing must be excluded. Hence we see very plainly that warlike pursuits, although generally to be deemed honourable, are not the supreme end of all things, but only means. And the good lawgiver should inquire how states and races of men and communities may participate in a good life, and in the happiness which is attainable by them. His enactments will not be always the same; and where there are neighbours he will have to see what sort of studies should be practised in relation to their several characters, or how the measures appropriate in relation to each are to be adopted. The end at which the best form of government should aim may be properly made a matter of future consideration.

Let us now address those who, while they agree that the life of virtue is the most eligible, differ about the manner of practising it. For some renounce political power, and think that the life of the freeman is different from the life of the statesman and the best of all; but others think the life of the statesman best. The argument of the latter is that he who does nothing cannot do well, and that virtuous activity is identical with happiness. To both we say: 'you are partly right and partly wrong.' The first class are right in affirming that the life of the freeman is better than the life of the despot; for there is nothing grand or noble in having the use of a slave, in so far as he is a slave; or in issuing commands about necessary things. But it is an error to suppose that every sort of rule is despotic like that of a master over slaves, for there is as great a difference between the rule over freemen and the rule over slaves as there is between slavery by nature and freedom by nature, about which I have said enough at the commencement of this treatise. And it is equally a mistake to place inactivity above action, for happiness is activity, and the actions of the just and wise are the realization of much that is noble.

But perhaps some one, accepting these premises, may still maintain that supreme power is the best of all things, because the possessors of it are able to perform the greatest number of noble actions. If so, the man who is able to rule, instead of giving up anything to his neighbour, ought rather to take away his power; and the father should make no account of his son, nor the son of his father, nor friend of friend; they should not bestow a thought on one another in comparison with this higher object, for the best is the most eligible and 'doing well' is the best. There might be some truth in such a view if we assume that robbers and plunderers attain the chief good. But this can never be; their hypothesis is false. For the actions of a ruler cannot really be honourable, unless he is as much superior to other men as a husband is to a wife, or a father to his children, or a master to his slaves. And therefore he who violates the law can never recover by any success, however great, what he has already lost in departing from virtue. For equals the honourable and the just consist in sharing alike, as is just and equal. But that the unequal should be given to equals, and the unlike to those who are like, is contrary to nature, and nothing which is contrary to nature is good. If therefore, there is any one superior in virtue and in the power of performing the best actions, him we ought to follow and obey, but he must have the capacity for action as well as virtue.

If we are right in our view, and happiness is assumed to be virtuous activity, the active life will be the best, both for every city collectively, and for individuals. Not that a life of action must necessarily have relation to others, as some persons think, nor are those ideas only to be regarded as practical which are pursued for the sake of practical results, but much more the thoughts and contemplations which are independent and complete in themselves; since virtuous activity, and therefore a certain kind of action, is an end, and even in the case of external actions the directing mind is most truly said to act. Neither, again, is it necessary that states which are cut off from others and choose to live alone should be inactive; for activity, as well as other things, may take place by sections; there are many ways in which the sections of a state act upon one another. The same thing is equally true of every individual. If this were otherwise, God and the universe, who have no external actions over and above their own energies, would be far enough from perfection. Hence it is evident that the same life is best for each individual, and for states and for mankind collectively.

Thus far by way of introduction. In what has preceded I have discussed other forms of government; in what remains the first point to be considered is what should be the conditions of the ideal or perfect state; for the perfect state cannot exist without a due supply of the means of life. And therefore we must pre-suppose many purely imaginary conditions, but nothing impossible. There will be a certain number of citizens, a country in which to place them, and the like. As the weaver or shipbuilder or any other artisan must have the material proper for his work (and in proportion as this is better prepared, so will the result of his art be nobler), so the statesman or legislator must also have the materials suited to him.

First among the materials required by the statesman is population: he will consider what should be the number and character of the citizens, and then what should be the size and character of the country. Most persons think that a state in order to be happy ought to be large; but even if they are right, they have no idea what is a large and what a small state. For they judge of the size of the city by the number of the inhabitants; whereas they ought to regard, not their number, but their power. A city too, like an individual, has a work to do; and that city which is best adapted to the fulfillment of its work is to be deemed greatest, in the same sense of the word great in which Hippocrates might be called greater, not as a man, but as a physician, than some one else who was taller. And even if we reckon greatness by numbers, we ought not to include everybody, for there must always be in cities a multitude of slaves and sojourners and foreigners; but we should include those only who are members of the state, and who form an essential part of it. The number of the latter is a proof of the greatness of a city; but a city which produces numerous artisans and comparatively few soldiers cannot be great, for a great city is not to be confounded with a populous one. Moreover, experience shows that a very populous city can rarely, if ever, be well governed; since all cities which have a reputation for good government have a limit of population. We may argue on grounds of reason, and the same result will follow. For law is order, and good law is good order; but a very great multitude cannot be orderly: to introduce order into the unlimited is the work of a divine power—of such a power as holds together the universe. Beauty is realized in number and magnitude, and the state which combines magnitude with good order must necessarily be the most beautiful. To the size of states there is a limit, as there is to other things, plants, animals, implements; for none of these retain their natural power when they are too large or too small, but they either wholly lose their nature, or are spoiled. For example, a ship which is only a span long will not be a ship at all, nor a ship a quarter of a mile long; yet there may be a ship of a certain size, either too large or too small, which will still be a ship, but bad for sailing. In like manner a state when composed of too few is not, as a state ought to be, self-sufficing; when of too many, though self-sufficing in all mere necessaries, as a nation may be, it is not a state, being almost incapable of constitutional government. For who can be the general of such a vast multitude, or who the herald, unless he have the voice of a Stentor?

A state, then, only begins to exist when it has attained a population sufficient for a good life in the political community: it may indeed, if it somewhat exceed this number, be a greater state. But, as I was saying, there must be a limit. What should be the limit will be easily ascertained by experience. For both governors and governed have duties to perform; the special functions of a governor are to command and to judge. But if the citizens of a state are to judge and to distribute offices according to merit, then they must know each other's characters; where they do not possess this knowledge, both the election to offices and the decision of lawsuits will go wrong. When the population is very large they are manifestly settled at haphazard, which clearly ought not to be. Besides, in an over-populous state foreigners and metics will readily acquire the rights of citizens, for who will find them out? Clearly then the best limit of the population of a state is the largest number which suffices for the purposes of life, and can be taken in at a single view. Enough concerning the size of a state.

Much the same principle will apply to the territory of the state: every one would agree in praising the territory which is most entirely self-sufficing; and that must be the territory which is all-producing, for to have all things and to want nothing is sufficiency. In size and extent it should be such as may enable the inhabitants to live at once temperately and liberally in the enjoyment of leisure. Whether we are right or wrong in laying down this limit we will inquire more precisely hereafter, when we have occasion to consider what is the right use of property and wealth: a matter which is much disputed, because men are inclined to rush into one of two extremes, some into meanness, others into luxury.

It is not difficult to determine the general character of the territory which is required (there are, however, some points on which military authorities should be heard); it should be difficult of access to the enemy, and easy of egress to the inhabitants. Further, we require that the land as well as the inhabitants of whom we were just now speaking should be taken in at a single view, for a country which is easily seen can be easily protected. As to the position of the city, if we could have what we wish, it should be well situated in regard both to sea and land. This then is one principle, that it should be a convenient centre for the protection of the whole country: the other is, that it should be suitable for receiving the fruits of the soil, and also for the bringing in of timber and any other products that are easily transported.

Whether a communication with the sea is beneficial to a well-ordered state or not is a question which has often been asked. It is argued that the introduction of strangers brought up under other laws, and the increase of population, will be adverse to good order; the increase arises from their using the sea and having a crowd of merchants coming and going, and is inimical to good government. Apart from these considerations, it would be undoubtedly better, both with a view to safety and to the provision of necessaries, that the city and territory should be connected with the sea; the defenders of a country, if they are to maintain themselves against an enemy, should be easily relieved both by land and by sea; and even if they are not able to attack by sea and land at once, they will have less difficulty in doing mischief to their assailants on one element, if they themselves can use both. Moreover, it is necessary that they should import from abroad what is not found in their own country, and that they should export what they have in excess; for a city ought to be a market, not indeed for others, but for herself.

Those who make themselves a market for the world only do so for the sake of revenue, and if a state ought not to desire profit of this kind it ought not to have such an emporium. Nowadays we often see in countries and cities dockyards and harbours very conveniently placed outside the city, but not too far off; and they are kept in dependence by walls and similar fortifications. Cities thus situated manifestly reap the benefit of intercourse with their ports; and any harm which is likely to accrue may be easily guarded against by the laws, which will pronounce and determine who may hold communication with one another, and who may not.

There can be no doubt that the possession of a moderate naval force is advantageous to a city; the city should be formidable not only to its own citizens but to some of its neighbours, or, if necessary, able to assist them by sea as well as by land. The proper number or magnitude of this naval force is relative to the character of the state; for if her function is to take a leading part in politics, her naval power should be commensurate with the scale of her enterprises. The population of the state need not be much increased, since there is no necessity that the sailors should be citizens: the marines who have the control and command will be freemen, and belong also to the infantry; and wherever there is a dense population of Perioeci and husbandmen, there will always be sailors more than enough. Of this we see instances at the present day. The city of Heraclea, for example, although small in comparison with many others, can man a considerable fleet. Such are our conclusions respecting the territory of the state, its harbours, its towns, its relations to the sea, and its maritime power.

Having spoken of the number of the citizens, we will proceed to speak of what should be their character. This is a subject which can be easily understood by any one who casts his eye on the more celebrated states of Hellas, and generally on the distribution of races in the habitable world. Those who live in a cold climate and in Europe are full of spirit, but wanting in intelligence and skill; and therefore they retain comparative freedom, but have no political organization, and are incapable of ruling over others. Whereas the natives of Asia are intelligent and inventive, but they are wanting in spirit, and therefore they are always in a state of subjection and slavery. But the Hellenic race, which is situated between them, is likewise intermediate in character, being high-spirited and also intelligent. Hence it continues free, and is the best-governed of any nation, and, if it could be formed into one state, would be able to rule the world. There are also similar differences in the different tribes of Hellas; for some of them are of a one-sided nature, and are intelligent or courageous only, while in others there is a happy combination of both qualities. And clearly those whom the legislator will most easily lead to virtue may be expected to be both intelligent and courageous. Some say that the guardians should be friendly towards those whom they know, fierce towards those whom they do not know. Now, passion is the quality of the soul which begets friendship and enables us to love; notably the spirit within us is more stirred against our friends and acquaintances than against those who are unknown to us, when we think that we are despised by them; for which reason Archilochus, complaining of his friends, very naturally addresses his soul in these words,

'For surely thou art plagued on account of friends.'

The power of command and the love of freedom are in all men based upon this quality, for passion is commanding and invincible. Nor is it right to say that the guardians should be fierce towards those whom they do not know, for we ought not to be out of temper with any one; and a lofty spirit is not fierce by nature, but only when excited against evil-doers. And this, as I was saying before, is a feeling which men show most strongly towards their friends if they think they have received a wrong at their hands: as indeed is reasonable; for, besides the actual injury, they seem to be deprived of a benefit by those who owe them one. Hence the saying,

'Cruel is the strife of brethren,'

and again,

'They who love in excess also hate in excess.'

Thus we have nearly determined the number and character of the citizens of our state, and also the size and nature of their territory. I say 'nearly,' for we ought not to require the same minuteness in theory as in the facts given by perception.

As in other natural compounds the conditions of a composite whole are not necessarily organic parts of it, so in a state or in any other combination forming a unity not everything is a part, which is a necessary condition. The members of an association have necessarily some one thing the same and common to all, in which they share equally or unequally; for example, food or land or any other thing. But where there are two things of which one is a means and the other an end, they have nothing in common except that the one receives what the other produces. Such, for example, is the relation in which workmen and tools stand to their work; the house and the builder have nothing in common, but the art of the builder is for the sake of the house. And so states require property, but property, even though living beings are included in it, is no part of a state; for a state is not a community of living beings only, but a community of equals, aiming at the best life possible. Now, whereas happiness is the highest good, being a realization and perfect practice of virtue, which some can attain, while others have little or none of it, the various qualities of men are clearly the reason why there are various kinds of states and many forms of government; for different men seek after happiness in different ways and by different means, and so make for themselves different modes of life and forms of government. We must see also how many things are indispensable to the existence of a state, for what we call the parts of a state will be found among the indispensables. Let us then enumerate the functions of a state, and we shall easily elicit what we want:

First, there must be food; secondly, arts, for life requires many instruments; thirdly, there must be arms, for the members of a community have need of them, and in their own hands, too, in order to maintain authority both against disobedient subjects and against external assailants; fourthly, there must be a certain amount of revenue, both for internal needs, and for the purposes of war; fifthly, or rather first, there must be a care of religion, which is commonly called worship; sixthly, and most necessary of all, there must be a power of deciding what is for the public interest, and what is just in men's dealings with one another.

These are the services which every state may be said to need. For a state is not a mere aggregate of persons, but a union of them sufficing for the purposes of life; and if any of these things be wanting, it is as we maintain impossible that the community can be absolutely self-sufficing. A state then should be framed with a view to the fulfilment of these functions. There must be husbandmen to procure food, and artisans, and a warlike and a wealthy class, and priests, and judges to decide what is necessary and expedient.

Having determined these points, we have in the next place to consider whether all ought to share in every sort of occupation. Shall every man be at once husbandman, artisan, councillor, judge, or shall we suppose the several occupations just mentioned assigned to different persons? or, thirdly, shall some employments be assigned to individuals and others common to all? The same arrangement, however, does not occur in every constitution; as we were saying, all may be shared by all, or not all by all, but only by some; and hence arise the differences of constitutions, for in democracies all share in all, in oligarchies the opposite practice prevails. Now, since we are here speaking of the best form of government, i.e. that under which the state will be most happy (and happiness, as has been already said, cannot exist without virtue), it clearly follows that in the state which is best governed and possesses men who are just absolutely, and not merely relatively to the principle of the constitution, the citizens must not lead the life of mechanics or tradesmen, for such a life is ignoble, and inimical to virtue. Neither must they be husbandmen since leisure is necessary both for the development of virtue and the performance of political duties.

Again, there is in a state a class of warriors, and another of councillors, who advise about the expedient and determine matters of law, and these seem in an especial manner parts of a state. Now, should these two classes be distinguished, or are both functions to be assigned to the same persons? Here again there is no difficulty in seeing that both functions will in one way belong to the same, in another, to different persons. To different persons in so far as these employments are suited to different primes of life, for the one requires wisdom and the other strength. But on the other hand, since it is an impossible thing that those who are able to use or to resist force should be willing to remain always in subjection, from this point of view the persons are the same; for those who carry arms can always determine the fate of the constitution. It remains therefore that both functions should be entrusted by the ideal constitution to the same persons, not, however, at the same time, but in the order prescribed by nature, who has given to young men strength and to older men wisdom. Such a distribution of duties will be expedient and also just, and is founded upon a principle of conformity to merit. Besides, the ruling class should be the owners of property, for they are citizens, and the citizens of a state should be in good circumstances; whereas mechanics or any other class which is not a producer of virtue have no share in the state. This follows from our first principle, for happiness cannot exist without virtue, and a city is not to be termed happy in regard to a portion of the citizens, but in regard to them all. And clearly property should be in their hands, since the husbandmen will of necessity be slaves or barbarian Perioeci.

Of the classes enumerated there remain only the priests, and the manner in which their office is to be regulated is obvious. No husbandman or mechanic should be appointed to it; for the Gods should receive honour from the citizens only. Now since the body of the citizens is divided into two classes, the warriors and the councillors, and it is beseeming that the worship of the Gods should be duly performed, and also a rest provided in their service for those who from age have given up active life, to the old men of these two classes should be assigned the duties of the priesthood.

We have shown what are the necessary conditions, and what the parts of a state: husbandmen, craftsmen, and labourers of all kinds are necessary to the existence of states, but the parts of the state are the warriors and councillors. And these are distinguished severally from one another, the distinction being in some cases permanent, in others not.

Aristotle

9

Poetics

Although Aristotle's extant writings resemble unrevised lecture notes and are not generally valued as literature, Aristotle was, paradoxically, author of the earliest book of literary criticism. Literature was a major subject of study at the Lyceum, and Aristotle sought to reduce it to the same methodical system found in his *Ethics* and *Politics*.

The Greeks had a profound sense of form; as the men of Aristotle's time looked back a hundred years or more, they wondered at the mastery displayed by the great tragedians of the fifth century B.C. If their secret could be analyzed and a formula arrived at, great tragedies might then be produced at will. The origin of this theory of art as deliberate imitation rather than unconscious inspiration had its roots, like so much of Plato's and Aristotle's thought, in Hellenic traditional ways of thinking and doing—ways which the two philosophers tried to invest with universal meaning and validity. In this case the root is linguistic: the Greek verb from which our word *poetry* is derived (*poiein*) means *to make*. Aristotle reasoned that inasmuch as Sophocles had not *made* Oedipus's disaster (in the sense of causing it), he had imitated it. Others might do the same, and Aristotle explains why men take pleasure in these imitations.

The *Poetics,* dating from *ca.* 330 B.C., is unfinished and is confined largely to a definition of tragedy and to an analysis of what makes tragedy. Nevertheless, by clarifying such matters as language, plot, and construction, on the basis of literature known to Aristotle, the *Poetics* established a canon of literary criticism and dramaturgy that has endured until modern times. As in other areas of learning, the authority of Aristotle—even his tentative conclusions—carried enormous weight. For many centuries, literary critics regarded his dicta as "classic" rules, laid down for all time; their own originality was, therefore, inhibited by this formal expression.

S. H. Butcher, *Aristotle's Theory of Poetry and Fine Art* (New York: Dover Publications, Inc., 1951), 23, 25, 27, 33, 35, 37, 39, 45, 47, 49, 51, 53, 55, 57. Reprinted through the permission of the publisher.

Tragedy is an imitation of an action that is serious, complete, and of a certain magnitude; in language embellished with each kind of artistic ornament, the several kinds being found in separate parts of the play; in the form of action, not of narrative; through pity and fear effecting the proper purgation of these emotions. By "language embellished," I mean language into which rhythm, "harmony," and song enter. By "the several kinds in separate parts," I mean, that some parts are rendered through the medium of verse alone, others again with the aid of song.

Now as tragic imitation implies persons acting, it necessarily follows, in the first place, that Spectacular equipment will be a part of Tragedy. Next, Song and Diction, for these are the medium of imitation. By "Diction" I mean the mere metrical arrangement of the words: as for "Song," it is a term whose sense every one understands.

Again, Tragedy is the imitation of an action; and an action implies personal agents, who necessarily possess certain distinctive qualities both of character and thought; for it is by these that we qualify actions themselves, and these—thought and character—are the two natural causes from which actions spring, and on actions again all success or failure depends. Hence, the Plot is the imitation of the action:—for by plot I here mean the arrangement of the incidents. By Character I mean that in virtue of which we ascribe certain qualities to the agents. Thought is required wherever a statement is proved, or, it may be, a general truth enunciated. Every Tragedy, therefore, must have six parts, which parts determine its quality—namely, Plot, Character, Diction, Thought, Spectacle, Song. Two of the parts constitute the medium of imitation, one the manner, and three the objects of imitation. And these complete the list. These elements have been employed, we may say, by the poets to a man; in fact, every play contains Spectacular elements as well as Character, Plot, Diction, Song, and Thought.

But most important of all is the structure of the incidents. For Tragedy is an imitation, not of men, but of an action and of life, and life consists in action, and its end is a mode of action, not a quality. Now character determines men's qualities, but it is by their actions that they are happy or the reverse. . . .

Unity of plot does not, as some persons think, consist in the unity of the hero. For infinitely various are the incidents in one man's life which cannot be reduced to unity; and so, too, there are many actions of one man out of which we cannot make one action. Hence the error, as it appears, of all poets who have composed a *Heracleid,* a *Theseid,* or other poems of the kind. They imagine that as Heracles was one man, the story of Heracles must also be a unity. But Homer, as in all else he is of surpassing merit, here too—whether from art or natural genius—seems to have happily discerned the truth. In composing the *Odyssey* he did not include all the adventures of Odysseus—such as his wound on Parnassus, or his feigned madness at the mustering of the host— incidents between which there was no necessary or probable connexion: but he made the *Odyssey,* and likewise the *Iliad,* to centre round an action that in our sense of the word is one. . . .

It is, moreover, evident from what has been said, that it is not the function of the poet to relate what has happened, but what may happen,—what is possible according to the law of probability or necessity. The poet and the historian differ not by writing in verse or in prose. The work of Herodotus might be put into verse, and it would still be a species of history, with metre no less than without it. The true difference is that one relates what has happened, the other what may happen. Poetry, therefore, is a more philosophical and a higher thing than history: for poetry tends to express the universal, history the particular. By the universal I mean how a person of a certain type will on occasion speak or act, according to the law of probability or necessity; and it is this universality at which poetry aims in the names she attaches to the personages. . . .

Of all plots and actions the epeisodic are the worst. I call a plot "epeisodic" in which the episodes or acts succeed one another without probable or necessary sequence. Bad poets compose such pieces by their own fault, good poets, to please the players; for, as they write show pieces for competition, they stretch the plot beyond its capacity, and are often forced to break the natural continuity.

But again, Tragedy is an imitation not only of a complete action, but of events inspiring fear or pity. Such an effect is best produced when the events come on us by surprise; and the effect is heightened when, at the same time, they follow as cause and effect. The tragic wonder will then be greater than if they happened of themselves or by accident; for even coincidences are most striking when they have an air of design. We may instance the statue of Mitys at Argos, which fell upon his murderer while he was a spectator at a festival, and killed him. Such events seem not to be due to mere chance. Plots, therefore, constructed on these principles are necessarily the best. . . .

As the sequel to what has already been said, we must proceed to consider what the poet should aim at, and what he should avoid, in constructing his plots; and by what means the specific effect of Tragedy will be produced.

A perfect tragedy should, as we have seen, be arranged not on the simple but on the complex plan. It should, moreover, imitate actions which excite pity and fear, this being the distinctive mark of tragic imitation. It follows plainly, in the first place, that the change of fortune presented must not be the spectacle of a virtuous man brought from prosperity to adversity: for this moves neither pity nor fear; it merely shocks us. Nor, again, that of a bad man passing from adversity to prosperity: for nothing can be more alien to the spirit of Tragedy; it possesses no single tragic quality; it neither satisfies the moral sense nor calls forth pity or fear. Nor, again, should the downfall of the utter villain be exhibited. A plot of this kind would, doubtless, satisfy the moral sense, but it would inspire neither pity nor fear; for pity is aroused by unmerited misfortune, fear by the misfortune of a man like ourselves. Such an event, therefore, will be neither pitiful nor terrible. There remains, then, the character between these two extremes,— that of a man who is not eminently good and just, yet whose misfortune is brought about not by vice or depravity, but by some error or frailty. He must be one who is highly renowned and prosperous,—a personage like Oedipus, Thyestes, or other illustrious men of such families.

A well constructed plot should, therefore, be single in its issue, rather than double as some maintain. The change of fortune should be not from bad to good, but, reversely, from good to bad. It should come about as the result not of vice, but of some great error or frailty, in a character either such as we have described, or better rather than worse. The practice of the stage bears out our view. At first the poets recounted any legend that came in their way. Now, the best tragedies are founded on the story of a few houses,—on the fortunes of Alcmaeon, Oedipus, Orestes, Meleager, Thyestes, Telephus, and those others who have done or suffered something terrible. A tragedy, then, to be perfect according to the rules of art should be of this construction. Hence they are in error who censure Euripides just because he follows this principle in his plays, many of which end unhappily. It is, as we have said, the right ending. The best proof is that on the stage and in dramatic competition, such plays, if well worked out, are the most tragic in effect; and Euripides, faulty though he may be in the general management of his subject, yet is felt to be the most tragic of the poets.

In the second rank comes the kind of tragedy which some place first. Like the *Odyssey,* it has a double thread of plot, and also an opposite catastrophe for the good and for the bad. It is accounted the best because of the weakness of the spectators; for the poet is guided in what he writes by the wishes of his audience. The pleasure, however, thence derived is not the true tragic pleasure. It is proper rather to Comedy, where those who, in the piece, are the deadliest enemies—like Orestes and Aegisthus—quit the stage as friends at the close, and no one slays or is slain.

Fear and pity may be aroused by spectacular means; but they may also result from the inner structure of the piece, which is the better way, and indicates a superior poet. For the plot ought to be so constructed that, even without the aid of the eye, he who hears the tale told will thrill with horror and melt to pity at what takes place. This is the impression we should receive from hearing the story of the *Oedipus.* But to produce this effect by the mere spectacle is a less artistic method, and dependent on extraneous aids. Those who employ spectacular means to create a sense not of the terrible but only of the monstrous, are strangers to the purpose of Tragedy; for we must not demand of Tragedy any and every kind of pleasure, but only that which is proper to it. And since the pleasure which the poet should afford is that which comes from pity and fear through imitation, it is evident that this quality must be impressed upon the incidents.

Let us then determine what are the circumstances which strike us as terrible or pitiful.

Actions capable of this effect must happen between persons who are either friends or enemies or indifferent to one another. If an enemy kills an enemy, there is nothing to excite pity either in the act or the intention,—except so far as the suffering in itself is pitiful. So again with indifferent persons. But when the tragic incident occurs between those who are near or dear to one another —if, for example, a brother kills, or intends to kill, a brother, a son his father, a mother her son, a son his mother, or any other deed of the kind is done—these are the situations to be looked for by the poet. He may not indeed destroy the framework of the received legends—the fact, for instance, that Clytemnestra was slain by Orestes and Eriphyle by Alcmaeon—but he ought to show invention of his own, and skilfully handle the traditional material. Let us explain more clearly what is meant by skilful handling.

The action may be done consciously and with knowledge of the persons, in the manner of the older poets. It is thus too that Euripides makes Medea slay her children. Or, again, the deed of horror may be done, but done in ignorance, and the tie of kinship or friendship be discovered afterwards. The *Oedipus* of Sophocles is an example. Here, indeed, the incident is outside the drama proper; but cases occur where it falls within the action of the play: one may cite the *Alcmaeon* of Astydamas, or Telegonus in the *Wounded Odysseus*. Again, there is a third case,—to be about to act with knowledge of the persons and then not to act. The fourth case is when some one is about to do an irreparable deed through ignorance, and makes the discovery before it is done. These are the only possible ways. For the deed must either be done or not done,—and that wittingly or unwittingly. But of all these ways, to be about to act knowing the persons, and then not to act, is the worst. It is shocking without being tragic, for no disaster follows. It is, therefore, never, or very rarely, found in poetry. One instance, however, is in the *Antigone,* where Haemon threatens to kill Creon. The next and better way is that the deed should be perpetrated. Still better, that it should be perpetrated in ignorance, and the discovery made afterwards. There is then nothing to shock us, while the discovery produces a startling effect. The last case is the best, as when in the *Cresphontes* Merope is about to slay her son; but, recognising who he is, spares his life. So in the *Iphigenia,* the sister recognises the brother just in time. Again in the *Helle,* the son recognises the mother when on the point of giving her up. This, then, is why a few families only, as has been already observed, furnish the subjects of tragedy. It was not art, but happy chance, that led the poets in search of subjects to impress the tragic quality upon their plots. They are compelled, therefore, to have recourse to those houses whose history contains moving incidents like these.

Enough has now been said concerning the structure of the incidents, and the right kind of plot.

In respect of Character there are four things to be aimed at. First, and most important, it must be good. Now any speech or action that manifests moral purpose of any kind will be expressive of character: the character will be good if the purpose is good. This rule is relative to each class. Even a woman may be good, and also a slave; though the woman may be said to be an inferior being, and the slave quite worthless. The second thing to aim at is propriety. There is a type of manly valour; but valour in a woman, or unscrupulous cleverness, is inappropriate. Thirdly, character must be true to life: for this is a distinct thing from goodness and propriety, as here described. The fourth point is consistency: for though the subject of the imitation, who suggested the type, be inconsistent, still he must be consistently inconsistent. As an example of motiveless degradation of character, we have Menelaus in the *Orestes:* of character indecorous and inappropriate, the lament of Odysseus in the Scylla, and the speech of Melanippe: of inconsistency, the *Iphigenia at Aulis,*—for Iphigenia the suppliant in no way resembles her later self.

As in the structure of the plot, so too in the portraiture of character, the poet should always aim either at the necessary or the probable. Thus a person of a given character should speak or act in a given way, by the rule either of necessity or of probability; just as this event should follow that by necessary or probable sequence. It is therefore evident that the unravelling of the plot, no less than the complication, must arise out of the plot itself, it must not be brought about by the *Deus ex Machina*—as in the *Medea*, or in the Return of the Greeks in the *Iliad*. The *Deus ex Machina* should be employed only for events external to the drama,—for antecedent or subsequent events, which lie beyond the range of human knowledge, and which require to be reported or foretold; for to the gods we ascribe the power of seeing all things. Within the action there must be nothing irrational. If the irrational cannot be excluded, it should be outside the scope of the tragedy. Such is the irrational element in the *Oedipus* of Sophocles.

Again, since Tragedy is an imitation of persons who are above the common level, the example of good portrait-painters should be followed. They, while reproducing the distinctive form of the original, make a likeness which is true to life and yet more beautiful. So too the poet, in representing men who are irascible or indolent, or have other defects of character, should preserve the type and yet ennoble it. In this way Achilles is portrayed by Agathon and Homer.

These then are rules the poet should observe. Nor should he neglect those appeals to the senses, which, though not among the essentials, are the concomitants of poetry; for here too there is much room for error. But of this enough has been said in our published treatises.

Plutarch

10

Lives: Marcus Cato

Greek literature did not end with the decline of the polis; however it remained the interest of the privileged and bookish few. Literature continued to grow, and from the fourth century B.C. a new genre made its appearance: the short biography, presenting not a "type," as previously, but a unique person with traits of his own. As Greek letters took a new lease on life in the early Roman Empire, this "modern" kind of biographical writing came into vogue and may even have provided a pattern for the Christian gospels. Certainly the form reached its peak in Plutarch (*ca.* 46 A.D.–*ca.* 120).

Little is known of Plutarch's own life. After student days in Athens, he spent some years lecturing in Rome. An amiable man of wide interests, broad learning, and cultivated taste, he was on close terms with the "mighty"; the Emperor Trajan made him a consul and provincial governor. Plutarch, however, preferred the life of a country gentleman; he returned to his native Chaeronea, in Greece, where he happily filled its petty offices and priesthoods. It was then that he composed his major work, the *Parallel Lives,* a biographical study of famous Greek soldiers and statesmen, paired with their Roman counterparts, in which, above all, he sought to inculcate the ethical ideals of Hellenic culture.

The following selection from the *Lives* is taken from the life of Marcus Porcius Cato (234–149 B.C.), usually known as Cato the Elder, or the Censor. It is a memorable picture of one of the Roman Republic's great personalities and national heroes who, throughout his private and public life, sought to stem the alien cultural tide that was eroding the ancestral ways of the Roman people—once the most puritanical of antiquity.

If only because they are based on sources now lost to us, the *Lives* are invaluable. But Plutarch's wide popularity among readers over the cen-

Plutarch, *Lives,* trans. called Dryden's, corr. and rev. A. H. Clough (Boston: Little, Brown, 1875), II, 316–18, 321–34, 341–47, 350–51.

turies eventually gave him first place among the Greek authors who shaped the image of the ancient world in the minds of Western men. Among men of letters, Shakespeare, Montaigne, Corneille, and Racine were all indebted to him.

Marcus Cato, we are told, was born at Tusculum, though (till he betook himself to civil and military affairs) he lived and was bred up in the country of the Sabines, where his father's estate lay. His ancestors seeming almost entirely unknown, he himself praises his father Marcus, as a worthy man and a brave soldier, and Cato, his great grandfather too, as one who had often obtained military prizes, and who, having lost five horses under him, received, on the account of his valor, the worth of them out of the public exchequer. Now it being the custom among the Romans to call those who, having no repute by birth, made themselves eminent by their own exertions, new men or upstarts, they called even Cato himself so, and so he confessed himself to be as to any public distinction or employment, but yet asserted that in the exploits and virtues of his ancestors he was very ancient. His third name originally was not Cato, but Priscus, though afterwards he had the surname of Cato, by reason of his abilities; for the Romans call a skilful or experienced man, *Catus*. He was of a ruddy complexion, and grey-eyed; as the writer, who, with no good-will, made the following epigram upon him, lets us see:—

> Porcius, who snarls at all in every place,
> With his grey eyes, and with his fiery face,
> Even after death will scarce admitted be
> Into the infernal realms by Hecate.

He gained, in early life, a good habit of body by working with his own hands, and living temperately, and serving in war; and seemed to have an equal proportion both of health and strength. And he exerted and practised his eloquence through all the neighborhood and little villages; thinking it as requisite as a second body, and an all but necessary organ to one who looks forward to something above a mere humble and inactive life. He would never refuse to be counsel for those who needed him, and was, indeed, early reckoned a good lawyer, and, ere long, a capable orator.

Hence his solidity and depth of character showed itself gradually, more and more to those with whom he was concerned, and claimed, as it were, employment in great affairs, and places of public command. Nor did he merely abstain from taking fees for his counsel and pleading, but did not even seem to put any high price on the honor which proceeded from such kind of combats, seeming much more desirous to signalize himself in the camp and in real fights; and while yet but a youth, had his breast covered with scars he had received from the enemy; being (as he himself says) but seventeen years old, when he made his first campaign; in the time when Hannibal, in the height of his success, was burning and pillaging all Italy. In engagements he would strike boldly, without flinching, stand firm to his ground, fix a bold countenance upon his enemies, and with a harsh threatening voice accost them, justly thinking himself and telling others, that such a rugged kind of behavior sometimes terrifies the enemy more than the sword itself. In his marches, he bore his own arms on foot, whilst one servant only followed, to carry the provisions for his table, with whom he is said never to have been angry or hasty, whilst he made ready his dinner or supper, but would, for the most part, when he was free from military duty, assist and help him himself to dress it. When he was with the army, he used to drink only water; unless, perhaps, when extremely thirsty, he might mingle it with a little vinegar; or if he found his strength fail him, take a little wine.

The little country house of Manius Curius, who had been thrice carried in triumph, happened to be near his farm; so that often going thither, and contemplating the small compass of the place, and plainness of the dwelling, he formed an idea of the mind of the person, who, being one of the greatest of the Romans, and having subdued the most warlike nations, nay, had driven Pyrrhus out of Italy, now, after three triumphs, was contented to dig in so small a piece of ground, and live in such a cottage. Here it was that the ambassadors of the Samnites, finding him boiling turnips in the chimney corner, offered him a present of gold; but he sent them away with this saying; that he, who was content with such a supper, had no need of gold; and that he thought it more honorable to conquer those who possessed the gold, than to possess the gold itself. Cato, after reflecting upon these things, used to return, and reviewing his own farm, his servants, and housekeeping, increase his labor, and retrench all superfluous expenses.

.   .   .

He himself says, that he never wore a suit of clothes which cost more than a hundred drachmas; and that, when he was general and consul, he drank the same wine which his workmen did; and that the meat or fish which was bought in the market for his dinner, did not cost above thirty *asses*. All which was for the sake of the commonwealth, that so his body might be the hardier for the war. Having a piece of embroidered Babylonian tapestry left him, he sold it; because none of his farm-houses were so much as plastered. Nor did he ever buy a slave for above fifteen hundred drachmas; as he did not seek for effeminate and handsome ones, but able, sturdy workmen, horse-keepers and cow-herds: and these he thought ought to be sold again, when they grew old, and no useless servants fed in a house. In short, he reckoned nothing a good bargain, which was superfluous; but whatever it was, though sold for a farthing, he would think it a great price, if you had no need of it; and was for the purchase of lands for sowing and feeding, rather than grounds for sweeping and watering.

Some imputed these things to petty avarice, but others approved of him, as if he had only the more strictly denied himself for the rectifying and amending of others. Yet certainly, in my judgment, it marks an over-rigid temper, for a man to take the work out of his servants as out of brute beasts, turning them off and selling them in their old age, and thinking there ought to be no further commerce between man and man, than whilst there arises some profit by it. . . . As to myself, I would not so much as sell my draught ox on the account of his age, much less for a small piece of money sell a poor old man, and so chase him, as it were, from his own country, by turning him not only out of the place where he has lived a long while, but also out of the manner of living he has been accustomed to, and that more especially when he would be as useless to the buyer as to the seller. Yet Cato for all this glories that he left that very horse in Spain, which he used in the wars when he was consul, only because he would not put the public to the charge of his freight. Whether these acts are to be ascribed to the greatness or pettiness of his spirit, let every one argue as they please.

For his general temperance, however, and self-control, he really deserves the highest admiration. For when he commanded the army, he never took for himself, and those that belonged to him, above three bushels of wheat for a month, and somewhat less than a bushel and a half a day of barley for his baggage-cattle. And when he entered upon the government of Sardinia, where his predecessors had been used to require tents, bedding, and clothes upon the public account, and to charge the state heavily with the cost of provisions and entertainments for a great train of servants and friends, the difference he showed in his economy was something incredible. There was nothing of any sort for which he put the public to expense; he would walk without a carriage to visit the cities, with one only of the common town officers, who carried his dress, and a cup to offer libation with. Yet, though he seemed thus easy and sparing to all who were under his power, he, on the other hand, showed most inflexible severity and strictness, in what related to public justice, and was rigorous and precise in what concerned the ordinances of the commonwealth; so that the Roman government, never seemed more terrible, nor yet more mild, than under his administration.

. . .

He was also a good father, an excellent husband to his wife, and an extraordinary economist; and as he did not manage his affairs of this kind carelessly, and as things of little moment, I think I ought to record a little further whatever was commendable in him in these points. He married a wife more noble than rich; being of opinion, that the rich and the high-born are equally haughty and proud; but that those of noble blood, would be more ashamed of base things, and consequently more obedient to their husbands in all that was fit and right. A man who beat his wife or child, laid violent hands, he said, on what was most sacred; and a good husband he reckoned worthy of more praise than a great senator; and he admired the ancient Socrates for nothing so much, as for having lived a temperate and contented life with a wife who was a scold, and children who were half-witted.

As soon as he had a son born, though he had never such urgent business upon his hands, unless it were some public matter, he would be by when his wife washed it, and dressed it in its swaddling clothes. For she herself suckled it, nay, she often too gave her breast to her servants' children, to produce, by sucking the same milk, a

kind of natural love in them to her son. When he began to come
to years of discretion, Cato himself would teach him to read, although he had a servant, a very good grammarian, called Chilo,
who taught many others; but he thought not fit, as he himself said,
to have his son reprimanded by a slave, or pulled, it may be, by
the ears when found tardy in his lesson: nor would he have him
owe to a servant the obligaton of so great a thing as his learning;
he himself, therefore, (as we were saying,) taught him his grammar,
law, and his gymnastic exercises. Nor did he only show him, too,
how to throw a dart, to fight in armor, and to ride, but to box
also and to endure both heat and cold, and to swim over the most
rapid and rough rivers. He says, likewise, that he wrote histories, in
large characters, with his own hand, that so his son, without stirring
out of the house, might learn to know about his countrymen and
forefathers: nor did he less abstain from speaking any thing obscene
before his son, than if it had been in the presence of the sacred
virgins, called vestals. Nor would he ever go into the bath with
him; which seems indeed to have been the common custom of the
Romans. Sons-in-law used to avoid bathing with fathers-in-law,
disliking to see one another naked: but having, in time, learned
of the Greeks to strip before men, they have since taught the Greeks
to do it even with the women themselves.

Thus, like an excellent work, Cato formed and fashioned his
son to virtue; nor had he any occasion to find fault with his readiness and docility; but as he proved to be of too weak a constitution
for hardships, he did not insist on requiring of him any very austere
way of living. However, though delicate in health, he proved a
stout man in the field, and behaved himself valiantly when Paulus
Aemilius fought against Perseus. . . . Afterwards he married Ter-
tia, Aemilius Paulus's daughter, and sister to Scipio; nor was he
admitted into this family less for his own worth than his father's.
So that Cato's care in his son's education came to a very fitting
result.

He purchased a great many slaves out of the captives taken in
war, but chiefly bought up the young ones, who were capable to
be, as it were, broken and taught like whelps and colts. None of
these ever entered another man's house, except sent either by Cato
himself or his wife. If any one of them were asked what Cato did,
they answered merely, that they did not know. When a servant
was at home, he was obliged either to do some work or sleep; for

indeed Cato loved those most who used to lie down often to sleep, accounting them more docile than those who were wakeful, and more fit for any thing when they were refreshed with a little slumber. Being also of opinion, that the great cause of the laziness and mis- behavior of slaves was their running after their pleasures, he fixed a certain price for them to pay for permission amongst themselves, but would suffer no connections out of the house. At first, when he was but a poor soldier, he would not be difficult in any thing which related to his eating, but looked upon it as a pitiful thing to quarrel with a servant for the belly's sake; but afterwards, when he grew richer, and made any feasts for his friends and colleagues in office, as soon as supper was over he used to go with a leathern thong and scourge those who had waited or dressed the meat carelessly. He always contrived, too, that his servants should have some difference one among another, always suspecting and fearing a good understanding between them. Those who had committed any thing worthy of death, he punished, if they were found guilty by the verdict of their fellow-servants. But being after all much given to the desire of gain, he looked upon agriculture rather as a pleasure than profit; resolving, therefore, to lay out his money in safe and solid things, he purchased ponds, hot baths, grounds full of fuller's earth, remunerative lands, pastures, and woods; from all which he drew large returns, nor could Jupiter himself, he used to say, do him much damage. He was also given to the form of usury, which is considered most odious, in traffic by sea; and that thus:—he desired that those whom he put out his money to, should have many partners; and when the number of them and their ships came to be fifty, he himself took one share through Quintio his freedman, who therefore was to sail with the adventurers, and take a part in all their proceedings; so that thus there was no danger of losing his whole stock, but only a little part, and that with a prospect of great profit. He likewise lent money to those of his slaves who wished to borrow, with which they bought also other young ones, whom, when they had taught and bred up at his charges, they would sell again at the year's end; but some of them Cato would keep for himself, giving just as much for them as another had offered. To incline his son to be of this kind of temper, he used to tell him, that it was not like a man, but rather like a widow woman, to lessen an estate. But the strongest indication of Cato's avaricious humor was when he took the boldness to affirm, that

he was a most wonderful, nay, a godlike man, who left more behind him than he had received.

He was now grown old, when Carneades the Academic, and
Diogenes the Stoic, came as deputies from Athens to Rome, praying for release from a penalty of five hundred talents laid on the
Athenians, in a suit, to which they did not appear, in which the
Oropians were plaintiffs, and Sicyonians judges. All the most studious youth immediately waited on these philosophers, and frequently, with admiration, heard them speak. But the gracefulness
of Carneades's oratory, whose ability was really greatest, and his
reputation equal to it, gathered large and favorable audiences,
and erelong filled, like a wind, all the city with the sound of it.
So that it soon began to be told, that a Greek, famous even to
admiration, winning and carrying all before him, had impressed so
strange a love upon the young men, that quitting all their pleasures
and pastimes, they ran mad, as it were, after philosophy; which indeed much pleased the Romans in general; nor could they but with
much pleasure see the youth receive so welcomely the Greek literature, and frequent the company of learned men. But Cato, on the
other side, seeing this passion for words flowing into the city,
from the beginning, took it ill, fearing lest the youth should be
diverted that way, and so should prefer the glory of speaking well
before that of arms, and doing well. And when the fame of the
philosophers increased in the city, and Caius Acilius, a person of
distinction, at his own request, became their interpreter to the
senate at their first audience, Cato resolved, under some specious
pretence, to have all philosophers cleared out of the city; and, coming into the senate, blamed the magistrates for letting these deputies
stay so long a time without being despatched, though they were
persons that could easily persuade the people to what they pleased;
that therefore in all haste something should be determined about
their petition, that so they might go home again to their own
schools, and declaim to the Greek children, and leave the Roman
youth, to be obedient, as hitherto, to their own laws and governors.

Yet he did this not out of any anger, as some think, to Carneades;
but because he wholly despised philosophy, and out of a kind of
pride, scoffed at the Greek studies and literature; as, for example,
he would say, that Socrates was a prating seditious fellow, who did
his best to tyrannize over his country, to undermine the ancient
customs, and to entice and withdraw the citizens to opinions con-

trary to the laws. Ridiculing the school of Isocrates, he would add, that his scholars grew old men before they had done learning with him, as if they were to use their art and plead causes in the court of Minos in the next world. And to frighten his son from any thing that was Greek, in a more vehement tone than became one of his age, he pronounced, as it were, with the voice of an oracle, that the Romans would certainly be destroyed when they began once to be infected with Greek literature; though time indeed has shown the vanity of this his prophecy; as, in truth, the city of Rome has risen to its highest fortune, while entertaining Grecian learning.

Nor had he an aversion only against the Greek philosophers, but the physicians also; for having, it seems, heard how Hippocrates, when the king of Persia sent for him, with offers of a fee of several talents, said, that he would never assist barbarians who were enemies to the Greeks; he affirmed, that this was now become a common oath taken by all physicians, and enjoined his son to have a care and avoid them; for that he himself had written a little book of prescriptions for curing those who were sick in his family; he never enjoined fasting to any one, but ordered them either vegetables, or the meat of a duck, pigeon, or leveret; such kind of diet being of light digestion, and fit for sick folks, only it made those who ate it, dream a little too much; and by the use of this kind of physic, he said, he not only made himself and those about him well, but kept them so.

•   •   •

Some will have the overthrow of Carthage to have been one of his last acts of state; when, indeed, Scipio the younger, did by his valor give it the last blow, but the war, chiefly by the counsel and advice of Cato, was undertaken on the following occasion. Cato was sent to the Carthaginians and Masinissa, king of Numidia, who were at war with one another, to know the cause of their difference. He, it seems, had been a friend of the Romans from the beginning; and they, too, since they were conquered by Scipio, were of the Roman confederacy, having been shorn of their power by loss of territory, and a heavy tax. Finding Carthage, not (as the Romans thought) low and in an ill condition, but well manned, full of riches and all sorts of arms and ammunition, and perceiving the Carthaginians carry it high, he conceived that it was not a time for the Romans to adjust affairs between them and Masinissa;

but rather that they themselves would fall into danger, unless they should find means to check this rapid new growth of Rome's ancient irreconcilable enemy. Therefore, returning quickly to Rome, he acquainted the senate, that the former defeats and blows given to the Carthaginians, had not so much diminished their strength, as it had abated their imprudence and folly; that they were not become weaker, but more experienced in war, and did only skirmish with the Numidians, to exercise themselves the better to cope with the Romans: that the peace and league they had made was but a kind of suspension of war which awaited a fairer opportunity to break out again.

Moreover, they say that, shaking his gown, he took occasion to let drop some African figs before the senate. And on their admiring the size and beauty of them, he presently added, that the place that bore them was but three days' sail from Rome. Nay, he never after this gave his opinion, but at the end he would be sure to come out with this sentence, "Also, Carthage, methinks, ought utterly to be destroyed." . . . For seeing his countrymen to be grown wanton and insolent, and the people made, by their prosperity, obstinate and disobedient to the senate, and drawing the whole city, whither they would, after them, he would have had the fear of Carthage to serve as a bit to hold in the contumacy of the multitude; and he looked upon the Carthaginians as too weak to overcome the Romans, and too great to be despised by them. On the other side, it seemed a perilous thing to Cato, that a city which had been always great, and was now grown sober and wise, by reason of its former calamities, should still lie, as it were, in wait for the follies and dangerous excesses of the overpowerful Roman people; so that he thought it the wisest course to have all outward dangers removed, when they had so many inward ones among themselves.

Cicero

================================ 11 ================================

De Legibus

With Cicero we come not only to the vastly wider world of Rome but to
Rome in the golden age of its literature (70 B.C.–14 A.D.). Cicero gave perfect expression to the dominant tradition of classical man, for all his
works—oratorical, philosophical, epistolary, and poetic—are pervaded by
the highest sense of public interest and duty. We find in them also a
supreme regard for *humanitas,* a word coined by Cicero, meaning the
mental and moral qualities that make for civilized living.

Marcus Tullius Cicero (106–43 B.C.) was born in Arpinum in Latium
to a family of only local note; as a "new man" (the Roman term for a
parvenu), he had to make his way against aristocratic prejudice. After
schooling in Rome, Athens, and Rhodes, he quickly rose to leadership
of the bar; in 63 B.C. he became a consul and later a provincial governor.
After the murder of Caesar in 44 B.C. he backed the senatorial party, and,
as a consequence, the following year he was put to death by the order of
Marcus Antonius, whom he had offended.

Cicero's writings are more voluminous than those of any other author
of ancient times, and his role as selector and transmitter of Greco-Roman
thought and values is of enormous importance. He was a master of Latin
prose and rhetorical form, and his stylistic influence (Ciceronianism), especially strong during the Renaissance, has descended to our own time.

Cicero's *De Legibus* (*On the Laws*), which he began *ca.* 52 B.C. but
never finished, is an exposition of his ideal state in the form of a dialogue
between himself, his brother Quintus, and his friend Pomponius Atticus.
Book I, from which the following selection is drawn, sets forth the thesis
(previously advanced by the Stoic philosophers) that divine justice is the
source of all law, everywhere. Existing codes and statutes, constituting

Cicero, *De Legibus,* trans. Clinton W. Keyes (Loeb Classical Library—London:
Heinemann and New York: Putnam, 1928), 311, 313, 315, 317, 319, 321, 323,
325, 327, 329, 331, 333, 335, 341, 343, 345, 347, 351, 353. Reprinted by permission
of Harvard University Press.

"positive" law, therefore derive their validity and justification from this "higher" or "natural" law, which is also identical with right reason. This doctrine of natural law, with its ideals of freedom and equality, was to have a long and influential life, becoming the *jus naturale* of Roman jurisprudence, finding embodiment in the laws of the medieval Church, and reaching its acme of influence in the the eighteenth century—as the foundation for the American and French Revolutions.

ATTICUS   Why do you not, then, in the present "odds and ends of time," as you call them, expound this very subject to us, and compose a treatise on the civil law, going into it more deeply than your predecessors? For I remember that you were interested in law even in your early youth, when I too was studying with Scaevola, and it has never seemed to me that you have become so absorbed in oratory as to turn your back completely upon the civil law.

MARCUS   You are urging me to a long discussion, Atticus, but nevertheless I will undertake it, unless Quintus prefers some other occupation; and, as we are at leisure, I will state my views on this topic.

QUINTUS   I should be very glad to listen to you; for what occupation could I prefer, or how could I spend the day more profitably?

M.   Then let us go to those promenades and seats of ours, so that when we have enough of walking, we may rest. Surely we shall not lack entertainment as we take up one question after another.

A.   We agree; and indeed, if you approve, we might walk here by the Liris, in the shade along its bank. But kindly begin without delay the statement of your opinions on the civil law.

M.   My opinions? Well then, I believe that there have been most eminent men in our State whose customary function it was to interpret the law to the people and answer questions in regard to it, but that these men, though they have made great claims, have spent their time on unimportant details. What subject indeed is so vast as the law of the State? But what is so trivial as the task of those who give legal advice? It is, however, necessary for the people. But, while I do not consider that those who have applied themselves to this profession have lacked a conception of universal law, yet they have carried their studies of this civil law, as it is called, only far enough to accomplish their purpose of being useful to the people. Now all this amounts to little so far as learning is concerned, though for practical purposes it is indispensable. What subject is it, then, that you are asking me to expound? To what task are you urging me? Do you want me to write a treatise on the law of eaves and house-walls? Or to compose formulas for contracts and court procedure? These subjects have been carefully treated by many writers, and are of a humbler character, I believe, than what is expected of me.

A. Yet if you ask what I expect of you, I consider it a logical thing that, since you have already written a treatise on the constitution of the ideal State, you should also write one on its laws. For I note that this was done by your beloved Plato, whom you admire, revere above all others, and love above all others.

M. Is it your wish, then, that, as he discussed the institutions of States and the ideal laws with Clinias and the Spartan Megillus in Crete on a summer day amid the cypress groves and forest paths of Cnossus, sometimes walking about, sometimes resting—you recall his description—we, in like manner, strolling or taking our ease among these stately poplars on the green and shady river bank, shall discuss the same subjects along somewhat broader lines than the practice of the courts calls for?

A. I should certainly like to hear such a conversation.

M. What does Quintas say?

Q. No other subject would suit me better.

M. And you are wise, for you must understand that in no other kind of discussion can one bring out so clearly what Nature's gifts to man are, what a wealth of most excellent possessions the human mind enjoys, what the purpose is, to strive after and accomplish which we have been born and placed in this world, what it is that unites men, and what natural fellowship there is among them. For it is only after all these things have been made clear that the origin of Law and Justice can be discovered.

A. Then you do not think that the science of law is to be derived from the praetor's edict, as the majority do now, or from the Twelve Tables, as people used to think, but from the deepest mysteries of philosophy?

M. Quite right; for in our present conversation, Pomponius, we are not trying to learn how to protect ourselves legally, or how to answer clients' questions. Such problems may be important, and in fact they are; for in former times many eminent men made a specialty of their solution, and at present one person performs this duty with the greatest authority and skill. But in our present investigation we intend to cover the whole range of universal Justice and Law in such a way that our own civil law, as it is called, will be confined to a small and narrow corner. For we must explain the nature of Justice, and this must be sought for in the nature of man; we must also consider the laws by which States ought to be governed; then we must deal with the enactments and decrees of nations which are already formulated and put in writing; and among these the civil law, as it is called, of the Roman people will not fail to find a place.

q. You probe deep, and seek, as you should, the very fountain-head, to find what we are after, brother. And those who teach the civil law in any other way are teaching not so much the path of justice as of litigation.

m. There you are mistaken, Quintus, for it is rather ignorance of the law than knowledge of it that leads to litigation. But that will come later; now let us investigate the origins of Justice.

Well then, the most learned men have determined to begin with Law, and it would seem that they are right, if, according to their definition, Law is the highest reason, implanted in Nature, which commands what ought to be done and forbids the opposite. This reason, when firmly fixed and fully developed in the human mind, is Law. And so they believe that Law is intelligence, whose natural function it is to command right conduct and forbid wrongdoing. . . .

Now if this is correct, as I think it to be in general, then the origin of Justice is to be found in Law, for Law is a natural force; it is the mind and reason of the intelligent man, the standard by which Justice and Injustice are measured. But since our whole discussion has to do with the reasoning of the populace, it will sometimes be necessary to speak in the popular manner, and give the name of law to that which in written form decrees whatever it wishes either by command or prohibition. For such is the crowd's definition of law. But in determining what Justice is, let us begin with that supreme Law which had its origin ages before any written law existed or any State had been established.

q. Indeed that will be preferable and more suitable to the character of the conversation we have begun.

M.   Well, then, shall we seek the origin of Justice itself at its fountain-head? For when that is discovered we shall undoubtedly have a standard by which the things we are seeking may be tested.

Q.   I think that is certainly what we must do.

.   .   .

M.   I will not make the argument long. Your admission leads us to this: that animal which we call man, endowed with foresight and quick intelligence, complex, keen, possessing memory, full of reason and prudence, has been given a certain distinguished status by the supreme God who created him; for he is the only one among so many different kinds and varieties of living beings who has a share in reason and thought, while all the rest are deprived of it. But what is more divine, I will not say in man only, but in all heaven and earth, than reason? And reason, when it is full grown and perfected, is rightly called wisdom. Therefore, since there is nothing better than reason, and since it exists both in man and God, the first common possession of man and God is reason. But those who have reason in common must also have right reason in common. And since right reason is Law, we must believe that men have Law also in common with the gods. Further, those who share Law must also share Justice; and those who share these are to be regarded as members of the same commonwealth. If indeed they obey the same authorities and powers, this is true in a far greater degree; but as a matter of fact they do obey this celestial system, the divine mind, and the God of transcendent power. Hence we must now conceive of this whole universe as one commonwealth of which both gods and men are members.

And just as in States distinctions in legal status are made on account of the blood relationships of families, according to a system which I shall take up in its proper place, so in the universe the same thing holds true, but on a scale much vaster and more splendid, so that men are grouped with Gods on the basis of blood relationship and descent.

For when the nature of man is examined, the theory is usually advanced (and in all probability it is correct) that through constant changes and revolutions in the heavens, a time came which was suitable for sowing the seed of the human race. And when this seed was scattered and sown over the earth, it was granted the divine gift of the soul. For while the other elements of which man consists were derived from what is mortal, and are therefore fragile and perishable, the soul was generated in us by God. Hence we are justified in saying that there is a blood relationship between ourselves and the celestial beings; or we may call it a common ancestry or origin. Therefore among all the varieties of living beings, there is no creature except man which has any knowledge of God, and among men themselves there is no race either so highly civilized or so savage as not to know that it must believe in a god, even if it does not know in what sort of god it ought to believe. Thus it is clear that man recognizes God because, in a way, he remembers and recognizes the source from which he sprang.

Moreover, virtue exists in man and God alike, but in no other creature besides; virtue, however, is nothing else than Nature perfected and developed to its highest point; therefore there is a likeness between man and God. As this is true, what relationship could be closer or clearer than this one? For this reason, Nature has lavishly yielded such a wealth of things adapted to man's convenience and use that what she produces seems intended as a gift to us, and not brought forth by chance; and this is true, not only of what the fertile earth bountifully bestows in the form of grain and fruit, but also of the animals; for it is clear that some of them have been created to be man's slaves, some to supply him with their products, and others to serve as his food. Moreover innumerable arts have been discovered through the teachings of Nature; for it is by a skilful imitation of her that reason has acquired the necessities of life. Nature has likewise not only equipped man himself with nimbleness of thought, but has also given him the senses, to be, as it were, his attendants and messengers; she has laid bare the obscure and none too [obvious] meanings of a great many things, to serve as the foundations of knowledge, as we may call them; and she has granted us a bodily form which is convenient and well suited to the human mind. For while she has bent the other creatures down toward their food, she has made man alone erect, and has challenged him to look up toward heaven, as being, so to speak, akin to him, and his first home. In addition, she has so formed his features as to portray therein the character that lies hidden deep within him; for not only do the eyes declare with exceeding clearness the innermost feelings of our hearts, but also the countenance, as we Romans call it, which can be found in no living thing save man, reveals the character. (The Greeks are familiar with the meaning which this

word "countenance" conveys, though they have no name for it.)
I will pass over the special faculties and aptitudes of the other
parts of the body, such as the varying tones of the voice and the
power of speech, which is the most effective promoter of human
intercourse; for all these things are not in keeping with our present
discussion or the time at our disposal; and besides, this topic has
been adequately treated, as it seems to me, by Scipio in the books
which you have read. But, whereas God has begotten and equipped
man, desiring him to be the chief of all created things, it should
now be evident, without going into all the details, that Nature,
alone and unaided, goes a step farther; for, with no guide to point
the way, she starts with those things whose character she has learned
through the rudimentary beginnings of intelligence, and, alone and
unaided, strengthens and perfects the faculty of reason.

A. Ye immortal gods, how far back you go to find the origins of
Justice! And you discourse so eloquently that I not only have no
desire to hasten on to the consideration of the civil law, concerning
which I was expecting you to speak, but I should have no objection
to your spending even the entire day on your present topic; for the
matters which you have taken up, no doubt, merely as preparatory
to another subject, are of greater import than the subject itself to
which they form an introduction.

M. The points which are now being briefly touched upon are
certainly important; but out of all the material of the philosophers'
discussions, surely there comes nothing more valuable than the
full realization that we are born for Justice, and that right is
based, not upon men's opinions, but upon Nature. This fact will
immediately be plain if you once get a clear conception of man's
fellowship and union with his fellow-men. For no single thing is so
like another, so exactly its counterpart, as all of us are to one another. Nay, if bad habits and false beliefs did not twist the weaker
minds and turn them in whatever direction they are incline, no one
would be so like his own self as all men would be like all others.
And so, however, we may define man, a single definition will apply
to all. This is a sufficient proof that there is no difference in kind
between man and man; for if there were, one definition could not
be applicable to all men; and indeed reason, which alone raises us
above the level of the beasts and enables us to draw inferences, to
prove and disprove, to discuss and solve problems, and to come to
conclusions, is certainly common to us all, and, though varying

in what it learns, at least in the capacity to learn it is invariable. For the same things are invariably perceived by the senses, and those things which stimulate the senses, stimulate them in the same way in all men; and those rudimentary beginnings of intelligence to which I have referred, which are imprinted on our minds, are imprinted on all minds alike; and speech, the mind's interpreter, though differing in the choice of words, agrees in the sentiments expressed. In fact, there is no human being of any race who, if he finds a guide, cannot attain to virtue.

The similarity of the human race is clearly marked in its evil tendencies as well as in its goodness. For pleasure also attracts all men; and even though it is an enticement to vice, yet it has some likeness to what is naturally good. For it delights us by its lightness and agreeableness; and for this reason, by an error of thought, it is embraced as something wholesome. It is through a similar misconception that we shun death as though it were a dissolution of nature, and cling to life because it keeps us in the sphere in which we were born; and that we look upon pain as one of the greatest of evils, not only because of its cruelty, but also because it seems to lead to the destruction of nature. In the same way, on account of the similarity between moral worth and renown, those who are publicly honoured are considered happy, while those who do not attain fame are thought miserable. Troubles, joys, desires, and fears haunt the minds of all men without distinction, and even if different men have different beliefs, that does not prove, for example, that it is not the same quality of superstition that besets those races which worship dogs and cats as gods, as that which torments other races. But what nation does not love courtesy, kindliness, gratitude, and remembrance of favours bestowed? What people does not hate and despise the haughty, the wicked, the cruel, and the ungrateful? Inasmuch as these considerations prove to us that the whole human race is bound together in unity, it follows, finally, that knowledge of the principles of right living is what makes men better.

If you approve of what has been said, I will go on to what follows. But if there is anything that you care to have explained, we will take that up first.

A. We have no questions, if I may speak for both of us.

M. The next point, then, is that we are so constituted by Nature as to share the sense of Justice with one another and to pass it on to all men. And in this whole discussion I want it understood that what I shall call Nature is [that which is implanted in us by Nature]; that, however, the corruption caused by bad habits is so great that the sparks of fire, so to speak, which Nature has kindled in us are extinguished by this corruption, and the vices which are their opposites spring up and are established. But if the judgments of men were in agreement with Nature, so that, as the poet says, they considered "nothing alien to them which concerns mankind," then Justice would be equally observed by all. For those creatures who have received the gift of reason from Nature have also received right reason, and therefore they have also received the gift of Law, which is right reason applied to command and prohibition. And if they have received Law, they have received Justice also. Now all men have received reason; therefore all men have received Justice. Consequently Socrates was right when he cursed, as he often did, the man who first separated utility from Justice; for this separation, he complained, is the source of all mischief. For what gave rise to Pythagoras' famous words about friendship? . . . From this it is clear that, when a wise man shows toward another endowed with equal virtue the kind of benevolence which is so widely diffused among men, that will then have come to pass which, unbelievable as it seems to some, is after all the inevitable result—namely, that he loves himself no whit more than he loves another. For what difference can there be among things which are all equal? But if the least distinction should be made in friendship, then the very name of friendship would perish forthwith; for its essence is such that, as soon as either friend prefers anything for himself, friendship ceases to exist.

Now all this is really a preface to what remains to be said in our discussion, and its purpose is to make it more easily understood that Justice is inherent in Nature. After I have said a few words more on this topic, I shall go on to the civil law, the subject which gives rise to all this discourse.

.   .   .

But if it were a penalty and not Nature that ought to keep men from injustice, what anxiety would there be to trouble the wicked when the danger of punishment was removed? But in fact there has never been a villain so brazen as not to deny that he had committed a crime, or else invent some story of just anger to excuse its commission, and seek justification for his crime in some natural principle of right. Now if even the wicked dare to appeal to such principles, how jealously should they be guarded by the good! But if it is a penalty, the fear of punishment, and not the wickedness itself, that is to keep men from a life of wrongdoing and crime, then no one can be called unjust, and wicked men ought rather to be regarded as imprudent; furthermore, those of us who are not influenced by virtue itself to be good men, but by some consideration of utility and profit, are merely shrewd, not good. For to what lengths will that man go in the dark who fears nothing but a witness and a judge? What will he do if, in some desolate spot, he meets a helpless man, unattended, whom he can rob of a fortune? Our virtuous man, who is just and good by nature, will talk with such a person, help him, and guide him on his way; but the other, who does nothing for another's sake, and measures every act by the standard of his own advantage—it is clear enough, I think, what he will do! If, however, the latter does deny that he would kill the man and rob him of his money, he will not deny it because he regards it as a naturally wicked thing to do, but because he is afraid that his crime may become known—that is, that he may get into trouble. Oh, what a motive, that might well bring a blush of shame to the cheek, not merely of the philosopher, but even of the simple rustic!

But the most foolish notion of all is the belief that everything is just which is found in the customs or laws of nations. Would that be true, even if these laws had been enacted by tyrants? If the well-known Thirty had desired to enact a set of laws at Athens, or if the Athenians without exception were delighted by the tyrants' laws, that would not entitle such laws to be regarded as just, would it? No more, in my opinion, should that law be considered just which a Roman interrex proposed, to the effect that a dictator might put to death with impunity any citizen he wished, even without a trial. For Justice is one; it binds all human society, and is based on one Law, which is right reason applied to command and prohibition. Whoever knows not this Law, whether it has been recorded in writing anywhere or not, is without Justice.

But if Justice is conformity to written laws and national customs, and if, as the same persons claim, everything is to be tested by the standard of utility, then anyone who thinks it will be profitable to him will, if he is able, disregard and violate the laws. It follows that Justice does not exist at all, if it does not exist in Nature, and if that form of it which is based on utility can be overthrown by that very utility itself. And if Nature is not to be considered the foundation of Justice, that will mean the destruction [of the virtues on which human society depends]. For where then will there be a place for generosity, or love of country, or loyalty, or the inclination to be of service to others or to show gratitude for favours received? For these virtues originate in our natural inclination to love our fellow-men, and this is the foundation of Justice. Otherwise not merely consideration for men but also rites and pious observances in honour of the gods are done away with; for I think that these ought to be maintained, not through fear, but on account of the close relationship which exists between man and God. But if the principles of Justice were founded on the decrees of peoples, the edicts of princes, or the decisions of judges, then Justice would sanction robbery and adultery and forgery of wills, in case these acts were approved by the votes or decrees of the populace. But if so great a power belongs to the decisions and decrees of fools that the laws of Nature can be changed by their votes, then why do they not ordain that what is bad and baneful shall be considered good and salutary? Or, if a law can make Justice out of Injustice, can it not also make good out of bad? But in fact we can perceive the difference between good laws and bad by referring them to no other standard than Nature; indeed, it is not merely Justice and Injustice which are distinguished by Nature, but also and without exception things which are honourable and dishonourable. For since an intelligence common to us all makes things known to us and formulates them in our minds, honourable actions are ascribed by us to virtue, and dishonourable actions to vice; and only a madman would conclude that these judgments are matters of opinion, and not fixed by Nature.

. . .

To close now our discussion of this whole subject, the conclusion, which stands clearly before our eyes from what has already been said, is this: Justice and all things honourable are to be sought for their own sake. And indeed all good men love fairness in itself and Justice in itself, and it is unnatural for a good man to make such a mistake as to love what does not deserve love for itself alone. Therefore Justice must be sought and cultivated for her own sake; and if this is true of Justice, it is also true of equity; and if this is the case with equity, then all the other virtues are also to be cherished for their own sake. What of generosity? Is it disinterested or does it look to a recompense? If a man is kind without any reward, then it is disinterested; but if he receives payment then it is hired. It cannot be doubted that he who is called generous or kind answers the call of duty, not of gain. Therefore equity also demands no reward or price; consequently it is sought for its own sake. And the same motive and purpose characterize all the virtues.

In addition, if it be true that virtue is sought for the sake of other benefits and not for its own sake, there will be only one virtue, which will most properly be called a vice. For in proportion as anyone makes his own advantage absolutely the sole standard of all his actions, to that extent he is absolutely not a good man; therefore those who measure virtue by the reward it brings believe in the existence of no virtue except vice. For where shall we find a kindly man, if no one does a kindness for the sake of anyone else than himself? Who can be considered grateful, if even those who repay favours have no real consideration for those to whom they repay them? What becomes of that sacred thing, friendship, if even the friend himself is not loved for his own sake, "with the whole heart," as people say? Why, according to this theory, a friend should even be deserted and cast aside as soon as there is no longer hope of benefit and profit from his friendship! But what could be more inhuman than that? If, on the other hand, friendship is to be sought for its own sake, then the society of our fellow-men, fairness, and Justice, are also to be sought for their own sake. If this is not the case then there is no such thing as Justice at all, for the very height of injustice is to seek pay for Justice. But what shall we say of sobriety, moderation, and self-restraint; of modesty, self-respect, and chastity? Is it for fear of disgrace that we should not be wanton, or for fear of the laws and the courts? In that case men are innocent and modest in order to be well spoken of, and they blush in order to gain a good reputation! I am ashamed even to mention chastity! Or rather I am ashamed of those philosophers who believe it honourable to avoid condemnation for a crime without having avoided the crime itself.

Livy

12

The History of Rome

Neither Herodotus nor Thucydides wrote merely to encourage patriotism and ancestral ways. The greatness of the Hellenic founders of history lay in their emphasis upon the spirit of impartial inquiry.

Quite the opposite was true, however, of the great Roman historian, Titus Livius (59 B.C.–17 A.D.). Livy was born at Patavium (the modern Padua) in northern Italy. Apparently of aristocratic stock, he seems to have had the means to devote his long life to the writing of *The History of Rome,* or, as he called it, *From the Founding of the City.* This prose epic traces the story of Rome from the mythical Father Aeneas to Livy's time.

His upbringing in an old-fashioned country town seems to have instilled in him an enduring love of the simple life and traditional moral discipline—a rare virtue in Rome during the ugly last years of the Republic. Thus equipped, Livy was thoroughly in harmony with the official moral and religious revival promoted by the Emperor Augustus, and the two men came to be and remained on terms of friendly intimacy.

Livy's *History,* then, is a long glorification of the Roman Republic; of its heroes, such as King Romulus, Lucius Junius Brutus, and Titus Manlius Torquatus; and of its heroines, such as Lucretia, whose characters and deeds are celebrated in the following selection. Livy's picture of the hazy past of Rome is often fabulous and always idealized, and his use of source material is uncritical. He lacked the practical knowledge of war and politics necessary to describe the rise of a community of soldier-farmers to world domination. But a scholarly treatise was not what he intended; rather, he created a morally edifying work of literature. Livy hoped that its style and content would inspire his countrymen to imitate the high old Roman virtues, arouse their sense of national destiny, and seal their determination to rule the world.

Livy, *The History of Rome,* trans. D. Spillan (London: Bell & Daldy, 1850–1872), I, 2–4, 8–11, 14–16, 65, 71–78, 510–13.

Whether in tracing the history of the Roman people, from the foundation of the city, I shall employ myself to a useful purpose, I am neither very certain, nor, if I were, dare I say: inasmuch as I observe, that it is both an old and hackneyed practice, later authors always supposing that they will either adduce something more authentic in the facts, or, that they will excel the less polished ancients in their style of writing.

Be that as it may, it will, all events, be a satisfaction to me, that I too have contributed my share to perpetuate the achievements of a people, the lords of the world; and if, amidst so great a number of historians, my reputation should remain in obscurity, I may console myself with the celebrity and lustre of those who shall stand in the way of my fame. Moreover, the subject is both of immense labour, as being one which must be traced back for more than seven hundred years, and which, having set out from small beginnings, has increased to such a degree that it is now distressed by its own magnitude.

And, to most readers, I doubt not but that the first origin and the events immediately succeeding, will afford but little pleasure, while they will be hastening to these later times, in which the strength of this overgrown people has for a long period been working its own destruction. I, on the contrary, shall seek this, as a reward of my labour, viz. to withdraw myself from the view of the calamities, which our age has witnessed for so many years, so long as I am reviewing with my whole attention these ancient times, being free from every care that may distract a writer's mind, though it cannot warp it from the truth.

The traditions which have come down to us of what happened before the building of the city, or before its building was contemplated, as being suitable rather to the fictions of poetry than to the genuine records of history, I have no intention either to affirm or refute. This indulgence is conceded to antiquity, that by blending things human with divine, it may make the origin of cities appear more venerable; and if any people might be allowed to consecrate their origin, and to ascribe it to the gods as its authors, such is the renown of the Roman people in war, that when they represent Mars, in particular, as their own parent and that of their founder, the nations of the world may submit to this as patiently as they submit to their sovereignty.

But in whatever way these and such like matters shall be attended to, or judged of, I shall not deem of great importance. I would have every man apply his mind seriously to consider these points, viz. what their life and what their manners were; through what men and by what measures, both in peace and in war, their empire was acquired and extended; then, as discipline gradually declined, let him follow in his thoughts their morals, at first as slightly giving way, anon how they sunk more and more, then began to fall head-long, until he reaches the present times, when we can neither endure our vices, nor their remedies. This it is which is particularly salutary and profitable in the study of history, that you behold instances of every variety of conduct displayed on a conspicuous monument; that from thence you may select for yourself and for your country that which you may imitate; thence *note* what is shameful in the undertaking, and shameful in the result, which you may avoid. But either a fond partiality for the task I have undertaken deceives me, or there never was any state either greater, or more moral, or richer in good examples, nor one into which luxury and avarice made their entrance so late, and where poverty and frugality were so much and so long honoured; so that the less wealth there was, the less desire was there. Of late, riches have introduced avarice, and excessive pleasures a longing for them, amidst luxury and a passion for ruining ourselves and destroying every thing else. But let complaints, which will not be agreeable even then, when perhaps they will be also necessary, be kept aloof at least from the first stage of commencing so great a work. We should rather, if it was usual with us (historians) as it is with poets, begin with good omens, vows and prayers to the gods and goddesses to vouchsafe good success to our efforts in so arduous an undertaking.

. . .

In my opinion, the origin of so great a city, and the establishment of an empire next in power to that of the gods, was due to the Fates. The vestal Rhea, being deflowered by force, when she had brought forth twins, declares Mars to be the father of her illegitimate off-spring, either because she believed it to be so, or because a god was a more creditable author of her offence. But neither gods nor men protect her or her children from the king's cruelty: the priestess is bound and thrown into prison; the children he commands to be thrown into the current of the river. By some interposition of providence, the Tiber having overflowed its banks in stagnant pools, did not admit of any access to the regular bed of the river; and the bearers supposed that the infants could be drowned in water however still; thus, as if they had effectually executed the king's orders, they expose the boys in the nearest land-flood, where now stands the ficus Ruminalis (they say that it was called Romularis).

The country thereabout was then a vast wilderness. The tradition is, that when the water, subsiding, had left the floating trough, in which the children had been exposed, on dry ground, a thirsty she-wolf, coming from the neighbouring mountains, directed her course to the cries of the infants, and that she held down her dugs to them with so much gentleness, that the keeper of the king's flock found her licking the boys with her tongue. It is said his name was Faustulus; and that they were carried by him to his homestead to be nursed by his wife Laurentia. Some are of opinion that she was called Lupa among the shepherds, from her being a common prostitute, and that this gave rise to the surprising story. The children thus born and thus brought up, when arrived at the years of manhood, did not loiter away their time in tending the folds or following the flocks, but roamed and hunted in the forests. Having by this exercise improved their strength and courage, they not only encountered wild beasts, but even attacked robbers laden with plunder, and afterwards divided the spoil among the shepherds. And in company with these, the number of their young associates daily increasing, they carried on their business and their sports.

They say, that the festival of the lupercal, as now celebrated, was even at that time solemnized on the Palatine hill . . . in such manner, that young men ran about naked in sport and wantonness, doing honour to Pan Lycaeus, whom the Romans afterwards called Inuus. That the robbers, through rage at the loss of their booty, having lain in wait for them whilst intent on this sport, as the festival was now well known, whilst Romulus vigorously defended himself, took Remus prisoner; that they delivered him up, when taken, to king Amulius, accusing him with the utmost effrontery. They principally alleged it as a charge against them, that they had made incursions upon Numitor's lands, and plundered them in a hostile manner, having assembled a band of young men for the purpose. Upon this Remus was delivered to Numitor to be punished.

Now, from the very first, Faustulus had entertained hopes that the boys whom he was bringing up were of the blood royal; for he both knew that the children had been exposed by the king's orders, and that the time at which he had taken them up agreed exactly with that period: but he had been unwilling that the matter, as not being yet ripe for discovery, should be disclosed, till either a fit opportunity or necessity should arise. Necessity came first; accordingly, compelled by fear, he discovers the whole affair to Romulus. By accident also, whilst he had Remus in custody, and had heard that the brothers were twins, on comparing their age, and *observing* their turn of mind entirely free from servility, the recollection of his grand-children struck Numitor; and on making inquiries he arrived at the same conclusion, so that he was well nigh recognising Remus. Thus a plot is concerted for the king on all sides. Romulus, not accompanied by a body of young men, (for he was unequal to open force,) but having commanded the shepherds to come to the palace by different roads at a fixed time, forces his way to the king; and Remus, with another party from Numitor's house, assists his brother, and so they kill the king.

Numitor . . . when he saw the young men, after they had killed the king, advancing to congratulate him, immediately called an assembly of the people, and represented to them the unnatural behaviour of his brother towards him, the extraction of his grand-children, the manner of their birth and education, and how they came to be discovered; then he informed them of the king's death, and that he was killed by his orders. When the young princes, coming up with their band through the middle of the assembly, saluted their grandfather king, an approving shout, following from all the people present, ratified to him both that title and the sovereignty.

Thus the government of Alba being committed to Numitor, a desire seized Romulus and Remus to build a city on the spot where they had been exposed and brought up. And there was an overflowing population of Albans and of Latins. The shepherds too had come into that design, and all these readily inspired hopes, that Alba and Lavinium would be but petty places in comparison with the city which they intended to build. But ambition of the sovereignty, the bane of their grandfather, interrupted these designs, and thence arose a shameful quarrel from a beginning sufficiently amicable. For as they were twins, and the respect due to seniority could not determine the point, they agreed to leave to the tutelary gods of the place to choose, by augury, which should give a name to the new city, which govern it when built.

Romulus chose the Palatine and Remus the Aventine hill as their stands to make their observations. It is said, that to Remus an omen came first, six vultures; and now, the omen having been declared, when double the number presented itself to Romulus, his own party saluted each king; the former claimed the kingdom on the ground of priority of time, the latter on account of the number of birds. Upon this, having met in an altercation, from the contest of angry feelings they turn to bloodshed; there Remus fell from a blow received in the crowd. A more common account is, that Remus, in derision of his brother, leaped over his new-built wall, and was, for that reason, slain by Romulus in a passion; who, after sharply chiding him, added words to this effect: "So shall every one fare, who shall dare to leap over my fortifications." Thus Romulus got the sovereignty to himself; the city, when built, was called after the name of its founder.

. . .

And now the Roman state was become so powerful, that it was a match for any of the neighbouring nations in war, but, from the paucity of women, its greatness could only last for one age of man; for they had no hope of issue at home, nor had they any intermarriages with their neighbours. Therefore, by the advice of the Fathers, Romulus sent ambassadors to the neighbouring states to solicit an alliance and the privilege of intermarriage for his new subjects. . . .

No where did the embassy obtain a favourable hearing: so much did they at the same time despise, and dread for themselves and their posterity, so great a power growing up in the midst of them. They were dismissed by the greater part with the repeated question, "Whether they had opened any asylum for women also, for that such a plan only could obtain them suitable matches?"

The Roman youth resented this conduct bitterly, and the matter unquestionably began to point towards violence. Romulus, in order that he might afford a favourable time and place for this, dissembling his resentment, purposely prepares games in honour of Neptunus Equestris; he calls them Consualia. He then orders the spectacle to be proclaimed among their neighbours; and they prepare for the celebration with all the magnificence they were then acquainted with, or were capable of doing, that they might render the matter famous, and an object of expectation. Great numbers assembled, from a desire also of seeing the new city; especially their nearest neighbours, the Caeninenses, Crustumini, and Antemnates. Moreover the whole multitude of the Sabines came, with their wives and children. Having been hospitably invited to the different houses, when they had seen the situation, and fortifications, and the city crowded with houses, they became astonished that the Roman power had increased so rapidly.

When the time of the spectacle came on, and while their minds and eyes were intent upon it, according to concert a tumult began, and upon a signal given the Roman youth ran different ways to carry off the virgins by force. A great number were carried off at hap-hazard, according as they fell into their hands. Persons from the common people, who had been charged with the task, conveyed to their houses some women of surpassing beauty, destined for the leading senators. . . .

The festival being disturbed by this alarm, the parents of the young women retire in grief, appealing to the compact of violated hospitality, and invoking the god, to whose festival and games they had come, deceived by the pretence of religion and good faith. Neither had the ravished virgins better hopes of their condition, or less indignation. But Romulus in person went about and declared, "That what was done was owing to the pride of their fathers, who had refused to grant the privilage of marriage to their neighbours; but notwithstanding, they should be joined in lawful wedlock, participate in all their possessions and civil privileges, and, than which nothing can be dearer to the human heart, in their common children. He begged them only to assuage the fierceness of their anger, and cheerfully surrender their affections to those to whom fortune had consigned their persons." [He added,] "That from injuries love and friendship often arise; and that they should find them kinder husbands on this account, because each of them, besides the performance of his conjugal duty, would endeavour to the utmost of his power to make up for the want of their parents and native country." To this the caresses of the husbands were added, excusing what they had done on the plea of passion and love, arguments that work most successfully on women's hearts.

. . . . .

After this period Tarquin began his reign, whose actions pro-
cured him the surname of the Proud. . . . He surrounded his person with armed men, for he had no claim to the kingdom except
force, inasmuch as he reigned without either the order of the people
or the sanction of the senate. To this was added (the fact) that, as
he reposed no hope in the affection of his subjects, he found it
necessary to secure his kingdom by terror; and in order to strike
this into the greater number, he took cognizance of capital cases
solely by himself without assessors; and under that pretext he had
it in his power to put to death, banish, or fine, not only those who
were suspected or hated, but those also from whom he could obtain
nothing else but plunder. The number of the fathers more especially being thus diminished, he determined to elect none into the
senate, in order that the order might become contemptible by their
very paucity, and that they might feel the less resentment at no
business being transacted by them. For he was the first king who
violated the custom derived from his predecessors of consulting the
senate on all subjects; he administered the public business by
domestic counsels. War, peace, treaties, alliances, he contracted and
dissolved with whomsoever he pleased, without the sanction of the
people and senate. The nation of the Latins in particular he wished
to attach to him, so that by foreign influence also he might be more
secure among his own subjects; and he contracted not only ties of
hospitality but affinities also with their leading men.

· · ·

Then he turned his thoughts to the business of the city. The
chief whereof was that of leaving behind him the temple of Jupiter
on the Tarpeian mount, as a monument of his name and reign.
. . . It is reported that the head of a man, with the face entire,
appeared to the workmen when digging the foundation of the
temple. The sight of this phenomenon unequivocally presaged
that this temple should be the metropolis of the empire, and the
head of the world; and so declared the soothsayers, both those who
were in the city, and those whom they had sent for from Etruria, to
consult on this subject. . . .

Tarquin, intent upon finishing this temple, having sent for workmen from all parts of Etruria, employed on it not only the public
money, but the manual labour of the people; and when this labour,
by no means inconsiderable in itself, was added to their military

service, still the people murmured less at their building the temples of the gods with their own hands; they were afterwards transferred to other works, which, whilst less in show, (required) still greater toil: such as the erecting benches in the circus, and conducting under ground the principal sewer, the receptacle of all the filth of the city; to which two works even modern splendour can scarcely produce any thing equal. . . .

While he was thus employed a frightful prodigy appeared to him. A serpent sliding out of a wooden pillar, after causing dismay and a run into the palace, not so much struck the king's heart with sudden terror, as filled him with anxious solicitude. Accordingly . . . he determined on sending persons to Delphos to the most celebrated oracle in the world; and not venturing to intrust the responses of the oracle to any other person, he despatched his two sons to Greece through lands unknown at that time, and seas still more so. Titus and Aruns were the two who went. To them were added, as a companion, L. Junius Brutus, the son of Tarquinia, sister to the king, a youth of an entirely different quality of mind from that the disguise of which he had assumed.

Brutus, on hearing that the chief men of the city, and among others his own brother, had been put to death by his uncle, resolved to leave nothing in his intellects that might be dreaded by the king, nor any thing in his fortune to be coveted, and thus to be secure in contempt, where there was but little protection in justice. Therefore designedly fashioning himself to the semblance of foolishness, after he suffered himself and his whole estate to become a prey to the king, he did not refuse to take even the surname of Brutus, that, concealed under the cover of such a cognomen, that genius that was to liberate the Roman people might await its proper time. He, being brought to Delphos by the Tarquinii rather as a subject of sport than as a companion, is said to have brought with him as an offering to Apollo a golden rod, enclosed in a staff of cornel-wood hollowed out for the purpose, a mystical emblem of his own mind.

When they arrived there, their father's commission being executed, a desire seized the young men of inquiring on which of them the sovereignty of Rome should devolve. They say that a voice was returned from the bottom of the cave, "Young men, whichever of you shall first kiss his mother shall enjoy the sovereign power at Rome." The Tarquinii order the matter to be kept secret with the utmost care, the Sextus, who had been left behind at Rome, might be ignorant of the response, and have no share in the kingdom; they cast lots among themselves, as to which of them should first kiss his mother, after they had returned to Rome. Brutus, thinking that the Pythian response had another meaning, as if he had stumbled and fallen, touched the ground with his lips; she being, forsooth, the common mother of all mankind. After this they all returned to Rome, where preparations were being made with the greatest vigour for a war against the Rutulians.

The Rutulians, a nation very wealthy, considering the country and age they lived in, were at that time in possession of Ardea. Their riches gave occasion to the war; for the king of the Romans, being exhausted of money by the magnificence of his public works, was desirous both to enrich himself, and by a large booty to soothe the minds of his subjects, who, besides other instances of his tyranny, were incensed against his government, because they were indignant that they had been kept so long a time by the king in the employments of mechanics, and in labour fit for slaves.

An attempt was made to take Ardea by storm; when that did not succeed, the enemy began to be distressed by a blockade, and by works raised around them. As it commonly happens in standing camps, the war being rather tedious than violent, furloughs were easily obtained, more so by the officers, however, than the common soldiers. The young princes sometimes spent their leisure hours in feasting and entertainments. One day as they were drinking in the tent of Sextus Tarquin, where Collatinus Tarquinius, the son of Egerius, was also at supper, mention was made of wives. Every one commended his own in an extravagant manner, till a dispute arising about it, Collatinus said, "There was no occasion for words, that it might be known in a few hours how far his Lucretia excelled all the rest. If then, added he, we have any share of the vigour of youth, let us mount our horses and examine the behaviour of our wives; that must be most satisfactory to every one, which shall meet his eyes on the unexpected arrival of the husband." They were heated with wine; "Come on, then," say all. They immediately galloped to Rome, where they arrived in the dusk of the evening. From thence they went to Collatia, where they find Lucretia, not like the king's daughters-in-law, whom they had seen spending their time in luxurious entertainments with their equals, but though at an advanced time of night, employed at her wool, sitting in the middle

of the house amid her maids working around her. The merit of
the contest regarding the ladies was assigned to Lucretia. Her husband on his arrival, and the Tarquinii, were kindly received; the
husband, proud of his victory, gives the young princes a polite in-
vitation. There the villanous passion for violating Lucretia by force
seizes Sextus Tarquin; both her beauty, and her approved purity,
act as incentives. And then, after this youthful frolic of the night,
they return to the camp.

A few days after, without the knowledge of Collatinus, Sextus
came to Collatia with one attendant only; where, being kindly received by them, as not being aware of his intention, after he had
been conducted after supper into the guests' chamber, burning with
passion, when every thing around seem sufficiently secure, and all
fast asleep, he comes to Lucretia, as she lay asleep, with a naked
sword, and with his left hand pressing down the woman's breast, he
says, "Be silent, Lucretia; I am Sextus Tarquin; I have a sword
in my hand; you shall die, if you utter a word." When awaking
terrified from sleep, the woman beheld no aid, impending death
nigh at hand; then Tarquin acknowledged his passion, entreated,
mixed threats with entreaties, tried the female's mind in every
possible way. When he saw her inflexible, and that she was not
moved even by the terror of death, he added to terror the threat of
dishonour; he says that he will lay a murdered slave naked by her
side when dead, so that she may be said to have been slain in infamous adultery.

When by the terror of this disgrace his lust, as it were victorious,
had overcome her inflexible chastity, and Tarquin had departed,
exulting in having triumphed over a lady's honour, Lucretia, in
melancholy distress at so dreadful a misfortune, despatches the same
messenger to Rome to her father, and to Ardea to her husband,
that they would come each with one trusty friend; that it was necessary to do so, and that quickly. Sp. Lucretius comes with P.
Valerius, the son of Volesus, Collatinus with L. Junius Brutus, with
whom, as he was returning to Rome, he happened to be met by
his wife's messenger. They find Lucretia sitting in her chamber in
sorrowful dejection. On the arrival of her friends the tears burst
from her eyes; and to her husband, on his inquiry "whether all was
right," she says, "By no means, for what can be right with a woman
who has lost her honour? The traces of another man are on your
bed, Collatinus. But the body only has been violated, the mind is

guiltless; death shall be my witness. But give me your right hands, and your honour, that the adulterer shall not come off unpunished. It is Sextus Tarquin, who, an enemy in the guise of a guest, has borne away hence a triumph fatal to me, and to himself, if you are men."

They all pledge their honour; they attempt to console her, distracted as she was in mind, by turning away the guilt from her, constrained by force, on the perpetrator of the crime; that it is the mind sins, not the body; and that where intention was wanting guilt could not be. "It is for you to see," says she, "what is due to him. As for me, though I acquit myself of guilt, from punishment I do not discharge myself; nor shall any woman survive her dishonour pleading the example of Lucretia." The knife, which she kept concealed beneath her garment, she plunges into her heart, and falling forward on the wound, she dropped down expiring. The husband and father shriek aloud.

Brutus, while they were overpowered with grief, having drawn the knife out of the wound, and holding it up before him reeking with blood, said, "By this blood, most pure before the pollution of royal villany, I swear, and I call you, O gods, to witness my oath, that I shall pursue Lucius Tarquin the Proud, his wicked wife, and all their race, with fire, sword, and all other means in my power; nor shall I ever suffer them or any other to reign at Rome." Then he gave the knife to Collatinus, and after him to Lucretius and Valerius, who were surprised at such extraordinary mind in the breast of Brutus. However, they all take the oath as they were directed, and converting their sorrow into rage, follow Brutus as their leader, who from that time ceased not to solicit them to abolish the regal power. . . .

Nor does the heinousness of the circumstance excite less violent emotions at Rome than it had done at Collatia; accordingly they run from all parts of the city into the forum, whither, when they came, the public crier summoned them to attend the tribune of the celeres, with which office Brutus happened to be at that time vested. There an harangue was delivered by him, by no means of that feeling and capacity which had been counterfeited up to that day, concerning the violence and lust of Sextus Tarquin, the horrid violation of Lucretia and her lamentable death, the bereavement of Tricipitinus, to whom the cause of his daughter's death was more exasperating and deplorable than the death itself. To this was added the haughty insolence of the king himself, and the sufferings and toils of the people, buried in the earth in cleansing sinks and sewers; that the Romans, the conquerors of all the surrounding states, instead of warriors had become labourers and stone-cutters. . . .

By stating these and other, I suppose, more exasperating circumstances, which though by no means easily detailed by writers, the heinousness of the case suggested at the time, he persuaded the multitude, already incensed, to deprive the king of his authority, and to order the banishment of L. Tarquin with his wife and children. He himself having selected and armed some of the young men, who readily gave in their names, set out for Ardea to the camp to excite the army against the king. . . .

News of these transactions having reached the camp when the king, alarmed at this sudden revolution, was going to Rome to quell the commotions, Brutus, for he had notice of his approach, turned out of the way, that he might not meet him; and much about the same time Brutus and Tarquin arrived by different routes, the one at Ardea, the other at Rome. The gates were shut against Tarquin, and an act of banishment passed against him; the deliverer of the state the camp received with great joy, and the king's sons were expelled. Two of them followed their father, and went into banishment to Caere, a city of Etruria. Sextus Tarquin, having gone to Gabii, as to his own kingdom, was slain by the avengers of the old feuds, which he had raised against himself by his rapines and murders.

Lucius Tarquin the Proud reigned twenty-five years: the regal form of government continued from the building of the city to this period of its deliverance, two hundred and forty-four years. Two consuls, viz. Lucius Junius Brutus and Lucius Tarquinius Collatinus, were elected by the prefect of the city at the comitia by centuries, according to the commentaries of Servius Tullius.

.   .   .

The consuls, after raising two armies, marched into the territories of the Marsians and Pelignians, the army of the Samnites having joined them, and pitched their camp near Capua, where the Latins and their allies had now assembled. . . .

What excited their attention particularly was, that they had to contend against Latins, who coincided with themselves in language,

manners, in the same kind of arms, and more especially in military
institutions; soldiers had been mixed with soldiers, centurions with
centurions, tribunes with tribunes, as comrades and colleagues, in
the same armies, and often in the same companies. Lest in consequence of this the soldiers should be involved in any mistake, the
consuls issue orders that no one should fight against an enemy out
of his post.

It happened that among the other prefects of the troops, who had
been sent out in all directions to reconnoitre, Titus Manlius, the
consul's son, came with his troop to the back of the enemy's camp,
so near that he was scarcely distant a dart's throw from the next post.
In that place were some Tusculan cavalry; they were commanded by
Geminus Metius, a man distinguished among his countrymen both
by birth and exploits. When he recognised the Roman cavalry,
and conspicuous among them the consul's son marching at their
head, (for they were all known to each other, especially the men of
note,) "Romans, are ye going to wage war with the Latins and
allies with a single troop? What in the interim will the consuls,
what will the two consular armies be doing?" "They will be here in
good time," says Manlius, "and with them will be Jupiter himself,
as a witness of the treaties violated by you, who is stronger and more
powerful. If we fought at the lake Regillus until you had quite
enough, here also we shall so act, that a line of battle and an encounter with us may afford you no very great gratification." In
reply to this, Geminus, advancing some distance from his own party,
says, "Do you choose then, until that day arrives on which you are
to put your armies in motion with such mighty labour, to enter the
lists with me, that from the result of a contest between us both,
it may be seen how much a Latin excels a Roman horseman?"

Either resentment, or shame at declining the contest, or the invincible power of fate, arouses the determined spirit of the youth.
Forgetful therefore of his father's command, and the consul's edict,
he is driven headlong to that contest, in which it made not much
difference whether he conquered or was conquered. The other horsemen being removed to a distance as if to witness the sight, in the
space of clear ground which lay between them they spurred on
their horses against each other; and when they were together in
fierce encounter, the spear of Manlius passed over the helmet of
his antagonist, that of Metius across the neck of the other's horse.

Then wheeling round their horses, when Manlius arose to repeat the blow, he fixed his javelin between the ears of his opponent's horse. When, by the pain of this wound, the horse, having raised his fore-feet on high, tossed his head with great violence, he shook off his rider, whom, when he was raising himself from the severe fall, by leaning on his spear and buckler, Manlius pierced through the throat, so that the steel passed out through the ribs, and pinned him to the earth; and having collected the spoils, he returned to his own party, and with his troop, who were exulting with joy, he proceeds to the camp, and thence to the general's tent to his father, ignorant of what awaited him, whether praise or punishment had been merited. "Father," says he, "that all may truly represent me as sprung from your blood; when challenged, I slew my adversary, and have taken from him these equestrian spoils."

When the consul heard this, immediately turning away from his son, he ordered an assembly to be summoned by sound of trumpet. When these assembled in great numbers, "Since you, Titus Manlius," says he, "revering neither the consular power nor a father's majesty, have fought against the enemy out of your post contrary to our orders, and, as far as in you lay, have subverted military discipline, by which the Roman power has stood to this day, and have brought me to this necessity, that I must either forget the republic, or myself and mine; we shall expiate our own transgressions rather than the republic should sustain so serious a loss for our misdeeds. We shall be a melancholy example, but a profitable one, to the youth of future ages. As for me, both the natural affection for my children, as well as that instance of bravery which has led you astray by the false notion of honour, affects me for you. But since either the authority of consuls is to be established by your death, or by your forgiveness to be for ever annulled; I do not think that even you, if you have any of our blood in you, will refuse to restore, by your punishment, the military discipline which has been subverted by your misconduct. Go, lictor, bind him to the stake. All became motionless, more through fear than discipline, astounded by so cruel an order, each looking on the axe as if drawn against himself. Therefore when they stood in profound silence, suddenly, when the blood spouted from his severed neck, their minds recovering, as it were, from a state of stupefaction, then their voices arose together in free expressions of complaint, so that they spared neither lamentations nor execrations: and the body of the youth, being covered with the spoils, was burned on a pile erected outside the rampart, with all the military zeal with which any funeral could be celebrated: and Manlian orders were considered with horror, not only for the present, but of the most austere severity for future times.

The severity of the punishment however rendered the soldiers more obedient to the general; and besides that the guards and watches and the regulation of the posts were every where more strictly attended to, such severity was also profitable in the final struggle when they came into the field of battle.

Horace

13

Odes

Propaganda contributed as much to the triumph of the Emperor Augustus as force, and once he was master of the world he centralized and systematized the influencing of opinion. Augustus spared no effort in reconciling men to his new order and in proclaiming the mission of a regenerated Rome. Fortunately for him and for the world, the age produced writers of genius who lent themselves to his purposes.

Among these was Quintus Horatius Flaccus (65–8 B.C.), born at Venusia in southern Italy, the son of a freedman who gave him the education of a gentleman. While at school in Athens, Horace joined the losing cause of Brutus in the civil war and returned home to poverty. His bitter early verses brought him to the attention of the great epic poet Vergil, who helped him to meet some influential people; in 33 B.C. the gift of a farm from the rich patron, Maecenas, made him financially independent and showed that he had accepted the Augustan regime.

The 103 lyrics called the *Odes,* his finest work, must not, however, be regarded as a mere product of patronage. They are the voice of true Roman feeling, devoted to the ideals of the Augustan age: love of the soil, martial virtues, and traditional religious and moral values. But not all the *Odes* are grave in tone; some are graceful, witty, or trivial expressions of Horace's personality, giving first place to the pleasures of friendship, vintage wine, and a life of leisure on his beloved farm. All these interests find a place in the following selections. Though the *Odes* show the same derivative relationship to Greek prototypes as does Latin literature in general, they strike a distinctive Roman note of their own.

In 23 B.C., when most of the *Odes* were first published, Horace boasted that he had "erected a monument more enduring than bronze." Certainly, since Petrarch "rediscovered" him, he has been the most popular of Latin poets, mainly, perhaps, because of his quotability and Roman common sense.

I: 5

What slender Youth, bedew'd with liquid odours,
Courts thee on Roses in some pleasant Cave,
   Pyrrha? For whom bind'st thou
   In wreaths thy golden Hair,
Plain in thy neatness? O how oft shall he
On Faith and changed Gods complain, and Seas
   Rough with black winds, and storms
   Unwonted shall admire!
Who now enjoys thee credulous, all Gold,
Who always vacant, always amiable
   Hopes thee, of flattering gales
   Unmindful. Hapless they
T'whom thou untried seem'st fair. Me in my vow'd
Picture the sacred wall declares t'have hung
      My dank and dripping weeds
      To the stern God of Sea.

I: 20

Our common Sabine wine shall be
The only drink I'll give to thee.
      In modest goblets, too;
'Twas stored in crock of Grecian delf,
Dear knight Maecenas by myself,
      That very day when through
The theatre thy plaudits rang,
And sportive echo caught the clang,
      And answered from the banks

I: 5. Horace, *Odes*, trans. John Milton, in *The Poetical Works of John Milton*, ed. Helen Darbishire (London: Oxford University Press, 1958), 440.

I: 20. Horace, *The Odes of Horace*, trans. Theodore Martin (London: Parker, 1860), 11, 36, 89–92, 108–11, 119–21, 196–97.

Of thine own dear paternal stream,
Whilst Vatican renewed the theme
    Of homage and of thanks!
Old Caecuban, the very best,
And juice in vats Falernian pressed,
    You drink at home, I know.
My cups no choice Falernian fills,
Nor unto them do Formiae's hills
    Impart a tempered glow.

II: 15

Idle the plough, since the rich men's lordly piles
    Usurped the fruitful acres; pond and stew,
Broad as the Lucrine water, miles on miles,
    Make sights for tourists gaping at the view.

The spinster plane drives out the wedded elm;
    Myrtle and violet, every odious weed,
Dispense their perfumes in the olive's realm,
    Whose erstwhile masters fed the public need,

And close-bough'd laurels weave luxurious shade—
    Not thus our bearded fathers built the State,
When Romulus or Cato were obeyed,
    An in her rugged plainness Rome was great.

Wealth for the City, not the citizen,
    Was massed; no upstart burgess felled his trees
And with nice compass plotted on the plain
    Verandahs cool to take the northern breeze.

Men roofed their homes with turves from every field,
    While at the general charge their towns grew fine
With stately buildings, and the quarry's field
    With new-cut stone adorned each holy shrine.

II: 15. Horace, *The Odes of Horace,* trans. Edward Marsh (London: Macmillan & Company Ltd. and St. Martin's Press, Inc., 1941), 80. Reprinted by permission of the publishers.

II: 16

Peace, he begs of the gods, caught on the open
Aegean, with black clouds holding the moon in
hiding, and the stars no longer steadily
          shining for sailors;

peace is the prayer of battle-maddened Thrace;
peace, beg Parthians with their painted quivers:
it is not bought, Grosphus, with purple cloths, with
          jewels or with gold.

No, neither royal treasures nor a consul's
lictor can clear the crowd of worries away
from the mind, and the troubles that flutter near
          the paneled ceilings.

He lives well with little, the man whose fathers'
salt dish shines on his impoverished table,
and whose easy sleep is not stolen by fear
          or by filthy greed.

Why do we try for so much so hard with such
little time? Why do we turn to countries warmed
by a different sun? What exile from home
          escapes himself too?

The disease of worry boards the bronze-prowed ship,
and troops of horsemen cannot leave it behind,
swifter than stags and swifter than the Eastwind
          driving the stormclouds.

Joyful here and now, may the spirit despise
concern for what lies beyond and dilute the
bitter with a calm smile. Nothing is wholly
          filled with happiness.

Sudden death took Achilles in his glory,
his long old age wasted Tithonus away,
and to me perhaps this hour will offer
          what you are denied.

II: 16. Reprinted from *The Odes and Epodes of Horace, A Modern English Verse Translation*, by Joseph P. Clancy, by permission of The University of Chicago Press. © 1960 by The University of Chicago. [Pp. 95–96.]

You are surrounded by a hundred mooing
herds of Sicilian cattle, you can hear
your racehorse whinny, you are dressed in wool
          double-dyed with Af-

rican purple; I was not cheated by Fate,
who gave me a little farm and a spirit
sensitive to Grecian poetry, above
          the crowd and its spite.

                              III: 6

You, the guiltless, will pay for your fathers' sins,
Roman, until you repair the decaying
          temples and shrines of the gods and their
                    images, filthy with blackening smoke.

When you act as servant of the gods, you rule:
from them all beginning, leave them the ending;
          neglected, the gods have brought many
                    sorrows to suffering Italy.

Twice now Monaeses and Pacorus' army,
when omens were evil, have smashed our attack
          to bits, and they grin as they fasten
                    our trophies to their skimpy necklaces.

In the grip of civil conflicts the city
was nearly wiped out by Egypt and Dacia,
          the one with a frightening fleet, and
                    the other with superior archers.

Breeder of vices, our age has polluted
first marriage vows and the children and the home;
          from this spring, a river of ruin
                    has flooded our country and our people.

The blossoming virgin enjoys her course in
Ionic dancing, and even now practices
          all the tricks, and thoughts of sinful loves
                    fill her to the tender tips of her toes.

III: 6. Reprinted from *The Odes and Epodes of Horace, A Modern English Verse Translation,* by Joseph P. Clancy, by permission of The University of Chicago Press. © 1960 by The University of Chicago. [Pp. 117–18.]

Soon she is after, at her husband's parties,
younger lovers, and is not particular
about the one she hastily gives
the forbidden thrills when the lights go out;

then called for, her husband there and knowing it,
she responds, whether a salesman summons her
or the master of a Spanish ship,
a wealthy trader in adulteries.

Not from parents like these were the young men born
who stained the sea with Carthaginian blood
and struck down Pyrrhus and the mighty
Antiochus and dreadful Hannibal;

no, they were men, the descendants of farm-bred
soldiers, who were raised to turn over the clods
with their Sabine hoes, and to chop wood
and carry it in at their stern mother's

orders, as the Sungod shifted the shadows
of the mountains, and gave the weary oxen
relief from the yoke, bringing an hour
of rest as his chariot departed.

What does time's decaying leave undiminished?
Our parent's age, worse than their parents', brought forth
us, who are still worse, who soon will breed
descendants even more degenerate.

IV: 15

Of stricken fields and conquered towns I planned
High singing; but Apollo on his lyre
Twanged a warning, not to aspire
So high, nor risk my skiff too far from land.

Thine age, great Caesar, to our fields restores
Their fatness; now in Jove's avengèd shrine
Once more the captured eagles shine
That blazed our shame on Parthia's temple doors,

IV: 15. Horace, *The Odes of Horace,* trans. Edward Marsh (London: Macmillan & Company Ltd. and St. Martin's Press, Inc., 1941), 181–82. Reprinted by permission of the publishers.

And Janus' Gates of War stand shut. Thy rein
Hath curbed the froward passions that had brought
    Our honour and our pride to nought,
And to the ancient arts we turn again

Which nursed the strength of Italy, and spread
Far forth her empire's majesty and fame,
    Emblazoning the Latin name
From the sun's rising to his Western bed.

Under thy guardian hand, no storm of hate
Shall banish peace, no kindred blood outpoured,
    Nor wrath, fell anvil of the sword,
Mover of woeful strife in city and state,

No tribe that drinks of Danube or of Don,
Nor Tartar fire nor Persian treachery,
    The Julian edict shall defy;
No Thracian highland but thy sway shall own.

And we, on work-a-day and holy days,
Blessing good Bacchus for his gifts of mirth,
    With wives and children round our hearth,
Paying the Gods their due of prayer and praise,

Will sing our storied names with rites of yore
And jocund harmony of voice and lyre,
    Telling of Troy and our great sire
Whom bounteous Venus to Anchises bore.

Lucretius

══ 14 ══

De Rerum Natura

Whatever the private opinions of educated Romans during the last century of the Republic (influenced as they were by critical Hellenic thought), publicly they endorsed the cult of the gods. Not only were all citizens morally obliged to uphold the state religion, but its support was recognized by the ruling minority as a prop to their privileged status. Rarely, then, does Roman literature express sentiments subversive of ancestral beliefs.

Titus Lucretius Carus (*ca.* 96–55 B.C.) was perhaps the most remarkable exception to this Roman conformism. Not that he was an immoral or irreligious man—quite the contrary. He has been described, rather, as "the most sincere religious enthusiast in the whole of Roman literature." Indeed, his attack on superstition puts him in line with the great moral and religious mentors of history.

Of his life we know only that, unlike the typical Roman of good birth, he renounced a public career in favor of philosophy and found the meaning of things in the teachings of Epicurus, the Hellenistic thinker. Hailing Epicurus as "father" and "glory of the Greek race," Lucretius gave himself with missionary fervor to proclaiming Epicurus's liberating gospel; he set it forth in a long philosophic poem, *De Rerum Natura* (*On the Nature of Things*). The following selections present some of Lucretius's views regarding nature, the soul, happiness, and death. He himself adopted a poetic form to please the taste of his own age, but to suit the taste of ours, a prose version seems better here.

In all these selections may be seen a single-minded aim: to deliver the human spirit from imaginary fears by presenting a purely naturalistic interpretation of phenomena. True piety, Lucretius held, consisted in permitting one to "contemplate all things with a tranquil mind." He

Lucretius, *De Rerum Natura,* ed. and trans. Cyril Bailey (Oxford: Clarendon Press, 1947), I, 179–81, 183–89, 193–95, 197–203, 237–39, 303–13, 345–53, 357. Reprinted by permission of the publisher.

believed that fear of the supernatural and "the dread of something after death" were the greatest of all terrors. Once released from these by his materialistic philosophy of atomism, men might, as Epicurus said, "go dancing round the world in unclouded happiness." But authentic Epicureanism did not fit the Roman temper. Even in antiquity Lucretius's views attracted little notice; throughout the Middle Ages until the Renaissance, he was scorned as the devil's disciple. However, with the scientific revolution that began in the seventeenth century, his doctrine of atoms (translated in the selections as "first bodies") was taken up as never before, and his great poem gained recognition as a unique expression of the many-sided Roman genius.

When the life of man lay foul to see and grovelling upon the earth, crushed by the weight of religion, which showed her face from the realms of heaven, lowering upon mortals with dreadful mien, 'twas a man of Greece who dared first to raise his mortal eyes to meet her, and first to stand forth to meet her: him neither the stories of the gods nor thunderbolts checked, nor the sky with its revengeful roar, but all the more spurred the eager daring of his mind to yearn to be the first to break through the close-set bolts upon the doors of nature. And so it was that the lively force of his mind won its way, and he passed on far beyond the fiery walls of the world, and in mind and spirit traversed the boundless whole; whence in victory he brings us tidings what can come to be and what cannot, yea and in what way each thing has its power limited, and its deep-set boundary-stone. And so religion in revenge is cast beneath men's feet and trampled, and victory raises us to heaven.

Herein I have one fear, lest perchance you think that you are starting on the principles of some unholy reasoning, and setting foot upon the path of sin. Nay, but on the other hand, again and again our foe, religion, has given birth to deeds sinful and unholy. Even as at Aulis the chosen chieftains of the Danai, the first of all the host, foully stained with the blood of Iphianassa the altar of the Virgin of the Cross-Roads. For as soon as the band braided about her virgin locks streamed from her either cheek in equal lengths, as soon as she saw her sorrowing sire stand at the altar's side, and near him the attendants hiding their knives, and her countrymen shedding tears at the sight of her, tongue-tied with terror, sinking on her knees she fell to earth. Nor could it avail the luckless maid at such a time that she first had given the name of father to the king. For seized by men's hands, all trembling was she led to the altars, not that, when the ancient rite of sacrifice was fulfilled, she might be escorted by the clear cry of 'Hymen,' but in the very moment of marriage, a pure victim she might foully fall beneath a father's slaughtering stroke in sorrow herself, that a happy and hallowed starting might be granted to the fleet. Such evil deeds could religion prompt.

.   .   .

This terror then of the mind, this darkness must needs be scattered not by the rays of the sun and the gleaming shafts of day, but by the outer view and the inner law of nature; whose first rule shall take its start for us from this, that nothing is ever begotten of nothing by divine will. Fear, forsooth, so constrains all mortal men, because they behold many things come to pass on earth and in the sky, the cause of whose working they can by no means see, and think that a divine power brings them about. Therefore, when we have seen that nothing can be created out of nothing, then more rightly after that shall we discern that for which we search, both whence each thing can be created, and in what way all things come to be without the aid of gods.

For if things came to being from nothing, every kind might be born from all things, nought would need a seed. Firstly, men might arise from the sea, and from the land the race of scaly creatures, and birds burst forth from the sky; cattle and other herds, and all the tribe of wild beasts, with no fixed law of birth, would haunt tilth and desert. Nor would the same fruits stay constant to the trees, but all would change: all trees might avail to bear all fruits. Why, were there not bodies to bring each thing to birth, how could things have a fixed unchanging mother? But as it is, since all things are produced from fixed seeds, each thing is born and comes forth into the coasts of light out of that which has in it the substance and first-bodies of each; and 'tis for this cause that all things cannot be begotten of all, because in fixed things there dwells a power set apart. Or again, why do we see the roses in spring, and the corn in summer's heat, and the vines bursting

out when autumn summons them, if it be not that when, in their
own time, the fixed seeds of things have flowed together, then is
disclosed each thing that comes to birth, while the season is at
hand, and the lively earth in safety brings forth the fragile things
into the coasts of light? But if they sprang from nothing, suddenly
would they arise at uncertain intervals and in hostile times of
year, since indeed there would be no first-beginnings which might
be kept apart from creative union by an ill-starred season. Nay
more, for the increase of things, there would be no need for lapse
of time for the meeting of the seed, if they could grow from nothing. For little children would grow suddenly to youths, and at once
trees would come forth, leaping from the earth. But of this it is
well seen that nothing comes to pass, since all things grow slowly,
as is natural from a fixed seed, and as they grow preserve their
kind: so that you can know that each thing grows great, and is
fostered out of its own substance. There is this too, that without
fixed rain-showers in the year the earth could not put forth its
gladdening produce, nor again kept apart from food could the
nature of living things renew its kind or preserve its life; so that
rather you may think that many bodies are common to many things,
as we see letters are to words, than that without first-beginnings
anything can come to being. Once more, why could not nature
produce men so large that on their feet they might wade through
the waters of ocean or rend asunder mighty mountains with their
hands, or live to overpass many generations of living men, if it be
not because fixed substance has been appointed for the begetting
of things, from which it is ordained what can arise? Therefore, we
must confess that nothing can be brought to being out of nothing,
inasmuch as it needs a seed for things, from which each may be
produced and brought forth into the gentle breezes of the air.
Lastly, inasmuch as we see that tilled grounds are better than the
untilled, and when worked by hands yield better produce, we must
know that there are in the earth first-beginnings of things, which
we call forth to birth by turning the teeming sods with the plough-
share and drilling the soil of the earth. But if there were none such,
you would see all things without toil of ours of their own accord
come to be far better.

Then follows this, that nature breaks up each thing again into
its own first-bodies, nor does she destroy ought into nothing. For
if anything were mortal in all its parts together, each thing would

on a sudden be snatched from our eyes and pass away. For there would be no need of any force such as might cause disunion in its parts and unloose its fastenings. But as it is, because all things are put together of everlasting seeds, until some force has met them to batter things asunder with its blow, or to make its way inward through the empty voids and break things up, nature suffers not the destruction of anything to be seen. Moreover, if time utterly destroys whatsoever through age it takes from sight, and devours all its substance, how is it that Venus brings back the race of living things after their kind into the light of life, or how, when she has, does earth, the quaint artificer, nurse and increase them, furnishing food for them after their kind? how is it that its native springs and the rivers from without, coming from afar, keep the sea full? how is it that the sky feeds the stars? For infinite time and the days that are gone by must needs have devoured all things that are of mortal body. But if in all that while, in the ages that are gone by, those things have existed, of which this sum of things consists and is replenished, assuredly they are blessed with an immortal nature; all things cannot then be turned to nought. And again, the same force and cause would destroy all things alike, unless an eternal substance held them together, part with part interwoven closely or loosely in its fastenings. For in truth a touch would be cause enough of death, seeing that there would be no particles of lasting body, whose texture a special force would be needed to break asunder. But as it is, because the fastenings of the first-elements are variously put together, and their substance is everlasting, things endure with body unharmed, until there meets them a force proved strong enough to overcome the texture of each. No single thing then passes back to nothing, but all by dissolution pass back into the first-bodies of matter. Lastly, the rains pass away, when the sky, our father, has cast them headlong into the lap of earth, our mother; but the bright crops spring up, and the branches grow green upon the trees, the trees too grow and are laden with fruit; by this next our race and the race of beasts is nourished, through this we see glad towns alive with children, and leafy woods on every side ring with the young birds' cry; through this the cattle wearied with fatness lay their limbs to rest over the glad pastures, and the white milky stream trickles from their swollen udders; through this a new brood with tottering legs sports wanton among the soft grass, their baby hearts thrilling with the pure milk. Not

utterly then perish all things that are seen, since nature renews
one thing from out another, nor suffers anything to be begotten,
unless she be requited by another's death.

.   .   .

And yet all things are not held close pressed on every side by
the nature of body; for there is void in things. To have learnt
this will be of profit to you in dealing with many things; it will
save you from wandering in doubt and always questioning about
the sum of things, and distrusting my words. There is then a void,
mere space untouchable and empty. For if there were not, by no
means could things move; for that which is the office of body, to
offend and hinder, would at every moment beset all things; nothing, therefore, could advance, since nothing could make a start of
yielding place. But as it is, through seas and lands and the high
tracts of heaven, we descry many things by many means moving
in diverse ways before our eyes, which, if there were not void, would
not so much be robbed and baulked of restless motion, but rather
could in no way have been born at all, since matter would on
every side be in close-packed stillness. Again, however solid things
may be thought to be, yet from this you can discern that they are
of rare body. In rocky caverns the liquid moisture of water trickles
through, and all weeps with copious dripping: food spreads itself
this way and that into the body of every living thing: trees grow
and thrust forth their fruit in due season, because the food is
dispersed into every part of them from the lowest roots through
the stems and all the branches. Noises creep through walls and
fly through the shut places in the house, stiffening cold works its
way to the bones: but were there no empty spaces, along which each
of these bodies might pass, you would not see this come to pass
by any means. Again, why do we see one thing surpass another in
weight, when its size is no whit bigger? For if there is as much
body in a ball of wool as in lead, it is natural it should weigh as
much, since 'tis the office of body to press all things downwards,
but on the other hand the nature of void remains without weight.
So because it is just as big, yet is seen to be lighter, it tells us, we
may be sure, that it has more void; but on the other hand the
heavier thing avows that there is more body in it and that it
contains far less empty space within. Therefore, we may be sure,

that which we are seeking with keen reasoning, does exist mingled in things—that which we call void.

. . .

But now, to weave my task again in words, all nature then, as it is of itself, is built of these two things: for there are bodies and the void, in which they are placed and where they move hither and thither. For that body exists is declared by the sensation which all share alike; and unless faith in this sensation be firmly grounded at once and prevail, there will be nought to which we can make appeal about things hidden, so as to prove ought by the reasoning of the mind. And next, were there not room and empty space, which we call void, nowhere could bodies be placed, nor could they wander at all hither and thither in any direction; and this I have above shown to you but a little while before. Besides these there is nothing which you could say is parted from all body and sundered from void, which could be discovered as it were a third nature in the list. For whatever shall exist, must needs be something in itself; and if it suffer touch, however small and light, it will swell the sum of body by an increase great or maybe small, provided it exist at all, and be added to its total. But if it is not to be touched, inasmuch as it cannot on any side check anything from wandering through it and passing on its way, in truth it will be that which we call empty void. Or again, whatsoever exists by itself, will either act on something or suffer itself while other things act upon it, or it will be such that things may exist and go on in it. But nothing can act or suffer without body, nor afford room again, unless it be void and empty space. And so besides void and bodies no third nature by itself can be left in the list of things, which might either at any time fall within the purview of our senses, or be grasped by anyone through reasoning of the mind.

For all things that have a name, you will find either properties linked to these two things or you will see them to be their accidents. That is a property which in no case can be sundered or separated without the fatal disunion of the thing, as is weight to rocks, heat to fire, moisture to water, touch to all bodies, intangibility to the void. On the other hand, slavery, poverty, riches, liberty, war, concord, and other things by whose coming and going the nature of things abides untouched, these we are used, as is right,

to call accidents. Even so time exists not by itself, but from actual
things comes a feeling, what was brought to a close in time past,
then what is present now, and further what is going to be hereafter. And it must be avowed that no man feels time by itself
apart from the motion or quiet rest of things. Then again, when
men say that 'the rape of Tyndarus' daughter,' or 'the vanquishing
of the Trojan tribes in war' exist, beware that they do not perchance constrain us to avow that these things exist in themselves,
just because the past ages have carried off beyond recall those
races of men, of whom, in truth, these were the accidents. For
firstly, we might well say that whatsoever has happened is an accident in one case of the countries, in another even of the regions
of space. Or again, if there had been no substance of things nor
place and space, in which all things are carried on, never would the
flame have been fired by love through the beauty of Tyndaris,
nor swelling deep in the Phrygian heart of Alexander have kindled
the blazing battles of savage war, nor unknown of the Trojans
would the timber horse have set Pergama aflame at dead of night,
when the sons of the Greeks issued from its womb. So that you may
see clearly that all events from first to last do not exist by themselves and are not like body, nor can they be spoken of in the same
way as the being of the void, but rather so that you might justly
call them the accidents of body and place, in which they are carried
on, one and all.

Bodies, moreover, are in part the first-beginnings of things, in
part those which are created by the union of first-beginnings. Now
the true first-beginnings of things, no force can quench; for they
by their solid body prevail in the end. Albeit it seems hard to believe that there can be found among things anything of solid body.
For the thunderbolt of heaven passes through walled houses, as do
shouts and cries; iron grows white hot in the flame, and stones
leap asunder in fierce fiery heat; both the hardness of gold is relaxed
and softened by heat, and the ice of brass yields beneath the flame
and melts; warmth and piercing cold ooze through silver, since
when we have held cups duly in our hands we have felt both
alike, when the dewy moisture of water was poured in from above.
So true is it that in things there is seen to be nothing solid. But
yet because true reasoning and the nature of things constrains us,
give heed, until in a few verses we set forth that there are things

which exist with solid and everlasting body, which we show to be
the seeds of things and their first-beginnings, out of which the
whole sum of things now stands created.

First, since we have found existing a twofold nature of two things
far differing, the nature of body and of space, in which all things
take place, it must needs be that each exists alone by itself and
unmixed. For wherever space lies empty, which we call the void,
body is not there; moreover, wherever body has its station, there
is by no means empty void. Therefore the first bodies are solid and
free from void. Moreover, since there is void in things created, solid
matter must needs stand all round, nor can anything by true reasoning be shown to hide void in its body and hold it within, except
you grant that what keeps it in is solid. Now it can be nothing but
a union of matter, which could keep in the void in things. Matter
then, which exists with solid body, can be everlasting, when all
else is dissolved. Next, if there were nothing which was empty and
void, the whole would be solid; unless on the other hand there were
bodies determined, to fill all the places that they held, the whole
universe would be but empty void space. Body, then, we may be
sure, is marked off from void turn and turn about, since there is
neither a world utterly full nor yet quite empty. There are therefore bodies determined, such as can mark off void space from what
is full. These cannot be broken up when hit by blows from without,
nor again can they be pierced to the heart and undone, nor by any
other way can they be assailed and made to totter; all of which I
have above shown to you but a little while before. For it is clear
that nothing could be crushed in without void, or broken or cleft
in twain by cutting, nor admit moisture nor likewise spreading cold
or piercing flame, whereby all things are brought to their end. And
the more each thing keeps void within it, the more is it assailed
within by these things and begins to totter. Therefore, if the first
bodies are solid and free from void, as I have shown, they must be
everlasting. Moreover, if matter had not been everlasting, ere this
all things had wholly passed away to nothing, and all that we see
had been born again from nothing. But since I have shown above
that nothing can be created from nothing, nor can what has been
begotten be summoned back to nothing, the first-beginnings must
needs be of immortal body, into which at their last day all things
can be dissolved, that there may be matter enough for renewing

things. Therefore the first-beginnings are of solid singleness, nor in any other way can they be preserved so through the ages from infinite time now gone and renew things.

.   .   .

And since I have shown of what kind are the beginnings of all things, with what diverse shapes they differ, and how of their own accord they fly on, impelled by everlasting motion, and in what manner each several thing can be created out of them; next after this it seems that the nature of the mind and the soul must now be displayed in my verses, and the old fear of Acheron driven headlong away, which utterly confounds the life of men from the very root, clouding all things with the blackness of death, and suffering no pleasure to be pure and unalloyed. For, although men often declare that disease and a life of disgrace are more to be feared than the lower realm of death, and that they know that the soul's nature is of blood, or else of wind, if by chance their whim so wills it, and that so they have no need at all of our philosophy, you may be sure by this that all is idly vaunted to win praise, and not because the truth is itself accepted. These same men, exiled from their country and banished far from the sight of men, stained with some foul crime, beset with every kind of care, live on all the same, and, spite of all, to whatever place they come in their misery, they make sacrifice to the dead, and slaughter black cattle and dispatch offerings to the gods of the dead, and in their bitter plight far more keenly turn their hearts to religion. Wherefore it is more fitting to watch a man in doubt and danger, and to learn how he behaves in adversity; for then at last a real cry is wrung from the bottom of his heart: the mask is torn off, and the truth remains behind. Moreover, avarice and the blind craving for office, which constrain wretched men to overleap the boundaries of right, and sometimes as comrades or accomplices in crime to struggle night and day with surpassing toil to rise up to the height of power—these sores in life are fostered in no small degree by the fear of death. For most often foul disgrace and biting poverty are seen to be far removed from pleasant settled life, and are, as it were, a present dallying before the gates of death; and while men, spurred by a false fear, desire to flee far from them, and to remove themselves far away from them, they amass substance by civil bloodshed and greedily multiply their riches, heaping slaughter on slaughter. Hardening their heart they revel in a brother's bitter death, and hate and fear their kinsmen's board. In like manner, often through the same fear, they waste with envy that he is powerful, he is regarded, who walks clothed with bright renown; while they complain that they themselves are wrapped in darkness and the mire. Some of them come to ruin to win statues and a name; and often through fear of death so deeply does the hatred of life and the sight of the light possess men, that with sorrowing heart they compass their own death, forgetting that it is this fear which is the source of their woes; it persuades one man to besmirch his honour, another to burst the bonds of friendship and in fine to overthrow his natural ties. For often ere now men have betrayed country and beloved parents, seeking to shun the realms of Acheron. For even as children tremble and fear everything in blinding darkness, so we sometimes dread in the light things that are no whit more to be feared than what children shudder at in the dark, and imagine will come to pass. This terror then, this darkness of the mind, must needs be scattered, not by the rays of the sun and the gleaming shafts of day, but by the outer view and the inner law of nature.

First I say that the mind, which we often call the understanding, in which is placed the reasoning and guiding power of life, is a part of a man no whit the less than hand and foot and eyes are created parts of the whole living being. [Yet many wise men have thought] that the sensation of the mind is not placed in any part determined, but is a certain vital habit of the body, which the Greeks call a harmony, and think that it makes us live with sensation, although in no part does an understanding exist; as when often good health is said to belong to the body, and yet it is not itself any part of a healthy man. In this wise they do not set the sensation of the mind in any part determined; and in this they seem to me to wander very far astray. Thus often the body, which is clear to see, is sick, when all the same we feel pleasure in some other hidden part; and contrariwise it happens that the reverse often comes to be in turn, when one wretched in mind feels pleasure in all his body; in no other wise than if, when a sick man's foot is painful, all the while, maybe, his head is in no pain. Moreover, when the limbs are given up to soft sleep, and heavy body lies slack and senseless, yet there is something else in us, which at that very time is stirred in many ways, and admits within itself all the motions of joy and baseless cares of heart. Now that you may be able

to learn that the soul too is in the limbs, and that it is not by a
harmony that the body is wont to feel, first of all it comes to pass
that when a great part of the body is removed yet often the life
lingers on in our limbs; and then again, when a few particles of
heat are scattered abroad and some air has been given out through
the mouth, that same life of a sudden abandons the veins and leaves
the bones; so that you may be able to know from this that not all
particles have an equal part to play, nor do all equally support
existence, but that rather those, which are the seeds of wind and
burning heat, are the cause that life lingers in the limbs. There is
then heat and a life-giving wind in the very body, which abandons
our dying frame. . . .

Now I say that mind and soul are held in union one with the
other, and form of themselves a single nature, but that the head,
as it were, and lord in the whole body is the reason, which we call
mind or understanding, and it is firmly seated in the middle region
of the breast. For here it is that fear and terror throb, around these
parts are soothing joys; here then is the understanding and the
mind. The rest of the soul, spread abroad throughout the body,
obeys and is moved at the will and inclination of the understanding. The mind alone by itself has understanding for itself, it rejoices for itself, when no single thing stirs either soul or body.
And just as, when head or eye hurts within us at the attack of
pain, we are not tortured at the same time in all our body; so the
mind sometimes feels pain by itself or waxes strong with joy, when
all the rest of the soul through the limbs and frame is not roused
by any fresh feeling. Nevertheless, when the understanding is stirred
by some stronger fear, we see that the whole soul feels with it
throughout the limbs, and then sweat and pallor break out over all
the body, and the tongue is crippled and the voice is choked, the
eyes grow misty, the ears ring, the limbs give way beneath us, and
indeed we often see men fall down through the terror in their mind;
so that anyone may easily learn from this that the soul is linked in
union with the mind; for when it is smitten by the force of the
mind, straightway it strikes the body and pushes it on.

This same reasoning shows that the nature of mind and soul is
bodily. For when it is seen to push on the limbs, to pluck the body
from sleep, to change the countenance, and to guide and turn the
whole man—none of which things we see can come to pass without
touch, nor touch in its turn without body—must we not allow that

mind and soul are formed of bodily nature? Moreover, you see that our mind suffers along with the body, and shares our feelings together in the body. If the shuddering shock of a weapon, driven within and laying bare bones and sinews, does not reach the life, yet faintness follows, and a pleasant swooning to the ground, and a turmoil of mind which comes to pass on the ground, and from time to time, as it were, a hesitating will to rise. Therefore it must needs be that the nature of the mind is bodily, since it is distressed by the blow of bodily weapons.

Now of what kind of body this mind is, and of what parts it is formed, I will go on to give account to you in my discourse. First of all I say that it is very fine in texture, and is made and formed of very tiny particles. That this is so, if you give attention, you may be able to learn from this. Nothing is seen to come to pass so swiftly as what the mind pictures to itself coming to pass and starts to do itself. Therefore the mind bestirs itself more quickly than any of the things whose nature is manifest for all to see. But because it is so very nimble, it is bound to be formed of exceeding round and exceeding tiny seeds, so that its particles may be able to move when smitten by a little impulse. For so water moves and oscillates at the slightest impulse, seeing it is formed of little particles, quick to roll. But, on the other hand, the nature of honey is more close-packed, its fluid more sluggish, and its movement more hesitating; for the whole mass of its matter clings more together, because, we may be sure, it is not formed of bodies so smooth, nor so fine and round. For a light trembling breath can constrain a high heap of poppy-seed to scatter from top to bottom before your eyes: but, on the other hand, a pile of stones or corn-ears it can by no means separate. Therefore, in proportion as bodies are tinier and smoother, so they are gifted with nimbleness. But, on the other hand, all things that are found to be of greater weight or more spiky, the more firm set they are. Now, therefore, since the nature of the mind has been found nimble beyond the rest, it must needs be formed of bodies exceeding small and smooth and round. And this truth, when known to you, will in many things, good friend, prove useful, and will be reckoned of service. This fact, too, shows the nature of the mind, of how thin a texture it is formed, and in how small a place it might be contained, could it be gathered in a mass; that as soon as the unruffled peace of death has laid hold on a man, and the nature of mind and soul has passed away, you could discern nothing there, that sight or weight can test, stolen from the entire body; death preserves all save the feeling of life, and some warm heat. And so it must needs be that the whole soul is made of very tiny seeds, and is linked on throughout veins, flesh, and sinews; inasmuch as, when it is all already gone from the whole body, yet the outer contour of the limbs is preserved unbroken, nor is a jot of weight wanting. Even so it is, when the flavour of wine has passed away or when the sweet breath of a perfume is scattered to the air, or when its savour is gone from some body; still the thing itself seems not a whit smaller to the eyes on that account, nor does anything seem withdrawn from its weight, because, we may be sure, many tiny seeds go to make flavours and scent in the whole body of things. Wherefore once and again you may know that the nature of the understanding and the soul is formed of exceeding tiny seeds, since when it flees away it carries with it no jot of weight.

*   *   *

Sweet it is, when on the great sea the winds are buffeting the waters, to gaze from the land on another's great struggles; not because it is pleasure or joy that anyone should be distressed, but because it is sweet to perceive from what misfortune you yourself are free. Sweet is it too, to behold great contests of war in full array over the plains, when you have no part in the danger. But nothing is more gladdening than to dwell in the calm regions, firmly embattled on the heights by the teaching of the wise, whence you can look down on others, and see them wandering hither and thither, going astray as they seek the way of life, in strife matching their wits or rival claims of birth, struggling night and day by surpassing effort to rise up to the height of power and gain possession of the world. Ah! miserable minds of men, blind hearts! in what darkness of life, in what great dangers ye spend this little span of years! to think that ye should not see that nature cries aloud for nothing else but that pain may be kept far sundered from the body, and that, withdrawn from care and fear, she may enjoy in mind the sense of pleasure! And so we see that for the body's nature but few things at all are needful, even such as can take away pain, yea, and can also supply many delights; nor does human nature itself from time to time need anything more acceptable, if there are not golden images of youths about the halls, grasping fiery torches in their right hands, that light may be supplied to banquets at night, if the house does not glow with silver or gleam with gold, nor do fretted and gilded rafters re-echo to the lute, but yet men lie in friendly groups on the soft grass near some stream of water under the branches of a tall tree, and at no great cost delightfully refresh their bodies, above all when the weather smiles on them, and the season of the year bestrews the green grass with flowers. Nor do fiery fevers more quickly quit the body, if you toss on broidered pictures and blushing purple, than if you must lie on the poor man's plaid. Wherefore since in our body riches are of no profit, nor high birth nor the glories of kingship, for the rest, we must believe that they avail nothing for the mind as well; unless perchance, when you see your legions swarming over the spaces of the Campus and provoking a mimic war, when you draw them up equipped with arms, all alike eager for the fray, strengthened with hosts in reserve and forces of cavalry, when you see the army wandering far wide in busy haste, then alarmed by all this the scruples of religion fly in panic from your mind, and the dread of death then leaves your heart empty and free from care. But if we see that these thoughts are mere mirth and mockery, and in very truth the fears of men and the cares that dog them fear not the clash of arms nor the weapons of war, but pass boldly among kings and lords of the world, nor dread the glitter that comes from gold nor the bright sheen of the purple robe, can you doubt that all such power belongs to reason alone, above all when the whole of life is but a struggle in darkness? For even as children tremble and fear everything in blinding darkness, so we sometimes dread in the light things that are no whit more to be feared than what children shudder at in dark, and imagine will come to pass. This terror of the mind then, this darkness, must needs be scattered not by the rays of the sun and the gleaming shafts of day, but by the outer view and the inner law of nature.

. . .

If only men, even as they clearly feel a weight in their mind, which wears them out with its heaviness, could learn too from what causes that comes to be, and whence so great a mass, as it were, of ill lies upon their breast, they would not pass their lives, as now for the most part we see them; knowing not each one of them what he wants, and longing ever for change of place, as though he could thus lay aside the burden. The man who is tired of staying at home, often goes out abroad from his great mansion, and of a sudden returns again, for indeed abroad he feels no better. He races to his country home, furiously driving his ponies, as though he were hurrying to bring help to a burning house; he yawns at once, when he has set foot on the threshold of the villa, or sinks into a heavy sleep and seeks forgetfulness, or even in hot haste makes for town, eager to be back. In this way each man struggles to flee from himself: yet, despite his will he clings to the self, which, we may be sure, in fact he cannot escape, and hates himself, because in his sickness he knows not the cause of his malady; but if he saw it clearly, every man would leave all else, and study first to learn the nature of things, since it is his state for all eternity, and not for a single hour, that is in question, the state in which mortals must expect all their being, that is to come after their death.

.   .   .

Death, then, is nought to us, nor does it concern us a whit, inasmuch as the nature of the mind is but a mortal possession. And even as in the time gone by we felt no ill, when the Poeni came from all sides to the shock of battle, when all the world, shaken by the tremorous turmoil of war, shuddered and reeled beneath the high coasts of heaven, in doubt to which people's sway must fall all human power by land and sea; so, when we shall be no more, when there shall have come the parting of body and soul, by whose union we are made one, you may know that nothing at all will be able to happen to us, who then will be no more, or stir our feeling; no, not if earth shall be mingled with sea, and sea with sky. And even if the nature of mind and the power of soul has feeling, after it has been rent asunder from our body, yet it is nought to us, who are made one by the mating and marriage of body and soul. Nor, if time should gather together our substance after our decease and bring it back again as it is now placed, if once more the light of life should be vouchsafed to us, yet, even were that done, it would not concern us at all, when once the remembrance of our former selves were snapped in twain. And even now we care not at all for the selves that we once were, not at all are we touched by any torturing pain for them. For when you look back over all the lapse of immeasurable time that now is gone, and think how manifold are the motions of matter, you could easily believe this too, that these same seeds, whereof we now are made, have often been placed in the same order as they are now; and yet we cannot recall that in our mind's memory; for in between lies a break in life, and all the motions have wandered everywhere far astray from sense. For, if by chance there is to be grief and pain for a man, he must needs himself too exist at that time, that ill may befall him. Since death forestalls this, and prevents the being of him on whom these misfortunes might crowd, we may know that we have nought to fear in death, and that he who is no more cannot be wretched, and that it were no whit different if he had never at any time been born, when once immortal death has stolen away mortal life.

And so, when you see a man chafing at his lot, that after death he will either rot away with his body laid in earth, or be destroyed by flames or the jaws of wild beasts, you may be sure that his words do not ring true, and that deep in his heart lies some secret pang, however much he deny himself that he believes that he will have any feeling in death. For he does not, I think, grant what he professes, nor the grounds of his profession, nor does he remove and cast himself root and branch out of life, but all unwitting supposes something of himself to live on. For when in life each man pictures to himself that it will come to pass that birds and wild beasts will mangle his body in death, he pities himself; for neither does he separate himself from the corpse, nor withdraw himself enough from the outcast body, but thinks that it is he, and, as he stands watching, taints it with his own feeling. Hence he chafes that he was born mortal, and sees not that in real death there will be no second self, to live and mourn to himself his own loss, or to stand there and be pained that he lies mangled or burning. For if it is an evil in death to be mauled by the jaws and teeth of wild beasts, I cannot see how it is not sharp pain to be laid upon hot flames and cremated, or to be placed in honey and stifled, and to grow stiff with cold, lying on the surface on the top of an icy rock, or to be crushed and ground by a weight of earth above.

'Now no more shall thy glad home welcome thee, nor thy good wife and sweet children run up to snatch the first kisses, and touch thy heart with a silent thrill of joy. No more shalt thou have power to prosper in thy ways, or to be a sure defence to thine own. Pitiful thou art,' men say, 'and pitifully has one malignant day taken from thee all the many prizes of life.' Yet to this they add not: 'nor does there abide with thee any longer any yearning for these things.'

But if they saw this clearly in mind, and followed it out in their words, they would free themselves from great anguish and fear of mind. 'Thou, indeed, even as thou art now fallen asleep in death, shalt so be for all time to come, released from every pain and sorrow. But 'tis we who have wept with tears unquenchable for thee, as thou wert turned to ashes hard by us on the awesome place of burning, and that unending grief no day shall take from our hearts.' But of him who speaks thus we should ask what there is so exceeding bitter, if it comes at the last to sleep and rest, that anyone should waste away in never-ending lamentation.

This too men often do, when they are lying at the board, and hold their cups in their hands, and shade their brows with garlands: they say from the heart, 'Brief is this enjoyment for us puny men: soon it will be past, nor ever thereafter will it be ours to call it back.' As though in death this were to be foremost among their ills, that thirst would burn the poor wretches and parch them with its drought, or that there would abide with them a yearning for any other thing. For never does any man long for himself and life, when mind and body alike rest in slumber. For all we care sleep may then be never-ending, nor does any yearning for ourselves then beset us. And yet at that time those first-beginnings stray not at all far through our frame away from the motions that bring sense, when a man springs up from sleep and gathers himself together. Much less then should we think that death is to us, if there can be less than what we see to be nothing; for at our dying there follows a greater scattering abroad of the turmoil of matter, nor does anyone wake and rise again whom the chill breach of life has once overtaken.

Again, suppose that the nature of things should of a sudden lift up her voice, and thus in these words herself rebuke some one of us: 'Why is death so great a thing to thee, mortal, that thou dost give way overmuch to sickly lamentation? Why groan and weep at death? For if the life that is past and gone has been pleasant to thee, nor have all its blessings, as though heaped in a vessel full of holes, run through and perished unenjoyed, why dost thou not retire like a guest sated with the banquet of life, and with calm mind embrace, thou fool, a rest that knows no care? But if all thou hast reaped hath been wasted and lost, and life is a stumbling-block, why seek to add more, all to be lost again foolishly and pass away unenjoyed; why not rather make an end of life and trouble?

For there is nought more which I can devise or discover to please thee: all things are ever as they were. If thy body is not yet wasted with years, nor thy limbs worn and decayed, yet all things remain as they were, even if thou shouldst live on to overpass all generations, nay rather, if thou shouldst never die.' What answer can we make, but that nature brings a just charge against us, and sets out in her pleading a true plaint? But if now some older man, smitten in years, should make lament, and pitifully bewail his decease more than is just, would she not rightly raise her voice and chide him in sharp tones? 'Away hence with tears, thou rascal, set a bridle on thy laments. Thou hast enjoyed all the prizes of life and now dost waste away. But because thou yearnest ever for what is not with thee, and despisest the gifts at hand, uncompleted and unenjoyed thy life has slipped from thee, and, ere thou didst think it, death is standing by thy head, before thou hast the heart to depart filled and sated with good things. Yet now give up all these things so ill-fitted for thy years, and with calm mind, come, yield them [to thy sons]: for so thou must.' She would be right, I think, in her plea, right in her charge and chiding. For the old ever gives place, thrust out by new things, and one thing must be restored at the expense of others: nor is anyone sent down to the pit and to black Tartarus. There must needs be substance that the generations to come may grow; yet all of them too will follow thee, when they have had their fill of life; yea, just as thyself, the generations have passed away before now, and will pass away again. So one thing shall never cease to rise up out of another, and life is granted to none for freehold, to all on lease. Look back again to see how the past ages of everlasting time, before we were born, have been as nought to us. These then nature holds up to us as a mirror of the time that is to come, when we are dead and gone. Is there ought that looks terrible in this, ought that seems gloomy? Is it not a calmer rest than any sleep?

Suetonius

─────── *15* ───────

The Lives of the Twelve Caesars: Augustus

The Romans had always been absorbed in the lives of their great men, as shown by the preservation of commemorative death masks and the development of portrait sculpture. When autocrats dominated all other men under the Empire, it was natural that their biographies should be written, and for a long time this genre eclipsed narrative history.

This trend began with Gaius Suetonius Tranquillus (*ca.* 69–*ca.* 140 A.D.), the son of a well-to-do family. Even more than Plutarch, he is known almost entirely through his books, for, apart from the fact that he was secretary to the Emperor Hadrian for a time, we known little of him. Although he wrote other works, the only one surviving is his *Lives of the Twelve Caesars,* published in 120 A.D.

Suetonius was an industrious scholar and through his official post had access to archival materials now lost forever, but he makes no attempt to present well-rounded portraits of his subjects, to set them in the background of their times, or even to comment upon them. If we knew nothing more of the Emperor Augustus than what Suetonius tells us, we would be left wondering that this man should have been the master of the world— the man referred to in a provincial inscription as "the savior of the whole human race . . . god of god . . . Zeus of father Zeus."

In this respect Suetonius differs from Plutarch, his Greek contemporary, who offers lessons in conduct rather than informatory sketches. But, although his studies lack style and insight, they abound in lively anecdotes and gossipy details, often sensational in nature. And, of course, they deal with twelve extraordinary men. These features account in large measure for the enduring popularity of Suetonius.

Suetonius, *The Lives of the Twelve Caesars,* trans. Alexander Thomson, rev. and corr. T. Forester (London: Bell, 1893), 75–76, 80–82, 84–85, 87, 91–100, 109–10, 112, 114–16, 128–30.

He lost his father when he was only four years of age; and, in his twelfth year, pronounced a funeral oration in praise of his grandmother Julia. Four years afterwards, having assumed the robe of manhood, he was honoured with several military rewards by Caesar in his African triumph, although he took no part in the war on account of his youth. Upon his uncle's expedition to Spain against the sons of Pompey, he was followed by his nephew, although he was scarcely recovered from a dangerous sickness; and after being shipwrecked at sea, and travelling with very few attendants through roads that were infested with the enemy, he at last came up with him. This activity gave great satisfaction to his uncle, who soon conceived an increasing affection for him, on account of such indications of character. After the subjugation of Spain, while Caesar was meditating an expedition against the Dacians and Parthians, he was sent before him to Apollonia, where he applied himself to his studies; until receiving intelligence that his uncle was murdered, and that he was appointed his heir, he hesitated for some time whether he should call to his aid the legions stationed in the neighbourhood; but he abandoned the design as rash and premature. However, returning to Rome, he took possession of his inheritance, although his mother was apprehensive that such a measure might be attended with danger, and his step-father, Marcius Philippus, a man of consular rank, very earnestly dissuaded him from it. From this time, collecting together a strong military force, he first held the government in conjunction with Mark Antony and Marcus Lepidus, then with Antony only for nearly twelve years, and at last in his own hands during a period of four and forty.

Having thus given a very short summary of his life, I shall prosecute the several parts of it, not in order of time, but arranging his acts into distinct classes, for the sake of perspicuity. He was engaged in five civil wars, namely those of Modena, Philippi, Perugia, Sicily, and Actium; the first and last of which were against Antony, and the second against Brutus and Cassius; the third against Lucius Antonius, the triumvir's brother, and the fourth against Sextus Pompeius, the son of Cneius Pompeius.

The motive which gave rise to all these wars was the opinion he entertained that both his honour and interest were concerned in revenging the murder of his uncle, and maintaining the state of affairs he had established.

.   .   .

The alliance between him and Antony, which had always been precarious, often interrupted, and ill cemented by repeated reconciliations, he at last entirely dissolved. And to make it known to the world how far Antony had degenerated from patriotic feelings, he caused a will of his, which had been left at Rome, and in which he had nominated Cleopatra's children, amongst others, as his heirs, to be opened and read in an assembly of the people. . . . And not long afterwards he defeated him in a naval engagement near Actium, which was prolonged to so late an hour, that, after the victory, he was obliged to sleep on board his ship.

From Actium he went to the isle of Samos to winter; but being alarmed with the accounts of a mutiny amongst the soldiers he had selected from the main body of his army sent to Brundisium after the victory, who insisted on their being rewarded for their service and discharged, he returned to Italy. . . .

He remained only twenty-seven days at Brundisium, until the demands of the soldiers were settled, and then went, by way of Asia and Syria, to Egypt, where laying siege to Alexandria, whither Antony had fled with Cleopatra, he made himself master of it in a short time. He drove Antony to kill himself, after he had used every effort to obtain conditions of peace, and he saw his corpse. Cleopatra he anxiously wished to save for his triumph; and when she was supposed to have been bit to death by an asp, he sent for the Psylli to endeavor to suck out the poison. He allowed them to be buried together in the same grave, and ordered a mausoleum, begun by themselves, to be completed. The eldest of Antony's two sons by Fulvia he commanded to be taken by force from the statue of Julius Caesar, to which he had fled, after many fruitless supplications for his life, and put him to death. The same fate attended Caesario, Cleopatra's son by Caesar, as he pretended, who had fled for his life, but was retaken. The children which Antony had by Cleopatra he saved, and brought up and cherished in a manner suitable to their rank, just as if they had been his own relations.

.   .   .

He conducted in person only two foreign wars; the Dalmatian, whilst he was yet but a youth; and, after Antony's final defeat, the Cantabrian. He was wounded in the former of these wars; in one battle he received a contusion in the right knee from a stone—and in another, he was much hurt in one leg and both arms, by the fall of a bridge. His other wars he carried on by his lieutenants; but occasionally visited the army, in some of the wars of Pannonia and Germany, or remained at no great distance, proceeding from Rome as far as Ravenna, Milan, or Aquileia.

He conquered, however, partly in person, and partly by his lieutenants, Cantabria, Aquitania and Pannonia, Dalmatia, with all Illyricum and Rhaetia, besides the two Alpine nations, the Vindelici and the Salassii. He also checked the incursions of the Dacians, by cutting off three of their generals with vast armies, and drove the Germans beyond the river Elbe; removing two other tribes who submitted, the Ubii and Sicambri, into Gaul, and settling them in the country bordering on the Rhine. Other nations also, which broke into revolt, he reduced to submission. But he never made war upon any nation without just and necessary cause; and was so far from being ambitious either to extend the empire, or advance his own military glory, that he obliged the chiefs of some barbarous tribes to swear in the temple of Mars the Avenger, that they would faithfully observe their engagements, and not violate the peace which they had implored. Of some he demanded a new description of hostages, their women, having found from experience that they cared little for their men when given as hostages; but he always afforded them the means of getting back their hostages whenever they wished it.

Even those who engaged most frequently and with the greatest perfidy in their rebellion, he never punished more severely than by selling their captives, on the terms of their not serving in any neighbouring country, nor being released from their slavery before the expiration of thirty years. By the character which he thus acquired, for virtue and moderation, he induced even the Indians and Scythians, nations before known to the Romans by report only, to solicit his friendship, and that of the Roman people, by ambassadors. The Parthians readily allowed his claim to Armenia; restoring at his demand, the standards which they had taken from Marcus Crassus and Mark Antony, and offering him hostages besides. Afterwards, when a contest arose between several pretenders to the

crown of that kingdom, they refused to acknowledge any one who
was not chosen by him.

. . .

In military affairs he made many alterations, introducing some
practices entirely new, and reviving others, which had become
obsolete. He maintained the strictest discipline among the troops;
and would not allow even his lieutenants the liberty to visit their
wives, except reluctantly, and in the winter season only. A Roman
knight having cut off the thumbs of his two young sons, to render
them incapable of serving in the wars, he exposed both him and
his estate to public sale. But upon observing the farmers of the
revenue very greedy for the purchase, he assigned him to a freedman
of his own, that he might send him into the country, and suffer him
to retain his freedom. The tenth legion becoming mutinous, he disbanded it with ignominy; and did the same by some others which
petulantly demanded their discharge; withholding from them the
rewards usually bestowed on those who had served their stated
time in the wars. The cohorts which yielded their ground in time
of action, he decimated, and fed with barley. Centurions, as well as
common sentinels, who deserted their posts when on guard, he
punished with death. For other misdemeanors he inflicted upon
them various kinds of disgrace; such as obliging them to stand all
day before the praetorium, sometimes in their tunics only, and
without their belts, sometimes to carry poles ten feet long, or sods
of turf.

. . .

He twice entertained thoughts of restoring the republic; first,
immediately after he had crushed Antony, remembering that he had
often charged him with being the obstacle to its restoration. The
second was in consequence of a long illness, when he sent for the
magistrates and the senate to his own house, and delivered them a
particular account of the state of the empire. But reflecting at the
same time that it would be both hazardous to himself to return to
the condition of a private person, and might be dangerous to the
public to have the government placed again under the control of the
people, he resolved to keep it in his own hands, whether with the
better event or intention, is hard to say. His good intentions he
often affirmed in private discourse, and also published an edict,

in which it was declared in the following terms: "May it be permitted me to have the happiness of establishing the commonwealth on a safe and sound basis, and thus enjoy the reward of which I am ambitious, that of being celebrated for moulding it into the form best adapted to present circumstances; so that, on my leaving the world, I may carry with me the hope that the foundations which I have laid for its future government, will stand firm and stable."

The city, which was not built in a manner suitable to the grandeur of the empire, and was liable to inundations of the Tiber, as well as to fires, was so much improved under his administration, that he boasted, not without reason, that he "found it of brick, but left it of marble." He also rendered it secure for the time to come against such disasters, as far as could be effected by human foresight.

A great number of public buildings were erected by him, the most considerable of which were a forum, containing the temple of Mars the Avenger, the temple of Apollo on the Palatine hill, and the temple of Jupiter Tonans in the capitol. The reason of his building a new forum was the vast increase in the population, and the number of causes to be tried in the courts, for which, the two already existing not affording sufficient space, it was thought necessary to have a third. It was therefore opened for public use before the temple of Mars was completely finished; and a law was passed, that causes should be tried, and judges chosen by lot, in that place. The temple of Mars was built in fulfilment of a vow made during the war of Philippi, undertaken by him to avenge his father's murder. He ordained that the senate should always assemble there when they met to deliberate respecting wars and triumphs; that thence should be despatched all those who were sent into the provinces in the command of armies; and that in it those who returned victorious from the wars, should lodge the trophies of their triumphs. He erected the temple of Apollo in that part of his house on the Palatine hill which had been struck with lightning, and which, on that account, the soothsayers declared the God to have chosen. He added porticos to it, with a library of Latin and Greek authors; and when advanced in years, used frequently there to hold the senate, and examine the rolls of the judges.

He dedicated the temple to Apollo Tonans, in acknowledgment of his escape from a great danger in his Cantabrian expedition; when, as he was travelling in the night, his litter was struck by lightning, which killed the slave who carried a torch before him.

He likewise constructed some public buildings in the name of others; for instance, his grandsons, his wife, and sister. Thus he built the portico and basilica of Lucius and Caius, and the porticos of Livia and Octavia, and the theatre of Marcellus. He also often exhorted other persons of rank to embellish the city by new buildings, or repairing and improving the old, according to their means. In consequence of this recommendation, many were raised; such as the temple of Hercules and the Muses, by Marcius Philippus; a temple of Diana by Lucius Cornificius; the Court of Freedom by Asinius Pollio; a temple of Saturn by Munatius Plancus; a theatre by Cornelius Balbus; an amphitheatre by Statilius Taurus; and several other noble edifices by Marcus Agrippa.

He divided the city into regions and districts, ordaining that the annual magistrates should take by lot the charge of the former; and that the latter should be superintended by wardens chosen out of the people of each neighbourhood. He appointed a nightly watch to be on their guard against accidents from fire; and, to prevent the frequent inundations, he widened and cleansed the bed of the Tiber, which had in the course of years been almost dammed up with rubbish, and the channel narrowed by the ruins of houses. To render the approaches to the city more commodious, he took upon himself the charge of repairing the Flaminian way as far as Ariminum, and distributed the repairs of the other roads amongst several persons who had obtained the honour of a triumph; to be defrayed out of the money arising from the spoils of war. Temples decayed by time, or destroyed by fire, he either repaired or rebuilt; and enriched them, as well as many others, with splendid offerings. On a single occasion, he deposited in the cell of the temple of Jupiter Capitolinus, sixteen thousand pounds of gold, with jewels and pearls to the amount of fifty millions of sesterces.

*   *   *

He restored the calendar, which had been corrected by Julius Caesar, but through negligence was again fallen into confusion, to its former regularity; and upon that occasion called the month Sextilis by his own name, August, rather than September, in which he was born; because in it he had obtained his first consulship, and all his most considerable victories. He increased the number, dignity, and revenues of the priests, and especially those of the Vestal Virgins. And when, upon the death of one of them, a new one was to be taken, and many persons made interest that their daughters' names might be omitted in the lists for election, he replied with an oath, "If either of my own grand-daughters were old enough, I would have proposed her."

He likewise revived some old religious customs, which had become obsolete; as the augury of public health, the office of high priest of Jupiter, the religious solemnity of the Lupercalia, with the Secular, and Compitalian games. He prohibited young boys from running in the Lupercalia; and in respect of the Secular games, issued an order, that no young persons of either sex should appear at any public diversions in the night-time, unless in the company of some elderly relation. He ordered the household gods to be decked twice a year with spring and summer flowers, in the Compitalian festival.

Next to the immortal gods, he paid the highest honours to the memory of those generals who had raised the Roman state from its low origin to the highest pitch of grandeur. He accordingly repaired or rebuilt the public edifices erected by them; preserving the former inscriptions, and placing statues of them all, with triumphal emblems, in both the porticos of his forum, issuing an edict on the occasion, in which he made the following declaration: "My design in so doing is, that the Roman people may require from me, and all succeeding princes, a conformity to those illustrious examples." He likewise removed the statue of Pompey from the senate-house, in which Caius Caesar had been killed, and placed it under a marble arch, fronting the palace attached to Pompey's theatre.

He corrected many ill practices, which, to the detriment of the public, had either survived the licentious habits of the late civil wars, or else originated in the long peace. Bands of robbers shewed themselves openly, completely armed, under colour of self-defence; and in different parts of the country, travellers, freemen and slaves without distinction, were forcibly carried off, and kept to work in the houses of correction. Several associations were formed under the specious name of a new college, which banded together for the perpetration of all kinds of villany. The banditti he quelled by establishing posts of soldiers in suitable stations for the purpose; the houses of correction were subjected to a strict superintendence; all associations, those only excepted which were of ancient standing, and recognised by the laws, were dissolved.

He burnt all the notes of those who had been a long time in arrear with the treasury, as being the principal source of vexatious suits and prosecutions. Places in the city claimed by the public, where the right was doubtful, he adjudged to the actual possessors. He struck out of the list of criminals the names of those over whom prosecutions had been long impending, where nothing further was intended by the informers than to gratify their own malice, by seeing their enemies humiliated; laying it down as a rule, that if any one chose to renew a prosecution, he should incur the risk of the punishment which he sought to inflict. And that crimes might not escape punishment, nor business he neglected by delay, he ordered the courts to sit during the thirty days which were spent in celebrating honorary games. . . .

He was himself assiduous in his functions as a judge, and would sometimes prolong his sittings even into the night: if he were indisposed, his litter was placed before the tribunal, or he administered justice reclining on his couch at home; displaying always not only the greatest attention, but extreme lenity. To save a culprit, who evidently appeared guilty of parricide, from the extreme penalty of being sewn up in a sack, because none were punished in that manner but such as confessed the fact, he is said to have interrogated him thus: "Surely you did not kill your father, did you?" And when, in a trial of a cause about a forged will, all those who had signed it were liable to the penalty of the Cornelian law, he ordered that his colleagues on the tribunal should not only be furnished with the two tablets by which they decided, "guilty or not guilty," but with a third likewise, ignoring the offence of those who should appear to have given their signatures through any deception or mistake. All appeals in causes between inhabitants of Rome, he assigned every year to the praetor of the city; and where provincials were concerned, to men of consular rank, to one of whom the business of each province was referred.

Some laws he abrogated, and he made some new ones; such as the sumptuary law, that relating to adultery and the violation of chastity, the law against bribery in elections, and likewise that for the encouragement of marriage. Having been more severe in his reform of this law than the rest, he found the people utterly averse to submit to it, unless the penalties were abolished or mitigated, besides allowing an interval of three years after a wife's death, and increasing the premiums on marriage. . . . But finding that the force of the law was eluded by marrying girls under the age of puberty and by frequent change of wives, he limited the time for consummation after espousals, and imposed restrictions on divorce.

By two separate scrutinies he reduced to their former number and splendour the senate, which had been swamped by a disorderly crowd; for they were now more than a thousand and some of them very mean persons, who, after Caesar's death, had been chosen by dint of interest and bribery, so that they had the nickname of Orcini among the people. The first of these scrutinies was left to themselves, each senator naming another; but the last was conducted by himself and Agrippa. On this occasion he is believed to have taken his seat as he presided, with a coat of mail under his tunic, and a sword by his side, and with ten of the stoutest men of senatorial rank, who were his friends, standing round his chair. Cordus Cremutius relates that no senator was suffered to approach him, except singly, and after having his bosom searched [for secreted daggers]. Some he obliged to have the grace of declining the office; these he allowed to retain the privileges of wearing the distinguishing dress, occupying the seats at the solemn spectacles, and of feasting publicly, reserved to the senatorial order.

That those who were chosen and approved of, might perform their functions under more solemn obligations, and with less inconvenience, he ordered that every senator, before he took his seat in the house, should pay his devotions, with an offering of frankincense and wine, at the altar of that God in whose temple the senate then assembled, and that their stated meetings, should be only twice in the month, namely, on the calends and ides; and that in the months of September and October, a certain number only, chosen by lot, such as the law required to give validity to a decree, should be required to attend. For himself, he resolved to choose every six months a new council, with whom he might consult previously upon such affairs as he judged proper at any time to lay before the full senate. He also took the votes of the senators upon any subject of importance, not according to custom, nor in regular order, but as he pleased; that every one might hold himself ready to give his opinion, rather than a mere vote of assent.

.　.　.

Having thus regulated the city and its concerns, he augmented the population of Italy by planting in it no less than twenty-eight colonies, and greatly improved it by public works, and a beneficial application of the revenues. In rights and privileges, he rendered it in a measure equal to the city itself, by inventing a new kind of suffrage, which the principal officers and magistrates of the colonies might take at home, and forward under seal to the city, against the time of the elections. To increase the number of persons of condition, and of children among the lower ranks, he granted the petitions of all those who requested the honour of doing military service on horseback as knights, provided their demands were seconded by the recommendation of the town in which they lived; and when he visited the several districts of Italy, he distributed a thousand sesterces a head to such of the lower class as presented him with sons or daughters.

The more important provinces, which could not with ease or safety be entrusted to the government of annual magistrates, he reserved for his own administration: the rest he distributed by lot amongst the proconsuls: but sometimes he made exchanges, and frequently visited most of both kinds in person. Some cities in alliance with Rome, but which by their great licentiousness were hastening to ruin, he deprived of their independence. Others, which were much in debt, he relieved, and rebuilt such as had been destroyed by earthquakes. To those that could produce any instance of their having deserved well of the Roman people, he presented the freedom of Latium, or even that of the City. There is not, I believe, a province, except Africa and Sardinia, which he did not visit. . . .

Kingdoms, of which he had made himself master by the right of conquest, a few only excepted, he either restored to their former possessors, or conferred upon aliens. Between kings in alliance with Rome, he encouraged most intimate union; being always ready to promote or favour any proposal of marriage or friendship amongst them; and, indeed, treated them all with the same consideration, as if they were members and parts of the empire. To such of them as were minors or lunatics he appointed guardians, until they arrived at age, or recovered their senses; and the sons of many of them he brought up and educated with his own.

With respect to the army, he distributed the legions and auxiliary troops throughout the several provinces. He stationed a fleet at Misenum, and another at Ravenna, for the protection of the Upper and Lower Seas. A certain number of the forces were selected, to occupy the posts in the city, and partly for his own body-guard; but he dismissed the Spanish guard, which he retained about him till the fall of Antony; and also the Germans, whom he had amongst his guards, until the defeat of Varus. Yet he never permitted a greater force than three cohorts in the city, and had no (praetorian) camps. The rest he quartered in the neighbourhood of the nearest towns, in winter and summer camps.

All the troops throughout the empire he reduced to one fixed model with regard to their pay and their pensions; determining these according to their rank in the army, the time they had served, and their private means; so that after their discharge, they might not be tempted by age or necessities to join the agitators for a revolution. For the purpose of providing a fund always ready to meet their pay and pensions, he instituted a military exchequer, and appropriated new taxes to that object. In order to obtain the earliest intelligence of what was passing in the provinces, he established posts, consisting at first of young men stationed at moderate distances along the military roads, and afterwards of regular couriers with fast vehicles; which appeared to him the most commodious, because the persons who were the bearers of dispatches, written on the spot, might then be questioned about the business, as occasion occurred.

* * *

He always abhorred the title of *Lord,* as ill-omened and offensive. And when, in a play, performed at the theatre, at which he was present, these words were introduced, "O just and gracious lord," and the whole company, with joyful acclamations, testified their approbation of them, as applied to him, he instantly put a stop to their indecent flattery, by waving his hand, and frowning sternly, and next day publicly declared his displeasure, in a proclamation. He never afterwards would suffer himself to be addressed in that manner, even by his own children or grand-children, either in jest or earnest and forbad them the use of all such complimentary expressions to one another.

He rarely entered any city or town, or departed from it, except in the evening or the night, to avoid giving any person the trouble of complimenting him. During his consulships, he commonly walked the streets on foot; but at other times, rode in a closed carriage. He admitted to court even plebeians, in common with people of the higher ranks; receiving the petitions of those who approached him with so much affability, that he once jocosely rebuked a man, by telling him, "You present your memorial with as much hesitation as if you were offering money to an elephant." On senate days, he used to pay his respects to the Conscript Fathers only in the house, addressing them each by name as they sat, without any prompter; and on his departure, he bade each of them farewell, while they retained their seats. In the same manner, he maintained with many of them a constant intercourse of mutual civilities, giving them his company upon occasions of any particular festivity in their families; until he became advanced in years, and was incommoded by the crowd at a wedding.

. . .

How much he was beloved for his worthy conduct in all these respects, it is easy to imagine. I say nothing of the decrees of the senate in his honour, which may seem to have resulted from compulsion or deference. The Roman knights voluntarily, and with one accord, always celebrated his birth for two days together; and all ranks of the people, yearly, in performance of a vow they had made, threw a piece of money into the Curtian lake, as an offering for his welfare. They likewise, on the calends [first] of January, presented for his acceptance new-year's gifts in the capitol, though he was not present: with which donations he purchased some costly images of the Gods, which he erected in several streets of the city; as that of Apollo Sandaliarius, Jupiter Tragoedus, and others.

When his house on the Palatine hill was accidentally destroyed by fire, the veteran soldiers, the judges, the tribes, and even the people, individually, contributed, according to the ability of each, for rebuilding it; but he would accept only of some small portion out of the several sums collected, and refused to take from any one person more than a single denarius. Upon his return home from any of the provinces, they attended him not only with joyful acclamations, but with songs. It is also remarked, that as often as he entered the city, the infliction of punishment was suspended for the time.

The whole body of the people, upon a sudden impulse, and with unanimous consent, offered him the title of Father of His Country. It was announced to him first at Antium, by a deputation from the people, and upon his declining the honour, they repeated their offer on his return to Rome, in a full theatre, when they were crowned with laurel. The senate soon afterwards adopted the proposal.

. . .

Having thus given an account of the manner in which he filled his public offices both civil and military, and his conduct in the government of the empire, both in peace and war; I shall now describe his private and domestic life.

. . .

He ate sparingly (for I must not omit even this), and commonly used a plain diet. He was particularly fond of coarse bread, small fishes, new cheese made of cow's milk, and green figs of the sort which bear fruit twice a year. He did not wait for supper, but took food at any time, and in any place, when he had an appetite. The following passages relative to this subject, I have transcribed from his letters. "I ate a little bread and some small dates, in my carriage." Again. "In returning home from the palace in my litter, I ate an ounce of bread, and a few raisins." Again. "No Jew, my dear Tiberius, ever keeps such strict fast upon the Sabbath, as I have to-day; for while in the bath, and after the first hour of the night, I only ate two biscuits, before I began to be rubbed with oil." From this great indifference about his diet, he sometimes supped by himself, before his company began, or after they had finished, and would not touch a morsel at table with his guests.

He was by nature extremely sparing in the use of wine. Cornelius Nepos says that he used to drink only three times at supper in the camp at Modena; and when he indulged himself the most, he never exceeded a pint; or if he did, his stomach rejected it. Of all wines, he gave the preference to the Rhaetian, but scarcely ever drank any in the day-time. Instead of drinking, he used to take a piece of bread dipped in cold water, or a slice of cucumber, or some leaves of lettuce, or a green, sharp, juicy apple.

After a slight repast at noon, he used to seek repose, dressed as he was, and with his shoes on, his feet covered, and his hand held before his eyes. After supper he commonly withdrew to his study, a small closet, where he sat late, until he had put down in his diary all or most of the remaining transactions of the day, which he had not before registered. He would then go to bed, but never slept above seven hours at most, and that not without interruption; for he would wake three or four times during that time. If he could not again fall asleep, as sometimes happened, he called for some one to read or tell stories to him, until he became drowsy, and then his sleep was usually protracted till after day-break. He never liked to lie awake in the dark, without somebody to sit by him. Very early rising was apt to disagree with him. On which account, if he was obliged to rise betimes, for any civil or religious functions, in order to guard as much as possible against the inconvenience resulting from it, he used to lodge in some apartment near the spot, belonging to any of his attendants. If at any time a fit of drowsiness seized him in passing along the streets, his litter was set down while he snatched a few moments' sleep.

In person he was handsome and graceful, through every period of his life. But he was negligent in his dress; and so careless about dressing his hair, that he usually had it done in great haste by several barbers at a time. His beard he sometimes clipped, and sometimes shaved; and either read or wrote during the operation. His countenance, either when discoursing or silent, was so calm and serene that a Gaul of the first rank declared amongst his friends that he was so softened by it, as to be restrained from throwing him down a precipice, in his passage over the Alps, when he had been admitted to approach him, under pretence of conferring with him. His eyes were bright and piercing; and he was willing it should be thought that there was something of a divine vigour in them. He was likewise not a little pleased to see people, upon his looking stedfastly at them, lower their countenances, as if the sun shone in their eyes. But in his old age, he saw very imperfectly with his left eye. His teeth were thin set, small and scaly, his hair a little curled, and inclining to a yellow colour. His eye-brows met; his ears were small, and he had an aquiline nose. His complexion was betwixt brown and fair; his stature but low; though Julius Marathus, his freedman, says he was five feet and nine inches in height. This, however, was so much concealed by the just proportion of his limbs, that it was only perceivable upon comparison with some taller person standing by him.

He is said to have been born with many spots upon his breast and belly, answering to the figure, order, and number of the stars in the constellation of the Bear. He had besides several callosities resembling scars, occasioned by an itching in his body, and the constant and violent use of the strigil in being rubbed. He had a weakness in his left hip, thigh, and leg, insomuch that he often halted on that side; but he received much benefit from the use of sand and reeds. He likewise sometimes found the fore-finger of his right hand so weak that, when it was benumbed and contracted with cold, to use it in writing he was obliged to have recourse to a circular piece of horn. He had occasionally a complaint in the bladder; but upon voiding some stones in his urine, he was relieved from that pain.

Juvenal

— 16 —

Satires: The Third Satire

The wealthy aristocracy of the Empire, deprived of any real participation
in its government and of any serious public responsibilities, often led a
parasitic and meaningless existence. The dangers of such luxurious idle-
ness had been pointed out by others, but it remained for a poet of the
early second century to voice a revulsion and disgust unequaled outside
the Christian writings of his day.

This poet was Decimus Junius Juvenalis (*ca.* 60–*ca.* 140 A.D.), born to
a middle-class family of Latium. Little is known of his life; but a tentative reconstruction presents him as a man who, failing of advancement in
a military career, published a lampoon against the corrupt imperial court
and so was exiled to Egypt. Returning to Rome in 96 A.D., with career
gone and fortune confiscated, he led the life of an embittered man, spong-
ing upon wealthy patrons. After fifteen years of this wretched existence,
he somehow acquired a farm near Tivoli, perhaps at the Emperor
Hadrian's bounty. Secure now, but still full of bile, he wrote his poems
between 110 and 130.

The theme of the third satire is the age-old fear and hatred of megalop-
olis, the vast city, with its venality and vice. The keynote is struck in the
setting of the poem. In search of quiet, Juvenal meets a friend, Umbricius,
another hanger-on, in a once-sacred grove, only to find that it has been
"improved" and vulgarized by rapacious foreigners, with whom the city
swarms. The poem then takes the form of a tough, frankly spoken mono-
logue by Umbricius, satirizing the bored, selfish, sex-crazy rich in the city
he is leaving forever.

The moral chaos depicted helps to explain the growing appeal of
Christianity to Romans during the poet's later years. Juvenal offered
escape into the idealized Roman past; Christianity proposed a new way of
life.

Juvenal, *The Satires of Juvenal,* trans. Rolfe Humphries (Bloomington: Indiana
University Press, 1958), 33–45. Reprinted by permission of the publisher.

AGAINST THE CITY OF ROME

Troubled because my old friend is going, I still must commend him
For his decision to settle down in the ghost town of Cumae,
Giving the Sibyl one citizen more. That's the gateway to Baiae
There, a pleasant shore, a delightful retreat. I'd prefer
Even a barren rock in that bay to the brawl of Subura.
Where have we ever seen a place so dismal and lonely
We'd not be better off there, than afraid, as we are here, of fires,
Roofs caving in, and the thousand risks of this terrible city
Where the poets recite all through the dog days of August?

While they are loading his goods on one little four-wheeled wagon,
Here he waits, by the old archways which the aqueducts moisten.
This is where Numa, by night, came to visit his goddess.
That once holy grove, its sacred spring, and its temple,
Now are let out to the Jews, if they have some straw and a basket.
Every tree, these days, has to pay rent to the people.
Kick the Muses out; the forest is swarming with beggars.
So we go down to Egeria's vale, with its modern improvements.
How much more close the presence would be, were there lawns by
    the water,
Turf to the curve of the pool, not this unnatural marble!

Umbricius has much on his mind. "Since there's no place in the
    city,"
He says, "For an honest man, and no reward for his labors,
Since I have less today than yesterday, since by tomorrow
That will have dwindled still more, I have made my decision. I'm
    going
To the place where, I've heard, Daedalus put off his wings,
While my white hair is still new, my old age in the prime of its
    straightness,
While my fate spinner still has yarn on her spool, while I'm able
Still to support myself on two good legs, without crutches.
Rome, good-bye! Let the rest stay in the town if they want to,
Fellows like A, B, and C, who make black white at their pleasure,
Finding it easy to grab contracts for rivers and harbors,

Putting up temples, or cleaning out sewers, or hauling off corpses,
Or, if it comes to that, auctioning slaves in the market.
Once they used to be hornblowers, working the carneys;
Every wide place in the road knew their puffed-out cheeks and their
    squealing.
Now they give shows of their own. Thumbs up! Thumbs down! And
    the killers
Spare or slay, and then go back to concessions for private privies.
Nothing they won't take on. Why not?—since the kindness of For-
    tune
(Fortune is out for laughs) has exalted them out of the gutter.

"What should I do in Rome? I am no good at lying.
If a book's bad, I can't praise it, or go around ordering copies.
I don't know the stars; I can't hire out as assassin
When some young man wants his father knocked off for a price; I
    have never
Studied the guts of frogs, and plenty of others know better
How to convey to a bride the gifts of the first man she cheats with.
I am no lookout for thieves, so I cannot expect a commission
On some governor's staff. I'm a useless corpse, or a cripple.
Who has a pull these days, except your yes men and stooges
With blackmail in their hearts, yet smart enough to keep silent?
No honest man feels in debt to those he admits to his secrets,
But your Verres must love the man who can tattle on Verres
Any old time that he wants. Never let the gold of the Tagus,
Rolling under its shade, become so important, so precious
You have to lie awake, take bribes that you'll have to surrender,
Tossing in gloom, a threat to your mighty patron forever.

"Now let me speak of the race that our rich men dote on most
    fondly.
These I avoid like the plague, let's have no coyness about it.
Citizens, I can't stand a Greekized Rome. Yet what portion
Of the dregs of our town comes from Achaia only?
Into the Tiber pours the silt, the mud of Orontes,
Bringing its babble and brawl, its dissonant harps and its timbrels,
Bringing also the tarts who display their wares at the Circus.
Here's the place, if your taste is for hat-wearing whores, brightly
    colored!
What have they come to now, the simple souls from the country

Romulus used to know? They put on the *trechedipna*
(That might be called, in our tongue, their running-to-dinner out-
    fit),
Pin on their *niketeria* (medals), and smell *ceromatic*
(Attar of wrestler). They come, trooping from Samos and Tralles,
Andros, wherever that is, Azusa and Cucamonga,
Bound for the Esquiline or the hill we have named for the vineyard,
Termites, into great halls where they hope, some day, to be tyrants.
Desperate nerve, quick wit, as ready in speech as Isaeus,
Also a lot more long-winded. Look over there! See that fellow?
What do you take him for? He can be anybody he chooses,
Doctor of science or letters, a vet or a chiropractor,
Orator, painter, masseur, palmologist, tightrope walker.
If he is hungry enough, your little Greek stops at nothing.
Tell him to fly to the moon and he runs right off for his space ship.
Who flew first? Some Moor, some Turk, some Croat, or some
    Slovene?
Not on your life, but a man from the very center of Athens.

"Should I not run away from these purple-wearing freeloaders?
Must I wait while they sign their names? Must their couches always
    be softer?
Stowaways, that's how they got here, in the plums and figs from
    Damascus.
I was here long before they were: my boyhood drank in the sky
Over the Aventine hill; I was nourished by Sabine olives.
Agh, what lackeys they are, what sycophants! See how they flatter
Some ignoramus's talk, or the looks of some horrible eyesore,
Saying some Ichabod Crane's long neck reminds them of muscles
Hercules strained when he lifted Antaeus aloft on his shoulders,
Praising some cackling voice that really sounds like a rooster's
When he's pecking a hen. We can praise the same objects that they
    do,
Only, they are believed. Does an actor do any better
Mimicking Thais, Alcestis, Doris without any clothes on?
It seems that a woman speaks, not a mask; the illusion is perfect
Down to the absence of bulge and the little cleft under the belly.
Yet they win no praise at home, for all of their talent.
Why?—Because Greece is a stage, and every Greek is an actor.
Laugh, and he splits his sides; weep, and his tears flow in torrents

Though he's not sad; if you ask for a little more fire in the winter
He will put on his big coat; if you say 'I'm hot,' he starts sweating.
We are not equals at all; he always has the advantage,
Able, by night or day, to assume, from another's expression,
This or that look, prepared to throw up his hands, to cheer loudly
If his friend gives a good loud belch or doesn't piss crooked,
Or if a gurgle comes from his golden cup when inverted
Straight up over his nose—a good deep swig, and no heeltaps!

"Furthermore, nothing is safe from his lust, neither matron nor
    virgin,
Not her affianced spouse, or the boy too young for the razor.
If he can't get at these, he would just as soon lay his friend's
    grandma.
(Anything, so he'll get in to knowing the family secrets!)
Since I'm discussing the Greeks, let's turn to their schools and pro-
    fessors,
The crimes of the hood and gown. Old Dr. Egnatius, informant,
Brought about the death of Barea, his friend and his pupil,
Born on that riverbank where the pinion of Pegasus landed.
No room here, none at all, for any respectable Roman
Where a Protogenes rules, or a Diphilus, or a Hermarchus,
Never sharing their friends—a racial characteristic!
Hands off! He puts a drop of his own, or his countryside's poison
Into his patron's ear, an ear which is only too willing
And I am kicked out of the house, and all my years of long service
Count for nothing. Nowhere does the loss of a client mean less.

"Let's not flatter ourselves. What's the use of our service?
What does a poor man gain by hurrying out in the nighttime,
All dressed up before dawn, when the praetor nags at his troopers
Bidding them hurry along to convey his respects to the ladies.
Barren, of course, like Albina, before any others can get there?
Sons of men freeborn give right of way to a rich man's
Slave, a crack, once or twice, at Calvina or Catiena
Costs an officer's pay, but if you like the face of some floozy
You hardly have money enough to make her climb down from her
    high chair.
Put on the stand, at Rome, a man with a record unblemished,
No more a perjurer than Numa was, or Metellus,
What will they question? His wealth, right away, and possibly, later,

(Only possibly, though) touch on his reputation.
'How many slaves does he feed? What's the extent of his acres?
How big are his platters? How many? What of his goblets and wine
  bowls?'
His word is as good as his bond—if he has enough bonds in his
  strongbox.
But a poor man's oath, even if sworn on all altars
All the way from here to the farthest Dodecanese island,
Has no standing in court. What has he to fear from the lightnings
Of the outraged gods? He has nothing to lose; they'll ignore him.

"If you're poor, you're a joke, on each and every occasion.
What a laugh, if your cloak is dirty or torn, if your toga
Seems a little bit soiled, if your shoe has a crack in the leather,
Or if more than one patch attests to more than one mending!
Poverty's greatest curse, much worse than the fact of it, is that
It makes men objects of mirth, ridiculed, humbled, embarrassed.
'Out of the front-row seats!' they cry when you're out of money,
Yield your place to the sons of some pimp, the spawn of some cat-
  house,
Some slick auctioneer's brat, or the louts some trainer has fathered
Or the well-groomed boys whose sire is a gladiator.
Such is the law of place, decreed by the nitwitted Otho:
All the best seats are reserved for the classes who have the most
  money.
Who can marry a girl if he has less money than she does?
What poor man is an heir, or can hope to be? Which of them ever
Rates a political job, even the meanest and lowest?
Long before now, all poor Roman descendants of Romans
Ought to have marched out of town in one determined migration.
Men do not easily rise whose poverty hinders their merit.
Here it is harder than anywhere else: the lodgings are hovels,
Rents out of sight; your slaves take plenty to fill up their bellies
While you make do with a snack. You're ashamed of your earthen-
  ware dishes—
Ah, but that wouldn't be true if you lived content in the country,
Wearing a dark-blue cape, and the hood thrown back on your
  shoulders.

"In a great part of this land of Italy, might as well face it,
No one puts on a toga unless he is dead. On festival days

Where the theater rises, cut from green turf, and with great pomp
Old familiar plays are staged again, and a baby,
Safe in his mother's lap, is scared of the grotesque mask,
There you see all dressed alike, the balcony and the front rows,
Even His Honor content with a tunic of simple white.
Here, beyond our means, we have to be smart, and too often
Get our effects with too much, an elaborate wardrobe, on credit!
This is a common vice; we must keep up with neighbors,
Poor as we are. I tell you, everything here costs you something.
How much to give Cossus the time of day, or receive from Veiento
One quick glance, with his mouth buttoned up for fear he might
    greet you?
One shaves his beard, another cuts off the locks of his boy friend,
Offerings fill the house, but these, you find, you will pay for.
Put this in your pipe and smoke it—we have to pay tribute
Giving the slaves a bribe for the prospect of bribing their masters.

"Who, in Praeneste's cool, or the wooded Volsinian uplands,
Who, on Tivoli's heights, or a small town like Gabii, say,
Fears the collapse of his house? But Rome is supported on pipe-
    stems,
Matchsticks; it's cheaper, so, for the landlord to shore up his ruins,
Patch up the old cracked walls, and notify all the tenants
They can sleep secure, though the beams are in ruins above them.
No, the place to live is out there, where no cry of *Fire!*
Sounds the alarm of the night, with a neighbor yelling for water,
Moving his chattels and goods, and the whole third story is smoking.
This you'll never know: for if the ground floor is scared first,
You are the last to burn, up there where the eaves of the attic
Keep off the rain, and the doves are brooding over their nest eggs.

Codrus owned one bed, too small for a midget to sleep on,
Six little jugs he had, and a tankard adorning his sideboard,
Under whose marble (clay), a bust or a statue of Chiron,
Busted, lay on its side; an old locker held Greek books
Whose divinest lines were gnawed by the mice, those vandals.
Codrus had nothing, no doubt, and yet he succeeded, poor fellow,
Losing that nothing, his all. And this is the very last straw—
No one will help him out with a meal or lodging or shelter.
Stripped to the bone, begging for crusts, he still receives nothing.

"Yet if Asturicus' mansion burns down, what a frenzy of sorrow!
Mothers dishevel themselves, the leaders dress up in black,
Courts are adjourned. We groan at the fall of the city, we hate
The fire, and the fire still burns, and while it is burning,
Somebody rushes up to replace the loss of the marble,
Some one chips in toward a building fund, another gives statues,
Naked and shining white, some masterpiece of Euphranor
Or Polyclitus' chef d'oeuvre; and here's a fellow with bronzes
Sacred to Asian gods. Books, chests, a bust of Minerva,
A bushel of silver coins. *To him that hath shall be given!*
This Persian, childless, of course, the richest man in the smart set,
Now has better things, and more, than before the disaster.
How can we help but think he started the fire on purpose?

"Tear yourself from the games, and get a place in the country!
One little Latian town, like Sora, say, or Frusino,
Offers a choice of homes, at a price you pay here, in one year,
Renting some hole in the wall. Nice houses, too, with a garden,
Springs bubbling up from the grass, no need for a windlass or bucket,
Plenty to water your flowers, if they need it, without any trouble.
Live there, fond of your hoe, an independent producer,
Willing and able to feed a hundred good vegetarians.
Isn't it something, to feel, wherever you are, how far off,
You are a monarch? At least, lord of a single lizard.

"Here in town the sick die from insomnia mostly.
Undigested food, on a stomach burning with ulcers,
Brings on listlessness, but who can sleep in a flophouse?
Who but the rich can afford sleep and a garden apartment?
That's the source of infection. The wheels creak by on the narrow
Streets of the wards, the drivers squabble and brawl when they're
        stopped,
More than enough to frustrate the drowsiest son of a sea cow.
When his business calls, the crowd makes way, as the rich man,
Carried high in his car, rides over them, reading or writing,
Even taking a snooze, perhaps for the motion's composing.
Still, he gets where he wants before we do; for all of our hurry
Traffic gets in our way, in front, around and behind us.
Somebody gives me a shove with an elbow, or two-by-four scantling.

One clunks my head with a beam, another cracks down with a beer
  keg.
Mud is thick on my shins, I am trampled by somebody's big feet.
Now what?—a soldier grinds his hobnails into my toes.

"Don't you see the mob rushing along to the handout?
There are a hundred guests, each one with his kitchen servant.
Even Samson himself could hardly carry those burdens,
Pots and pans some poor little slave tries to keep on his head, while
  he hurries
Hoping to keep the fire alive by the wind of his running.
Tunics, new-darned, are ripped to shreds; there's the flash of a fir
  beam
Huge on some great dray, and another carries a pine tree,
Nodding above our heads and threatening death to the people.
What will be left of the mob, if that cart of Ligurian marble
Breaks its axle down and dumps its load on these swarms?
Who will identify limbs or bones? The poor man's cadaver,
Crushed, disappears like his breath. And meanwhile, at home, his
  household
Washes the dishes, and puffs up the fire, with all kinds of a clatter
Over the smeared flesh-scrapers, the flasks of oil, and the towels.
So the boys rush around, while their late master is sitting,
Newly come to the bank of the Styx, afraid of the filthy
Ferryman there, since he has no fare, not even a copper
In his dead mouth to pay for the ride through that muddy whirl-
  pool.

"Look at other things, the various dangers of nighttime.
How high it is to the cornice that breaks, and a chunk beats my
  brains out,
Or some slob heaves a jar, broken or cracked, from a window.
Bang! It comes down with a crash and proves its weight on the side-
  walk.
You are a thoughtless fool, unmindful of sudden disaster,
If you don't make your will before you go out to have dinner.
There are as many deaths in the night as there are open windows
Where you pass by; if you're wise, you will pray, in your wretched
  devotions,
People may be content with no more than emptying slop jars.

"There your hell-raising drunk, who has had the bad luck to kill no
   one,
Tosses in restless rage, like Achilles mourning Patroclus,
Turns from his face to his back, can't sleep, for only a fracas
Gives him the proper sedation. But any of these young hoodlums,
All steamed up on wine, watches his step when the crimson
Cloak goes by, a lord, with a long, long line of attendants,
Torches and brazen lamps, warning him, *Keep your distance!*
Me, however, whose torch is the moon, or the feeblest candle
Fed by a sputtering wick, he absolutely despises.
Here is how it all starts, the fight, if you think it is fighting
When he throws all the punches, and all I do is absorb them.
He stops. He tells me to stop. I stop. I have to obey him.
What can you do when he's mad and bigger and stronger than you
   are?
'Where do you come from?' he cries, 'you wino, you bean-bloated
   bastard?
Off what shoemaker's dish have you fed on chopped leeks and boiled
   lamb-lip?
What? No answer? Speak up, or take a swift kick in the rear.
Tell me where you hang out—in some praying-house with the Jew-
   boys?'
If you try to talk back, or sneak away without speaking,
All the same thing: you're assaulted, and then put under a bail bond
For committing assault. This is a poor man's freedom.
Beaten, cut up by fists, he begs and implores his assailant,
Please, for a chance to go home with a few teeth left in his mouth.

"This is not all you must fear. Shut up your house or your store,
Bolts and padlocks and bars will never keep out all the burglars,
Or a holdup man will do you in with a switch blade.
If the guards are strong over Pontine marshes and pinewoods
Near Volturno, the scum of the swamps and the filth of the forest
Swirl into Rome, the great sewer, their sanctuary, their haven.
Furnaces blast and anvils groan with the chains we are forging:
What other use have we for iron and steel? There is danger
We will have little left for hoes and mattocks and ploughshares.
Happy the men of old, those primitive generations
Under the tribunes and kings, when Rome had only one jailhouse!

"There is more I could say, I could give you more of my reasons,
But the sun slants down, my oxen seem to be calling,
My man with the whip is impatient, I must be on my way.
So long! Don't forget me. Whenever you come to Aquino
Seeking relief from Rome, send for me. I'll come over
From my bay to your hills, hiking along in my thick boots
Toward your chilly fields. What's more, I promise to listen
If your satirical verse esteems me worthy the honor."

Marcus Aurelius

— 17 —

Thoughts

Plato had dreamed of the possibility of wisdom and political authority meeting in the same man, and the early Stoics taught the idea of a cosmopolis or "universal city" of gods and men. Although the Roman Empire fell far short of these ideals, the reigning philosophy, Stoicism, did provide its autocrats with moral justification, and its thinkers with the concept of natural law. The second century of the Empire may not have been "the period in the history of the world in which the condition of the human race was most happy and prosperous," as the historian Edward Gibbon thought; but for a portion of that century supreme power rested in the hands of the Stoics, and Marcus Aurelius Antoninus (121–180 A.D.) personified Plato's ideal of the philosopher-king.

Born and reared in Rome, Marcus so impressed Emperor Antoninus that he legally adopted him, named him his successor, and in 145 began to share with him the government of the Empire. After Marcus became sole ruler (161–180 A.D.) there was hard fighting on the northern frontier against the barbarians; finally a plague carried off Marcus Aurelius together with a quarter of his subjects. Marcus Aurelius was the last of the "good emperors," and his reign was the end of an epoch. "At heart," wrote the nineteenth-century French historian, Ernest Renan, "all of us mourn Marcus Aurelius as if he had died yesterday."

This selection is no Stoic tract appealing for the improvement of others, but the unaffected private diary of a man communing with his own soul, recording at the end of each busy day as soldier and administrator his innermost thoughts and feelings. As such, it is unique, and its very survival remains a mystery. For centuries at a time it disappeared from view, and only during the Renaissance was it recognized for what it is: one of the priceless treasures of humanity.

Written when the emperor was somewhat past fifty, the *Thoughts* re-

Marcus Aurelius, *The Thoughts of the Emperor Marcus Aurelius,* trans. George Long (Boston: Little, Brown, 1892), 97–231, *passim.*

veal a man not brilliant but modest, unselfish, high-minded, and imbued with the highest sense of duty. The selected passages (here rearranged in a topical order) reveal the principles of Roman Stoicism: a religion without revelation, a lofty ethic without hope of reward or fear of punishment to come—one of the last and finest products of the classical mind.

ON NATURE

All things are implicated with one another, and the bond is holy; and there is hardly anything unconnected with any other thing. For things have been co-ordinated, and they combine to form the same universe [order]. For there is one universe made up of all things, and one god who pervades all things, and one substance, and one law, [one] common reason in all intelligent animals, and one truth; if indeed there is also one perfection for all animals which are of the same stock and participate in the same reason.

ON LIVING IN HARMONY WITH NATURE

Everything harmonizes with me, which is harmonious to thee, O Universe. Nothing for me is too early nor too late, which is in due time for thee. Everything is fruit to me which thy seasons bring, O Nature: from thee are all things, in thee are all things, to thee all things return. The poet says, Dear city of Cecrops; and wilt not thou say, Dear city of Zeus?

. . .

Judge every word and deed which are according to nature to be fit for thee; and be not diverted by the blame which follows from any people nor by their words, but if a thing is good to be done or said, do not consider it unworthy of thee. For those persons have their peculiar leading principle and follow their peculiar movement; which things do not thou regard, but go straight on, following thy own nature and the common nature; and the way of both is one.

ON REASON

A man should always have these two rules in readiness; the one to do only whatever the reason of the ruling and legislating faculty may suggest for the use of men; the other, to change thy opinion, if there is any one at hand who sets thee right and moves thee from any opinion. But this change of opinion must proceed only from a certain persuasion, as of what is just or of common advantage, and the like, not because it appears pleasant or brings reputation.

Hast thou reason? I have.—Why then dost not thou use it? For if this does its own work, what else dost thou wish?

. . .

Remember that the ruling faculty is invincible, when self-collected it is satisfied with itself, if it does nothing which it does not choose to do, even if it resist from mere obstinacy. What then will it be when it forms a judgment about anything aided by reason and deliberately? Therefore the mind which is free from passions is a citadel, for man has nothing more secure to which he can fly for refuge and for the future be inexpugnable. He then who has not seen this is an ignorant man; but he who has seen it and does not fly to this refuge is unhappy.

ON DUTY AND RESPONSIBILITY

Every moment think steadily as a Roman and a man to do what thou hast in hand with perfect and simple dignity, and feeling of affection, and freedom, and justice, and to give thyself relief from all other thoughts. And thou wilt give thyself relief if thou doest every act of thy life as if it were the last, laying aside all carelessness and passionate aversion from the commands of reason, and all hypocrisy, and self-love, and discontent with the portion which has been given to thee. Thou seest how few the things are, the which if a man lays hold of, he is able to live a life which flows in quiet, and is like the existence of the gods; for the gods on their part will require nothing more from him who observes these things.

. . .

Do not disturb thyself by thinking of the whole of thy life. Let not thy thoughts at once embrace all the various troubles which thou mayest expect to befall thee: but on every occasion ask thyself, What is there in this which is intolerable and past bearing? for thou wilt be ashamed to confess. In the next place remember that neither the future nor the past pains thee, but only the present. But this is reduced to a very little, if thou only circumscribest it, and chidest thy mind if it is unable to hold out against even this.

. . .

If thou workest at that which is before thee, following right reason seriously, vigorously, calmly, without allowing anything else to distract thee, but keeping thy divine part pure, as if thou shouldst be bound to give it back immediately; if thou holdest to this, expecting nothing, fearing nothing, but satisfied with thy present activity according to nature, and with heroic truth in every word and sound which thou utterest, thou wilt live happy. And there is no man who is able to prevent this.

ON THE MORAL LIFE

If thou findest in human life anything better than justice, truth, temperance, fortitude, and, in a word, anything better than thy own mind's self-satisfaction in the things which it enables thee to do according to right reason, and in the condition that is assigned to thee without thy own choice; if, I say, thou seest anything better than this, turn to it with all thy soul, and enjoy that which thou hast found to be the best. But if nothing appears to be better than the Deity which is planted in thee, which has subjected to itself all thy appetites, and carefully examines all the impressions, and, as Socrates said, has detached itself from the persuasions of sense, and has submitted itself to the gods, and cares for mankind; if thou findest everything else smaller and of less value than this, give place to nothing else, for if thou dost once diverge and incline to it, thou wilt no longer without distraction be able to give the preference to that good thing which is thy proper possession and thy own; for it is not right that anything of any other kind, such as praise from the many, or power, or enjoyment of pleasure, should come into competition with that which is rationally and politically [or, practically] good. All these things, even though they may seem to adapt themselves [to the better things] in a small degree, obtain the superiority all at once, and carry us away. But do thou, I say, simply and freely choose the better, and hold to it.—But that which is useful is the better.—Well, then, if it is useful to thee as a rational being, keep to it; but if it is only useful to thee as an animal, say so, and maintain thy judgment without arrogance: only take care that thou makest the inquiry by a sure method.

Never value anything as profitable to thyself which shall compel thee to break thy promise, to lose thy self-respect, to hate any man, to suspect, to curse, to act the hypocrite, to desire anything which needs walls and curtains: for he who has preferred to everything else his own intelligence and daemon and the worship of its excellence, acts no tragic part, does not groan, will not need either solitude or much company; and, what is chief of all, he will live without either pursuing or flying from [death]; but whether for a longer or a shorter time he shall have the soul enclosed in the body, he cares not at all: for even if he must depart immediately, he will go as readily as if he were going to do anything else which can be done with decency and order; taking care of this only all through life, that his thoughts turn not away from anything which belongs to an intelligent animal and a member of a civil community.

ON HUMILITY AND FORBEARANCE

When thou art offended with any man's shameless conduct, immediately ask thyself, Is it possible, then, that shameless men should not be in the world? It is not possible. Do not, then, require what is impossible. For this man also is one of those shameless men who must of necessity be in the world. Let the same considerations be present to thy mind in the case of the knave, and the faithless man, and of every man who does wrong in any way. For at the same time that thou dost remind thyself that it is impossible that such kind of men should not exist, thou wilt become more kindly disposed towards every one individually. It is useful to perceive this, too, immediately when the occasion arises, what virtue nature has given to man to oppose to every wrongful act. For she has given to man, as an antidote against the stupid man, mildness, and against another kind of man some other power. And in all cases it is possible for thee to correct by teaching the man who is gone astray; for every man who errs misses his object and is gone astray. Besides, wherein hast thou been injured? For thou wilt find that no one among those against whom thou art irritated has done anything by which thy mind could be made worse; but that which is evil to thee and harmful has its foundation only in the mind. And what harm is done or what is there strange, if the man who has not been instructed does the acts of an uninstructed man? Consider whether thou shouldst not rather blame thyself, because thou didst not expect such a man to err in such a way. For thou hadst means given thee by thy reason to suppose that it was likely that he would commit this error, and yet thou hast forgotten and art amazed that he has erred. But most of all when thou blamest a man as faithless or ungrateful, turn to thyself. For the fault is manifestly thy own, whether thou didst trust that a man who had such a disposition would keep his promise, or when conferring thy kindness thou didst not confer it absolutely, nor yet in such way as to have received from thy very act all the profit. For what more dost thou want when thou hast done a man a service? art thou not content that thou hast done something conformable to thy nature, and dost thou seek to be paid for it? just as if the eye demanded a recompense for seeing, or the feet for walking. For as these members are formed for a particular purpose, and by working according to their several constitutions obtain what is their own; so also as man is formed by nature to acts of benevolence, when he has done anything benevolent or in any other way conducive to the common interest, he has acted conformably to his constitution, and he gets what is his own.

ON EQUANIMITY AND IMPERTURBABILITY

Hippocrates, after curing many diseases, himself fell sick and died. The Chaldaei foretold the deaths of many, and then fate caught them too. Alexander and Pompeius and Caius Caesar, after so often completely destroying whole cities, and in battle cutting to pieces many ten thousands of cavalry and infantry, themselves too at last departed from life. Heraclitus, after so many speculations on the conflagration of the universe, was filled with water internally and died smeared all over with mud. And lice destroyed Democritus; and other lice killed Socrates. What means all this? Thou has embarked, thou hast made the voyage, thou art come to shore; get out. If indeed to another life, there is no want of gods, not even there; but if to a state without sensation, thou wilt cease to be held by pains and pleasures, and to be a slave to the vessel, which is as much inferior as that which serves it is superior: for the one is intelligence and deity; the other is earth and corruption.

. . .

This is the chief thing: Be not perturbed, for all things are according to the nature of the universal; and in a little time thou wilt be nobody and nowhere, like Hadrianus and Augustus. In the next place, having fixed thy eyes steadily on thy business look at it, and at the same time remembering that it is thy duty to be a good man, and what man's nature demands, do that without turning aside; and speak as it seems to thee most just, only let it be with a good disposition and with modesty and without hypocrisy.

ON RETIREMENT INTO ONE'S SELF

Men seek retreats for themselves, houses in the country, sea-shores, and mountains; and thou too art wont to desire such things very much. But this is altogether a mark of the most common sort of men, for it is in thy power whenever thou shalt choose to retire into thyself. For nowhere either with more quiet or more freedom from trouble does a man retire than into his own soul, particularly when he has within him such thoughts that by looking into them he is immediately in perfect tranquillity; and I affirm that tranquillity is nothing else than the good ordering of the mind. Constantly then give to thyself this retreat, and renew thyself; and let thy principles be brief and fundamental, which, as soon as thou shalt recur to them, will be sufficient to cleanse the soul completely, and to send thee back free from all discontent with the things to which thou returnest. For with what art thou discontented? With the badness of men? Recall to thy mind this conclusion, that rational animals exist for one another, and that to endure is a part of justice, and that men do wrong involuntarily; and consider how many already, after mutual enmity, suspicion, hatred, and fighting, have been stretched dead, reduced to ashes; and be quiet at last.— But perhaps thou art dissatisfied with that which is assigned to thee out of the universe.—Recall to thy recollection this alternative; either there is providence or atoms [fortuitous concurrence of things]; or remember the arguments by which it has been proved that the world is a kind of political community [and be quiet at last].—But perhaps corporeal things will still fasten upon thee.—

Consider then further that the mind mingles not with the breath, whether moving gently or violently, when it has once drawn itself apart and discovered its own power, and think also of all that thou hast heard and assented to about pain and pleasure [and be quiet at last].—But perhaps the desire of the thing called fame will torment thee.—See how soon everything is forgotten, and look at the chaos of infinite time on each side of [the present], and the emptiness of applause, and the changeableness and want of judgment in those who pretend to give praise, and the narrowness of the space within which it is circumscribed [and be quiet at last]. For the whole earth is a point, and how small a nook in it is this thy dwelling, and how few are there in it, and what kind of people are they who will praise thee.

This then remains: Remember to retire into this little territory of thy own, and above all do not distract or strain thyself, but be free, and look at things as a man, as a human being, as a citizen, as a mortal. But among the things readiest to thy hand to which thou shalt turn, let there be these, which are two. One is that things do not touch the soul, for they are external and remain immovable; but our perturbations come only from the opinion which is within. The other is that all these things, which thou seest, change immediately and will no longer be; and constantly bear in mind how many of these changes thou hast already witnessed. The universe is transformation: life is opinion.

Old Testament

The Old Testament, as the Jewish sacred books are called by Christians, is venerated as the divinely inspired account of God's dealings
with his chosen witnesses, the Jews. In a wider sense it is accepted by be-
lievers as the revelation of the mind and purpose of God to all mankind. Dating from much earlier times, the Old Testament is presented
here at this point because it was accepted from the first by Christians as
the prologue of their own evangel, and only through them did it come
to be known outside Jewish circles in the early days of the Roman Empire. The following selections represent the Jewish account of certain
crises in the tremendous encounter between the human and the divine,
and man's painfully slow comprehension of God's presence and designs.

The drama begins in a garden, typifying the world as God had planned
it—a world full of good things, where man enjoys the intimacy of his
creator. This right relationship is ruptured by man's mutinous self-will,
the primordial sin, followed by the first murder. Evil, then, is inherent
in man's nature, and judgment falls upon him in the Flood, from which
only Noah and his family are rescued. Thus the themes that run all
through the Judeo-Christian epic are prefigured: a recurring pattern of
sin, divine judgment, and—because of the merits of one only, or of a few—
divine mercy.

God then selects the Jewish people as the instrument of his purposes.
They pledge obedience to him and through Moses are given the Law.
But once more man proves unequal to the divine challenge. Exposed to
the contaminating influences of their neighbors, the Jews follow strange
gods and adopt a life of self-indulgence. God's anger is expressed through
his spokesmen, the prophets, who warn and threaten in his name. Gradually they give shape and direction to the religious experience of the
Jews. The books named for the prophets constitute no fewer than a third

The Holy Bible, revised (Oxford: University Press, 1885), I, 4–8, 11–12, 165–76:
IV, 68–70, 80–82, 94–95, 448–51, 453–55, 458–59.

of those in the Old Testament. The first of these prophets—figures peculiar to the Semitic religions—was Amos, who, in the eighth century B.C., denounced the luxury and social injustice of the Jews and predicted the judgment to come.

First the northern kingdom, Israel, was wiped out by the Assyrians in 722 B.C. Later the southern kingdom, Judah, fell to the Babylonians, and its leading citizens were carried into captivity. Reflecting upon these disasters and guided by the insights of the "Second Isaiah," a prophet who wrote about 540 B.C., the Jews acquired a clearer understanding of God's nature and of their role in history. This ultimate awareness marked the acme of their religious experience and, so Christians believe, prepared the way for God's further revelation.

GENESIS

The Creation and Fall
2:4–4:17

These are the generations of the heaven and of the earth when they were created, in the day that the Lord God made earth and heaven. And no plant of the field was yet in the earth, and no herb of the field had yet sprung up: for the Lord God had not caused it to rain upon the earth, and there was not a man to till the ground; but there went up a mist from the earth, and watered the whole face of the ground. And the Lord God formed man of the dust of the ground, and breathed into his nostrils the breath of life; and man became a living soul. And the Lord God planted a garden eastward, in Eden; and there he put the man whom he had formed. And out of the ground made the Lord God to grow every tree that is pleasant to the sight, and good for food; the tree of life also in the midst of the garden, and the tree of the knowledge of good and evil. And a river went out of Eden to water the garden; and from thence it was parted, and became four heads. The name of the first is Pishon: that is it which compasseth the whole land of Havilah, where there is gold; and the gold of that land is good: there is bdellium and the onyx stone. And the name of the second river is Gihon: the same is it that compasseth the whole land of Cush. And the name of the third river is Hiddekel: that is it which goeth in front of Assyria. And the fourth river is Euphrates. And the Lord God took the man, and put him into the garden of Eden to dress it and to keep it. And the Lord God commanded the man, saying, Of every tree of the garden thou mayest freely eat: but of the tree of the knowledge of good and evil, thou shalt not eat of it: for in the day that thou eatest thereof thou shalt surely die.

And the Lord God said, It is not good that the man should be alone; I will make him an help meet for him. And out of the ground the Lord God formed every beast of the field, and every fowl of the air; and brought them unto the man to see what he would call them: and whatsoever the man called every living creature, that was the name thereof. And the man gave names to all cattle, and to the fowl of the air, and to every beast of the field; but for man there was not found an help meet for him. And the Lord God caused a deep sleep to fall upon the man, and he slept; and he took one of his ribs, and closed up the flesh instead thereof: and the rib, which the Lord God had taken from the man, made he a woman, and brought her unto the man. And the man said, This is now bone of my bones, and flesh of my flesh: she shall be called Woman, because she was taken out of Man. Therefore shall a man leave his father and his mother, and shall cleave unto his wife: and they shall be one flesh. And they were both naked, the man and his wife, and were not ashamed.

Now the serpent was more subtil than any beast of the field which the Lord God had made. And he said unto the woman, Yea, hath God said, Ye shall not eat of any tree of the garden? And the woman said unto the serpent, Of the fruit of the trees of the garden we may eat: but of the fruit of the tree which is in the midst of the garden, God hath said, Ye shall not eat of it, neither shall ye touch it, lest ye die. And the serpent said unto the woman, Ye shall not surely die: for God doth know that in the day ye eat thereof, then your eyes shall be opened, and ye shall be as God, knowing good and evil. And when the woman saw that the tree was good for food, and that it was a delight to the eyes, and that the tree was to be desired to make one wise, she took of the fruit thereof, and did eat; and she gave also unto her husband with her, and he did eat. And the eyes of them both were opened, and they knew that they were naked; and they sewed fig leaves together, and made themselves aprons. And they heard the voice of the Lord God walking in the garden in the cool of the day: and the man and his wife hid themselves from the presence of the Lord God amongst the trees of the garden. And the Lord God called unto the man, and said unto him, Where art thou? And he said, I heard thy voice in the garden, and I was afraid, because I was naked; and I hid myself. And he said, Who told thee that thou wast naked? Hast thou eaten of the tree, whereof I commanded thee that thou shouldest not eat? And the man said, The woman whom thou gavest to be with me, she gave me of the tree, and I did eat. And the Lord God said unto the woman, What is this thou hast done? And the woman said, The serpent beguiled me, and I did eat. And the Lord God said unto the serpent, Because thou has done this, cursed art thou above all cattle, and above every beast of the field; upon thy belly shalt thou go, and dust shalt thou eat all the days of thy life: and I will put enmity between thee and the woman, and between thy seed and her seed: it shall bruise thy head, and thou shalt bruise his heel. Unto the woman he said, I will greatly multiply thy sorrow and thy conception; in sorrow thou shalt bring forth children; and thy desire shall be to thy husband, and he shall rule over thee. And unto Adam he said, Because thou hast hearkened unto the voice of thy wife, and hast eaten of the tree, of which I commanded thee, saying, Thou shalt not eat of it: cursed is the ground for thy sake; in toil shalt thou eat of it all the days of thy life; thorns also and thistles shall it bring forth to thee; and thou shalt eat the herb of the field; in the sweat of thy face shalt thou eat bread, till thou return unto the ground; for out of it wast thou taken: for dust thou art, and unto dust shalt thou return. And the man called his wife's name Eve; because she was the mother of all living. And the Lord God made for Adam and for his wife coats of skins, and clothed them.

And the Lord God said, Behold, the man is become as one of us, to know good and evil; and now, lest he put forth his hand, and take also of the tree of life, and eat, and live for ever: therefore the Lord God sent him forth from the garden of Eden, to till the ground from whence he was taken. So he drove out the man; and he placed at the east of the Garden of Eden the Cherubim, and the flame of a sword which turned every way, to keep the way of the tree of life.

And the man knew Eve his wife; and she conceived, and bare Cain, and said, I have gotten a man with *the help of* the Lord. And again she bare his brother Abel. And Abel was a keeper of sheep, but Cain was a tiller of the ground. And in process of time it came to pass, that Cain brought of the fruit of the ground an offering unto the Lord. And Abel, he also brought of the firstlings of his flock and of the fat thereof. And the Lord had respect unto Abel and to his offering: but unto Cain and to his offering he had not respect. And Cain was very wroth, and his countenance fell. And the Lord said unto Cain, Why art thou wroth? and why is thy countenance fallen? If thou doest well, shalt thou not be accepted? and if thou doest not well, sin coucheth at the door: and unto thee shall be his desire, and thou shalt rule over him. And Cain told Abel his brother. And it came to pass, when they were in the field, that Cain rose up against Abel his brother, and slew him. And the Lord said unto Cain, Where is Abel thy brother? And he said, I know not: am I my brother's keeper? And he said, What hast thou done? the voice of thy brother's blood crieth unto me from the ground. And now cursed art thou from the ground, which hath opened her mouth to receive thy brother's blood from thy hand; when thou tillest the ground, it shall not henceforth yield unto thee her strength; a fugitive and a wanderer shalt thou be in the earth. And Cain said unto the Lord, My punishment is greater than I can bear. Behold, thou hast driven me out this day from the face of the ground; and from thy face shall I be hid; and I shall be a fugitive and a wanderer in the earth; and it shall come to pass, that whosoever findeth me shall slay me. And the Lord said unto him, Therefore whosoever slayeth Cain, vengeance shall be taken on him sevenfold. And the Lord appointed a sign for Cain, lest any finding him should smite him.

And Cain went out from the presence of the Lord and dwelt in the land of Nod, on the east of Eden. And Cain knew his wife; and she conceived, and bare Enoch: and he builded a city, and called the name of the city, after the name of his son, Enoch.

The Flood
6:1–22

And it came to pass, when men began to multiply on the face of the ground, and daughters were born unto them, that the sons of God saw the daughters of men that they were fair; and they took them wives of all that they chose. And the Lord said, My spirit shall not strive with man for ever, for that he also is flesh: yet shall his days be an hundred and twenty years. The Nephilim were in the earth in those days, and also after that, when the sons of God came in unto the daughters of men, and they bare children to them: the same were the mighty men which were of old, the men of renown. And the Lord saw that the wickedness of man was great in the earth, and that every imagination of the thoughts of his heart was only evil continually. And it repented the Lord that he had made man on the earth, and it grieved him at his heart. And the Lord said, I will destroy man whom I have created from the face of the ground; both man, and beast, and creeping thing, and fowl of the air; for it repenteth me that I have made them. But Noah found grace in the eyes of the Lord.

These are the generations of Noah. Noah was a righteous man, *and* perfect in his generations: Noah walked with God. And Noah begat three sons, Shem, Ham, and Japheth. And the earth was corrupt before God, and the earth was filled with violence. And God saw the earth, and, behold, it was corrupt; for all flesh had corrupted his way upon the earth.

And God said unto Noah, The end of all flesh is come before me; for the earth is filled with violence through them; and, behold, I will destroy them with the earth. Make thee an ark of gopher wood; rooms shalt though make in the ark, and shalt pitch it within and without with pitch. And this is how thou shalt make it: the length of the ark three hundred cubits, the breadth of it fifty cubits, and the height of it thirty cubits. A light shalt thou make to the ark, and to a cubit shalt thou finish it upward; and the door of the ark shalt thou set in the side thereof; with lower, second, and third stories shalt thou make it. And I, behold, I do bring the flood of waters upon the earth, to destroy all flesh, wherein is the breath of life, from under heaven; every thing that is in the earth shall die. But I will establish my convenant with thee; and thou shalt come into the ark, thou, and thy sons, and thy wife, and thy sons' wives with thee. And of every living thing of all flesh, two of every sort shalt thou bring into the ark, to keep them alive with thee; they shall be male and female. Of the fowl after their kind, and of the cattle after their kind, of every creeping thing of the ground after its kind, two of every sort shall come unto thee, to keep them alive. And take thou unto thee of all food that is eaten, and gather it to thee; and it shall be for food for thee, and for them. Thus did Noah; according to all that God commanded him, so did he.

EXODUS

The Covenant

19:1–20:21

In the third month after the children of Israel were gone forth out of the land of Egypt, the same day came they into the wilderness of Sinai. And when they were departed from Rephidim, and were come to the wilderness of Sinai, they pitched in the wilderness; and there Israel camped before the mount. And Moses went up unto God, and the Lord called unto him out of the mountain, saying, Thus shalt thou say to the house of Jacob, and tell the children of Israel; Ye have seen what I did unto the Egyptians, and how I bare you on eagles' wings, and brought you unto myself. Now therefore, if ye will obey my voice indeed, and keep my covenant, then ye shall be a peculiar treasure unto me from among all peoples: for all the earth is mine: and ye shall be unto me a kingdom of priests, and an holy nation. These are the words which thou shalt speak unto the children of Israel. And Moses came and called for the elders of the people, and set before them all these words which the Lord commanded him. And all the people answered together, and said, All that the Lord hath spoken we will do. And Moses reported the words of the people unto the Lord. And the Lord said unto Moses, Lo, I come unto thee in a thick cloud, that the people may hear when I speak with thee, and may also believe thee for ever. And Moses told the words of the people unto the Lord. And the Lord said unto Moses, Go unto the people, and sanctify them to-day and to-morrow, and let them wash their garments, and be ready against the third day: for the third day the Lord will come down in the sight of all the people upon mount Sinai. And thou shalt set bounds unto the people round about, saying, Take heed to yourselves, that ye go not up into the mount, or touch the border of it: whosoever toucheth the mount shall be surely put to death: no hand shall touch him, but he shall surely be stoned, or shot through; whether it be beast or man, it shall not live: when the trumpet soundeth long, they shall come up to the mount. And Moses went down from the mount unto the people, and sanctified the people; and they washed their garments. And he said unto the people, Be ready against the third day: come not near a woman. And it came to pass on the third day, when it was morning, that there were thunders and lightnings, and a thick cloud upon the mount, and the voice of a trumpet exceeding loud; and all the people that were in the camp trembled. And Moses brought forth the people out of the camp to meet God; and they stood at the nether part of the mount. And mount Sinai was altogether on smoke, because the Lord descended upon it in fire: and the smoke thereof ascended as the smoke of a furnace, and the whole mount quaked greatly. And when the voice of the trumpet waxed louder and louder, Moses spake, and God answered him by a voice. And the Lord came down upon mount Sinai, to the top of the mount: and the Lord called Moses to the top of the mount; and Moses went up. And the Lord said unto Moses, Go down, charge the people, lest they break through unto the Lord to gaze, and many of them perish. And let the priests also, which come near to the Lord, sanctify themselves, lest the Lord break forth upon them. And Moses said unto the Lord, The people cannot come up to mount Sinai: for thou didst charge us, saying, Set bounds about the mount, and sanctify it. And the Lord said unto him, Go, get thee down; and thou shalt come up, thou, and Aaron with thee: but let not the priests and the people break through to come up unto the Lord, lest he break forth upon them. So Moses went down unto the people, and told them.

And God spake all these words, saying,

I AM the Lord thy God, which brought thee out of the land of Egypt, out of the house of bondage.

THOU shalt have none other gods before me.

THOU shalt not make unto thee a graven image, nor *the likeness of* any form that is in heaven above, or that is in the earth beneath, or that is in the water under the earth: thou shalt not bow down thyself unto them, nor serve them: for I the Lord thy God am a jealous God, visiting the iniquity of the fathers upon the children, upon the third and upon the fourth generation of them that hate me; and shewing mercy unto thousands, of them that love me and keep my commandments.

THOU shalt not take the name of the Lord thy God in vain; for the Lord will not hold him guiltless that taketh his name in vain.

REMEMBER the sabbath day, to keep it holy. Six days shalt thou labour, and do all thy work; but the seventh day is a sabbath

unto the Lord thy God: *in it* thou shalt not do any work, thou,
nor thy son, nor thy daughter, thy manservant, nor thy maidservant, nor thy cattle, nor thy stranger that is within thy gates:
for in six days the Lord made heaven and earth, the sea, and
all that in them is, and rested the seventh day: wherefore the
Lord blessed the sabbath day, and hallowed it.

HONOUR thy father and thy mother: that thy days may be long
upon the land which the Lord thy God giveth thee.

THOU shalt do no murder.

THOU shalt not commit adultery.

THOU shalt not steal.

THOU shalt not bear false witness against thy neighbour.

THOU shalt not covet thy neighbour's house, thou shalt not covet
thy neighbour's wife, nor his manservant, nor his maidservant,
nor his ox, nor his ass, nor any thing that is thy neighbour's.

And all the people saw the thunderings, and the lightnings, and
the voice of the trumpet, and the mountain smoking: and when
the people saw it, they trembled, and stood afar off. And they said
unto Moses, Speak thou with us, and we will hear: but let not God
speak with us, lest we die. And Moses said unto the people, Fear
not: for God is come to prove you, and that his fear may be before
you, that ye sin not. And the people stood afar off, and Moses drew
near unto the thick darkness where God was.

The Torah or Law
20:22–23:19

And the Lord said unto Moses, Thus thou shalt say unto the
children of Israel, Ye yourselves have seen that I have talked with
you from heaven. Ye shall not make *other gods* with me; gods of
silver, or gods of gold, ye shall not make unto you. An altar of earth
thou shalt make unto me, and shalt sacrifice thereon thy burnt
offerings, and thy peace offerings, thy sheep, and thine oxen: in
every place where I record my name I will come unto thee and I
will bless thee. And if thou make me an altar of stone, thou shalt
not build it of hewn stones: for if thou lift up thy tool upon it,
thou hast polluted it. Neither shalt thou go up by steps unto mine
altar, that thy nakedness be not discovered thereon.

Now these are the judgements which thou shalt set before them.

If thou buy an Hebrew servant, six years he shall serve: and in the seventh he shall go out free for nothing. If he come in by himself, he shall go out by himself: if he be married, then his wife shall go out with him. If his master give him a wife, and she bear him sons or daughters; the wife and her children shall be her master's, and he shall go out by himself. But if the servant shall plainly say, I love my master, my wife, and my children; I will not go out free: then his master shall bring him unto God, and shall bring him to the door, or unto the door post; and his master shall bore his ear through with an awl; and he shall serve him for ever.

And if a man sell his daughter to be a maidservant, she shall not go out as the menservants do. If she please not her master, who hath espoused her to himself, then shall he let her be redeemed: to sell her unto a strange people he shall have no power, seeing he hath dealt deceitfully with her. And if he espouse her unto his son, he shall deal with her after the manner of daughters. If he take him another *wife;* her food, her raiment, and her duty of marriage, shall he not diminish. And if he do not these three unto her, then shall she go out for nothing, without money.

He that smiteth a man, so that he die, shall surely be put to death. And if a man lie not in wait, but God deliver *him* into his hand; then I will appoint thee a place whither he shall flee. And if a man come presumptuously upon his neighbour, to slay him with guile; thou shalt take him from mine altar, that he may die.

And he that smiteth his father, or his mother, shall be surely put to death.

And he that stealeth a man, and selleth him, or if he be found in his hand, he shall surely be put to death.

And he that curseth his father, or his mother, shall surely be put to death.

And if men contend, and one smiteth the other with a stone, or with his fist and he die not, but keep his bed: if he rise again, and walk abroad upon his staff, then shall he that smote him be quit: only he shall pay for the loss of his time, and shall cause him to be thoroughly healed.

And if a man smite his servant, or his maid, with a rod, and he die under his hand; he shall surely be punished. Notwithstanding, if he continue a day or two, he shall not be punished: for he is his money.

And if men strive together, and hurt a woman with child, so that her fruit depart, and yet no mischief follow: he shall be surely fined, according as the woman's husband shall lay upon him; and he shall pay as the judges determine. But if any mischief follow, then thou shalt give life for life, eye for eye, tooth for tooth, hand for hand, foot for foot, burning for burning, wound for wound, stripe for stripe.

And if a man smite the eye of his servant, or the eye of his maid, and destroy it; he shall let him go free for his eye's sake. And if he smite out his manservant's tooth, or his maidservant's tooth; he shall let him go free for his tooth's sake.

And if an ox gore a man or a woman, that they die, the ox shall be surely stoned, and his flesh shall not be eaten; but the owner of the ox shall be quit. But if the ox were wont to gore in time past, and it hath been testified to his owner, and he hath not kept him in, but that he hath killed a man or a woman; the ox shall be stoned, and his owner also shall be put to death. If there be laid on him a ransom, then he shall give for the redemption of his life whatsoever is laid upon him. Whether he have gored a son, or have gored a daughter, according to this judgement shall it be done unto him. If the ox gore a manservant or a maidservant he shall give unto their master thirty shekels of silver, and the ox shall be stoned.

And if a man shall open a pit, or if a man shall dig a pit and not cover it, and an ox or an ass fall therein, the owner of the pit shall make it good; he shall give money unto the owner of them, and the dead *beast* shall be his.

And if one man's ox hurt another's, that he die; then they shall sell the live ox, and divide the price of it; and the dead also they shall divide. Or if it be known that the ox was wont to gore in time past, and his owner hath not kept him in; he shall surely pay ox for ox, and the dead *beast* shall be his own.

If a man shall steal an ox, or a sheep, and kill it, or sell it; he shall pay five oxen for an ox, and four sheep for a sheep. If the thief be found breaking in, and be smitten that he die, there shall be no bloodguiltiness for him. If the sun be risen upon him, there shall be bloodguiltiness for him: he should make restitution; if he have nothing, then he shall be sold for his theft. If the theft be found in his hand alive, whether it be ox, or ass, or sheep; he shall pay double.

If a man shall cause a field or vineyard to be eaten, and shall let his beast loose, and it feed in another man's field; of the best of his own field, and of the best of his own vineyard, shall he make restitution.

If fire break out, and catch in thorns, so that the shocks of corn, or the standing corn, or the field, be consumed; he that kindled the fire shall surely make restitution.

If a man shall deliver unto his neighbour money or stuff to keep, and it be stolen out of the man's house; if the thief be found, he shall pay double. If the thief be not found, then the master of the house shall come near unto God, *to see* whether he have not put his hand unto his neighbour's goods. For every matter of trespass, whether it be for ox, for ass, for sheep, for raiment, *or* for any manner of lost thing, whereof one saith, This is it, the cause of both parties shall come before God; he whom God shall condemn shall pay double unto his neighbour.

If a man deliver unto his neighbour an ass, or an ox, or a sheep, or any beast, to keep; and it die, or be hurt, or driven away, no man seeing it: the oath of the Lord shall be between them both, whether he hath not put his hand unto his neighbour's goods; and the owner thereof shall accept it, and he shall not make restitution. But if it be stolen from him, he shall make restitution unto the owner thereof. If it be torn in pieces, let him bring it for witness; he shall not make good that which was torn.

And if a man borrow aught of his neighbour, and it be hurt, or die, the owner thereof not being with it, he shall surely make restitution. If the owner thereof be with it, he shall not make it good: if it be an hired thing, it came for its hire.

And if a man entice a virgin that is not betrothed, and lie with her, he shall surely pay a dowry for her to be his wife. If her father utterly refuse to give her unto him, he shall pay money according to the dowry of virgins.

Thou shalt not suffer a sorceress to live.

Whosoever lieth with a beast shall surely be put to death.

He that sacrificeth unto any god, save unto the Lord only, shall be utterly destroyed. And a stranger shalt thou not wrong, neither shalt thou oppress him: for ye were strangers in the land of Egypt. Ye shall not afflict any widow, or fatherless child. If thou afflict them in any wise, and they cry at all unto me, I will surely hear their cry; and my wrath shall wax hot, and I will kill you with the sword; and your wives shall be widows, and your children fatherless.

If thou lend money to any of my people with thee that is poor, thou shalt not be to him as a creditor; neither shall ye lay upon him usury. If thou at all take thy neighbour's garment to pledge, thou shalt restore it unto him by that the sun goeth down: for that is his only covering, it is his garment for his skin: wherein shall he sleep? and it shall come to pass, when he crieth unto me, that I will hear; for I am gracious.

Thou shalt not revile God, nor curse a ruler of thy people. Thou shalt not delay to offer of the abundance of thy fruits, and of thy liquors. The firstborn of thy sons shalt thou give unto me. Likewise shalt thou do with thine oxen, *and* with thy sheep: seven days it shall be with its dam; on the eighth day thou shalt give it me. And ye shall be holy men unto me: therefore ye shall not eat any flesh that is torn of beasts in the field; ye shall cast it to the dogs.

Thou shalt not take up a false report: put not thine hand with the wicked to be an unrighteous witness. Thou shalt not follow a multitude to do evil; neither shalt thou speak in a cause to turn aside after a multitude to wrest *judgement:* neither shalt thou favour a poor man in his cause.

If thou meet thine enemy's ox or his ass going astray, thou shalt surely bring it back to him again. If thou see the ass of him that hateth thee lying under his burden, and wouldest forbear to help him, thou shalt surely help with him.

Thou shalt not wrest the judgement of thy poor in his cause. Keep thee far from a false matter; and the innocent and righteous slay thou not: for I will not justify the wicked. And thou shalt take no gift: for a gift blindeth them that have sight, and perverteth the words of the righteous. And a stranger shalt thou not oppress: for ye know the heart of a stranger, seeing ye were strangers in the land of Egypt.

And six years thou shalt sow thy land, and shalt gather in the increase thereof: but the seventh year thou shalt let it rest and lie fallow; that the poor of thy people may eat: and what they leave the beast of the field shall eat. In like manner thou shalt deal with thy vineyard, *and* with thy oliveyard. Six days thou shalt do thy work, and on the seventh day thou shalt rest: that thine ox and thine ass may have rest, and the son of thy handmaid, and the stranger, may be refreshed. And in all things that I have said unto you take ye heed: and make no mention of the name of other gods, neither let it be heard out of thy mouth.

Three times thou shalt keep a feast unto me in the year. The feast of unleavened bread shalt thou keep: seven days thou shalt eat unleavened bread, as I commanded thee, at the time appointed in the month Abib (for in it thou camest out from Egypt); and none shall appear before me empty: and the feast of harvest, the firstfruits of thy labours, which thou sowest in the field: and the feast of ingathering, at the end of the year, when thou gatherest in thy labours out of the field. Three times in the year all thy males shall appear before the Lord God.

Thou shalt not offer the blood of my sacrifice with leavened bread; neither shall the fat of my feast remain all night until the morning. The first of the firstfruits of thy ground thou shalt bring into the house of the Lord thy God. Thou shalt not seethe a kid in its mother's milk.

ISAIAH

The Prophecy
40:1–41:14; 45:8–25; 52:13–53:12

Comfort ye, comfort ye my people, saith your God. Speak ye comfortably to Jerusalem, and cry unto her, that her warfare is accomplished, that her iniquity is pardoned; that she hath received of the Lord's hand double for all her sins.

The voice of one that crieth, Prepare ye in the wilderness the way of the Lord, make straight in the desert a high way for our God. Every valley shall be exalted, and every mountain and hill shall be made low: and the crooked shall be made straight, and the rough places plain: and the glory of the Lord shall be revealed, and all flesh shall see it together: for the mouth of the Lord hath spoken it. The voice of one saying, Cry. And one said, What shall I cry? All flesh is grass, and all the goodliness thereof is as the flower of the field: the grass withereth, the flower fadeth; because the breath of the Lord bloweth upon it: surely the people is grass. The grass withereth, the flower fadeth: but the word of our God shall stand for ever.

O thou that tellest good tidings to Zion, get thee up into the high mountain; O thou that tellest good tidings to Jerusalem, lift up thy voice with strength; lift it up, be not afraid; say unto the cities of Judah, Behold, your God! Behold, the Lord God will come as a mighty one, and his arm shall rule for him: behold, his reward is with him, and his recompence before him. He shall feed his flock like a shepherd, he shall gather the lambs in his arm, and carry them in his bosom, *and* shall gently lead those that give suck.

Who hath measured the waters in the hollow of his hand, and meted out heaven with the span, and comprehended the dust of the earth in a measure, and weighed the mountains in scales, and the hills in a balance? Who hath directed the spirit of the Lord, or being his counsellor hath taught him? With whom took he counsel, and who instructed him, and taught him in the path of judgement, and taught him knowledge, and shewed to him the way of understanding? Behold, the nations are as a drop of a bucket, and are counted as the small dust of the balance: behold, he taketh up the isles as a very little thing. And Lebanon is not sufficient to burn, nor the beasts thereof sufficient for a burnt offering. All the nations are as nothing before him; they are counted to him less than nothing, and vanity. To whom then will ye liken God? or what likeness will ye compare unto him? The graven image, a workman melted *it,* and the goldsmith spreadeth it over with gold, and casteth *for it* silver chains. He that is too impoverished for *such* an oblation chooseth a tree that will not rot; he seeketh unto him a cunning workman to set up a graven image, that shall not be moved. Have ye not known? have ye not heard? hath it not been told you from the beginning? have ye not understood from the foundations of the earth? *It is* he that sitteth upon the circle of the earth, and the inhabitants thereof are as grasshoppers; that stretcheth out the heavens as a curtain, and spreadeth them out as a tent to dwell in: that bringeth princes to nothing; he maketh the judges of the earth as vanity. Yea, they have not been planted; yea, they have not been sown; yea, their stock hath not taken root in the earth: moreover he bloweth upon them, and they wither, and the whirlwind taketh them away as stubble. To whom then will ye liken me, that I should be equal *to him?* saith the Holy One. Lift up your eyes on high, and see who hath created these, that bringeth out their host by number: he calleth them all by name; by the greatness of his might, and for that he is strong in power, not one is lacking.

Why sayest thou, O Jacob, and speakest, O Israel, My way is hid from the Lord, and my judgement is passed away from my God? Hast thou not known? hast thou not heard? the everlasting God, the Lord, the Creator of the ends of the earth, fainteth not, neither is weary; there is no searching of his understanding. He giveth power to the faint; and to him that hath no might he increaseth strength. Even the youths shall faint and be weary, and the young men shall utterly fall: but they that wait upon the Lord shall renew their strength; they shall mount up with wings as eagles; they shall run, and not be weary; they shall walk, and not faint.

Keep silence before me, O islands; and let the peoples renew their strength: let them come near; then let them speak: let us come near together to judgement. Who hath raised up one from the east, whom he calleth in righteousness to his foot? he giveth nations before him, and maketh him rule over kings; he giveth them as the dust to his sword, as the driven stubble to his bow. He pursueth them, and passeth on safely; even by a way that he had not gone with his feet. Who hath wrought and done it, calling the generations from the beginning? I the Lord, the first, and with the last, I am he. The isles saw, and feared; the ends of the earth trembled: they drew near, and came. They helped every one his neighbour; and *every one* said to his brother, Be of good courage. So the carpenter encouraged the goldsmith, *and* he that smootheth with the hammer him that smiteth the anvil, saying of the soldering, It is good: and he fastened it with nails, that it should not be moved.

But thou, Israel, my servant, Jacob whom I have chosen, the seed of Abraham my friend; thou whom I have taken hold of from the ends of the earth, and called thee from the corners thereof, and said unto thee, Thou art my servant, I have chosen thee and not cast thee away; fear thou not, for I am with thee; be not dismayed, for I am thy God: I will strengthen thee; yea, I will help thee; yea, I will uphold thee with the right hand of my righteousness. Behold, all they that are incensed against thee shall be ashamed and confounded: they that strive with thee shall be as nothing, and shall perish. Thou shalt seek them, and shalt not find them, even them that contend with thee: they that war against thee shall be as nothing, and as a thing of nought. For I the Lord thy God will hold thy right hand, saying unto thee, Fear not; I will help thee.

Fear not, thou worm Jacob, and ye men of Israel; I will help thee, saith the Lord, and thy redeemer is the Holy One of Israel.

. . .

Drop down, ye heavens, from above, and let the skies pour down righteousness: let the earth open, that they may bring forth salvation; and let her cause righteousness to spring up together; I the Lord have created it.

Woe unto him that striveth with his Maker! a potsherd among the potsherds of the earth! Shall the clay say to him that fashioneth it, What makest thou? or thy work, He hath no hands? Woe unto him that saith unto a father, What begettest thou? or to a woman, With what travailest thou? Thus saith the Lord, the Holy One of Israel, and his Maker: Ask me of the things that are to come; concerning my sons, and concerning the work of my hands, command ye me. I have made the earth, and created man upon it: I, even my hands, have stretched out the heavens, and all their host have I commanded. I have raised him up in righteousness, and I will make straight all his ways: he shall build my city, and he shall let my exiles go free, not for price nor reward, saith the Lord of hosts.

Thus saith the Lord, The labour of Egypt, and the merchandise of Ethiopia, and the Sabeans, men of stature, shall come over unto thee, and they shall be thine; they shall go after thee; in chains they shall come over: and they shall fall down unto thee, they shall make supplication unto thee, *saying*, Surely God is in thee; and there is none else, there is no God. Verily thou art a God that hidest thyself, O God of Israel, the Saviour. They shall be ashamed, yea, confounded, all of them: they shall go into confusion together that are makers of idols. *But* Israel shall be saved by the Lord with an everlasting salvation: ye shall not be ashamed nor confounded world without end.

For thus saith the Lord that created the heavens; he is God; that formed the earth and made it; he established it, he created it not a waste, he formed it to be inhabited: I am the Lord; and there is none else. I have not spoken in secret, in a place of the land of darkness; I said not unto the seed of Jacob, Seek ye me in vain: I the Lord speak righteousness, I declare things that are right. Assemble yourselves and come; draw near together, ye that are escaped of the nations: they have no knowledge that carry the wood of their graven image, and pray unto a god that cannot save. Declare ye, and bring *it* forth; yea, let them take counsel together: who hath shewed this from ancient time? who hath declared it of old? have not I the Lord? and there is no God else beside me; a just God and a saviour; there is none beside me. Look unto me, and be ye saved, all the ends of the earth: for I am God, and there is none else. By myself have I sworn, the word is gone forth from my mouth *in* righteousness, and shall not return, that unto me every knee shall bow, every tongue shall swear. Only in the Lord, shall one say unto me, is righteousness and strength: even to him shall men come, and all they that were incensed against him shall be ashamed. In the Lord shall all the seed of Israel be justified, and shall glory.

· · ·

Behold, my servant shall deal wisely, he shall be exalted and lifted up, and shall be very high. Like as many were astonied at thee, (his visage was so marred more than any man, and his form more than the sons of men,) so shall he sprinkle many nations; kings shall shut their mouths at him: for that which had not been told them shall they see; and that which they had not heard shall they understand.

Who hath believed our report? and to whom hath the arm of the Lord been revealed? For he grew up before him as a tender plant, and as a root out of a dry ground: he hath no form nor comeliness; and when we see him, there is no beauty that we should desire him. He was despised, and rejected of men; a man of sorrows, and acquainted with grief: and as one from whom men hide their face he was despised, and we esteemed him not.

Surely he hath borne our griefs, and carried our sorrows: yet we did esteem him stricken, smitten of God, and afflicted. But he was wounded for our transgressions, he was bruised for our iniquities: the chastisement of our peace was upon him; and with his stripes we are healed. All we like sheep have gone astray; we have turned every one to his own way; and the Lord hath laid on him the iniquity of us all.

He was oppressed, yet he humbled himself and opened not his mouth; as a lamb that is led to the slaughter, and as a sheep that before her shearers is dumb; yea, he opened not his mouth. By oppression and judgement he was taken away; and as for his generation, who *among them* considered that he was cut off out of the land of the living? for the transgression of my people was he stricken. And they made his grave with the wicked, and with the rich in his death; although he had done no violence, neither was any deceit in his mouth.

Yet it pleased the Lord to bruise him; he hath put him to grief: when thou shalt make his soul an offering for sin, he shall see *his* seed, he shall prolong his days, and the pleasure of the Lord shall prosper in his hand. He shall see of the travail of his soul, *and* shall be satisfied: by his knowledge shall my righteous servant justify many: and he shall bear their iniquities. Therefore will I divide him a portion with the great, and he shall divide the spoil with the strong; because he poured out his soul unto death, and was numbered with the transgressors: yet he bare the sin of many, and made intercession for the transgressors.

AMOS

The Prophecy
1:1–2; 2:4–3:8; 5:1–27; 8:1–10

The words of Amos, who was among the herdmen of Tekoa, which he saw concerning Israel in the days of Uzziah king of Judah, and in the days of Jeroboam the son of Joash king of Israel, two years before the earthquake.

And he said, The Lord shall roar from Zion, and utter his voice from Jerusalem; and the pastures of the shepherds shall mourn, and the top of Carmel shall wither.

.   .   .

Thus saith the Lord: For three transgressions of Judah, yea, for four, I will not turn away the punishment thereof; because they have rejected the law of the Lord, and have not kept his statutes, and their lies have caused them to err, after the which their fathers did walk: but I will send a fire upon Judah, and it shall devour the palaces of Jerusalem.

Thus saith the Lord: For three transgressions of Israel, yea, for four, I will not turn away the punishment thereof; because they have sold the righteous for silver, and the needy for a pair of shoes: that pant after the dust of the earth on the head of the poor and turn aside the way of the meek: and a man and his father will go unto the *same* maid, to profane my holy name: and they lay themselves down beside every altar upon clothes taken in pledge, and in the house of their God they drink the wine of such as have been fined. Yet destroyed I the Amorite before them, whose height was like the height of the cedars, and he was strong as the oaks; yet I destroyed his fruit from above, and his roots from beneath. Also I brought you up out of the land of Egypt, and led you forty years in the wilderness, to possess the land of the Amorite. And I raised up of your sons for prophets, and of your young men for Nazirites. Is it not even thus, O ye children of Israel? saith the Lord. But ye gave the Nazirites wine to drink; and commanded the prophets, saying, Prophesy not. Behold, I will press *you* in your place, as a cart presseth that is full of sheaves. And flight shall perish from the swift, and the strong shall not strengthen his force, neither shall the mighty deliver himself: neither shall he stand that handleth the bow; and he that is swift of foot shall not deliver *himself:* neither shall he that rideth the horse deliver himself: and he that is courageous among the mighty shall flee away naked in that day, saith the Lord.

Hear this word that the Lord hath spoken against you, O children of Israel, against the whole family which I brought up out of the land of Egypt, saying, You only have I known of all the families of the earth: therefore I will visit upon you all your iniquities. Shall two walk together, except they have agreed? Will a lion roar in the forest, when he hath no prey? Will a young lion cry out of his den, if he have taken nothing? Can a bird fall in a snare upon the earth, where no gin is *set* for him? Shall a snare spring up from the ground, and have taken nothing at all? Shall the trumpet be blown in a city, and the people not be afraid? Shall evil befall a city, and the Lord hath not done it? Surely the Lord God will do nothing, but he revealeth his secret unto his servants the prophets. The lion hath roared, who will not fear? the Lord God hath spoken, who can but prophesy?

. . .

Hear ye this word which I take up for a lamentation over you, O house of Israel. The virgin of Israel is fallen; she shall no more rise: she is cast down upon her land; there is none to raise her up. For thus saith the Lord God: The city that went forth a thou-

sand shall have an hundred left, and that which went forth an
hundred shall have ten left, to the house of Israel. For thus saith
the Lord unto the house of Israel, Seek ye me, and ye shall live:
but seek not Beth-el, nor enter into Gilgal, and pass not to Beer-
sheba: for Gilgal shall surely go into captivity, and Beth-el shall
come to nought. Seek the Lord, and ye shall live; lest he break out
like fire in the house of Joseph, and it devour and there be none
to quench it in Beth-el: ye who turn judgement to wormwood, and
cast down righteousness to the earth; *seek him* that maketh the
Pleiades and Orion, and turneth the shadow of death into the
morning, and maketh the day dark with night; that calleth for
the waters of the sea, and poureth them out upon the face of
the earth; the Lord is his name; that bringeth sudden destruction
upon the strong, so that destruction cometh upon the fortress. They
hate him that reproveth in the gate, and they abhor him that
speaketh uprightly. Forasmuch therefore as ye trample upon the
poor, and take exactions from him of wheat: ye have built houses
of hewn stone, but ye shall not dwell in them; ye have planted
pleasant vineyards, but ye shall not drink the wine thereof. For I
know how manifold are your transgressions and how mighty are
your sins; ye that afflict the just, that take a bribe, and that turn
aside the needy in the gate *from their right*. Therefore he that is
prudent shall keep silence in such a time; for it is an evil time.
Seek good, and not evil, that ye may live: and so the Lord, the
God of hosts, shall be with you, as ye say. Hate the evil, and love
the good, and establish judgement in the gate: it may be that the
Lord, the God of hosts, will be gracious unto the remnant of
Joseph. Therefore thus saith the Lord, the God of hosts, the Lord:
Wailing shall be in all the broad ways; and they shall say in all
the streets, Alas! alas! and they shall call the husbandman to
mourning, and such as are skilful of lamentation to wailing. And in
all vineyards shall be wailing: for I will pass through the midst
of thee, saith the Lord. Woe unto you that desire the day of the
Lord! wherefore would ye have the day of the Lord? it is darkness, and not light. As if a man did flee from a lion, and a bear
met him; or went into the house and leaned his hand on the wall,
and a serpent bit him. Shall not the day of the Lord be darkness,
and not light? even very dark, and no brightness in it? I hate, I
despise your feasts, and I will take no delight in your solemn as-
semblies. Yea, though ye offer me your burnt offerings and meal

offerings, I will not accept them: neither will I regard the peace offerings of your fat beasts. Take thou away from me the noise of thy songs; for I will not hear the melody of thy viols. But let judgement roll down as waters, and righteousness as a mighty stream. Did ye bring unto me sacrifices and offerings in the wilderness forty years, O house of Israel? Yea, ye have borne Siccuth your king and Chiun your images, the star of your god, which ye made to yourselves. Therefore will I cause you to go into captivity beyond Damascus, saith the Lord, whose name is the God of hosts.

. . .

Thus the Lord God shewed me: and behold, a basket of summer fruit. And he said, Amos, what seest thou? And I said, A basket of summer fruit. Then said the Lord unto me, The end is come upon my people Israel; I will not again pass by them any more. And the songs of the temple shall be howlings in that day, saith the Lord God: the dead bodies shall be many; in every place shall they cast them forth with silence. Hear this, O ye that would swallow up the needy, and cause the poor of the land to fail, saying, When will the new moon be gone, that we may sell corn? and the sabbath, that we may set forth wheat? making the ephah small, and the shekel great, and dealing falsely with balances of deceit; that we may buy the poor for silver, and the needy for a pair of shoes, and sell the refuse of the wheat. The Lord hath sworn by the excellency of Jacob, Surely I will never forget any of their works. Shall not the land tremble for this, and every one mourn that dwelleth therein? yea, it shall rise up wholly like the River; and it shall be troubled and sink again, like the River of Egypt. And it shall come to pass in that day, saith the Lord God, that I will cause the sun to go down at noon, and I will darken the earth in the clear day. And I will turn your feasts into mourning, and all your songs into lamentation; and I will bring up sackcloth upon all loins, and baldness upon every head; and I will make it as the mourning for an only son, and the end thereof as a bitter day.

New Testament

The New Testament is so called because the Christians claim that the
message of Jesus represents a *new* covenant or testament (the words are
the same in Greek), superseding the old one entered into between God
and the Jews. The twenty-seven books which make up the New Testament
were not written as a unified work but on a piecemeal basis, during the
second half of the first century, in each case to meet a particular practical
requirement. Moreover, they were not regarded as sacred, as were the
scriptures of the Jews, until the second century or later, and it was not
until 367 that the contents, as we know them now, were authoritatively
promulgated. The New Testament is the result of a slow winnowing-out
process from an extensive body of early Christian writings, some of which
still survive as the Apocrypha. Although, as with the Jewish scriptures,
the New Testament was not a *product* of the Western mind, it has pervaded it through and through, so that the Judeo-Christian tradition and
Western culture are now inseparable.

The following selections deal with some of the most fundamental
matters of Christian faith—convictions arrived at not by reasoning, as in
the philosophies, but by an intuitive response to the life and teachings
of a unique personality. As such, they are highly colored by the pre-
scientific thought-forms and terminology of the first century of our era.

These influences themselves underwent alteration from the outset. The
gospel was first preached in a Jewish atmosphere in Palestine, where ideas
of a "Messiah," a "Kingdom of God," and a "Son of Man" were current.
As the Christian movement became more and more identified with the
gentiles, its message was restated in a form intelligible to Greek-speaking
peoples. Such different terms as "Savior," "Son of God," and "Body of
Christ" then appeared. This development is to be seen especially in the
Gospel according to St. John (dating *ca.* 100), where Jesus appears not

The New Testament, revised (Oxford: University Press, 1881), 8–15, 208, 224–25,
248–49, 393–94, 396, 402–06.

merely as a human teacher and prophet favored by God, but as a divine being.

The Sermon on the Mount, from the Gospel according to St. Matthew (dating *ca.* 90), represents another aspect of Christian tradition—the ethical aspect. Jesus's words go beyond the Mosaic Law and summon men to an inwardness of religious life in place of the Jewish externalism of that day. The three chapters from St. Matthew included here are probably the best known in the Bible, and most popular despite the demands they make upon those who have chosen to commit themselves to God rather than to self.

Early Christianity developed its own ritual, and in I Corinthians (dating *ca.* 54) we see that the Last Supper of Jesus with his disciples has been transformed into a rite bearing the deepest mystical significance. In the same epistle, one of the most important New Testament books, Paul also sets forth what must have been Christianity's most powerful appeal in a world offering nothing beyond the bleak here-and-now. It is interesting to compare Socrates' view in the *Phaedo,* that the body and personal identity are obstacles to the life of the soul and to its absorption in the world-soul, with Paul's observations on the Resurrection.

ST. MATTHEW

The Sermon on the Mount
4:24–7:29

And the report of him went forth into all Syria: and they brought unto him all that were sick, holden with divers diseases and torments, possessed with devils, and epileptic, and palsied; and he healed them. And there followed him great multitudes from Galilee and Decapolis and Jerusalem and Judaea and *from* beyond Jordan.

And seeing the multitudes, he went up into the mountain: and when he had sat down, his disciples came unto him: and he opened his mouth and taught them, saying,

BLESSED are the poor in spirit:
for theirs is the kingdom of heaven.
BLESSED are they that mourn:
for they shall be comforted.

> BLESSED are the meek:
> for they shall inherit the earth.
> BLESSED are they that hunger and thirst after righteousness:
> for they shall be filled.
> BLESSED are the merciful:
> for they shall obtain mercy.
> BLESSED are the pure in heart:
> for they shall see God.
> BLESSED are the peacemakers:
> for they shall be called sons of God.

Blessed are they that have been persecuted for righteousness' sake: for theirs is the kingdom of heaven. Blessed are ye when *men* shall reproach you, and persecute you, and say all manner of evil against you falsely, for my sake. Rejoice, and be exceeding glad: for great is your reward in heaven: for so persecuted they the prophets which were before you.

Ye are the salt of the earth: but if the salt have lost its savour, wherewith shall it be salted? it is thenceforth good for nothing, but to be cast out and trodden under foot of men. Ye are the light of the world. A city set on a hill cannot be hid. Neither do *men* light a lamp, and put it under the bushel, but on the stand; and it shineth unto all that are in the house. Even so let your light shine before men, that they may see your good works, and glorify your Father which is in heaven.

Think not that I came to destroy the law or the prophets: I came not to destroy, but to fulfill. For verily I say unto you, Till heaven and earth pass away, one jot or one tittle shall in no wise pass away from the law, till all things be accomplished. Whosoever therefore shall break one of these least commandments, and shall teach men so, shall be called least in the kingdom of heaven: but whosoever shall do and teach them, he shall be called great in the kingdom of heaven. For I say unto you, that except your righteousness shall exceed *the righteousness* of the scribes and Pharisees, ye shall in no wise enter into the kingdom of heaven.

Ye have heard that it was said to them of old time, Thou shalt not kill; and whosoever shall kill shall be in danger of the judgement: but I say unto you, that every one who is angry with his brother shall be in danger of the judgement; and whosoever shall say to his brother, Raca, shall be in danger of the council; and whosoever shall say, Thou fool, shall be in danger of the hell of fire. If therefore thou are offering thy gift at the altar, and there rememberest that thy brother hath aught against thee, leave there thy gift before the altar, and go thy way, first be reconciled to thy brother, and then come and offer thy gift. Agree with thine adversary quickly, whiles thou art with him in the way; lest haply the adversary deliver thee to the judge, and the judge deliver thee to the officer, and thou be cast into prison. Verily I say unto thee, Thou shalt by no means come out thence, till thou have paid the last farthing.

Ye have heard that it was said, Thou shalt not commit adultery: but I say unto you, that every one that looketh on a woman to lust after her hath committed adultery with her already in his heart. And if thy right eye causeth thee to stumble, pluck it out, and cast it from thee: for it is profitable for thee that one of thy members should perish, and not thy whole body be cast into hell. And if thy right hand causeth thee to stumble, cut it off, and cast it from thee: for it is profitable for thee that one of thy members should perish, and not thy whole body go into hell. It was said also, Whosoever shall put away his wife, let him give her a writing of divorcement: but I say unto you, that every one that putteth away his wife, saving for the cause of fornication, maketh her an adulteress: and whosoever shall marry her when she is put away committeth adultery.

Again, ye have heard that it was said to them of old time, Thou shalt not forswear thyself, but shalt perform unto the Lord thine oaths: but I say unto you, Swear not at all; neither by the heaven, for it is the throne of God; nor by the earth, for it is the footstool of his feet; nor by Jerusalem, for it is the city of the great King. Neither shalt thou swear by thy head, for thou canst not make one hair white or black. But let your speech be, Yea, yea; Nay, nay: and whatsoever is more than these is of the evil *one*.

Ye have heard that it was said, An eye for an eye, and a tooth for a tooth: but I say unto you, Resist not him that is evil: but whosoever smiteth thee on thy right cheek, turn to him the other also. And if any man would go to law with thee, and take away thy coat, let him have thy cloke also. And whosoever shall compel thee to go one mile, go with him twain. Give to him that asketh thee, and from him that would borrow of thee turn not thou away.

Ye have heard that it was said, Thou shalt love thy neighbour, and hate thine enemy: but I say unto you, Love your enemies, and pray for them that persecute you; that ye may be sons of your Father which is in heaven: for he maketh his sun to rise on the evil and the good, and sendeth rain on the just and the unjust. For if ye love them that love you, what reward have ye? do not even the publicans the same? And if ye salute your brethren only, what do ye more *than others?* do not even the Gentiles the same? Ye therefore shall be perfect, as your heavenly Father is perfect.

Take heed that ye do not your righteousness before men, to be seen of them: else ye have no reward with your Father which is in heaven.

When therefore thou doest alms, sound not a trumpet before thee, as the hypocrites do in the synagogues and in the streets, that they may have glory of men. Verily I say unto you, They have received their reward. But when thou doest alms, let not thy left hand know what thy right hand doeth: that thine alms may be in secret: and thy Father which seeth in secret shall recompense thee.

And when ye pray, ye shall not be as the hypocrites: for they love to stand and pray in the synagogues and in the corners of the streets, that they may be seen of men. Verily I say unto you, They have received their reward. But thou, when thou prayest, enter into thine inner chamber, and having shut thy door, pray to thy Father which is in secret, and thy Father which seeth in secret shall recompense thee. And in praying use not vain repetitions, as the Gentiles do: for they think that they shall be heard for their much speaking. Be not therefore like unto them: for your Father knoweth what things ye have need of, before ye ask him. After this manner therefore pray ye: Our Father which art in heaven, Hallowed be thy name. Thy kingdom come. Thy will be done, as in heaven, so on earth. Give us this day our daily bread. And forgive us our debts, as we also have forgiven our debtors. And bring us not into temptation, but deliver us from the evil *one.* For if ye forgive men their trespasses, your heavenly Father will also forgive you. But if ye forgive not men their trespasses, neither will your Father forgive your trespasses.

Moreover when ye fast, be not, as the hypocrites, of a sad countenance: for they disfigure their faces, that they may be seen of men to fast. Verily I say unto you, They have received their reward. But thou, when thou fastest, anoint thy head, and wash thy face;

that thou be not seen of men to fast, but of thy Father which is in secret: and thy Father, which seeth in secret, shall recompense thee.

Lay not up for yourselves treasures upon the earth, where moth and rust doth consume, and where thieves break through and steal: but lay up for yourselves treasures in heaven, where neither moth nor rust doth consume, and where thieves do not break through nor steal: for where thy treasure is, there will thy heart be also. The lamp of the body is the eye: if therefore thine eye be single, thy whole body shall be full of light. But if thine eye be evil, thy whole body shall be full of darkness. If therefore the light that is in thee be darkness, how great is the darkness! No man can serve two masters: for either he will hate the one, and love the other; or else he will hold to one, and despise the other. Ye cannot serve God and mammon. Therefore I say unto you, Be not anxious for your life, what ye shall eat, or what ye shall drink; nor yet for your body, what ye shall put on. Is not the life more than the food, and the body than the raiment? Behold the birds of the heaven, that they sow not, neither do they reap, nor gather into barns; and your heavenly Father feedeth them. Are not ye of much more value than they? And which of you by being anxious can add one cubit unto his stature? And why are ye anxious concerning raiment? Consider the lilies of the field, how they grow; they toil not, neither do they spin: yet I say unto you, that even Solomon in all his glory was not arrayed like one of these. But if God doth so clothe the grass of the field, which to-day is, and to-morrow is cast into the oven, *shall he* not much more *clothe* you, O ye of little faith? Be not therefore anxious, saying, What shall we eat? or, What shall we drink? or, Wherewithal shall we be clothed? For after all these things do the Gentiles seek; for your heavenly Father knoweth that ye have need of all these things. But seek ye first his kingdom, and his righteousness; and all these things shall be added unto you. Be not therefore anxious for the morrow: for the morrow will be anxious for itself. Sufficient unto the day is the evil thereof.

Judge not, that ye be not judged. For with what judgement ye judge, ye shall be judged: and with what measure ye mete, it shall be measured unto you. And why beholdest thou the mote that is in thy brother's eye, but considerest not the beam that is in thine own eye? Or how wilt thou say to thy brother, Let me cast out the mote out of thine eye; and lo, the beam is in thine own eye? Thou hypocrite, cast out first the beam out of thine own eye; and then shalt thou see clearly to cast out the mote out of thy brother's eye.

Give not that which is holy unto the dogs, neither cast your pearls before the swine, lest haply they trample them under their feet, and turn and rend you.

Ask, and it shall be given you; seek, and ye shall find; knock, and it shall be opened unto you: for every one that asketh receiveth; and he that seeketh findeth; and to him that knocketh it shall be opened. Or what man is there of you, who, if his son shall ask him for a loaf, will give him a stone; or if he shall ask for a fish, will give him a serpent? If ye then, being evil, know how to give good gifts unto your children, how much more shall your Father which is in heaven give good things to them that ask him? All things therefore whatsoever ye would that men should do unto you, even so do ye also unto them: for this is the law and the prophets.

Enter ye in by the narrow gate: for wide is the gate, and broad is the way, that leadeth to destruction, and many be they that enter in thereby. For narrow is the gate, and straitened the way, that leadeth unto life, and few be they that find it.

Beware of false prophets, which come to you in sheep's clothing, but inwardly are ravening wolves. By their fruits ye shall know them. Do *men* gather grapes of thorns, or figs of thistles? Even so every good tree bringeth forth good fruit; but the corrupt tree bringeth forth evil fruit. A good tree cannot bring forth evil fruit, neither can a corrupt tree bring forth good fruit. Every tree that bringeth not forth good fruit is hewn down, and cast into the fire. Therefore by their fruits ye shall know them. Not every one that saith unto me, Lord, Lord, shall enter into the kingdom of heaven; but he that doeth the will of my Father which is in heaven. Many will say to me in that day, Lord, Lord, did we not prophesy by thy name, and by thy name cast out devils, and by thy name do many mighty works? And then will I profess unto them, I never knew you: depart from me, ye that work iniquity. Every one therefore which heareth these words of mine, and doeth them, shall be likened unto a wise man, which built his house upon the rock: and the rain descended, and the floods came, and the winds blew, and beat upon that house; and it fell not: for it was founded upon the rock. And every one that heareth these words of mine, and doeth them not, shall be likened unto a foolish man, which built his house upon the sand: and the rain descended. and the floods came, and the winds blew, and smote upon that house; and it fell: and great was the fall thereof.

And it came to pass, when Jesus ended these words, the multitudes were astonished at his teaching: for he taught them as *one* having authority, and not as their scribes.

Jesus the Divine Lord
1:1–16; 6:32–59; 13:36–14:11

In the beginning was the Word, and the Word was with God, and the Word was God. The same was in the beginning with God. All things were made by him; and without him was not anything made that hath been made. In him was life; and the life was the light of men. And the light shineth in the darkness; and the darkness apprehended it not. There came a man, sent from God, whose name was John. The same came for witness, that he might bear witness of the light, that all might believe through him. He was not the light, but *came* that he might bear witness of the light. There was the true light, *even the light* which lighteth every man, coming into the world. He was in the world, and the world was made by him, and the world knew him not. He came unto his own, and they that were his own received him not. But as many as received him, to them gave he the right to become children of God, *even* to them that believe on his name: which were born, not of blood, nor of the will of the flesh, nor of the will of man, but of God. And the Word became flesh, and dwelt among us (and we beheld his glory, glory as of the only begotten from the Father), full of grace and truth. John beareth witness of him, and crieth, saying, This was he of whom I said, He that cometh after me is become before me: for he was before me. For of his fulness we all received.

.   .   .

Jesus therefore said unto them, Verily, verily, I say unto you, It was not Moses that gave you the bread out of heaven; but my Father giveth you the true bread out of heaven. For the bread of God is that which cometh down out of heaven, and giveth life unto the world. They said therefore unto him, Lord, evermore give us this bread. Jesus said unto them, I am the bread of life: he that cometh to me shall not hunger, and he that believeth on me shall never thirst. But I said unto you, that ye have seen me, and yet believe not. All that which the Father giveth me shall come unto me; and him that cometh to me I will in no wise cast out. For I am come down from heaven, not to do mine own will, but the will of him that sent me. And this is the will of him that sent me, that of all that which he hath given me I should lose nothing, but should raise it up at the last day. For this is the will of my Father, that every one that beholdeth the Son, and believeth on him, should have eternal life; and I will raise him up at the last day.

The Jews therefore murmured concerning him, because he said, I am the bread which came down out of heaven. And they said, Is not this Jesus, the son of Joseph, whose father and mother we know? how doth he now say, I am come down out of heaven? Jesus answered and said unto them, Murmur not among yourselves. No man can come to me, except the Father which sent me draw him: and I will raise him up in the last day. It is written in the prophets, And they shall all be taught of God. Every one that hath heard from the Father, and hath learned, cometh unto me. Not that any man hath seen the Father, save he which is from God, he hath seen the Father. Verily, verily, I say unto you, He that believeth hath eternal life. I am the bread of life. Your fathers did eat the manna in the wilderness, and they died. This is the bread which cometh down out of heaven, that a man may eat thereof, and not die. I am the living bread which came down out of heaven: if any man eat of this bread, he shall live for ever: yea and the bread which I will give is my flesh, for the life of the world.

The Jews therefore strove one with another, saying, How can this man give us his flesh to eat? Jesus therefore said unto them, Verily, verily, I say unto you, Except ye eat the flesh of the Son of man and drink his blood, ye have not life in yourselves. He that eateth my flesh and drinketh my blood hath eternal life; and I will raise him up at the last day. For my flesh is meat indeed, and my blood is drink indeed. He that eateth my flesh and drinketh my blood abideth in me, and I in him. As the living Father sent me, and I live because of the Father; so he that eateth me, he also shall live because of me. This is the bread which came down out of heaven: not as the fathers did eat, and died: he that eateth this bread shall live for ever. These things said he in the synagogue, as he taught in Capernaum.

. . .

Simon Peter saith unto him, Lord, whither goest thou? Jesus answered, Whither I go, thou canst not follow me now; but thou shalt follow afterwards. Peter saith unto him, Lord, why cannot I follow thee even now? I will lay down my life for thee. Jesus answereth, Wilt thou lay down thy life for me? Verily, verily, I say unto thee, The cock shall not crow, till thou hast denied me thrice.

Let not your heart be troubled: ye believe in God, believe also in me. In my Father's house are many mansions; if it were not so, I would have told you; for I go to prepare a place for you. And if I go and prepare a place for you, I come again, and will receive you unto myself; that where I am, *there* ye may be also. And whither I go, ye know the way. Thomas saith unto him, Lord, we know not whither thou goest; how know we the way? Jesus saith unto him, I am the way, and the truth, and the life: no one cometh unto the Father, but by me. If ye had known me, ye would have known my Father also: from henceforth ye know him, and have seen him. Philip saith unto him, Lord, shew us the Father, and it sufficeth us. Jesus saith unto him, Have I been so long time with you, and dost thou not know me, Philip? he that hath seen me hath seen the Father; how sayest thou, Shew us the Father? Believest thou not that I am in the Father, and the Father in me? the words that I say unto you I speak not from myself: but the Father abiding in me doeth his works. Believe me that I am in the Father, and the Father in me.

I CORINTHIANS

Salutation

1:1-3

Paul, called to be an apostle of Jesus Christ through the will of God, and Sosthenes our brother, unto the Church of God which is at Corinth. . . . Grace to you and peace from God our Father, and the Lord Jesus Christ.

The Lord's Supper
10:1–4; 15–22; 11:20–28

For I would not, brethren, have you ignorant, how that our fathers were all under the cloud, and all passed through the sea; and were all baptized unto Moses in the cloud and in the sea; and did all eat the same spiritual meat; and did all drink the same spiritual drink: for they drank of a spiritual rock that followed them: and the rock was Christ.

. . .

I speak as to wise men; judge ye what I say. The cup of blessing which we bless, is it not a communion of the blood of Christ? The bread which we break, is it not a communion of the body of Christ? seeing that we, who are many, are one bread, one body: for we all partake of the one bread. Behold Israel after the flesh: have not they which eat the sacrifices communion with the altar? What say I then? that a thing sacrificed to idols is any thing, or that an idol is any thing? But *I say,* that the things which the Gentiles sacrifice, they sacrifice to devils, and not to God: and I would not that ye should have communion with devils. Ye cannot drink the cup of the Lord, and the cup of devils: ye cannot partake of the table of the Lord, and of the table of devils. Or do we provoke the Lord to jealousy? are we stronger than he?

. . .

When therefore ye assemble yourselves together, it is not possible to eat the Lord's supper: for in your eating each one taketh before *other* his own supper; and one is hungry, and another is drunken. What? have ye not houses to eat and to drink in? or despise ye the church of God, and put them to shame that have not? What shall I say to you? shall I praise you in this? I praise you not. For I received of the Lord that which also I delivered unto you, how that the Lord Jesus in the night in which he was betrayed took bread; and when he had given thanks, he brake it, and said, This is my body, which is for you: this do in remembrance of me. In like manner also the cup, after supper, saying, This cup is the new covenant in my blood: this do, as oft as ye drink *it,* in remembrance of me. For as often as ye eat this bread, and drink the cup, ye proclaim the Lord's death till he come. Wherefore whosoever shall eat the bread or drink the cup of the Lord unworthily, shall be guilty of the body and the blood of the Lord. But let a man prove himself, and so let him eat of the bread, and drink of the cup.

The Resurrection
15:1–58

Now I make known unto you, brethren, the gospel which I preached unto you, which also ye received, wherein also ye stand, by which also ye are saved; *I make known, I say,* in what words I preached it unto you, if ye hold it fast, except ye believed in vain. For I delivered unto you first of all that which also I received, how that Christ died for our sins according to the scriptures; and that he was buried; and that he hath been raised on the third day according to the scriptures; and that he appeared to Cephas; then to the twelve; then he appeared to above five hundred brethren at once, of whom the greater part remain until now, but some are fallen asleep; then he appeared to James; then to all the apostles; and last of all, as unto one born out of due time, he appeared to me also. For I am the least of the apostles, that am not meet to be called an apostle, because I persecuted the church of God. But by the grace of God I am what I am: and his grace which was bestowed upon me was not found vain; but I laboured more abundantly than they all: yet not I, but the grace of God which was with me. Whether then *it be* I or they, so we preach, and so ye believed.

Now if Christ is preached that he hath been raised from the dead, how say some among you that there is no resurrection of the dead? But if there is no resurrection of the dead, neither hath Christ been raised: and if Christ hath not been raised, then is our preaching vain, your faith also is vain. Yea, and we are found false witnesses of God; because we witnessed of God that he raised up Christ: whom he raised not up, if so be that the dead are not raised. For if the dead are not raised, neither hath Christ been raised: and if Christ hath not been raised, your faith is vain; ye are yet in your sins. Then they also which are fallen asleep in Christ have perished. If in this life only we have hoped in Christ, we are of all men most pitiable.

But now hath Christ been raised from the dead, the firstfruits of them that are asleep. For since by man *came* death, by man *came* also the resurrection of the dead. For as in Adam all die, so also in Christ shall all be made alive. But each in his own order: Christ the firstfruits; then they that are Christ's, at his coming. Then *cometh* the end, when he shall deliver up the kingdom to God, even the Father; when he shall have abolished all rule and all authority and power. For he must reign, till he hath put all his enemies under his feet. The last enemy that shall be abolished is death. For, He put all things in subjection under his feet. But when he saith, All things are put in subjection, it is evident that he is excepted who did subject all things unto him. And when all things have been subjected unto him, then shall the Son also himself be subjected to him that did subject all things unto him, that God may be all in all.

Else what shall they do which are baptized for the dead? If the dead are not raised at all, why then are they baptized for them? why do we also stand in jeopardy every hour? I protest by that glorying in you, brethren, which I have in Christ Jesus our Lord, I die daily. If after the manner of men I fought with beasts at Ephesus, what doth it profit me? If the dead are not raised, let us eat and drink, for tomorrow we die. Be not deceived: Evil company doth corrupt good manners. Awake up righteously, and sin not; for some have no knowledge of God: I speak *this* to move you to shame.

But some one will say, How are the dead raised? and with what manner of body do they come? Thou foolish one, that which thou thyself sowest is not quickened, except it die: and that which thou sowest, thou sowest not the body that shall be, but a bare grain, it may chance of wheat, or of some other kind; but God giveth it a body even as it pleased him, and to each seed a body of its own. All flesh is not the same flesh: but there is one *flesh* of men, and another flesh of beasts, and another flesh of birds, and another of fishes. There are also celestial bodies, and bodies terrestrial: but the glory of the celestial is one, and the *glory* of the terrestrial is another. There is one glory of the sun, and another glory of the moon, and another glory of the stars; for one star differeth from another star in glory. So also is the resurrection of the dead. It is sown in corruption; it is raised in incorruption: it is sown in dishonour; it is raised in glory: it is sown in weakness; it is raised in power: it is sown a natural body; it is raised a spiritual body. If there is a natural body, there is also a spiritual *body*. So also it is written, The first man Adam became a living soul. The last Adam *became* a life-giving spirit. Howbeit that is not first which is spiritual, but that which is natural; then that which is spiritual. The first man is of the earth, earthly: the second man is of heaven. As is the earthy, such are they also that are earthy: and as is the heavenly, such are they also that are heavenly. And as we have borne the image of the earthy, we shall also bear the image of the heavenly.

Now this I say, brethren, that flesh and blood cannot inherit the kingdom of God; neither doth corruption inherit incorruption. Behold, I tell you a mystery: We shall not all sleep, but we shall all be changed, in a moment, in the twinkling of an eye, at the last trump: for the trumpet shall sound, and the dead shall be raised incorruptible, and we shall be changed. For this corruptible must put on incorruption, and this mortal must put on immortality. But when this corruptible shall have put on incorruption, and this mortal shall have put on immortality, then shall come to pass the saying that is written, Death is swallowed up in victory. O death, where is thy victory? O death, where is thy sting? The sting of death is sin; and the power of sin is the law: but thanks be to God, which giveth us the victory through our Lord Jesus Christ. Wherefore, my beloved brethren, be ye stedfast, unmovable, always abounding in the work of the Lord, forasmuch as ye know that your labour is not vain in the Lord.

Tertullian

——— 20 ———

The Apparel of Women

The Fathers of the Church were writers, first in Greek and later in Latin, who came to be regarded as authentically testifying to or expounding the teachings of Christianity. Some came to be venerated as saints and martyrs; some belonged to the hierarchy of clergy; others were laymen.

In this last group is Quintus Septimius Florens Tertullianus (*ca.* 160–*ca.* 230 A.D.), born in Carthage, the son of a gentile military officer who provided him with a well-rounded education. About 195, while in legal practice in Rome, Tertullian was converted to Christianity; upon his return to Africa he threw himself wholeheartedly into the defense of the new faith. He is recognized as the ablest Christian apologist and theologian of the Latin West before Augustine.

Tertullian's Christianity was severe and puritanical, demanding renunciation of all vestiges of paganism and the rigid observance of Christian precepts as the guide to life. Christianity and paganism had nothing in common: "What has Athens to do with Jerusalem?" he demanded in a famous phrase. This straitlaced rigorism, which won Tertullian the title of "the Christian Juvenal," is reflected in his tract *The Apparel of Women,* which, though addressed to recent female converts in particular, has a more universal application. It represents one extreme of the ascetic impulse inherent in Christianity—an ideal to be contrasted with the rationality and moderation of the classical standard as set forth, for example, in the *Nicomachean Ethics.*

Tertullian was the first important Latin writer to defend Christianity with the instruments of learning traditional to paganism itself. But, unlike the pagan classics, always intended for the aristocratic few, his writings appealed to all men. Moreover, as a Christian publicist, obliged like Cicero

Tertullian, *The Apparel of Women,* in *Ante-Nicene Christian Library,* eds. Alexander Roberts and James Donaldson (Edinburgh: Clark, 1869), XI, 304–06, 308–11, 314–18, 320–27, 331–32.

to find a medium for expounding novel ideas, he coined new words and
turned old ones to new account, thus creating the Latin of the Church.

—————————————————   ■■■■■■■   —————————————————

If there dwelt upon earth a faith as great as is the reward of faith
which is expected in the heavens, no one of you at all, best beloved
sisters, from the time that she had first "known the Lord," and
learned [the truth] concerning her own (that is, woman's) condition,
would have desired too gladsome (not to say too ostentatious) a
style of dress; so as not rather to go about in humble garb, and
rather to affect meanness of appearance, walking about as Eve
mourning and repentant, in order that by every garb of penitence
she might the more fully expiate that which she derives from Eve,—
the ignominy, I mean, of the first sin, and the odium [attaching to
her as the cause] of human perdition. "In pains and in anxieties
dost thou bear [children], woman; and toward thine husband [is]
thy inclination, and he lords it over thee." And do you not know
that you are [each] an Eve? The sentence of God on this sex of
yours lives in this age: the guilt must of necessity live too. *You* are
the devil's gateway: *you* are the unsealer of that [forbidden] tree:
you are the first deserter of the divine law: *you* are she who persuaded him whom the devil was not valiant enough to attack. *You*
destroyed so easily God's image, man. On account of *your* desert
—that is, death—even the Son of God had to die.

.   .   .

For they, withal, who instituted [women's adornments] are assigned, under condemnation, to the penalty of death,—those angels,
to wit, who rushed from heaven on the daughters of men; so that
this ignominy also attaches to woman.

.   .   .

But why was it of so much importance to show these things as
well as to confer them? Was it that women, without material causes
of splendour, and without ingenious contrivances of grace, could
not please *men*, who, while still unadorned, and uncouth, and—
so to say—crude and rude, had moved [the mind of] *angels?* or was

it that the lovers would appear sordid and—through gratuitous use—contumelious, if they had conferred no [compensating] gift on the women who had been enticed into connubial connection with them? But these questions admit of no calculation. Women who possessed angels [as husbands] could desire nothing more; they had, forsooth, made a grand match!

. . .

Grant now that no mark of pre-condemnation has been branded on womanly pomp by the [fact of the] fate of its authors; let nothing be imputed to those angels besides their repudiation of heaven and [their] carnal marriage: let us examine the qualities of the things themselves, in order that we may detect the purposes also for which they are eagerly desired.

Female habit carries with it a twofold idea—dress and ornament. By "dress" we mean what they call "womanly gracing;" by "ornament," what it is suitable should be called "womanly *dis*gracing." The former is accounted [to consist] in gold, and silver, and gems, and garments; the latter in care of the hair, and of the skin, and of those parts of the body which attract the eye. Against the one we lay the charge of ambition, against the other of prostitution; so that even from this early stage [of our discussion] you may look forward and see what, out of [all] these, is suitable, handmaid of God, to *your* discipline, inasmuch as you are assessed on different principles [from other women],—those, namely, of humility and chastity.

. . .

Handmaids of the living God, my fellow-servants and sisters, the right which I enjoy with you—I, the most meanest in that right of fellow-servantship and brotherhood—emboldens me to address to you a discourse, not, of course, of affection, but paving the way for affection in the cause of your salvation.

That salvation—and not [the salvation] of women only, but likewise of men—consists in the exhibition principally of modesty. For since, by the introduction into and appropriation [in] us of the Holy Spirit, we are all "the temple of God," Modesty is the sacristan and priestess of that temple, who is to suffer nothing unclean or profane to be introduced [into it], for fear that the God who inhabits it should be offended, and quite forsake the polluted abode.

But on the present occasion we [are to speak] not about modesty, for the enjoining and exacting of which the divine precepts which press [upon us] on every side are sufficient; but about the matters which pertain to it, that is, the manner in which it behoves you to walk. For most women (which very thing I trust God may permit me, with a view, of course, to my own personal censure, to censure in all), either from simple ignorance or else from dissimulation, have the hardihood so to walk as if modesty consisted only in the [bare] integrity of the flesh, and in turning away from [actual] fornication, and there were no need for anything extrinsic to boot—in the matter (I mean) of the arrangement of dress and ornament, the studied graces of form and brilliance:—wearing in their gait the self-same appearance as the women of the nations, from whom the sense of *true* modesty is absent, because in those who know not God, the Guardian and Master of truth, there is *nothing* true.

For if any modesty can be believed [to exist] in Gentiles, it is plain that it must be imperfect and undisciplined to such a degree that, although it be actively tenacious of itself in the *mind* up to a certain point, it yet allows itself to relax into licentious extravagances of attire; just in accordance with Gentile perversity, in craving after that of which it carefully shuns the effect.

How many a one, in short, is there who does not earnestly desire even to look pleasing to strangers? who does not on that very account take care to have herself painted out, and denies that she has [ever] been an object of [carnal] appetite? And yet, granting that even this is a practice familiar to Gentile modesty—[namely,] not actually to *commit* the sin, but still to be *willing* to do so; or even not to be *willing*, yet still not *quite* to refuse—what wonder? for all things which are not God's are perverse. Let those women therefore look to it, who, by not holding fast the *whole* good, easily mingle with evil even what they do hold fast. Necessary it is that *you* turn aside from them, as in all other things, so also in your gait; since you ought to be "perfect, as [is] your Father who is in the heavens."

You must know that in the eye of perfect, that is, Christian, modesty, [carnal] desire of one's self [on the part of others] is not only not to be desired, but even execrated by you: first, because the study of making personal grace (which we know to be naturally the inviter of lust) a mean of pleasing does not spring from a sound conscience: why therefore excite toward yourself that evil [passion]? why invite [that] to which you profess yourself a stranger? secondly, because we ought not to open a way to temptations, which, by their instancy, sometimes achieve [a wickedness] which God expels from them who are His; [or,] at all events, put the spirit into a thorough tumult by [presenting] a stumbling-block [to it].

We ought indeed to walk so holily, and with so entire substantiality of faith, as to be confident and secure in regard of our own conscience, *desiring* that that [gift] may abide in us to the end, yet not *presuming* [that it will]. For he who presumes feels less apprehension; he who feels less apprehension takes less precaution; he who takes less precaution runs more risk. Fear is the foundation of salvation; presumption is an impediment to fear.

More useful, then, is it to apprehend that we may possibly fail than to presume that we cannot; for apprehending will lead us to fear, fearing to caution, and caution to salvation. On the other hand, if we presume, there will be neither fear nor caution to save us. He who acts securely, and not at the same time warily, possesses no safe and firm security; whereas he who is wary will be truly able to be secure. And for His own servants, may the Lord by His mercy take care that to *them* it may be lawful even to *presume* on His goodness!

But why are we a [source of] danger to our neighbour? why do we import concupiscence into . . . some other? For that other, as soon as he has felt concupiscence after your beauty, and has mentally already committed [the deed] which his concupiscence pointed to, perishes; and you have been made the sword which destroys him: so that, albeit you be free from the [actual] crime, you are not free from the odium [attaching to it]; as, when a robbery has been committed on some man's estate, the [actual] crime indeed will not be laid to the owner's charge, while yet the domain is branded with ignominy, [and] the owner himself aspersed with the infamy.

Are we to paint ourselves out that our neighbours may perish? Where, then, is [the command], "Thou shalt love thy neighbour as thyself?" "Care not merely about your own [things], but [about your] neighbour's?" No enunciation of the Holy Spirit ought to be [confined] to the subject immediately in hand merely, and not applied and carried out with a view to *every* occasion to which its application is useful. Since, therefore, both our own interest and that of others is implicated in the studious pursuit of most perilous

[outward] comeliness, it is time for you to know that not merely must
the pageantry of fictitious and elaborate beauty be rejected by you;
but that of even natural grace must be obliterated by concealment
and negligence, as equally dangerous to the glances of [the behold-
er's] eyes.

.   .   .

As if I were speaking to Gentiles, addressing you with a Gentile
precept and [one which is] common to all, [I would say,] "You
are bound to please your husbands only." But you will please *them*
in proportion as you take no care to please *others.* Be ye without
carefulness, blessed [sisters]: no wife is "ugly" to her own husband.
She "pleased" him enough when she was selected [by him as his
wife]; whether commended by form or by character. Let none of
you think that, if she abstain from the care of her person, she will
incur the hatred and aversion of husbands. Every husband is the
exactor of *chastity;* but *beauty* a believing [husband] does not require, because we are not captivated by the same graces which the
Gentiles think [to be] graces: an *un*believing, on the other hand,
even regards with suspicion, just from that infamous opinion of
us which the Gentiles have. For whom, then, is it that you cherish
your beauty? If for a believer, he does not exact it: if for an *un*believer, he does not believe in it unless it be artless. Why are you
eager to please either one who is suspicious, or else one who desires
no [such pleasing]?

These suggestions are not made to you, of course, to be developed
into an entire crudity and wildness of appearance; nor are we seeking to persuade you of the good of squalor and slovenliness; but
of the limit and norm and just measure of cultivation of the person.
There must be no overstepping of that line to which simple and
sufficient refinements limit their desires—that line which is pleasing
to God. For they who rub their skin with medicaments, stain their
cheeks with rouge, make their eyes prominent with antimony, sin
against Him.

To them, I suppose, the plastic skill of God is displeasing! In
their own persons, I suppose, they convict, they censure, the
Artificer of all things! For censure they do when they amend, when
they add to, [His work;] taking these their additions, of course, from

the adversary artificer. That adversary artificer is the devil. For who would show the way to change the *body*, but he who by wickedness transfigured man's *spirit?* He it is, undoubtedly, who adapted ingenious devices of this kind; that in your own persons it may be apparent that you do, in a certain sense, do violence to God. Whatever is *born* is the work of God. Whatever, then, is *plastered on* [that], is the devil's work. To superinduce on a divine work Satan's ingenuities, how criminal is it! Our servants borrow nothing from our personal enemies: soldiers eagerly desire nothing from the foes of their own general; for, to demand for [your own] use anything from the adversary of him in whose hand you are, is a transgression.

Shall a Christian be assisted in anything by that evil one? [If he do,] I know not whether this name [of "Christian"] will continue [to belong] to him; for he will be *his* in whose lore he eagerly desires to be instructed. But how alien from *your* schoolings and professions are [these things], how unworthy the Christian name, to wear a fictitious face, [you,] on whom simplicity in every form is enjoined!—to lie in your appearance, [you,] to whom [lying] with the tongue is not lawful!—to seek after what is another's, [you,] to whom is delivered [the precept of] abstinence from what is another's!—to practice adultery in your mien, [you,] who make modesty your study! Think, blessed [sisters], how will you keep God's precepts if you shall not keep in your own persons His lineaments?

I see some [women] turn [the colour of] their hair with saffron. They are ashamed even of their own nation, [ashamed] that their procreation did not assign them to Germany and to Gaul: thus, as it is, they transfer their *hair* [thither]! Ill, ay, *most* ill, do they augur for themselves with their flame-coloured head, and think that graceful which [in fact] they are polluting! Nay, moreover, the force of the cosmetics burns ruin into the hair; and the constant application of even any *un*drugged moisture, lays up a store of harm for the head; while the sun's warmth, too, so desirable for imparting to the hair at once growth and dryness, is hurtful. What "grace" is compatible with "injury?" What "beauty" with "impurities?" Shall a Christian woman heap saffron on her head, as upon an altar? For, whatever is wont to be burned to the honour of the unclean spirit, that—unless it is applied for honest and necessary and salutary uses, [to serve the end] for which God's creature was provided—may seem to be a sacrifice. But, however, God saith, "Which of you can make a white hair black, or out of a black a white?" And so they refute the Lord! "Behold!" say they, "instead of white or black, we make it *yellow*,—more winning in grace."

And yet such as repent of having lived to old age do *attempt* to change it even from white to black! O temerity! The age which is the object of our wishes and prayers blushes [for itself]! a theft is effected! youth, wherein we have sinned, is sighed after! the opportunity of sobriety is spoiled! Far from Wisdom's daughters be folly so great! The more old age tries to conceal itself, the more will it be detected. Here is a veritable eternity, in the [perennial] youth of your head! Here we have an "incorruptibility" to "put on," with a view to the new house of the Lord which the divine monarchy promises! Well do you speed toward the Lord, well do you hasten to be quit of this most iniquitous world, to whom to approach [your own] end is unsightly!

What service, again, does all the labour spent in *arranging* the hair render to [the cause of] salvation? Why is no rest allowed to your hair, which must now be bound, now loosed, now cultivated, now thinned out? Some are anxious to force their hair into curls, some to let it hang loose and flying; not with good simplicity: beside which, you affix I know not what enormities of subtle and textile perukes; now, after the manner of a helmet of undressed hide, as it were a sheath for the head and a covering for the crown; now, a mass [drawn] backward toward the neck. The wonder is, that there is no [open] contending against the Lord's prescripts!

It has been pronounced that no one can add to his own stature. *You,* however, *do* add to your *weight* some kind of rolls, or shield-bosses, to be piled upon your necks! If you feel no shame at the enormity [of the gear], feel some at the pollution; for fear you may be fitting on a holy and Christian head the slough of some one else's head, unclean perchance, guilty perchance and destined to hell. Nay, rather banish quite away from your "free" head all this slavery of ornamentation. In vain do you labour to seem adorned, in vain do you call in the aid of all the most skilful manufacturers of false hair. God bids you "be veiled." I believe [He does so] for fear the heads of some should be seen! And oh that in "that day" of Christian exultation, I, most miserable [as I am], may elevate my head, even though below [the level of] your heels! I shall [then] see whether you will rise with [your] ceruse and rouge and saffron, and in all that parade of head-gear: whether it will be women thus tricked out whom the angels carry up to meet Christ in the air! If these [decorations] are *now* good, and of God, they will *then* also present themselves to the rising bodies, and will recognise their several places. But nothing can rise except flesh and spirit sole and pure. Whatever, therefore, does not rise in [the form of] spirit and flesh is condemned, because it is not of God. From things which are condemned abstain, even at the present day. At the present day let God see you such as He will see you *then*.

Of course, now, I, a man, as being envious of women, am banishing them quite from their own [domains]. Are there, in our case too, some things which, in respect of the sobriety we are to maintain on account of the fear due to God, are disallowed? [There are,] if it is true, [as it is,] that in men, for the sake of women (just as in women for the sake of men), there is implanted, by a defect of nature, the will to please; and [if] this sex of ours acknowledges to itself deceptive trickeries of form peculiarly its own,—[such as] to cut the beard too sharply; to pluck it out here and there; to shave round about [the mouth]; to arrange the hair, and disguise its hoariness by dyes; to remove all the incipient down all over the body; to fix [each particular hair] in its place with [some] womanly pigment; to smooth all the rest of the body by the aid of some rough powder or other: then, further, to take every opportunity for consulting the mirror; to gaze anxiously into it.

.   .   .

Wherefore, with regard to clothing also, and all the remaining lumber of your self-elaboration, the like pruning off and retrenchment of too redundant splendour must be the object of your care.

.   .   .

Perhaps some [woman] will say: "To me it is not necessary to be approved by men; for I do not require the testimony of men: God is the inspector of the heart." [That] we all know; provided, however, we remember what the same [God] has said through the apostle: "Let your probity appear before men." For what purpose,

except that malice may have no access at all to you, or that you
may be an example and testimony to the evil? Else, what is [that]:
"Let your works shine?" Why, moreover, does the Lord call us
the light of the world; why has He compared us to a city built
upon a mountain if we do not shine in [the midst of] darkness
and stand eminent amid them who are sunk down? If you hide
your lamp beneath a bushel, you must necessarily be left quite in
darkness, and be run against by many.

The things which make us luminaries of the world are these—
our good works. What is *good,* moreover, provided it be true and
full, loves not darkness: it joys in being seen, and exults over the
very pointings which are made at it. To Christian modesty it is
not enough to *be* so, but to *seem* so too. For so great ought its
plenitude to be, that it may flow out from the mind to the garb,
and burst out from the conscience to the outward appearance; so
that even from the outside it may gaze, as it were, upon its own
furniture,—[a furniture] such as to be suited to retain faith as its
inmate perpetually. For such delicacies as tend by their softness
and effeminacy to unman the manliness of faith are to be dis-
carded. Otherwise, I know not whether the wrist that has been
wont to be surrounded with the palm-leaf-like bracelet will endure
till it grow into the numb hardness of its own chain! I know not
whether the leg that has rejoiced in the anklet will suffer itself to
be squeezed into the gyve! I fear the neck, beset with pearl and
emerald nooses, will give no room to the broadsword!

Wherefore, blessed [sisters], let us meditate on hardships, and we
shall not feel them; let us abandon luxuries, and we shall not regret
them. Let us stand ready to endure every violence, having nothing
which we may fear to leave behind. It is these things which are
the bonds which retard our hope. Let us cast away earthly ornaments
if we desire heavenly. Love not gold; in which [one substance] are
branded all the sins of the people of Israel. You ought to *hate* what
ruined your fathers; what was adored by them who were forsaking
God. Even *then* [we find] gold is food for the fire.

But Christians always, and now more than ever, pass their times
not in gold but in iron: the stoles of martyrdom are [now] preparing: the angels who are to carry us are [now] being awaited! Do
you go forth [to meet them] already arrayed in the cosmetics and
ornaments of prophets and apostles; drawing your whiteness from

simplicity, your ruddy hue from modesty; painting your eyes with bashfulness, and your mouth with silence; implanting in your ears the words of God; fitting on your necks the yoke of Christ. Submit your head to your husbands, and you will be enough adorned. Busy your hands with spinning; keep your feet at home; and you will "please" better than [by arraying yourselves] in gold. Clothe yourselves with the silk of uprightness, the fine linen of holiness, the purple of modesty. Thus painted, you will have God as your Lover!

Minucius Felix

21

Octavius

The Apostolic Age, ending *ca.* 100 A.D., was followed by the Age of the Fathers, or the Patristic Age, so called for the men who carried on the work of the apostles. Early in this period the Christian communities rose in social standing, many converts being drawn from the educated, privileged classes of gentiles. Those Christians who turned their talents to the defense of the faith against its detractors are known, in consequence, as apologists and their writings as apologetics.

One of the earliest literary attacks on Christianity, now lost, was the work of Marcus Cornelius Fronto, the tutor of Marcus Aurelius. It was in reply to this attack, late in the second century, that Marcus Minucius Felix (*fl. ca.* 200) wrote his dialogue *Octavius*, in which Fronto, because of his place of birth (Cirta), is referred to as "the Cirtensian." It is the first important apologetic work in Latin. Little is known of Minucius Felix except that he was probably of African birth, of pagan parentage, and well educated. His conversion to Christianity probably resulted from his contact, as a practicing lawyer, with evidence frequently given at trials of Christians as enemies of the state.

The introduction to the book (not included in this selection) presents Marcus Minucius and two lawyer-friends—L. Caecilius Natalis, the champion of paganism, and Octavius Januarius, a Christian—enjoying a holiday, away from the capital, by the seashore at Ostia. A friendly argument begins when Caecilius salutes a statue of the god Serapis; his attack on Christianity, which forms the second part of the dialogue, is included here to show the persistent beliefs of cultivated pagans concerning the strange new sect and to emphasize the differences between the Christian and pagan points of view. Following Octavius's defense, Caecilius acknowledges his errors and, as might be expected, embraces the faith.

The dialogue *Octavius*, as a whole, reveals the changing mental climate

Minucius Felix, *Octavius*, in *Ante-Nicene Christian Library*, eds. Alexander Roberts and James Donaldson (Edinburgh: Clark, 1869), XIII, 455–69.

and the trend of the times: the opening of the Christian offensive against pagan opposition, hitherto unchalleged, and the gradual abandonment of traditional philosophies and cults by the educated minority who governed the Roman world.

[Caecilius said,] "Let us be seated on those rocky barriers that are cast there for the protection of the baths, and that run far out into the deep, that we may be able both to rest after our journey, and to argue with more attention." And at his word we sat down, so that, by covering me on either side, they sheltered me in the midst of the three. Nor was this a matter of observance, or of rank, or of honour, because friendship always either receives or makes equals; but that, as an arbitrator, and being near to both, I might give my attention, and being in the middle, I might separate the two. Then Caecilius began thus:

"Although to you, Marcus my brother, the subject on which especially we are inquiring is not in doubt, inasmuch as, being carefully informed in both kinds of life, you have rejected the one and assented to the other, yet in the present case your mind must be so fashioned that you may hold the balance of a most just judge, nor lean with a disposition to one side [more than another], lest your decision may seem not to arise so much from our arguments, as to be originated from your own perceptions.

"Accordingly, if you sit in judgment on me, as a person who is new, and as one ignorant of either side, there is no difficulty in making plain that all things in human affairs are doubtful, uncertain, and unsettled, and that all things are rather probable than true. Wherefore it is the less wonderful that some, from the weariness of thoroughly investigating truth, should rashly succumb to any sort of opinion rather than persevere in exploring it with persistent diligence. And thus all men must be indignant, all men must feel pain, that certain persons—and these unskilled in learning, strangers to literature, without knowledge even of sordid arts—should dare to determine on any certainty concerning the nature at large, and the [divine] majesty, of which so many of the multitude of sects in all ages [are still in doubt], and philosophy itself deliberates still.

"Nor without reason; since the mediocrity of human intelligence is so far from [the capacity of] divine investigation, that neither is it given us to know, nor is it permitted to search, nor is it religious to ravish, the things that are supported in suspense in the heaven above us, nor the things which are deeply submerged below the earth; and we may rightly seem sufficiently happy and sufficiently prudent, if, according to that ancient oracle of the sage, we should know ourselves intimately. But even if we indulge in a senseless and useless labour, and wander away beyond the limits proper to our humility, and though, inclined towards the earth, we transcend with daring ambition heaven itself and the very stars, let us at least not entangle this error with vain and fearful opinions.

"Let the seeds of all things have been in the beginning condensed by a nature combining them in itself—what God is the author here? Let the members of the whole world be by fortuitous concurrences united, digested, fashioned—what God is the contriver? Although fire may have lit up the stars; although [the lightness of] its own material may have suspended the heaven; although its own material may have established the earth by its weight; and although the sea may have flowed in from moisture, whence is this religion? Whence this fear? What is this superstition?

"Man, and every animal which is born, inspired with life, and nourished, is as a voluntary concretion of the elements, into which again man and every animal is divided, resolved, and dissipated: so all things flow back again into their source, and are turned again into themselves, without any artificer, or judge, or creator. Thus the seeds of fires, being gathered together, cause other suns, and again others, always to shine forth. Thus the vapours of the earth, being exhaled, cause the mists always to grow, which being condensed and collected, cause the clouds to rise higher; and when they fall, cause the rains to flow, the winds to blow, the hail to rattle down; or when the clouds clash together, they cause the thunder to bellow, the lightnings to grow red, the thunderbolts to gleam forth. Therefore they fall everywhere, they rush on the mountains, they strike the trees; without any choice, they blast places sacred and profane; they smite mischievous men, and often, too, religious men.

"Why should I speak of tempests, various and uncertain, wherein the attack upon all things is tossed about without any order or discrimination?—in shipwrecks, that the fates of good and bad men are jumbled together, their deserts confounded?—in conflagrations, that the destruction of innocent and guilty is united?—and when with the plague-taint of the sky a region is stained, that all perish without distinction?—and when the heat of war is raging, that it is the better men who generally fall? In peace also, not only is wickedness put on the same level with [the lot of] those who are better, but it is also regarded in such esteem, that, in the case of many people, you know not whether their depravity is most to be detested, or their felicity to be desired.

"But if the world were governed by divine providence and by the authority of any deity, Phalaris and Dionysius would never have deserved to reign, Rutilius and Camillus would never have merited banishment, Socrates would never have merited the poison. Behold the fruit-bearing trees, behold the harvest already white, the vintage, already dropping, is destroyed by the rain, is beaten down by the hail. Thus either an uncertain truth is hidden from us, and kept back; or, which is rather to be believed, in these various and wayward chances, fortune, unrestrained by laws, is ruling over us.

"Since, then, either fortune is certain or nature is uncertain, how much more reverential and better it is, as the high priests of truth, to receive the teaching of your ancestors, to cultivate the religions handed down to you, to adore the gods whom you were first trained by your parents to fear rather than to know with familiarity; not to assert an opinion concerning the deities, but to believe your forefathers, who, while the age was still untrained in the birthtimes of the world itself, deserved to have gods either propitious to them, or as their kings.

"Thence, therefore, we see through all empires, and provinces, and cities, that each people has its national rites of worship, and adores its local gods: as the Eleusinians worship Ceres; the Phrygians, Mater; the Epidaurians, Aesculapius; the Chaldaeans, Belus; the Syrians, Astarte; the Taurians, Diana; the Gauls, Mercurius; the Romans, all divinities. Thus their power and authority has occupied the circuit of the whole world: thus it has propagated its empire beyond the paths of the sun and the bounds of the ocean itself; in that in their arms they practise a religious valour; in that they fortify their city with the religions of sacred rites, with chaste virgins, with many honours, and the names of priests; in that, when besieged and taken, all but the Capitol alone, they worship the gods which when angry any other people would have despised; and through the lines of the Gauls, marvelling at the audacity of their superstition, they move unarmed with weapons, but armed with the worship of their religion; while in the city of an enemy, when taken while still in the fury of victory, they venerate the conquered deities; while in all directions they seek for the gods of the strangers, and make them their own; while they build altars even to unknown divinities, and to the Manes.

"Thus, in that they acknowledge the sacred institutions of all nations, they have also deserved their dominion. Hence the perpetual course of their veneration has continued, which is not weakened by the long lapse of time but increased, because antiquity has been accustomed to attribute to ceremonies and temples so much of sanctity as it has ascribed of age.

"Nor yet by chance (for I would venture in the meantime even to take for granted [the point in debate], and so to err on the safe side) have our ancestors succeeded in their undertakings either by the observance of auguries, or by consulting the entrails, or by the institution of sacred rites, or by the dedication of temples. Consider what is the record of books. You will at once discover that they have inaugurated the rites of all kinds of religions, either that the divine indulgence might be rewarded, or that the threatening anger might be averted, or that the wrath already swelling and raging might be appeased. . . .

"I omit the old stories, which are many, and I pass by the songs of the poets about the births, and the gifts, and the rewards of the gods. Moreover, I hasten over the fates predicted by the oracles, lest antiquity should appear to you excessively fabulous. Look at the temples and fanes of the gods by which the Roman city is both protected and armed: they are more august by the deities which are their inhabitants, who are present and constantly dwelling in them, than opulent by the ensigns and gifts of worship. Thence therefore the prophets, filled with the god, and mingled with him, collect futurity beforehand, give caution for dangers, medicine for diseases, hope for the afflicted, help to the wretched, solace to calamities, alleviation to labours. Even in our repose we see, we hear, we acknowledge the gods, whom in the day-time we impiously deny, refuse, and abjure.

"Therefore, since the consent of all nations concerning the existence of the immortal gods remains established, although their nature or their origin remains uncertain, I suffer nobody swelling with such boldness, and with I know not what irreligious wisdom, who would strive to undermine or weaken this religion, so ancient, so useful, so wholesome, even although he may be Theodorus of Cyrene, or one who is before him, Diagoras the Melian, to whom antiquity applied the surname of Atheist,—both of whom, by asseverating that there were no gods, took away all the fear by which humanity is ruled, and all veneration absolutely; yet never will they prevail in this discipline of impiety, under the name and authority of their pretended philosophy.

"When the men of Athens both expelled Protagoras of Abdera, and in public assembly burnt his writings, because he disputed deliberately rather than profanely concerning the divinity, why is it not a thing to be lamented, that men (for you will bear with my making use pretty freely of the force of the plea that I have undertaken)—that men, I say, of a reprobate, unlawful, and desperate faction, should rage against the gods? who, having gathered together from the lowest dregs the more unskilled, and women, credulous and, by the facility of their sex, yielding, establish a herd of a profane conspiracy, which is leagued together by nightly meetings, and solemn fasts, and inhuman meats—not by any sacred rite, but by that which requires expiation—a people skulking and shunning the light, silent in public, but garrulous in corners.

"They despise the temples as dead-houses, they reject the gods, they laugh at sacred things; wretched, they pity, if they are allowed, the priests; half naked themselves, they despise honours and purple robes. Oh, wondrous folly and incredible audacity! they despise present torments, although they fear those which are uncertain and future; and while they fear to die after death, they do not fear to die for the present: so does a deceitful hope soothe their fear with the solace of revival [to come].

"And now, as wickeder things advance more fruitfully, and abandoned manners creep on day by day, those abominable shrines of an impious assembly are maturing themselves throughout the whole world. Assuredly this confederacy ought to be rooted out and execrated. They know one another by secret marks and insignia, and they love one another almost before they know one another; everywhere also there is mingled among them a certain religion of lust, and they call one another promiscuously brothers and sisters, that even a not unusual debauchery may by the intervention of that sacred name become incestuous: it is thus that their vain and senseless superstition glories in crimes.

"Nor, concerning these things, would intelligent report speak of things so great and various, and requiring to be prefaced by an apology, unless truth were at the bottom of it. I hear that they adore the head of an ass, that basest of creatures, consecrated by I know not what silly persuasion,—a worthy and appropriate religion for such manners. Some say that they worship the genitals of their pontiff and priest, and adore the nature, as it were, of their common parent. I know not whether these things are false; certainly suspicion is applicable to secret and nocturnal rites; and he who explains their ceremonies by reference to a man punished by extreme suffering for his wickedness, and to the deadly wood of the cross, appropriates fitting altars for reprobate and wicked men, that they may worship what they deserve.

"Now the story about the initiation of young novices is as much to be detested as it is well known. An infant covered over with meal, that it may deceive the unwary, is placed before him who is to be stained with their rites: this infant is slain by the young pupil, who has been urged on as if to harmless blows on the surface of the meal, with dark and secret wounds. Thirstily—O horror!—they lick up its blood; eagerly they divide its limbs. By this victim they are pledged together; with this consciousness of wickedness they are covenanted to mutual silence.

"Such sacred rites as these are more foul than any sacrileges. And of their banqueting it is well known all men speak of it everywhere; even the speech of our Cirtensian testifies to it. On a solemn day they assemble at the feast, with all their children, sisters, mothers, people of every sex and of every age. There, after much feasting, when the fellowship has grown warm, and the fervour of incestuous lust has grown hot with drunkenness, a dog that has been tied to the chandelier is provoked, by throwing a small piece of offal beyond the length of a line by which he is bound, to rush and spring; and thus the conscious light being overturned and extinguished in the shameless darkness, the connections of abominable lust involve them in the uncertainty of fate. Although not all in fact, yet in consciousness all are alike incestuous, since by the desire of all of them everything is sought for which can happen in the act of each individual.

"I purposely pass over many things, for those that I have mentioned are already too many; and that all these, or the greater part of them, are true, the obscurity of their vile religion declares. For why do they endeavour with such pains to conceal and to cloak whatever they worship, since honourable things always rejoice in publicity, while crimes are kept secret? Why have they no altars, no temples, no acknowledged images? Why do they never speak openly, never congregate freely, unless for the reason that what they adore and conceal is either worthy of punishment, or something to be ashamed of?

"Moreover, whence or who is he, or where is the *one* God, solitary, desolate, whom no free people, no kingdoms, and not even Roman superstition, have known? The lonely and miserable nationality of the Jews worshipped one God, and one peculiar to itself; but they worshipped him openly, with temples, with altars, with victims, and with ceremonies; and he has so little force or power, that he is enslaved, with his own special nation, to the Roman deities. But the Christians, moreover, what wonders, what monstrosities do they feign!—that he who is their God, whom they can neither show nor behold, inquires diligently into the character of all, the acts of all, and, in fine, into their words and secret thoughts; that he runs about everywhere, and is everywhere present: they make him out to be troublesome, restless, even shamelessly inquisitive, since he is present at everything that is done, wanders in and out in all places, although, being occupied with the whole, he cannot give attention to particulars, nor can he be sufficient for the whole while he is busied with particulars.

"What! because they threaten conflagration to the whole world, and to the universe itself, with all its stars, are they meditating its destruction?—as if either the eternal order constituted by the divine laws of nature would be disturbed, or the league of all the elements would be broken up, and the heavenly structure dissolved, and that fabric in which it is contained and bound together would be overthrown.

"And, not content with this wild opinion, they add to it and associate with it old women's fables: they say that they will rise again after death, and ashes, and dust; and with I know not what confidence, they believe by turns in one another's lies: you would think that they had already lived again. It is a double evil and a twofold madness to denounce destruction to the heaven and the stars, which we leave just as we find them, and to promise eternity to ourselves, who are dead and extinct—who, as we are born, so also perish!

"It is for this cause, doubtless, also that they execrate our funeral piles, and condemn our burials by fire, as if every body, even although it be withdrawn from the flames, were not, nevertheless, resolved into the earth by lapse of years and ages, and as if it mattered not whether wild beasts tore the body to pieces, or seas consumed it, or the ground covered it, or the flames carried it away; since for the carcases every mode of sepulture is a penalty if they feel it; if they feel it not, in the very quickness of their destruction there is relief. Deceived by this error, they promise to themselves, as being good, a blessed and perpetual life after their death; to others, as being unrighteous, eternal punishment.

"Many things occur to me to say in addition, if the limits of my discourse did not hasten me. I have already shown, and take no more pains to prove, that they themselves are unrighteous; although, even if I should allow them to be righteous, yet your agreement also concurs with the opinions of many, that guilt and innocence are attributed by fate. For whatever we do, as some ascribe it to fate, so you refer it to God: thus it is according to your sect to believe that men will, not of their own accord, but as elected to will. Therefore you feign an iniquitous judge, who punishes in men, not their will, but their destiny. Yet I should be glad to be informed whether or no you rise again with bodies; and if so, with what bodies—whether with the same or with renewed bodies? Without a body? Then, as far as I know, there will neither be mind, nor soul, nor life. With the same body? But this has already been previously destroyed. With another body? Then it is a new man who is born, not the former one restored; and yet so long a time has passed away, innumerable ages have flowed by, and what single individual has returned from the dead either by the fate of Protesilaus, with permission to sojourn even for a few hours, or that we might believe it for an example? All such figments of an unhealthy belief, and vain sources of comfort, with which deceiving poets have trifled in the sweetness of their verse, have been disgracefully remoulded by you, believing undoubtingly on your God.

"Neither do you at least take experience from things present, how the fruitless expectations of vain promise deceive you. Consider, wretched creatures, [from your lot] while you are yet living, what is threatening you after death. Behold, a portion of you—and, as you declare, the larger and better portion—are in want, are cold, are labouring in hard work and hunger; and God suffers it, He feigns; He either is not willing or not able to assist His people; and thus He is either weak or inequitable. Thou, who dreamest over a posthumous immortality, when thou art shaken by danger, when thou art consumed with fever, when thou art torn with pain, dost thou not then feel thy real condition? Dost thou not then acknowledge thy frailty? Poor wretch, art thou unwillingly convinced of thine infirmity, and wilt not confess it?

"But I omit matters that are common to all alike. Lo, for you there are threats, punishments, tortures, and crosses; and that no longer as objects of adoration, but as tortures to be undergone; fires also, which you both predict and fear. Where is that God who is able to help you when you come to life again, since he cannot help you while you are in this life? Do not the Romans, without any help from your God, govern, reign, have the enjoyment of the whole world, and have dominion over you?

"But you in the meantime, in suspense and anxiety, are abstaining from respectable enjoyments. You do not visit exhibitions; you have no concern in public displays; you reject the public banquets, and abhor the sacred contests; the meats previously tasted by, and the drinks made a libation of upon, the altars. Thus you stand in dread of the gods whom you deny. You do not wreath your heads with flowers; you do not grace your bodies with odours; you reserve unguents for funeral rites; you even refuse garlands to your sepulchres—pallid, trembling beings, worthy of the pity even of our gods!

"Thus, wretched as you are, you neither rise again, nor do you live in the meanwhile. Therefore, if you have any wisdom or modesty, cease from prying into the regions of the sky and the destinies and secrets of the world: it is sufficient to look before your feet, especially for untaught, uncultivated, boorish, rustic people: they who have no capacity for understanding civil matters, are much more denied the ability to discuss divine.

"However, if you have a desire to philosophize, let any one of you who is sufficiently great, imitate, if he can, Socrates the prince of wisdom. The answer of that man, whenever he was asked about ce-

lestial matters, is well known: 'What is above us is nothing to us.'
Well, therefore, did he deserve from the oracle the testimony of singular wisdom, which oracle he himself had a presentiment of, that he
had been preferred to all men for the reason, not that he had discovered all things, but because he had learnt that he knew nothing.

"And thus the confession of ignorance is the height of wisdom.
From this source flowed the safe doubting of Arcesilas, and long
after of Carneades, and of very many of the Academics, in questions of the highest moment, in which species of philosophy the
unlearned can do much with caution, and the learned can do
gloriously. What! is not the hesitation of Simonides the lyric poet to
be admired and followed by all? Which Simonides, when he was
asked by Hiero the tyrant what, and what like he thought the gods
to be, asked first of all for a day to deliberate; then postponed his
reply for two days; and then, when pressed, he added only another;
and finally, when the tyrant inquired into the causes of such a long
delay, he replied that, the longer his research continued, the
obscurer the truth became to him.

"In my opinion also, things which are uncertain ought to be left
as they are. Nor, while so many and so great men are deliberating,
should we rashly and boldly give an opinion in another direction,
lest either a childish superstition should be introduced, or all
religion should be overthrown."

St. Jerome

— 22 —

Letter CXXV

By the fourth century Christianity was making further inroads upon classical culture. Many devout Christian men and women of rank and fashion were abandoning civilized life in the cities and the civic and social responsibilities traditional to it—the supreme achievement of the ancient world—for a withdrawn life of solitude. The aspiration to pursue the "ascetic ideal," often in waste places, was fast becoming the greatest force in the life of the Church.

One of the most famous and influential of these ascetics was St. Jerome (Eusebius Hieronymus, *ca.* 340–420), born of Christian parents in the Roman province of Pannonia. Although a scholar and "intellectual," at twenty-eight St. Jerome retired to the Syrian desert near Antioch, sharing for five years the austerities of other Christian hermits there. In 382, he moved temporarily to Rome and became the fervid leader of a protest movement, not only against the secular world but against the increasing involvement of churchmen therein. When he left the metropolis, a pious group of aristocratic women accompanied him to Bethlehem, where he spent the remainder of his days in a monastery built with funds they provided. Devoted as ever to study and writing, he produced there (among other works) the famous Latin translation of the Bible known as the Vulgate.

Over 150 of his letters survive. The one reprinted here in part was written in 411 and represents a moderate expression of his asceticism. It furnishes the standard arguments for monasticism. Rusticus, whom St. Jerome addressed in the letter, took his advice, entered a monastery, and afterward became a bishop. The letter is notable also for revealing the decay of the classical spirit—that of Socrates and Plato, Cato and Cicero—and for illustrating the preoccupation of the kind of men who, in the pre-Christian era, would have served the state as generals and magistrates.

St. Jerome, *Select Letters*, trans. F. A. Wright (Loeb Classical Library—London: Heinemann and New York: Putnam, 1933), 407–19, 423–29, 435–39. Reprinted by permission of Harvard University Press.

If you wish to be, and not merely seem, a monk, have regard not
for your property—you began your vows by renouncing it—but for
your soul. Let a squalid garb be the evidence of a clean heart: let
a coarse tunic prove that you despise the world; provided only that
you do not pride yourself on such things nor let your dress and
language be at variance. Avoid hot baths: your aim is to quench
the heat of the body by the help of chilling fasts. But let your fasts
be moderate, since if they are carried to excess they weaken the
stomach, and by making more food necessary to make up for it
lead to indigestion, which is the parent of lust. A frugal, temperate
diet is good both for body and soul.

See your mother often, but do not be forced to see other women
when you visit her. Their faces may dwell in your heart and so

'A secret wound may fester in your breast.'

You must remember too that the maids who wait upon her are an
especial snare; the lower they are in rank, the easier it is to ruin
them. John the Baptist had a saintly mother and his father was a
priest; but neither his mother's love nor his father's wealth could
prevail upon him to live in his parents' house at the risk of his
chastity. He took up his abode in the desert, and desiring only to
see Christ refused to look at anything else. His rough garb, his
skin girdle, his diet of locusts and wild honey were all alike meant
to ensure virtue and self-restraint. The sons of the prophets, who
are the monks of the Old Testament, built huts for themselves by
the stream of Jordan, and leaving the crowded cities lived on por-
ridge and wild herbs.

As long as you stay in your native city, regard your cell as Paradise,
gather in it the varied fruits of the Scriptures, make them your delight, and rejoice in their embrace. If your eye or your foot or your
hand offend you, cast it off. Spare nothing, provided that you spare
your soul. 'Whosoever looketh on a woman to lust after her hath
committed adultery with her already in his heart.' 'Who can boast "I
have made my heart clean"?' The stars are not pure in God's sight:
how much less are men, whose life is one long temptation! Woe to
us, who commit fornication whenever we have lustful thoughts! 'My
sword,' says the Scripture, 'hath drunk its fill in heaven': much

more than will it on earth, which produces thorns and thistles. The chosen vessel, from whose mouth we hear Christ's own words, keeps his body under and brings it into subjection; but still he perceives that the natural heat of the body fights against his fixed purpose, and he is compelled to do what he will not. Like a man suffering violence he cries aloud and says: 'O wretched man that I am, who shall deliver me from the body of this death?' And do *you* think then that you can pass through life without a fall and without a wound, if you do not keep your heart with all diligence and say with the Saviour: 'My mother and my brethren are these which hear the word of God and do it'? Such cruelty as this is really love. Nay, what greater love can there be than to guard a holy son for a holy mother? She desires your eternal life: she is content not to see you for the moment, provided that she may see you for ever with Christ. She is like Hannah, who brought forth Samuel, not for her own comfort, but for the service of the tabernacle.

The sons of Jonadab drank no wine nor strong drink and lived in tents which they pitched whenever night came on. Of them the psalm says that they were the first to undergo captivity, for when the Chaldean host was devastating Judaea they were compelled to enter cities. Let others think as they will—every one follows his own bent—but to me a town is a prison, and the wilderness a paradise. What do we monks want with crowded cities, we whose very name bespeaks loneliness? Moses was trained for forty years in the desert to fit him for the task of leading the Jewish people, and from being a shepherd of sheep he became a shepherd of men. The apostles left their fishing on Lake Gennesaret to fish for human souls. Then they had a father, nets, and a little boat: but they followed the Lord straightway and abandoned everything, carrying their cross every day, without so much as a stick in their hands.

I say this, so that if you are tickled by a desire to become a clergyman, you may learn now what you will then be able to teach others, offering a reasonable sacrifice to Christ. You must not think yourself an old soldier while you are still a recruit, a master while you are still a pupil. It would not become my lowly rank to pass judgment on others, or to say anything unfavourable about those who serve in churches. Let them keep their proper place and station, and if you ever join them, my treatise written for Nepotian will show you how you ought to live in that position. For the moment I am discussing a monk's early training and character, a monk, moreover, who after a liberal education in his early manhood placed upon his neck the yoke of Christ.

The first point with which I must deal is whether you ought to live alone or in a monastery with others. I would prefer you to have the society of holy men and not to be your own teacher. If you set out on a strange road without a guide you may easily at the start take a wrong turning and make a mistake, going too far or not far enough, running till you weary yourself or delaying your journey for a sleep. In solitude pride quickly creeps in, and when a man has fasted for a little while and has seen no one, he thinks himself a person of some account. He forgets who he is, whence he comes, and where he is going, and lets his body run riot within, his tongue abroad. Contrary to the apostle's wishes, he judges another man's servants; he stretches out his hand for anything that his gullet craves; he does what he pleases and sleeps as long as he pleases; he fears no one, he thinks all men his inferiors, spends more time in cities than in his cell, and though among the brethren he makes a pretence of modesty, in the crowded squares he ruffles it with the best. What then, you will say? Do I disapprove of the solitary life? Not at all: I have often commended it. But I wish to see the soldiers who march out from a monastery-school men who have not been frightened by their early training, who have given proof of a holy life for many months, who have made themselves last that they might be first, who have not been overcome by hunger or satiety, who take pleasure in poverty, whose garb, conversation, looks and gait all teach virtue, and who have no skill—as some foolish fellows have—in inventing monstrous stories of their struggles with demons, tales invented to excite the admiration of the ignorant mob and to extract money from their pockets.

Just lately, to my sorrow, I saw the fortune of a Croesus brought to light at one man's death, and beheld a city's alms collected ostensibly for the poor's benefit left by will to his sons and their descendants. Then the iron which was hidden in the depths floated upon the surface, and amid the palm trees the bitter waters of Marah were seen. Nor need we wonder at his avarice: his partner and teacher was a man who turned the hunger of the needy into a source of wealth for himself, and to his own wretchedness kept back the legacies that were left to the wretched. But at last their cries reached heaven and were too much for God's patient ears, so that he sent an angel to say to this villainous Nabal the Carmelite: 'Thou fool, this night thy soul shall be required of thee: then whose shall those things be which thou has provided?'

For the reasons then which I have given above, I wish you not to live with your mother. And there are some further considerations. If she offers you a dainty dish, you would grieve her by refusing it, while if you take it you would be throwing oil on fire. Moreover, in a house that is full of girls you would see things in the day-time that you would think about in the night. Always have a book in your hand and before your eyes; learn the psalms word by word, pray without ceasing, keep your senses on the alert and closed against vain imaginings. Let your mind and body both strain towards the Lord, overcome wrath by patience; love the knowledge of the Scriptures and you will not love the sins of the flesh.

Do not let your mind offer a lodging to disturbing thoughts, for if they once find a home in your breast they will become your masters and lead you on into fatal sin. Engage in some occupation, so that the devil may always find you busy. If the apostles who had the power to make the Gospel their livelihood still worked with their hands that they might not be a burden on any man, and gave relief to others whose carnal possessions they had a right to enjoy in return for their spiritual benefits, why should you not provide for your own future wants? Make creels of reeds or weave baskets of pliant osiers. Hoe the ground and mark it out into equal plots, and when you have sown cabbage seed or set out plants in rows, bring water down in channels and stand by like the onlooker in the lovely lines:

'Lo, from the channelled slope he brings the stream,
Which falls hoarse murmuring o'er the polished stones
And with its bubbling flood allays the heat
Of sun-scorched fields.'

Graft barren trees with buds or slips, so that you may, after a little time, pluck sweet fruit as a reward for your labours. Make hives for bees, for to them the Proverbs of Solomon send you, and by watching the tiny creatures learn the ordinance of a monastery and the discipline of a kingdom. Twist lines too for catching fish, and copy out manuscripts, so that your hand may earn you food and your soul be satisfied with reading. 'Every one that is idle is a

prey to vain desires.' Monasteries in Egypt make it a rule not to take
any one who will not work, thinking not so much of the necessities
of life as of the safety of men's souls, lest they should be led astray
by dangerous imaginings, and be like Jerusalem in her whoredoms,
who opened her feet to every chance comer.

. . .

No art is learned without a master. Even dumb animals and herds
of wild beasts follow leaders of their own. Bees have rulers, and
cranes fly behind one of their number in the shape of the letter Y.
There is one emperor, and one judge for each province. When
Rome was founded it could not have two brothers reigning together,
and so it was inaugurated by an act of fratricide. Esau and Jacob
warred against one another in Rebecca's womb. Each church has
but one bishop, one arch-presbyter, one archdeacon; every ecclesiasti-
cal order is subjected to its own rulers. There is one pilot in a
ship, one master in a house; and however large an army may be, the
soldiers await one man's signal.

I will not weary my reader with further repetition, for the purpose
of all these examples is simply this. I want to show you that you
had better not be left to your own discretion, but should rather
live in a monastery under the control of one father and with many
companions. From one of them you may learn humility, from another patience; this one will teach you silence, that one meekness.
You will not do what you yourself wish; you will eat what you are
ordered; you will take what you are given; you will wear the dress
allotted to you; you will perform a set amount of work; you will
be subordinate to some one you do not like; you will come to bed
worn out with weariness and fall asleep as you walk about. Before
you have had your fill of rest, you will be forced to get out of
bed and take your turn in psalm-singing, a task where real emotion
is a greater requisite than a sweet voice.

The apostle says: 'I will pray with the spirit and I will pray with
the understanding also,' and, again: 'Make melody in your hearts,'
He had read the precept: 'Sing ye praises with understanding.' You
will serve the brethren; you will wash the feet of guests; if you
suffer wrong you will say nothing; the superior of the monastery
you will fear as a master and love as a father. Whatever precepts
he gives you will believe to be wholesome for you. You will not pass

judgment upon your elder's decisions, for it is your duty to be obedient and carry out orders, according to the words of Moses: 'Keep silence and hearken, O Israel.' You will be so busy with all these tasks that you will have no time for vain imaginings, and while you pass from one occupation to the next you will only have in mind the work that you are being forced to do.

I myself have seen some men who after they had renounced the world—in garb, at least, and in verbal professions, but not in reality —changed nothing of their former mode of life. Their household has increased rather than diminished; they have the same number of servants to wait upon them and keep the same elaborate table; though they drink from glass and eat from plates of earthenware, it is gold they swallow, and amidst crowds of servants swarming round them they claim the name of hermit. Others, who are poor and of slender means and think themselves full of wisdom, pass through the streets like the pageants in a procession, to practise a cynical eloquence. Others shrug their shoulders and croak indistinctly to themselves, and with glassy eyes fixed upon the earth they balance swelling words upon their tongues, so that if you add a crier, you might think it was his excellency the governor who was coming along. Some, too, by reason of damp cells and immoderate fasts, added to the weariness of solitude and excessive study, have a singing in their ears day and night, and turning melancholy mad need Hippocrates' fomentations more than any advice of mine.

Very many cannot forgo their previous trades and occupations, and though they change its name carry on the same pedlar's traffic as before, seeking for themselves not food and raiment, as the apostle directs, but greater profits than men of the world expect. In the past the mad greed of sellers was checked by the aediles, or as the Greeks call them, market-inspectors, and men could not cheat with impunity: to-day under the cloak of religion such men hoard up unjust gains, and the good name of Christianity does more wrong than it suffers. I am ashamed to say it, but I must—at least we ought to blush at our disgrace—we hold out our hands in public for alms while we have gold hidden under our rags, and to every one's surprise after living as poor men we die rich with purses well filled.

In your case, since you will be in a monastery, such conduct will not be allowed; habits will gradually grow on you, and finally you will do of your own accord what was at first a matter of compulsion; you will take pleasure in your labours, and forgetting what is behind you will reach out to that which is before; you will not think at all of the evil that others do, but only of the good which it is your duty to perform.

Do not be influenced by the number of those that sin, or disturbed by the host of the perishing, so as to have the unspoken thought: 'What? Shall all then perish who live in cities? Behold, they enjoy their property, they serve in the churches, they frequent the baths, they do not disdain unguents, and yet they flourish and are universally respected.' To such reasonings I have replied before, and will now do so briefly again, merely remarking that in this present short treatise I am not discussing the behaviour of the clergy, but laying down rules for a monk. The clergy are holy men, and in every case their life is worthy of praise. Go then and so live in your monastery that you may deserve to be a clergyman, that you may keep your youth free from all stain of defilement, and that you may come forth to Christ's altar as a virgin steps from her bower; that you may be well spoken of abroad, and that women may know your reputation but not your looks. When you come to ripe years, that is, if life be granted you, and have been appointed as a clergyman either by the people or by the bishop of the city, then act as becomes a cleric, and among your colleagues choose the better men as your models. In every rank and condition of life the very bad is mingled with the very good.

· · ·

Truth does not love corners nor does she seek out whisperers. To Timothy it is said: 'Against an elder receive not an accusation suddenly; but him that sinneth rebuke before all, that others also may fear.' When a man is of ripe years you should not readily believe evil of him; his past life is a defence and so is the honourable title of elder. Still, as we are but men and sometimes in spite of our mature age fall into the sins of youth, if I do wrong and you wish to correct me, rebuke me openly and do not indulge in secret backbiting. 'Let the righteous smite me, it shall be a kindness, and let him reprove me; but let not the oil of the sinner enrich my head.' 'Whom the Lord loveth, he chasteneth, and scourgeth every son whom he receiveth.' By the mouth of Isaiah God makes proclamation: 'O my people, they who call you happy cause you to err and destroy the way of your paths.' What benefit is it to me if you tell other people of my misdeeds, if without my knowledge you hurt another by the story of my sins or rather by your slanders, if while really eager to tell your tale to all you speak to each individual as though he were your only confidant? Such conduct seeks not my improvement but the satisfaction of your own vice. The Lord gave commandment that those who sin against us should be arraigned privately or else in the presence of a witness, and that if they refuse to listen they should be brought before the Church, and those who persist in wickedness should be regarded as heathens and publicans.

I have spoken thus definitely because I wish to free a young friend of mine from an itching tongue and itching ears, so that I may present him born again in Christ without spot or roughness as a chaste virgin, holy both in body and in mind. I would not have him boast in name alone, or be shut out by the Bridegroom because his lamp has gone out for want of the oil of good works. You have in your town a saintly and most learned prelate, Proculus, and he by the living sound of his voice can do more for you than any pages I can write. By daily homilies he will keep you in the straight path and not suffer you to turn right or left and leave the king's highway, whereby Israel undertakes to pass on its hasty journey to the promised land. May the voice of the Church's supplication be heard: 'Lord, ordain peace for us, for thou also hast wrought all our works for us.' May our renunciation of the world be a matter of free will and not of necessity! May we seek poverty as a glorious thing, not have it forced upon us as a punishment!

However, in our present miseries, with swords raging fiercely all around us, he is rich enough who is not in actual want of bread, he is more powerful than he needs be who is not reduced to slavery. Exuperius, the saintly bishop of Toulouse, like the widow of Zarephath feeds others and goes hungry himself. His face is pale with fasting, but it is the craving of others that torments him, and he has spent all his substance on those that are Christ's flesh. Yet none is richer than he; for in his wicker basket he carries the body of the Lord and in his glass cup His blood. He has driven greed from the temple; without scourge of ropes or chiding words he has overthrown the tables of mammon of those that sell doves, that is, the gifts of the Holy Spirit; he has scattered the money of the moneychangers, so that the house of God might be called a house of prayer and not a den of robbers.

Follow closely in his steps and in those of others like him in virtue, men whom their holy office only makes more humble and more poor. Or else, if you desire perfection, go out like Abraham from your native city and your kin, and travel whither you know not. If you have substance, sell it and give it to the poor. If you have none, you are free from a great burden. Naked yourself follow a naked Christ. The task is hard and great and difficult; but great also are the rewards.

St. Augustine

═══ 23 ═══

The City of God

As the heirs of Greco-Roman civilization, imbued with its forms of thought and expression, fourth-century Christians for the most part were unable to conceive of themselves outside its fold. Instead of turning their backs upon this civilization, as Tertullian did, Christian thinkers generally sought by mutual understanding to give it new moral and spiritual direction, thus achieving a kind of synthesis of Christianity and classicism. The most important of these, the greatest of the Latin Fathers, was Aurelius Augustinus (354–430).

Born near Carthage, St. Augustine received the best education his pagan father, a man of modest standing, could afford; afterward, he became a professor of rhetoric at Carthage, then Rome, and then Milan. There, about 387, he was converted to Christianity. A few years after his return to his birthplace, he was made bishop of Hippo, a minor coastal town in North Africa. But his personality and writings spread his fame far and wide so that he became the outstanding figure in the whole Western Church, and St. Jerome hailed him as the "second founder of the ancient faith."

His most important writing was *The City of God*, undertaken between 413 and 426 to "combat the blasphemies and errors" of those who, bewildered by the collapse of their old security, laid the blame for the capture of Rome by the Goths upon men's defection from the old gods. Deeply versed in the mind of the pagan world himself and admiring much of it, St. Augustine answered with the argument of the "two cities." This, "the most famous of all philosophic meditations on history," as it has been called, is set forth in our selection. Nothing illustrates better the process whereby a Semitic religion, and the Christian movement to which it gave rise, became domesticated in Greco-Roman culture.

St. Augustine, *The City of God.* From Volume II of *Basic Writings of Saint Augustine,* edited by Whitney J. Oates. Copyright 1948 by Random House, Inc. Reprinted by permission. [Pp. 38–40, 143, 257, 274–76, 278–79, 474–75, 493–94.]

The vast historical importance of this saint and doctor of the Church is suggested by the words of the historian, Terrot R. Glover:

> He gave to Christian thought . . . an impulse and direction the force of which is still unspent. He shaped the Catholic theory of the Church; he gave the great popes the idea of the City of God . . . he was the father of the mystics; the founder of the scholastic philosophy of the Middle Ages; and above all the hero and master of the Renaissance and the Reformation.*

THAT THE OVERTHROW OF ROME HAS NOT CORRECTED
THE VICES OF THE ROMANS

Oh infatuated men, what is this blindness, or rather madness, which possesses you? How is it that while, as we hear, even the eastern nations are bewailing your ruin, and while powerful states in the most remote parts of the earth are mourning your fall as a public calamity, ye yourselves should be crowding to the theatres, should be pouring into them and filling them; and, in short, be playing a madder part now than ever before? This was the foul plague-spot, this the wreck of virtue and honor that Scipio sought to preserve you from when he prohibited the construction of theatres; this was his reason for desiring that you might still have an enemy to fear, seeing as he did how easily prosperity would corrupt and destroy you. He did not consider that republic flourishing whose walls stand, but whose morals are in ruins. But the seductions of evil-minded devils had more influence with you than the precautions of prudent men. Hence the injuries you do, you will not permit to be imputed to you: but the injuries you suffer, you impute to Christianity. Depraved by good fortune, and not chastened by adversity, what you desire in the restoration of a peaceful and secure state, is not the tranquillity of the commonwealth, but the impunity of your own vicious luxury. Scipio wished you to be hard pressed by an enemy, that you might not abandon yourselves to luxurious manners; but so abandoned are you, that not even when crushed by the enemy is

---

* *Life and Letters in the Fourth Century* (New York: G. E. Stechert & Co., 1924), 194.

your luxury repressed. You have missed the profit of your calamity;
you have been made most wretched, and have remained most
profligate

OF GOD'S CLEMENCY IN MODERATING THE RUIN OF THE CITY

And that you are yet alive is due to God, who spares you that you
may be admonished to repent and reform your lives. It is He who
has permitted you, ungrateful as you are, to escape the sword of the
enemy, by calling yourselves His servants, or by finding asylum in
the sacred places of the martyrs.

It is said that Romulus and Remus, in order to increase the population of the city they founded, opened a sanctuary in which every
man might find asylum and absolution of all crime—a remarkable
foreshadowing of what has recently occurred in honor of Christ. The
destroyers of Rome followed the example of its founders. But it was
not greatly to their credit that the latter, for the sake of increasing
the number of their citizens, did that which the former have done,
lest the number of their enemies should be diminished.

OF THE SONS OF THE CHURCH WHO ARE HIDDEN
AMONG THE WICKED,
AND OF FALSE CHRISTIANS WITHIN THE CHURCH

Let these and similar answers (if any fuller and fitter answers can
be found) be given to their enemies by the redeemed family of the
Lord Christ, and by the pilgrim city of King Christ. But let this city
bear in mind, that among her enemies lie hid those who are destined
to be fellow-citizens, that she may not think it a fruitless labor to bear
what they inflict as enemies until they become confessors of the faith.
So, too, as long as she is a stranger in the world, the city of God has
in her communion, and bound to her by the sacraments, some who
shall not eternally dwell in the lot of the saints. Of these, some are
not now recognized; others declare themselves, and do not hesitate
to make common cause with our enemies in murmuring against God,
whose sacramental badge they wear. These men you may to-day see
thronging the churches with us, to-morrow crowding the theatres
with the godless. But we have the less reason to despair of the recla-
mation even of such persons, if among our most declared enemies

there are now some, unknown to themselves, who are destined to become our friends. In truth, these two cities are entangled together in this world, and intermixed until the last judgment effects their separation. I now proceed to speak, as God shall help me, of the rise, progress, and end of these two cities; and what I write, I write for the glory of the city of God, that, being placed in comparison with the other, it may shine with a brighter lustre.

WHAT SUBJECTS ARE TO BE HANDLED
IN THE FOLLOWING DISCOURSE

But I have still some things to say in confutation of those who refer the disasters of the Roman republic to our religion, because it prohibits the offering of sacrifices to the gods. For this end I must recount all, or as many as may seem sufficient, of the disasters which befell that city and its subject provinces, before these sacrifices were prohibited; for all these disasters they would doubtless have attributed to us, if at that time our religion had shed its light upon them, and had prohibited their sacrifices. I must then go on to show what social well-being the true God, in whose hand are all kingdoms, vouchsafed to grant to them that their empire might increase. I must show why He did so, and how their false gods, instead of at all aiding them, greatly injured them by guile and deceit. And, lastly, I must meet those who, when on this point convinced and confuted by irrefragable proofs, endeavor to maintain that they worship the gods, not hoping for the present advantages of this life, but for those which are to be enjoyed after death. And this, if I am not mistaken, will be the most difficult part of my task, and will be worthy of the loftiest argument; for we must then enter the lists with the philosophers, not the mere common herd of philosophers, but the most renowned, who in many points agree with ourselves, as regarding the immortality of the soul, and that the true God created the world, and by His providence rules all He has created. But as they differ from us on other points, we must not shrink from the task of exposing their errors, that, having refuted the gainsaying of the wicked with such ability as God may vouchsafe, we may assert the city of God, and true piety, and the worship of God, to which alone the promise of true and everlasting felicity is attached. Here, then, let us conclude, that we may enter on these subjects in a fresh book.

OF THIS PART OF THE WORK, WHEREIN WE BEGIN
TO EXPLAIN THE ORIGIN AND END OF THE TWO CITIES

The city of God we speak of is the same to which testimony is borne by that Scripture, which excels all the writings of all nations by its divine authority, and has brought under its influence all kinds of minds, and this not by a casual intellectual movement, but obviously by an express providential arrangement. For there it is written, "Glorious things are spoken of thee, O city of God." And in another psalm we read, "Great is the Lord, and greatly to be praised in the city of our God, in the mountain of His holiness, increasing the joy of the whole earth." And, a little after, in the same psalm, "As we have heard, so have we seen in the city of the Lord of hosts, in the city of our God. God has established it for ever." And in another, "There is a river the streams whereof shall make glad the city of our God, the holy place of the tabernacles of the Most High. God is in the midst of her, she shall not be moved." From these and similar testimonies, all of which it were tedious to cite, we have learned that there is a city of God, and its Founder has inspired us with a love which makes us covet its citizenship. To this Founder of the holy city the citizens of the earthly city prefer their own gods, not knowing that He is the God of gods, not of false, *i.e.*, of impious and proud gods, who, being deprived of His unchangeable and freely communicated light, and so reduced to a kind of poverty-stricken power, eagerly grasp at their own private privileges, and seek divine honors from their deluded subjects; but of the pious and holy gods, who are better pleased to submit themselves to one, than to subject many to themselves, and who would rather worship God than be worshipped as God. . . .

OF THE NATURE OF MAN'S FIRST SIN

If any one finds a difficulty in understanding why other sins do not alter human nature as it was altered by the transgression of those first human beings, so that on account of it this nature is subject to the great corruption we feel and see, and to death, and is distracted and tossed with so many furious and contending emotions, and is certainly far different from what it was before sin, even though it were then lodged in an animal body—if, I say, any one is moved by this, he ought not to think that that sin was a small and light one because it was committed about food, and that not bad nor noxious, except because it was forbidden; for in that spot of singular felicity God could not have created and planted any evil thing. But by the precept He gave, God commended obedience, which is, in a sort, the mother and guardian of all the virtues in the reasonable creature, which was so created that submission is advantageous to it, while the fulfillment of its own will in preference to the Creator's is destruction. And as this commandment enjoining abstinence from one kind of food in the midst of great abundance of other kinds was so easy to keep—so light a burden to the memory—and, above all, found no resistance to its observance in lust, which only afterwards sprung up as the penal consequence of sin, the iniquity of violating it was all the greater in proportion to the ease with which it might have been kept.

THAT IN ADAM'S SIN AN EVIL WILL PRECEDED THE EVIL ACT

Our first parents fell into open disobedience because already they were secretly corrupted; for the evil act had never been done had not an evil will preceded it. And what is the origin of our evil will but pride? For "pride is the beginning of sin." And what is pride but the craving for undue exaltation? And this is undue exaltation, when the soul abandons Him to whom it ought to cleave as its end, and becomes a kind of end to itself. This happens when it becomes its own satisfaction, and it does so when it falls away from that unchangeable good which ought to satisfy it more than itself. This falling away is spontaneous; for if the will had remained steadfast in the love of that higher and changeless good by which it was illumined to intelligence and kindled into love, it would not have turned away to find satisfaction in itself, and so become frigid and benighted. The woman would not have believed the serpent spoke the truth, nor would the man have preferred the request of his wife to the command of God, nor have supposed that it was a venial transgression to cleave to the partner of his life, even in a partnership of sin. The wicked deed, then,—that is to say the transgression of eating the forbidden fruit,—was committed by persons who were already wicked. . . .

OF THE NATURE OF THE TWO CITIES,
THE EARTHLY AND THE HEAVENLY

Accordingly, two cities have been formed by two loves: the earthly by the love of self, even to the contempt of God; the heavenly by the love of God, even to the contempt of self. The former, in a word, glories in itself, the latter in the Lord. For the one seeks glory from men; but the greatest glory of the other is God, the witness of conscience. The one lifts up its head in its own glory; the other says to its God, "Thou art my glory, and the lifter up of mine head." In the one, the princes and the nations it subdues are ruled by the love of ruling; in the other, the princes and the subjects serve one another in love, the latter obeying, while the former take thought for all. The one delights in its own strength, represented in the persons of its rulers; the other says to its God, "I will love Thee, O Lord, my strength." And therefore the wise men of the one city, living according to man, have sought for profit to their own bodies or souls, or both, and those who have known God "glorified Him not as God, neither were thankful, but became vain in their imaginations, and their foolish heart was darkened; professing themselves to be wise"—that is, glorying in their own wisdom, and being possessed by pride—"they became fools, and changed the glory of the incorruptible God into an image made like to corruptible man, and to birds, and four-footed beasts, and creeping things." For they were either leaders or followers of the people in adoring images, "and worshipped and served the creature more than the Creator, who is blessed for ever." But in the other city there is no human wisdom, but only godliness, which offers due worship to the true God, and looks for its reward in the society of the saints, of holy angels as well as holy men, that God may be all in all.

OF THE TWO LINES OF THE HUMAN RACE
WHICH FROM FIRST TO LAST DIVIDE IT

Of the bliss of Paradise, of Paradise itself, and of the life of our first parents there, and of their sin and punishment, many have thought much, spoken much, written much. We ourselves, too, have spoken of these things in the foregoing books, and have written either what we read in the Holy Scriptures, or what we could reasonably deduce from them. And were we to enter into a more detailed investigation of these matters, an endless number of endless questions would arise, which would involve us in a larger work than the present occasion admits. We cannot be expected to find room for replying to every question that may be started by unoccupied and captious men, who are ever more ready to ask questions than capable of understanding the answer. Yet I trust we have already done justice to these great and difficult questions regarding the beginning of the world, or of the soul, or of the human race itself.

This race we have distributed into two parts, the one consisting of those who live according to man, the other of those who live according to God. And these we also mystically call the two cities, or the two communities of men, of which the one is predestined to reign eternally with God, and the other to suffer eternal punishment with the devil. This, however, is their end, and of it we are to speak afterwards. At present, as we have said enough about their origin, whether among the angels, whose numbers we know not, or in the two first human beings, it seems suitable to attempt an account of their career, from the time when our two first parents began to propagate the race until all human generation shall cease. For this whole time or world-age, in which the dying give place and those who are born succeed, is the career of these two cities concerning which we treat.

Of these two first parents of the human race, then, Cain was the first-born, and he belonged to the city of men; after him was born Abel, who belonged to the city of God. For as in the individual the truth of the apostle's statement is discerned, "that is not first which is spiritual, but that which is natural, and afterward that which is spiritual," whence it comes to pass that each man, being derived from a condemned stock, is first of all born of Adam evil and carnal, and becomes good and spiritual only afterwards, when he is grafted into Christ by regeneration: so was it in the human race as a whole.

When these two cities began to run their course by a series of deaths and births, the citizen of this world was the first-born, and after him the stranger in this world, the citizen of the city of God, predestinated by grace, elected by grace, by grace a stranger below, and by grace a citizen above. By grace—for so far as regards himself he is sprung from the same mass, all of which is condemned in its origin: but God, like a potter (for this comparison is introduced by the apostle judiciously, and not without thought) of the same lump made one vessel to honor, another to dishonor. But first the vessel to dishonor was made, and after it another to honor. For in each individual, as I have already said, there is first of all that which is reprobate, that from which we must begin, but in which we need not necessarily remain; afterwards is that which is well-approved, to which we may by advancing attain, and in which, when we have reached it, we may abide. Not, indeed, that every wicked man shall be good, but that no one will be good who was not first of all wicked; but the sooner any one becomes a good man, the more speedily does he receive this title, and abolish the old name in the new. Accordingly, it is recorded of Cain that he built a city, but Abel, being a sojourner, built none. For the city of the saints is above, although here below it begets citizens, in whom it sojourns till the time of its reign arrives, when it shall gather together all in the day of the resurrection; and then shall the promised kingdom be given to them, in which they shall reign with their Prince, the King of the ages, time without end.

OF THE CONFLICT AND PEACE OF THE EARTHLY CITY

But the earthly city, which shall not be everlasting (for it will no longer be a city when it has been committed to the extreme penalty), has its good in this world, and rejoices in it with such joy as such things can afford. But as this is not a good which can discharge its devotees of all distresses, this city is often divided against itself by litigations, wars, quarrels, and such victories as are either life-destroying or short-lived. For each part of it that arms against another part of it seeks to triumph over the nations though itself in bondage to vice. If, when it has conquered, it is inflated with pride, its victory is life-destroying; but if it turns its thoughts upon the common casualties of our mortal condition, and is rather anxious concerning the disasters that may befall it than elated with the successes already achieved, this victory, though of a higher kind, is still only short-lived; for it cannot abidingly rule over those whom it has victoriously subjugated.

But the things which this city desires cannot justly be said to be evil, for it is itself, in its own kind, better than all other human good. For it desires earthly peace for the sake of enjoying earthly goods, and it makes war in order to attain to this peace; since, if it has conquered, and there remains no one to resist it, it enjoys a peace which it had not while there were opposing parties who contested for the enjoyment of those things which were too small to satisfy both. This peace is purchased by toilsome wars; it is obtained by what they style a glorious victory. Now, when victory remains with the party which had the juster cause, who hesitates to congratulate the victor, and style it a desirable peace? These things, then, are good things, and without doubt the gifts of God. But if they neglect the better things of the heavenly city, which are secured by eternal victory and peace never-ending, and so inordinately covet these present good things that they believe them to be the only desirable things, or love them better than those things which are believed to be better—if this be so, then it is necessary that misery follow and ever increase.

WHAT THE CHRISTIANS BELIEVE
REGARDING THE SUPREME GOOD AND EVIL,
IN OPPOSITION TO THE PHILOSOPHERS, WHO HAVE
MAINTAINED THAT THE SUPREME GOOD IS IN THEMSELVES

If, then, we be asked what the city of God has to say upon these points, and, in the first place, what its opinion regarding the supreme good and evil is, it will reply that life eternal is the supreme good, death eternal the supreme evil, and that to obtain the one and escape the other we must live rightly. And thus it is written, "The just lives by faith," for we do not as yet see our good, and must therefore live by faith; neither have we in ourselves power to live rightly, but can do so only if He who has given us faith to believe in His help do help us when we believe and pray. As for those who have supposed that the sovereign good and evil are to be found in this life and have placed it either in the soul or the body, or in both, or, to speak more explicitly, either in pleasure or in virtue, or in both; in repose or in virtue, or in both; in pleasure and repose, or in virtue, or in all combined; in the primary objects of nature, or in virtue, or in both—all these have, with a marvelous shallowness, sought to find their blessedness in this life and in themselves. Contempt has been poured upon such ideas by the Truth, saying by the prophet, "The Lord knoweth the thoughts of men" (or, as the Apostle Paul cites the passage, "The Lord knoweth the thoughts of the *wise*") "that they are vain."

WHAT PRODUCES PEACE, AND WHAT DISCORD, BETWEEN THE HEAVENLY AND EARTHLY CITIES

But the families which do not live by faith seek their peace in the earthly advantages of this life; while the families which live by faith look for those eternal blessings which are promised, and use as pilgrims such advantages of time and of earth as do not fascinate and divert them from God, but rather aid them to endure with greater ease, and to keep down the number of those burdens of the corruptible body which weigh upon the soul. Thus the things necessary for this mortal life are used by both kinds of men and families alike, but each has its own peculiar and widely different aim in using them.

The earthly city, which does not live by faith, seeks an earthly peace, and the end it proposes, in the well-ordered concord of civic obedience and rule, is the combination of men's wills to attain the things which are helpful to this life. The heavenly city, or rather the part of it which sojourns on earth and lives by faith, makes use of this peace only because it must, until this mortal condition which necessitates it shall pass away. Consequently, so long as it lives like a captive and a stranger in the earthly city, though it has already received the promise of redemption, and the gift of the Spirit as the earnest of it, it makes no scruple to obey the laws of the earthly city, whereby the things necessary for the maintenance of this mortal life are administered; and thus, as this life is common to both cities, so there is a harmony between them in regard to what belongs to it.

But, as the earthly city has had some philosophers whose doctrine is condemned by the divine teaching, who, being deceived either by their own conjectures or by demons, supposed that many gods must be invited to take an interest in human affairs, and assigned to each a separate function and a separate department—to one the body, to another the soul; and in the body itself, to one the head, to another the neck, and each of the other members to one of the gods; and in like manner, in the soul, to one god the natural capacity was assigned, to another education, to another anger, to another lust; so the various affairs of life were assigned—cattle to one, corn to another, wine to another, oil to another, the woods to another, money to another, navigation to another, wars and victories to another, marriages to another, births and fecundity to another, and other things to other gods.

The celestial city, on the other hand, knew that one God only was to be worshipped, and that to Him alone was due that service which the Greeks call [Latria], and which can be given only to a god, [so] it has come to pass that the two cities could not have common laws of religion, and that the heavenly city has been compelled in this matter to dissent, and to become obnoxious to those who think differently, and to stand the brunt of their anger and hatred and persecutions, except in so far as the minds of their enemies have been alarmed by the multitude of the Christians and quelled by the manifest protection of God accorded to them.

This heavenly city, then, while it sojourns on earth, calls citizens out of all nations, and gathers together a society of pilgrims of all languages, not scrupling about diversities in the manners, laws, and institutions whereby earthly peace is secured and maintained, but recognizing that, however various these are, they all tend to one and the same end of earthly peace. It therefore is so far from rescinding and abolishing these diversities, that it even preserves and adopts them, so long only as no hindrance to the worship of the one supreme and true God is thus introduced. Even the heavenly city, therefore, while in its state of pilgrimage, avails itself of the peace of earth, and, so far as it can without injuring faith and godliness, desires and maintains a common agreement among men regarding the acquisition of the necessaries of life, and makes this earthly peace bear upon the peace of heaven; for this alone can be truly called and esteemed the peace of the reasonable creatures, consisting as it does in the perfectly ordered and harmonious enjoyment of God and of one another in God. When we shall have reached that peace, this mortal life shall give place to one that is eternal, and our body shall be no more this animal body which by its corruption weighs down the soul, but a spiritual body feeling no want, and in all its members subjected to the will. In its pilgrim state the heavenly city possesses this peace by faith; and by this faith it lives righteously when it refers to the attainment of that peace every good action towards God and man; for the life of the city is a social life.